A PINE TREE IN A
BAMBOO FOREST

Five years in Japan & South Korea

By Brendan
Magone

Special thanks to assistant editors Patrick Nelson and Victoria Magone.

Cheers to all travellers – to those who depart the familiar to pursue the unfamiliar.

TABLE OF CONTENTS

PROLOGUE

Please permit me to start with two haiku, which may double as *mise en abymes*. (*Mise an abyme* is French term for a kind of story within a story, an image within an image, a reflection of a reflection, that often represents the whole.)

In brown leather boots,
I trek foreign green forests,
Passing known pale trees.

In a wood canoe,
I paddle fresh white waters,
Cresting old dark waves.

I taught English in Kyoto, Japan and Jeonju, South Korea for five years. Amidst these adventures, I travelled both countries extensively as well as excursions into Thailand. In addition, I befriended many intriguing foreigners who shared with me countless stories over late-night pints.

One year overseas was the original plan, yet as Robert Frost wrote, "way leads on to way." Eventually the foreign experience became a normal experience.

Living long-term in other countries, you don't simply learn about cultural differences and new mindsets. You embody them. First you discover exotic foods, fascinating architecture, and perplexing culture differences; later you find your everyday life, health, and mindset effected. For my work and time in Asia, these factors included business relations, personal relations, transportation, clothes, music, dating, sex, hairstyles, product packaging, furniture and silverware-sizing, posture, landscape, littering, eye contact (or not), personal space in public (or not), daily habits, general ethics, and, as you can tell, much more than one would think.

Japanese and South Koreans know a considerable amount about us (Americans & Westerners). They study English, listen to Western music, watch Hollywood movies, and peruse American websites. Yet the average Westerner has barely set foot into the true labyrinth of Asian cultures.

My sincere hope is that readers can find entertainment and education within these bumbling adventures and unusual reflections. In tandem with travel—as one moves forward and tackles new things—I've found the past is often present, in formative layers and in shadows; it sometimes requires a brave revisit with keen eyes.

I might also mention that working full-time in a foreign country is far different than traveling there for a few days or weeks on holiday; or, as some fortunate established writers have done, transplanting oneself in a new milieu with enough funds to simply live and enjoy, explore and dance around, and view the culture philosophically as privileged outsider. As an American I was in truth semi-privileged, but I worked full-time and depended directly on this income. I grappled seriously with money and business, in addition to relocating and exploring. In short, while other travel writers dated Asia, I lived with her.

In this sense, my work might resemble *River Town: Two Years on the Yangtze*, by Peter Hessler, who lived and taught English in China for several years. It is an elegant, insightful book for those of you who haven't read it.

Finally, please note that my time covered the years of 2000-2006. Most likely much has changed. Still, my tales and impressions should take a few steps towards unraveling the Japanese and Korean mystery.

Please brew a cup of strong green tea, preferably ceremonial matcha, and dig in.

Cheers, Brendan Magone

CHAPTER 1, KONICHIWA –
THE LANDING (JULY 21ST, 2000)

The plane's wheels hit the pavement, screeched down the runway, stopped. Osaka, Japan. We stepped off the plane and walked to a shuttle bus. The outside air, 40 degrees Celsius (104 Fahrenheit) with high humidity, slapped us like invisible waves of wet fire, and I laughed at the absurdity. How could people function in such conditions? Walking through the airport I started wading into the Japanese language and environment; the occasional English sign or announcement felt like looking back at familiar dry land. I pushed my two monster 70-lb bags on a wheeled cart and arrived at customs. The young Japanese official looked a bit frightened, perhaps timid about his grasp of English or scared of foreigners. He had a smooth boyish face, black slightly-spiked hair, bright black eyes: an Asian rock star in a pressed blue suit. When I didn't understand his attempts at English, he panicked, opened a large book, and showed me several pictures of various drugs, firearms, and other illegal items.

"Do you have these any?" he asked.

I laughed and said no.

Without even bothering to unzip my huge expedition pack or look closer at my giant duffle bag, he smiled and said, "Okay, welcome to Japan!"

"Thank you very much!" I shook his hand firmly. His words would be forever etched in my mind. As I passed through, I looked over at another line and noticed a little old harmless-looking Japanese lady with a simple light backpack. The customs officer was unpacking every item and examining each closely.

A representative from NOVA English School held several signs up in the air. One of them had my name in big black letters: MAGONE. I felt both relieved and important. I met a few other NOVA teachers from America and Canada who were heading to various cities and branches. We bonded quickly, savoring the newness of our surroundings. We counted our Japanese money—which looked strange, small, felt waxy—Monopoly money—and started trying out basic Japanese on airport information staff and passersby.

Osaka Airport is an artificial island. We hopped on a train, glided across the bridge and over bay waters, slipped quietly into the outskirts of the city and then its center. I had never seen so much concrete in my life! It was as if the city was one giant concrete mold, with buildings and streets carved into it. Not a blade of green grass. And more surprising, it was incredibly clean, not a scrap of trash.

The train looked impeccably neat, too. Female conductors were well-dressed and well-groomed: short, cropped hair under their solid navy-blue hats, perfect make-up, pressed navy-blue uniforms with shiny buttons. They made snappy announcements at each stop, topping it off with a bow.

Everything was dreamy, shiny, shimmering. And leaving Montana, the U.S., Western culture, Western rules, Western expectations, made it felt a little like summer camp without parents. Yet this was bigger, better, and more exotic. Newfound cultural freedom.

The other foreigners and I swapped stories. Even though we would be in different cities, we promised to email each other and create monthly meetings. (Actually, I would never see or hear from them again. Perhaps we would all get lost and dazzled in our new Japanese lives.)

At sunset, leaving the city and en route to Nagoya, the train slipped into the mountains; clouds of steam rose from various buildings and hillsides in the distance. *Onsen*, a train attendant told me, hot springs. I love hot springs. Montana and neighboring Idaho has hot springs all over, and I had soaked in both facilities and forests. I gazed out at the intense green of the bamboo, rising vapors, setting sun, and sharp-roofed Japanese houses that looked like old temples tucked between small winding roads. Perhaps I should have chosen a small town in the mountains instead of a large city? But then again, I wanted to save money, and had heard that one could get easy acting work in Japan—TV commercials, movies, and modeling jobs. Maybe I could make a few local and national commercials and pay off school loans. I had agreed to a large city with a good dose of nature and outdoor activities nearby. Or at least that's what the guidebook said.

Soon I grew tired and hunched over in my seat, laying my head against the window. Darkness fell fast. We passed through small cities, lights flickering and rolling by. I suddenly felt nervous. I tried not to think too much. The passing lights reminded me of taking the Greyhound bus as a child, riding back and forth between mother and father in different cities. That bus usually felt lonely and empty, yet it was safe, and my own private space. I usually packed too much for those trips, carrying well-worn clothes or favorite objects that gave me comfort; maybe that's why I had maxed out my two bags for this trip at 70 pounds each. I had weighed them both beforehand in order to bring all that I could.

I was finally falling asleep when the Nova representative shook my shoulder. "We are in Nagoya. You get off in two stops, at the downtown station. Another representative awaits you, Anthony, a good guy from New Zealand. He will be your contact in Nagoya." I shook my head a few times to wake up and collected my bags. 9 p.m. Japanese time, 6 a.m. Montana time. The train was gliding underground now. The other NOVA foreigners looked as bewildered as I, clothes wrinkled, hair disheveled, eyes bleary. After giving them all a hearty Montana handshake, I reiterated my promise to meet up once a month.

I stepped off the train into a shallow sea of Japanese people. Almost all wore suits or dress clothes. At 6'3, I towered above them. I saw another tall foreign figure in the distance, waving at me, obviously Anthony. Soon we ascended to the streets and walked briskly. Hello, Japan! I saw bright fantastical lights flashing, strange Japanese writing surrounding us on shops, billboards, and giant screen TVs; I heard choppy language everywhere along with the high-pitched, fast beat music coming from the bars; I smelled sushi mixed with oil and city grit. I felt the powerful and dense Japanese crowds moving around me like schools of fish. As my senses overloaded on this exotic environment, I could feel scores of eyes landing on me, dissecting me. I felt oddly fresh again, reborn, embracing the world anew. I wanted to share this all with Anthony, ask him a thousand questions, have a toast to this new world, but he quickly ushered me into a taxi and said he was running late. I guess it was ho-hum and old hat to him.

I wanted to dive into Japan more, yet my consciousness seemed to be stuttering. I resigned myself to casual conversation and looking out the window. Twenty minutes later we were in a suburb, Hibino, near Higashiyama station. Suddenly Japan looked drab and dreary, the buildings run-down, garbage piles laying outside of apartments. A light rotten smell crept into the cab. Not the best part of town.

"This is it," Anthony chimed. "Let me take you to your flat."

"Flat? Is that like an apartment?"

"Yes, that's what you Yanks call it. Let's see if some of your flatmates are home."

No one was home. Friday night. Anthony gave me an extra key and wished me luck. "Training starts Monday, mate." I ducked under the low door frame to get in, then hit my head hard on the second low frame, which separated the entryway from the living space. I ducked a few more times as I made my way around the apartment. Each area had a low door frame to negotiate, including the tiny bathroom, tiny living room, tiny kitchen, and tiny bedroom. The apartment was nearly all concrete. Thin sliding panels separated my room from the small living area and other bedrooms. My head hurt and I felt a little sick. Maybe it would look better in the morning? I found a note taped to the miniature fridge: "Welcome Brendan! Sorry we missed you, we are out drinking sake. Make yourself at home and we will show you around tomorrow, Daniel."

I had initially chosen to live by myself in a studio apartment. Two weeks before my arrival, NOVA had mistakenly scheduled me to live with two other teachers. Upon further consideration, having some roommates who knew the city and job might prove useful, so I went along with it. But now, as I observed the towering pile of dishes in the sink and brushed my teeth in a bathroom with clothes and towels scattered on the floor, I wondered if this would be like living with college freshmen. To make matters worse, the bathroom sink was so low it resembled a urinal.

I hit my head again on the room entryway, stumbled onto a stone-hard futon, and fell fast asleep.

CHAPTER 2, COMPRESSION –
FIRST WEEK

A blazing sun lit and scorched my tiny room. It felt so bright and hot, I thought I had slept till noon. I looked at the clock—5:12 am. No wonder they put the rising sun on the Japanese flag! Outside I heard a strange clicking and swishing noise that resembled a hundred automatic sprinklers going at once. That's annoying, I thought, how could they water their lawns so early? There was a screen door and a smallish square concrete patio outside my room. I put on shorts and a shirt and stuck my head outside. I started to sweat as it was hot and humid already. Concrete dominated the landscape with all the apartments squashed together and no lawns or sprinklers in sight. Nor a blade of grass. In the distance stood two withered trees...or perhaps they were giant shrubs. The clicking and buzzing sound was deafening and freaky (later I learned it to be cicadas). I went back inside, turned on the tiny fan in the room. I felt groggy and displaced, yet a kind of excitement pulsed through me, as though I were simultaneously intoxicated with alcohol and buzzed on caffeine.

I managed to sleep another hour, then unpacked my two carry-on bags and organized my little room. My two main bags would arrive Monday, sent delivery service from the airport. I had also shipped a few boxes by boat before departure, mainly books and knickknacks. I'm the kid who took a few golf clubs camping to practice with plastic balls around the lake, or when I cycled on a two-day, 226-mile bike tour, people passing me would note my brimming rear basket and say, "Where's the kitchen sink?" I guess I liked to be prepared. You never know when you might need a Leatherman, small first aid kit, notebook and pen, waterproof sac, headlamp, hacky sack, handgrip exerciser, or wool fingerless gloves, right?

That morning I met my flatmates—Darren, a Canadian, and Daniel, a New Zealander. Darren was tall, red-haired, lumbering, and rarely smiled. While showing me around the neighborhood he also emphasized several of America's bad points. He mentioned how American forces flattened Nagoya in WWII, that America had refused to sign the recent Kyoto Protocol to curb global warming, and that Americans were flagrantly excessive in lifestyle. He then remarked on several famous people that were Canadian— though many people mistook them for Americans—Michael J. Fox, Jim Carey, Bryan Adams, and Cory Hart. I told him that since Montana borders Canada, I often visited there as a child, and enjoyed the landscape and open spaces. I had always considered Canadians our friends. Guess a few of them felt otherwise.

Daniel was a few years younger than us, 24, a lean wily character, buzzed haircut, always listening to his headphones, always bouncing around. He worked as a deejay back home and was constantly "mixing a little something." They had both arrived a few months prior to me.

Above us were three female teachers: English, Canadian, New Zealander. I felt thrust into a tight-knit social life though appreciated the assistance in these new surroundings.

That first Saturday they took me to a sumo wrestling match inside Nagoya Castle. My timing was lucky, as Aiki Bono, one of the most revered sumo wrestlers in Japan, would wrestle there that night. His opponent, a famed rebel-rouser, held the moniker "The Saltshaker" due to his habit of throwing the ceremonial salt around the ring in an untraditional fashion instead of clapping it between his hands.

On our way to Nagoya Castle and then inside, the dreamscape continued. First, things were smaller: smaller streets, smaller buildings, smaller roads, smaller tables, smaller chairs, smaller food portions, smaller everything. At the sumo match I managed to find a miniscule can of coke in a vending machine, and it was one-third the size of a soda back home! It was as if everything had been shrunk down. The elderly people were so short (and sometimes steeply bent over) I had to worry about plowing them over when negotiating a crowd. I felt like a Montana bear in a Japanese tea shop. And the Japanese language flooded my consciousness. Soon I craved English, and found that speaking to my new foreign friends kept me sane. In fact, discussions about movies or American TV shows or nearly anything seemed far more interesting here than back home. It was just nice to hear English.

The sumo matches took place in a small concrete arena. The wrestlers clapped salt together, gestured to the crowd, performed traditional dances before fighting. When the two giant bodies slammed together, the sound reverberated throughout the castle. The audience sat on square colorful cushions. I learned that Aiki Bono was born in Hawaii, making him American by nationality, though of obvious Japanese descent. He overpowered and beat "The Saltshaker."

These huge wrestlers enchanted the Japanese. As I looked around at the small individuals in the crowd, and recalled my tiny apartment and tiny neighborhood stores, I wondered if in the land of so many small things they were fascinated with large objects? Godzilla was, after all, a Japanese creation. And Japanese often talked about how big America was, big in space and big in ideas, and my home state of Montana was the same geographical size as Japan, but with higher mountains and far more open spaces. Would I be another giant foreign object for them that provided entertainment?

At the end, per custom, the crowd threw and whirled their cushions in the air. Japan appeared highly unified, color-coordinated, even choreographed. Our group looked like an unruly pack of lost wild animals. Large wild animals.

Back outside, the intense heat made undulations in the air. We went to a tiny restaurant, ordered tiny food, and I tried to slip my legs under the tiny table. Outside the restaurant there were plastic replicas of the dishes you could order, so one had a rough idea of what you were getting, and could just point to a plate, usually whatever looked safest or most familiar. The Japanese staff were polite, patient, and kind; all wore crisp blue and white uniforms.

The Canadian woman, Anna, sat very close to Darren. She stared at me, puffing her cigarette. She looked chubby, and like the weight had recently been put on. She squirmed a lot. "Are you ready to be a slave for the English factory?"

"Slave? I'm excited to start teaching. And I look forward to learning more about Japanese culture—this place is like another planet! Everything feels like an adventure."

"Don't worry, it will wear off. The students are alright, but NOVA sucks, and we are all getting screwed in several ways."

Darren pitched in. "For starters, we are paying far too much for our lousy apartment. Maybe we can find something on our own later. And guess what NOVA stands for? 'No vacation.' We have to work a lot of Japanese holidays that most companies have off."

They continued to fill me in on the numerous evils of NOVA. Either I had made a large mistake or they were a bunch of whining sad sacks. But Dana, a New Zealander, appeared enthusiastic and looked at me intently with dough eyes. She was short, fair-skinned with shoulder-length brown hair, and cute thick curls. I told her about my train ride through sunset, passing hot springs in the mountain villages, seeing wisps of steam in the fading light near Buddhist temples.

"That's kind of romantic! Are you a poet?" she asked.

"Not published, but I try sometimes. I love Yeats and Frost."

"I thought so. You should come up to our flat some evening and show me your writing."

"Thanks, I will. It's always cool to share ideas, get another perspective. Maybe you could show me some pictures of New Zealand? I hear it's amazing."

She doubled her intensity, talking more and more, pouring attention on me like a waterfall. The others broke off in their own conversations. I felt a little cornered, but this kind of attention and obvious flirting happened rarely, so I enjoyed it.

Back home I was usually the nice guy who made lots of women friends, meanwhile they dated players. I developed crushes, meanwhile they complained to me about their aloof and promiscuous boyfriends.

Thus, getting attention like this from Dana felt good, though nerve-wracking. Her Kiwi accent (similar to a British accent) made her sound articulate and witty. But once we started talking extensively, she mostly complained about work like the others and didn't seem all that interested in Japanese culture. Didn't she notice the amazing temples on practically every street corner? How well-dressed everyone was? The interesting harmony, the ebb and flow of Japan? Why hadn't she made any Japanese friends yet? She seemed to hang out only with this gang of complaining foreigners. Plus, she lived upstairs from me, an easy recipe for drama. I decided to refrain for now. (Looking back, I know she wanted to hook me swiftly before I met any Japanese women.)

After walking back home, and looking around carefully, I figured out that although my apartment seemed like a run-down mini-submarine, it represented standard fare for Japanese living. I was living like everyone else. And later I would notice how safe the neighborhoods were – no one locked their bikes, despite being in a big city.

Rather than flat or apartment, perhaps I should say "compartment," like on a submarine or train.

A brighter note: the bedroom floors were tatami mat, rectangular pieces made from woven straw and rice. They looked golden, peaceful, and were quiet to walk on. They gave the sleeping compartments a traditional feel, like sleeping in a mountain temple.

Saturday night I slept four hours. Sunday was a wash, too. The upstairs girls kept popping in, thinking I felt rested up and ready for conversations and city outings, though I still struggled with jet lag (14-hour time difference) and the new surroundings.

For now just stepping outside my compartment provided enough adventure. My immediate neighborhood contained plenty of exotic sights. The local seafood markets were brimming with octopi, crabs, eels, oysters, mussels, sea urchins, sea cucumbers, scallops, shrimp, clams, and many creatures I had never laid eyes on; the markets looked like makeshift sea aquariums. Then I stumbled upon a slanted and rickety Japanese-Elvis bar on our block (the owner gave me a free afternoon shot and proudly displayed his Elvis memorabilia). Vending machines held razors, ties, beer, and condoms (what more does one need?). Around the corner from me were convenient though spooky underground walkways and various temples painted in bright oranges, purples, and reds.

That Sunday afternoon I strolled into my first Japanese supermarket. Inside looked ultrabright, colorful, super-clean, icy-cool. Was this a supermarket or an advertisement for a supermarket? It sparkled! Yet, I couldn't recognize a single item on the shelves or in the coolers. Where was the milk, peanut butter, bread and chicken soup? In the front aisles, where in America would perch candy bars and gum, I found funky tofu and dried squid.

Suddenly, amidst the weird Japanese music, came an old disco tune, sped-up and high-pitched but still recognizable...*Upside down, boy you turn me, inside out, and, round and round*...I couldn't believe it. It was like coming across a can of cold coke after landing on Mars. Admittedly I loved danced music and they were playing a song that described my new life. Suddenly there seemed an unusual connection between East and West—and an unusual connection within me. I felt good, I felt real. Maybe I could dance to this Japanese beat; maybe I could succeed in this new environment. A new fresh home, maybe a new woman? I put more spring in my step as I walked the aisles, tossed a few unknown foods in my basket. I walked to the counter, whipped out my Japanese phrasebook, greeted the lady cashier *Gokigen ikaga desu ka?* The woman giggled, turned to her friends with a smile, they all laughed. In my book this had translated as, "How are you?" (Later I would find out that my outdated formal phrase meant something like, "How is your life going now fine lady?").

I tried to hand her some money. She pointed to a little round dish on the counter between us. Was she afraid to touch a foreigner? Then after looking around, I noticed all the counters had these petite money dishes. I put a pile of money in it, she helped pick out the right ones. The total price was 2500 yen. Was that cheap or expensive? I wasn't sure yet. I gave her a deep bow and said domo arigato gozaimasu. They laughed again. (I had used an excessively polite term reserved for royalty or heartfelt thanks).

Back on the street, walking through intense heat, I continued to carry in my head that funky dance beat. I was ready for NOVA training tomorrow. I was ready for Japan!

CHAPTER 3, SEPPUKU

Two months here has felt like two years. Perhaps since I've absorbed an enormous amount regarding surroundings and culture. For example, Japanese people seem incredibly polite and accommodating. When I'm lost, and make the slightest attempt to get assistance, any pedestrian walking down the street will stop immediately and help me thoroughly. One even took me into a cafe, bought me a green tea soda and green tea snack, and sat down with me for twenty-five minutes. He made a few marks on my map and did his best to explain the city. Then he ushered me back outside, apologized excessively for his poor English, and bowed deeply as if wishing me good fortune on a grand and perilous journey. For several minutes he watched as I walked down the sidewalk to make sure I was headed in the right direction.

Or, take one night after my last day of NOVA training. My foreign coworkers took me out for a long evening of drinking sake and singing karaoke. I didn't pay for a drink or song all night. Come 4 a.m., we all left the karaoke room drunk, and scattered like leaves in a typhoon. I suddenly found myself alone, walking down a barren sidewalk, wondering how to get home, not a yen in my pocket. As I stumbled along, a car pulled alongside and offered me a lift. A Japanese couple, college students, then drove me forty-five minutes across the city to my apartment doorstep and wouldn't accept a single yen for payment (I had money inside my room). And they had to work at 8 a.m. They smiled and said, "Welcome to Japan!"

Was this first-class treatment because foreigners rarely visited Nagoya? Or was it their unique culture and honor code? At any rate, I needed the assistance, and am ashamed to say I started to enjoy the attention.

Then came the pen incident.

One afternoon, three weeks into my stay, I struggled with some lengthy foreign documents inside a small government building. Soon the head manager abandoned his rear office and stacks of paperwork to sit down alongside me and fill out the forms. He brewed fresh green tea and served green tea cookies. He showed me traditional paintings on the office walls and tried to explain their history. In short, the manager welcomed me and bid me adieu like a long-lost brother.

While walking down the sidewalk—finding my way back to the subway with a map—I discovered I had left my pen back in the building. I paused and checked my watch. I hated to bother them again after all they had done, but it was a good pen, and I had already lost too many good pens in my life. Maybe it was just sitting on the counter? Maybe they had already found it and were agonizing over how to get it to me?

Once inside, I tried to avoid the head manager, but he was quickly re-summoned and soon appeared before me. In a spontaneous attempt to justify my pettiness over a pen, I lied and said it was a gift from my brother. Big mistake! A look of quiet horror overtook his face. He sprang up some stairs to a tiny control room, switched on a loudspeaker, and made several booming announcements. Again I was directed to sit down, drink green tea and eat green tea snacks. Business was brought to a standstill. All employees were gathered to join the search; all offices and desks were ransacked. After fifteen minutes, I was red-faced and feeling guilty, and tried to bow out, literally. I slowly backed away towards the front door with my Japanese phrasebook in hand, stammering *sumimasen* (excuse me), *dijob* (that's okay), *domo arigato gozaimasu* (thank you very much). The head manager turned even more grave, rushed over to me, and pulled out his wallet. *Ikura deska? Ikura deska?* (How much? How much?) He tried handing me a 5,000 yen note, about $50. I refused again, and he insisted I leave all my contact information, including my Japanese home address, work address, and family's address back in America in case my pen turned up.

Twenty minutes later, on the subway home, I found the pen in the bottom of my backpack. I felt horrible. Had I had a small sword with me, I might have committed *seppuku* (*hara-kiri*) right there. From that moment forward, I pledged to be on my best behavior and serve as a shining American diplomat.

Several months later, I moved to the historical city of Kyoto. Just before leaving Nagoya, official business required my visiting that government office again. I tried to squeak in and out unnoticed, but the head manager recognized me immediately, leapt up from behind his desk, rushed over, and took both my hands into his. His words still echo in my American mind: "Your pen, your pen, is it okay?"

CHAPTER 4, JAPAN
JOURNAL HIGHLIGHTS

O ctober 10th, 2000: Through my American eyes Japan seems a cauldron of contrasts and contradictions, from its geography and landscape to its social climate and behavior. Where else is so much nature pressed up against so much city? Where else do so many people sip green tea in the mornings, eat a little rice and fish in the afternoons, then polish off three pitchers of beer and a pack of cigarettes in the evenings? Where else is politeness often adhered to like a religion in both customer service and interpersonal relations, only to be abandoned to the point of criminal behavior when operating a motorized vehicle? So far, living and working in Japan has been exciting, exotic, and rewarding, plus aggravating, difficult, and troubling, but most of all it's been interesting.

Fast-forwards in italics: After a full two years in Japan and three more in South Korea, I see my experiences a little differently now. Yes, this is all true, and yet, Asians are equally baffled by American contradictions. For example, we claim to be a free and independent country yet have the highest murder and crime rates. Things like "carjacking" don't even have a name in Asia, because they never happen (at least not during the time I lived there). This would seem to belie the freedom Americans are always trumpeting.

<u>November 4th, 2000:</u> Commuting to work I bike along the northern Takano and Kamo Rivers, a pleasant but sometimes perilous path, as one minute I'm observing a goose floating and bobbing quietly, sleeping with its beak nestled in its feathers, and the next minute I`m ducking under a bridge overhang, or dodging sharp, craggy, and undoubtedly centuries-old pieces of cobblestone. And from time to time great swarms of gnats (or the Japanese equivalent) descend upon any person walking or biking the river path. I've seen several cyclists wearing large plastic goggles, and I doubt it's to break the wind. Sure beats the subway, though. Perhaps one grows accustomed to the grave shortage of oxygen, the near absolute loss of personal space, and the warm smell of deodorant and alcohol, but I`d probably swim the rivers to work before purchasing another subway pass.

Now I would say to myself: You were blessed to grow up in the wide-open spaces of America and especially Montana. Remember the stone inscription at Ryoanji, the Japanese rock garden, "I learn only to be contented." You could learn something from the million Japanese who, riding the packed subway every morning and night, often two hours a day, find a calm, polite way to do so, not disturbing the group and allowing for harmony, or "wa", to exist within the heavy population density that makes up Japanese society.

<u>November 20th, 2000:</u>   The stereotype of Japanese people working extremely hard is accurate; they are up early, work at least 10-12 hours, and then often have work functions or engagements afterwards. Whenever I introduce the term "workaholic" to students, it's always interpreted as having a positive meaning, and rarely can I convince them otherwise.

We Westerners would call it a personal choice, and they would call it a cultural duty.

<u>December 2nd, 2000:</u>   Along with teaching English, I have dabbled in the Japanese entertainment business. I did a few voice-overs for some Toyota commercials, modeled for two bridal magazines, and played the lead spokesman in a regional commercial for Dr. Zeus Car Wax. Believe it or not, the car commercial was incredibly difficult work. It all started with my rewriting the whole script en route to location while crammed in the backseat of a tiny Mitsubishi. Next, most Japanese commercials and TV shows seem extremely plastic and melodramatic, and of course that's exactly what they wanted from me! Then, the language barrier complicated matters, as well as them

rushing everything. All good acting training, I guess, although I didn't enjoy the process nor have much pride in the finished product. With their cultural humbleness and brutal work ethic, they work even longer and harder without breaks and the treatment of talent (not to mention the rest of the crew) is comically poor. Yet, strangely enough, if you are turned down for an acting job, they give you this long apology and deep bow. That's Japan for you.

Speaking of the limelight, these days I sometimes forget about the *gaijin* (foreigner) spotlight that follows me wherever I go. The spotlight that shines: The Westerner, The English Person, the American, the American Diplomat, the tall guy, the big guy, the white guy, and even "Tyrone Power" from some of the older folks. So I'll be walking along and minding my own business, subconsciously thinking I blend in, and a passing crowd of school kids suddenly yell: "Hello, nice to meet you!" or "I'm fine how are you!?" or "Do you like pizza?" Or a little girl on the back of a bicycle points at me "*Eigo, Eigo*," which means "English, English"; or upon walking into a restaurant all eyes land upon me, then look away, while the bravest, or the least polite depending on how you look at it, keep staring and sneaking several long glances during the next hour.

This kind of thing was fun for the first few weeks, even the first few months, and I'm glad to have had the experience. It sure beats a fair number of other countries, where I'm liable to be kidnapped or shot. But sixteen months wore me down, and I remember really looking forward to the time when I could just slip back into the crowd again. I missed the anonymity and diversity of America.

<u>January 6th, 2001</u>: Kyoto's not as cold as Montana, and it snows rarely. But like many other things in this country, one must reconfigure and evaluate all conditions before issuing final judgment. It can be cold with a lot of moisture, which makes the chill far more penetrating; the wind blows more often than not; and as water is almost ubiquitous in Kyoto (ancient canals, waterways, and irrigating ditches crisscross the entire city), there is almost always a cool icy draft slipping up behind you or through you. My dorm-like room, with as much insulation as a shack in the woods, stays nearly consistent with outside temperature. Electric heat doesn't work well because the power circuits in my room are tiny and weak. Kerosene heat seems the best, and is what most Japanese use in winter, although it makes a room smell like a refueling garage for Lear jets. Then I learned they were banned by the landlord because of all the paper and wood in our building.

After a few weeks of trying other options, like a sleeping bag or electric blanket (difficult to find my size, among other complications), I decided to risk my landlord's fury and went back to using a cheap kerosene heater. Such a choice meant midnight runs every three or four days to the gas station for refueling; midnight runs since my landlord seemed to pop up every other day, sweeping the floors, scouring the shower (outside and coin-operated, mind you), or eyeing the tenants. More than once, on one of these midnight runs, I caught other Japanese tenants sneaking out with their kerosene tanks in hand, both of us a little startled by the other. Then we would exchange international, conspiratorial smiles.

January 27th, 2001: When you stay at an *onsen* (hot springs) resort, you are given a "yukata" at check-in. This is a soft and comfortable cotton robe that can be worn around the hotel and even to dinner. After a first soak with Japanese friends, my American friend Aaron and his girlfriend Naoko, we all went to a late dinner buffet in our yukatas, enjoying hearty portions of seafood. I was visiting Hokkaido, and their food is especially fresh, healthy, and excellent. And beer goes down extremely well after an hour-long soak, as does a glass of milk.

The next morning all of us were walking past the main relaxing area, and I saw a sight I will never forget. The time was just after 7 am, and a fifties-something Japanese couple were perched at a table playing cards. They looked clean cut, bright, and healthy, and both had a huge mug of frosty draft beer in hand (double pint size). Just as we passed, they clinked their mugs together with a cheerful "*kampai*"! Now, I have grown accustomed to the incredible amount of working and drinking that occurs in this country, and for a while even subscribed to both myself, but still it seemed a wee early in the morning for an alcoholic beverage. I mean the sun wasn't even close to being over the yardarm. I turned to Naoko and asked, "Why are they drinking so early?" And without a second's hesitation she replied, "Well, they are on vacation!"

Yes, it's amazing the amount of alcohol Japanese and Koreans consume. That said, they generally don't overeat, and have learned to enjoy much smaller portions, while Americans typically have monster portions and overeat with "comfort food". Studies indicate that the effects of overeating and obesity are usually more detrimental than alcohol abuse. Another check and balance, perhaps.

March 24th, 2001: I am constantly astonished by the absence of creative thinking. Even at the doctor's office, when seeking treatment for an old injury (stress fracture on foot), the doctors were stumped, and resolved that the only option was surgery. Then, to their amazement, I came up with a few ideas for a foot cast that they hadn't thought of but readily agreed to. Further, they called a few other doctors in to display the "revolutionary" ideas I proposed! No joke. As it turned out, the foot cast didn't work and I later underwent surgery, but at least I saw an alternative path to try first. Or, I'm in the bicycle shop guiding the repairman on something handmade. Or, I rearrange the entire class schedule for the Kyoto Biocollege. This kind of thing happens on a weekly basis. If I could somehow patent and sell all the creative ideas I've composed in this country I would return to Montana in retirement. I have to remind myself that America was built on creative thinking and independence, Japan the opposite.

Yes, most Asian societies are built on Confucian ideals, which stress group and public harmony over individual desires for the betterment of everyone. This foundation— plus the heavy population density in Japan and Korea— make self-sacrifice and group awareness a must. In America we often say, "the squeaky wheel gets the grease," while in Japan they say, "The nail that sticks out gets the hammer." Japanese are not taught to think creatively, but rather to conform. And it's not necessarily bad, just different. America was founded on independence, creativity, and the cowboy/maverick who rides alone and often must break the rules. That's how we broke away from England and later settled the American West.

<u>May 4th, 2001:</u> In the heart of spring, thousands of cherry blossoms make their bright and brilliant appearance. Cherry blossom season is short, maybe two or three weeks, and as hyped-up as a Hollywood blockbuster. Students and Japanese friends kept telling me all about it. Billboards and posters displayed families having picnics underneath their branches. Anti-hype as I am, I shrugged it off as a few pretty flowers that I had surely seen the likes of before. Certainly I wouldn't be having my picture taken

near them, or having dinner underneath them; I might as well put on a dress and swish around to the lilt of a Broadway musical. Four days into their bloom, though, I am eating my words. They are gorgeous. Every day I bike down two Kyoto rivers on my way to work, and it now seems a jungle of cherry blossom trees line the riverbanks, reds and pinks and whites so dazzling I need sunglasses even if it is cloudy. And coming home at night I can turn off my bike light, the moonlight shining so full and vivid within the reflective petals like thousands of little torches to illuminate my path. A light cherry perfume blankets the city. When you don't see the numerous blossoms floating down through the air in slow spirals, or being stirred-up by a warm wind, you can hear them rustling behind you or to the side of you. Yes, I too caught cherry blossom fever, and if you didn't find me sharing some sake after work underneath their branches, you might find me picking a few to give to a pretty girl later in the evening.

June 25th, 2001: It's about 100 degrees Fahrenheit and very humid. My room is so hot that I am sleep-deprived and mildly catatonic. The only time spent in a truly comfortable and climate-controlled environment is in the Berlitz classroom, which is good motivation for working overtime every week. But boy do I have to fight to stay awake! Every ounce of my flesh cries out for letting my eyes fall shut and leaning back into that flexible, cushioned chair. I have caught myself nodding off a few times, the student reading a paragraph, my mind just starting to slip into a dream, but somehow I've always caught myself. One other teacher, poor chap, did fall asleep in the classroom last summer. He awoke, seven minutes later, to the student keeping time on his stopwatch. And one forty-minute lesson at Berlitz costs 8000 yen, about $70. Of course both the teacher and Berlitz apologized, and offered the student a free lesson. The next week Berlitz installed another coffee vending machine in the tiny staff room.

<u>July 20th, 2001</u>:
THE TOP TEN REASONS YOU KNOW YOU'VE LIVED IN JAPAN FOR A YEAR...

10. You use the words "I'm sorry" or "excuse me" at least once in every conversation.

9. Even though you use the words "I'm sorry" or "excuse me" at least once in every conversation, you give strong consideration to yelling at or shoving old Japanese women, famous for throwing elbows in a crowd and doing whatever they want, whenever they please.

8. You don't mind eating fish and rice every day, nor do you think it's unusual.

7. After buying a bag of rice chips or Snickers bar at a convenience store, you thank the clerk three times and bow twice on the way out.

6. Most of your shoes are slip-ons.

5. At the movie theater you eat popcorn very carefully to not make too much noise.

4. Paying $12 for a Guinness and $3 for a Kit Kat in a convenience store seems reasonable.

3. Green tea cake, green tea granola bars, green tea ice cream, and green tea yogurt all taste great.

2. You speak simple and broken English constantly, reinforcing your words with hand gestures, even with other native English speakers.

AND THE NUMBER ONE REASON YOU KNOW YOU'VE LIVED IN JAPAN FOR ONE YEAR...

1. If you're tall, you duck at every doorway, whether it's too low or not!

July 25th, 2001: "Japanese-English" has become my nemesis. One day I'll be arrested for trying to rewrite someone's tee shirt with a Sharpie. There are mistakes everywhere, especially on clothing. Occasionally I do come across something clever or insightful, but I doubt the author is conscious of its full meaning. Something like "smiles enjoy fresh life" and "lovers make poetry paint." But in the worst cases, you encounter extremely vulgar phrases worn by someone obviously oblivious to its true meaning; and you know somewhere in a shirt shop sits a disheveled & burnt-out "gaijin" (foreigner) having a grand ole laugh. For example, you can imagine my surprise this morning when seeing on the subway a shy, well-groomed, and polite high school girl with a neon tee shirt exclaiming, "If it isn't hard I won't fuck it!" As politely as possible, I passed her a note saying her shirt had a negative meaning and she should consult her dictionary. There are many more examples like this, but you get the idea.

Great point, and yet again, Americans/ Westerners do the same to Asian language. We think anything with Kanji characters looks cool and mystical and ancient, and splash it all over the place with little knowledge of its true meaning.

<u>August 10th, 2001:</u> Elderly Japanese women who have abandoned all societal decorum are my second pet peeve. Even the Japanese joke about this. Half your size and double your age, they walk the streets like the newest members of WWF. They can own any foot path or road with their fully loaded and ever-swinging shopping bags (or over-packed double and triple-bike baskets), and if you don't give them enough space on the subway or bus they'll wedge up against you with bony hips, growl some guttural Japanese, and make no attempt to contain their foul breath. On my bicycle I've been toppled more than once when trying to play "chicken" with an old Japanese lady on a dark and narrow cobblestone street. And today, when I didn't buy a vacuum cleaner in a secondhand shop, but made the mistake of having the old woman (and owner) give me the full demo (it worked fine but I changed my mind), she barked a few things that I'm sure were anything but résumé builders, and then prodded me out of her store by

jabbing my butt with her two bony fingers! She continued her harangues until I was well out of sight on my bicycle. (Even my American friend, Mark, when visiting Kyoto, mentioned he was severely elbowed in the back by some short and feisty old ladies trying to pass through a dense crowd.) The best explanation for this phenomenon— my personal guess and one supported by a few Japanese friends—is that after fifty plus years of intense politeness and lower social rank, and after forever losing any remnants of beauty (no small thing in Japan's image-conscious culture), they finally snap and let everything fly. And with this in mind, I usually forgive them.

Yes, Japan has its own joke about these wild old women. But it is also understood that they have sacrificed an incredible amount for their husbands, family, and children, and deserve to be forgiven any rude behavior. Perhaps they've earned it. And when you were buying the vacuum, you were acting as a typical American, wanting to try everything out before buying, which was rude to the shop owner, saying you did not trust her business or products. In Japan rarely, if ever, would you find shop owners trying to swindle their patrons—another Confucian outcome—for it would bring shame upon their entire neighborhood and family.

CHAPTER 5,
MOUNTAINS AS SHIELDS

*Know from whence you came. If you know
whence you came, there are absolutely no
limitations to where you can go. –James Baldwin*

The Japanese city of Kyoto felt dense, like a big
American city packed into a mid-sized Montana town,
then surrounded by small mountains and steeped
heavily in Asian flavor. Large drab buildings and modern
development gradually parted to reveal a myriad of
mysterious wooden temples, Buddhist shrines, Zen rock
gardens, narrow meandering cobblestone streets, winding
waterways, and two main rivers. I lived at the northern
edge of the city with a few hills behind me and higher
mountains climbing in the distance. I often jogged these
hills or hiked the mountains. In the classroom, I showed
pictures of Montana to the adults I taught; these pictures
included the Rocky Mountains and other formidable
ranges. Students loved to see the open spaces and
prodigious peaks of Montana. Every New Year's Eve, Kyoto
residents lit five small fires on the surrounding low

mountains in the shape of Kanji characters called *Daimonji*. These signified spirits of recently deceased and assisted their smooth return to the spirit world. These five *Daimonji* burned bright and ushered in the New Year.

Even in the womb, mountains were a part of me. While pregnant, my mother skied down the long winding runs of Big Mountain in Whitefish, Montana. The cold, high altitude air reached my bloodstream by way of hers. Four months after my birth, my parents divorced, and my mother moved to Missoula; as I grew up I took the bus back and forth between mother and father, Missoula and Whitefish, riding on roads alongside the Rocky Mountains. Mountains are what I remember most. I watched them often, then later hiked them, skied them, sledded down them, swam near them, camped around them, and nearly always had them within my peripheral vision.

Kyoto mountains are far smaller than Montana mountains. Still, they offered a sense of solace, escape, and ascent. I climbed past Buddhist and Shinto temples with steeply curved roofs, wooden pillars, and giant wooden doors, opening to reveal golden statues illuminated by candles and incense dancing in a slight forest breeze. The

Buddha statues held a facial expression of stalwart content. While trekking I often passed bamboo groves amidst towering trees.

◆◆◆

In my childhood, memories of my mother are as hazy as the thick triple layers of cigarette smoke that often hung over the kitchen table and coffee table. I recall large jugs of cheap red wine next to packs of Virginia Slims. Sometimes she sent me to the neighborhood store, with a note, to purchase cigarettes. Things were often changing—husbands, boyfriends, vehicles, houses, schools, cities, jobs, religions. Multi-level marketing jobs like Amway and Herbalife never seemed to pan out. Her final religion was a controversial new age one, Church Universal and Triumphant, aka CUT.

One afternoon after school, around the age of ten, I came home to my mother practicing minor astral travel. A jug of Gallo wine sat on the table next to a pack of Virginia Slims, plus a few other objects. She would turn around in her chair, opposite the table, then ask me to quietly move one or two objects around behind her. She would try to lift herself as her soul above her body, turn around, and peer down at the objects, then slip back into her body and tell me which ones I had moved. We practiced this for an hour or more; I don't remember an instance of her guessing accurately.

Another time, late in the evening, I was woken up abruptly and told Satan had drifted inside our house, causing my mom to bring us all together and recite some prayers or chants; then apparently Satan slipped into our cat, Pete, and possessed him. She gave Pete away soon after, to some kind of minister that could speak in tongues and handle the possession.

Once in 6th grade, when I attended a school dance, my mother showed up and yanked me off the dance floor, reminding me that rock music would spin my chakras backwards and sometimes—when played in reverse—would utter Satanic messages.

1st – 6th grade was Missoula, in seven different houses and five different schools; 7th grade Whitefish; 8th grade Butte; 9th grade Bozeman; and 10th grade Whitefish again.

During these strange days, I often wandered nearby streams, hills, and mountains, usually alone or sometimes with neighborhood kids. Mountains were my favorite—clean, quiet, safe, stable.

Mountains didn't move.

Riding the Japanese subway...people, people, everywhere, and not a space to sit. The subways were crowded along with the streets, houses, schools, movie theaters, markets, classrooms, offices, and stores, people spilling out of the city and up into the mountains.

Montana and Japan comprise roughly the same geographical area, yet the population of Kyoto alone, 1.3 million people, is greater than the entire state of Montana. Most of Japan felt incredibly dense, compressed, compact. I didn't realize how much space Montana—and even the United States—provided until I lived in Japan. Open spaces promote individual thinking and a free spirit; small shared spaces promote group thinking and selflessness. More than an ideology, it becomes pragmatic. An only child in a large bedroom, a room of one's own, will probably grow up far more individualistic than four children forced to share a single room. But it was more than psychological.

Living in Japan I felt crushed physically. I stand 6'3 and weigh 190 pounds. The average Japanese person stands 5'3 and weighs 135. Doorways, ceilings, kitchens, sinks, bathrooms...all architecture felt miniature to me...requiring constant slumping, ducking, slouching, bending, squeezing, and a general compression of my physical being. Some Japanese called me "Gulliver." The landscape of Japan seemed to shrink my body and, for a while, my usage of creativity, at least in the external. Mentally and emotionally, however, I was expanding, absorbing, and comprehending these new cultural perspectives. Perhaps if I had only visited a few days, I would have felt as if I had grown several sizes, and like a giant; but living there required me to reduce my physical being.

Take an average person and put them atop a glorious mountain range; take another average person and have them sit in a tiny packed room on a small chair; who will have the more expansive thoughts? Only when I practiced maintaining the great openness of Montana like a vast endless sky inside me could I sit as a Zen student and think big amidst Japan's hyper-compression. And later I tried to hold both East and West in my internal being, balancing and drawing from two different perspectives, using whichever one was most applicable to a present situation.

◆◆◆

I don't recall my father saying much as I grew up, but I can see now that he partly communicated through mountains. To visit my father, I rode the Greyhound Bus north to Whitefish, skirting around Flathead Lake and viewing the long majestic chain of the Rockies capped with snow September through June. Weekend visits sometimes meant a hike into Glacier National Park or Jewel Basin. The Friday night before, about an hour after picking up me or me and my two brothers from the bus station, we prepared our hiking packs, rubbed mink oil into our hiking boots, set them near the fire, checked a few trail maps, and made sandwiches. The next morning at dawn we left for the mountains. After hiking several hours we arrived at a glacial lake campground in early afternoon, set up the tent, rolled out our sleeping bags. Now my brothers and I could scout the area, fish the icy waters, try throwing our hatchets into a tree, skip rocks, or build a fort. At night we cooked dinner—usually freshly-caught trout—and roasted marshmallows. Sleep was short and spotty due to uneven ground or small rocks under the camping pad. Breakfast consisted of granola, fruit, and funky clumps of powdered milk. We broke camp, hiked back, and by 6 p.m. Sunday I was back on the Greyhound bus headed for my mom's house.

In Japan I had to duck constantly. In my tiny two-room apartment I ducked to cross rooms. I ducked to step into the hallway and ducked again to enter the little communal kitchen; visiting the bathroom meant two more ducks; visiting the outside coin-operated shower meant four ducks. On any given day I ducked over a hundred times. Before I learned to duck well, I hit my head so many times that a small scar could be seen across my forehead. But after two or three months of accidental head-whacking, I could duck when half asleep in the middle of the night when visiting the bathroom down the hall. Amazing what a little pain and necessity can do.

Several times a year my father led my brothers and me into the winter mountains on snowshoes or snowmobiles. During Christmas breaks he took us night-skiing on Big Mountain. The steep runs glowed under gigantic yellow lights. I wondered about my mother and father skiing together before I was born; what were they like? I had never seen them together as a couple, and only twice in the same setting at a few tense points in my life.

The bus ride from Missoula to Whitefish takes three hours. Getting a window seat was easy since the bus was usually half-full or less. For most of the trip I watched mountains roll by in the distance. They comforted me and were always there.

On summer evenings in Whitefish, when I was perhaps seven or eight, I often walked down to the end of the gravel driveway and waited for my father to come home from work. I hid in the field and peered through the tall grass. I could see the road for a mile ahead, headlights coming, and kept waiting for those headlights to turn into a familiar Chevy truck. Above the road, far in the distance, stood Big Mountain and adjacent mountains, half dark, half light, during sunset. The waiting is what I remember most—burnt-yellow fields, occasional headlights, overhead looming mountains.

◆ ◆ ◆

After working a year in Kyoto, I planned to visit my friend Aaron in Otaru, Hokkaido for two weeks. He envied my living in Kyoto for all its history, temples, rock gardens, and festivals; however, he preferred Hokkaido as it resembled the Northwest of America in both unfettered open spaces and an outdoor-minded spirit. I envied him and Hokkaido for this, and after all the ducking and compressing, I was ready to stretch out.

◆◆◆

Missoula is a sunken hub of five valleys surrounded by mountains. The Clark Fork River runs through it. Before my Mom moved to Butte and then Bozeman, we lived in Missoula up the Rattlesnake, ten minutes from town, at the base of a few small mountains. After school or on weekends, I hiked these areas for hours. I passed horses in mountain pastures, listening to their husky snorts, watching them swish flies away with their tails; I followed clear rushing streams upwards hoping to find their magical source. In winter my friends and I sledded down the slopes on inner tubes. When we felt brave we built snow-packed jumps to launch off.

During my freshman year in high school, my mother settled in the outskirts of Bozeman. We lived in the basement of a Mexican woman's house at the base of a small mountain; my brothers had already graduated from high school several years before and moved out. I often climbed the mountain alone after school. The basement smelled of cigarette smoke, vodka, and religious incense. When I reached 14, the legal age to choose between living with either parent, I decided to move to Whitefish to live full-time with my father and step-mother.

I recall only strange fragments of the night I told my mother I was leaving. My sweating profusely and shaking; my mother conversely crying or swearing at me for several hours while drinking; my feeling hollowed out inside.

I remember she said I was abandoning her, like others had done. I remember pictures of Saint Germain and Guanyin, the "ascended masters" from Church Universal and Triumphant, staring at me from wood-paneled walls behind her. I remember the coffee-table scarred from cigarette burns. I remember she would sometimes yell "Shiva! Shiva! Shiva!" to ward off any evil spirits in the house. And I remember some chants playing over and over on the stereo... *And in full faith I consciously accept this manifest, manifest, manifest! And in full faith I consciously accept this manifest, manifest, manifest! And in full faith I consciously accept this manifest, manifest, manifest! Right here and now with full power, eternally sustained, all-powerfully active, ever-expanding and world-enfolding until all are wholly ascended in the light and free! Beloved I am! Beloved I am! Beloved I am!*

While dreaming of "real mountains," I booked a 15-hour ferry ride from Maizuru to Otaru, a small port city where Aaron taught, traveling north on the Sea of Japan. It was my first time on the open ocean. To be sure, it was a tiny boat with tiny rooms, but on the foredeck, looking out over dark mysterious waters under a melting sun, drinking a cold Sapporo beer, my soul suddenly unfolded and felt bigger than the ferry. I could better understand Melville's first chapter of Moby Dick and how the sea enchants us all. Space and time stretched out and seemed to move slowly and easily underneath shimmering curling waves. The horizon looked endless, cloudless, timeless. After it got dark, I ducked back into my tiny cabin.

While in Whitefish High School, I played on the golf team, and traveled to courses all over the state, usually at the base of scenic mountains, the occasional fairway climbing upwards with the next hole sloping down.

In Japan, Hokkaido is famous for mountains and hot springs. Geothermal activity brews over all five islands, forming hot springs everywhere, but Hokkaido has the most. When the ferry slipped into Otaru Bay at 6 AM, I could see the landscape as more open and less dense than most of Japan: larger spaces between buildings, bigger restaurants, wider roads, fewer people, healthier outdoorsy individuals, fewer business suits, a slight frontier-feeling in the air. Soon I was down to about twenty ducks a day. Aaron was of medium height at 5'7", and had far less trouble than I. A little short in America, he now stood the same as a tall Japanese man.

Two days later, we set out on a long day hike, planning to drop into mountain hot springs in the evening. We took a subway, bus, and train to reach our trailhead; they were all nearly empty. The mountains looked far bigger than those around Kyoto. Intense greens of many shades covered the landscape. My excitement grew. Ten minutes into our hike we entered a dense forest with thick brush overhead. I had to duck, then continued ducking. I stopped to examine the pathway. For as far as I could see, the path had been manmade, the brush cut at about six feet, reaching precisely to the middle of my forehead, matching my ducking scar. Aaron fit fine and gave a chuckle, then quieted down when he saw the expression on my face. "Sorry, buddy," he said, "I had no idea."

The hike became a three-mile long duck with a heavy day pack. I didn't talk much. When we finally rose above the tree line, near the top, I stood up straight. Aaron admired the rolling mountains that reached the sea, but I stood rubbing my lower back. I was in reasonable physical condition, but flexibility was my weak point. Rarely can I touch my toes with straight legs. I tried it that day and could put my hands flat on the ground. Aaron piped up, "See, now you are more flexible!" The descent became another long duck and, two hours later, I stretched out and nearly collapsed in the hot springs.

The day after graduating high school in early June of 1990, I packed up my '78 Volkswagen Dasher and left for Los Angeles, California. Similar to my mother's house, I had never felt quite right or comfortable at my father's house. By the time I reached Nevada to spend the night, the mountains faded, and desert took over. The next day, a few hours short of LA, I passed through the San Bernardino Mountains. They looked barren, dusty, and polluted. While I worked in Hollywood as a production assistant for television commercials and music videos, and as I navigated through nothing but sprawling concrete, highways, buildings, and factories, I carried around visions of Montana mountains in my mind's eye and in my heart. I remembered the taste of glacial water, the sound of alpine silence, the feeling of passing through forest undergrowth wet with dew. All of this carried me through a year and a half before I felt compelled to return to Montana for college. I had tried hiking once in the LA hills but it was a joke-- small lifeless slopes with loose dirt and gravel. My friend and I continually slipped just trying to walk their base, forget trying to ascend. Nothing was out there, no vegetation, no wildlife, no hiking trails. I went back to LA for work during the summers, always relishing the return north again, watching deserts and plains turn to pine forests and high peaks.

◆◆◆

While Montana hot springs can boast spectacular outdoor settings, Japan has become the master of refined indoor hot springs. The indoor area of a Japanese onsen is usually spacious and high, with wooden walls and marble floors, and several soaking pools ranging from bathwater warm to piping hot. You can also try the cold plunge. Some pools have jets with ultrasonic waves, varying in power; others have a light waterfall that you can sit under. And, of course, a few pools are for pure silent soaking. Then one moves to the *rotumbro*, outside bath. These have similar features to the inside pools, but with the environment of a Zen rock garden or other landscaped setting, which might include boulders, plants, flowers, waterfalls, and trees. If it rains you can take cover under the simple wooden awnings in and beside the pools. The posted signs say no alcohol, but almost no one obeys this, and cold sake or draft beer can be readily purchased. If the whole human race were able to soak in this on a weekly basis, surely the planet would be a more peaceful and relaxed place. Aaron and I did, however, experience one substantial drawback. A century or two ago, Western Puritanism seeped its way into Japanese culture and put an end to the common practice of nude bathing for all. Sad. Once or twice we did imagine climbing over the small wooden walls and saying *konbonwa*, good evening, to any female bathers on the other side. But we were so relaxed in the hot pools that these thoughts, like the rest of our concerns, evaporated into the evening air.

While attending the University of Montana in Missoula, I hiked Mount Sentinel two or three times a week, an impressive presence that starts on the edge of campus and climbs two thousand feet. Once a month, college friends and I drove two hours west for hot springs hidden in the Bitterroot National Forest. After a forty-minute hike we reached a small paradise. Campers had used rocks and logs to build numerous hot pools varying in size and temperature, all adjacent to a lovely ice-cold river. You could soak in open areas or under large pine boughs tucked in the forest, saunter down to the river for a cold dip to cool off, then pick up your wine or beer chilling in the river and bring it back to your friends for further outdoor decadence.

After 14 months of working in Japan, I had experienced several stages of the foreign living process. First the exotic stage: everything felt new, wild, interesting. Then came culture shock, having to navigate a completely different social and professional landscape along with the environmental differences. The hierarchy is supreme, and one not even dare "step on the boss's shadow," as the Japanese idiom goes. Usually following this stage was moderate acceptance and functionality. Then, after eight months, most foreigners felt deeply homesick, and started making plans to return home. For those of us who stayed longer, like me, the kaleidoscope continued to shift. I felt deep irritation, even prejudice, towards Japan and Japanese culture. I was sick of the group thinking and hyper-structure to everything, where reshaping the rules was never allowed; I was sick of hearing the monotone Japanese language all around me; I was sick of ducking, crouching, slouching, bending, and continually reducing my physique to fit the small surroundings; I was sick of the dark aspects of life being swept underneath a squeaky-clean Japanese surface; I was sick of Japanese ignorance and aloofness to the rest of the globe; I was sick of my own habits of broken, dumbed-down English, my brain and wit growing increasingly dull; I was sick of having to communicate with Japanese friends and coworkers in simplified terms while always avoiding more interesting, complicated subjects. True, there were numerous positives to staying this long, becoming intimate with the city and suburbs, growing closer to Japanese people and better understanding their customs, plus picking up lucrative private students. But the anger and resentment started grinding away at my internal landscape; it seemed I was carrying seven sacks of rice on my shoulders.

During Montana winters I often cross-country skied in mountain valleys, occasionally slipping on skins to scale up mountains and then telemark back down, taking easy, soft turns in fresh powder. Mountains were quiet, clean, and life made simple. They demanded warmer clothing like wool and fleece; the sensation of being wrapped up and protected in something was a feeling I came to crave and enjoy.

When my frustrations with Japan seemed near eruption, I took a day off and went hiking up Kurama Mountain, an hour north of Kyoto, planning to soak in hot springs that evening. After climbing two hours, I reached the summit. A temple and small museum were perched on top. The autumn air carried a light chill and the Japanese maples, Bloodgood and Crimson Queen, burst with deep purple, cherry-red, and pumpkin-yellow leaves. It was a Tuesday afternoon and I didn't see anyone around, a rarity in

Japan, but of course most Japanese people were working. Inside the museum I found several statues of ancient warriors—with weapons, armor, and artifacts—on three levels. I read the plaques recounting numerous battles, perils, and hardships of long-ago Japan. An audio recording played war-cries and swords clashing. A mock village displayed workers pumping water, weaving clothing, and cooking in a giant outdoor pit.

Then I visited the wooden temple. Its steeply-slanted roof protected three twenty-foot golden Buddhas. They sat cross-legged, quiet, as if in meditation. Candles and incense flickered in front. I reflected on Japan's long history and the many forces that shaped its present day. I found myself bowing, then removing my shoes and kneeling on the tatami mat floor. I whispered to the Buddhas, tears streaming down my face. I offered a prayer to the statues, to the ancient warriors, to the ancient culture of Japan, asking them to forgive the anger and prejudice swelling in my heart. I told them many aspects of their land were difficult to accept and understand. But now I would try again, try more deeply. Please help me comprehend the beauty and power of your way of life; help me understand the Japanese mindset; construct for me an internal Japanese temple from which I can sit, breathe, and flow like a Buddha. I sat with my tears. I felt alive and real again.

Awhile later I rose up, put my shoes back on, and walked out into the sunlight. I could hear my footsteps clearly. My mind carried a strange electric hum. Soon I was floating down the mountain trail and into the village. With ease I ducked into the changing room of Kurama Hot Springs. I soaked quietly during sunset. If I can make peace with Japan, and understand what forces created it, appreciate its positives and negatives, perhaps someday I could visit each of my parents' homes with the same intent and transcendence.

Wherever I am, I look for mountains.

CHAPTER 6, ENGLISH LESSONS (OR MOONRISE)

Japanese people have a saying about romance: "A man's heart has many rooms, while a woman's heart changes owners."

Sometimes I wonder if I created a strange *washitsu* (room) for Yoshiko. Or perhaps I strung her along for the money? I was 30, she 64. I do think about her occasionally, our long conversations, walks alongside hillside temples, sitting cross-legged on wooden platforms over small rivers while enjoying traditional dining in the heat of Japanese summer.

Japan itself seemed bathed in paradoxes. How could Japanese eat lean, light, healthy meals while simultaneously smoking and drinking excessively? How could the culture emphasize over-the-top-politeness while victims of crimes were rarely helped by passersby? How could Japanese keep their houses and city streets ultra-clean while littering in parks and nature preserves? How could most husbands visit brothels and keep mistresses on a regular basis while the wives never complained, provided all was kept discreet? How could some ancient samurai decapitate their enemies in daylight while writing nature poetry amidst bamboo groves under starlight?

The longer I lived in Japan, the more these contradictions began to make sense, and I started to view Western culture in a new light.

I worked as Yoshiko's private English instructor; our lessons involved sightseeing and fine dining around the city of Kyoto. One night, eight months into our lessons, she brought Japanese plums for desert, encircled by fragrant pink flowers. Her face looked different that evening, luminescent, daring. And everything would change.

◆◆◆

Our story begins in Kyoto, one of the most culturally-rich cities on the planet. Kyoto contains 1600 Buddhist temples, 400 Shinto shrines, dozens of palaces, museums, castles, and Zen rock gardens. It is the traditional setting for various festivals and ceremonies and holds 17 UNESCO World Heritage Sites. Kyoto served as Japan's imperial center and capital for nearly 1100 years until the role transferred to Tokyo in 1868. For cultural significance—and within the hearts of most Japanese—Kyoto remains the true jewel of Japan, the Paris of France, the Rome of Italy, the Prague of the Czech Republic, the St. Petersburg of Russia.

In the year 2000, I am working for the international language institute Berlitz, founded in 1878. Berlitz operates more than 450 schools in over 60 countries. The Kyoto branch employs French, Italian, Spanish, and German teachers, but mostly English teachers walk the hallways.

At first the atmosphere intimidates me—three stages of interviews and demonstration lessons to secure a position, monitoring devices in the classroom, multi-layered, level-specific instruction. And other high IQ teachers assume a rural Montanan doesn't belong in the cosmopolitan, erudite atmosphere of Berlitz. But now I walk the hallways with more confidence. Japanese generally like Americans and American culture, and they seem to like my methods. Truth be told, I don't always match the specific vocabulary with the student's level, nor do I follow the precise format during the forty-minute lessons. Ken, the head teacher, a fifty-year-old pompous Brit, frequently calls me into his office to reprimand my wayward instruction. He reminds me that the students are paying $75 for their forty-minute lessons. He hands me a few manuals that I must review and commit to memory. I nod and bow and agree, then tell him I'll work harder. But I've already tried several times; the manuals and rigorous methods don't work for me. Fortunately, the students seem to appreciate my other qualities: friendliness, passion, a spring in my step, a theatrical presence, a sincerity to connect. I throw in stories of snowboarding Montana glaciers, soaking in forest hot springs under autumn moonlight, enduring winters so cold that one's spit freezes before it reaches the ground. (I admit, that last tale I stole from Jack London. But how many Japanese have read 'To Build A Fire'? None that I meet.)

Rich Japanese businessmen stumble through our doors at 8 p.m., up since 6 a.m., impeccably dressed but now starting to unravel, here only because their companies and bosses require the continual study of English. They are tired, browbeaten, and miss their families. Do they want forty minutes of English drills and grammar stuffed into their heads? Do they want to be admonished for not doing their homework and forgetting their vocabulary? That's where my way works. I tell stories; I listen to theirs; I engage them and offer encouraging words. And it is all in English. Most often stone faces break into smiles and shyness turns to laughter. Amidst this I pepper in a few principles of English. What's more, if I bump into students on the streets of Kyoto, I take time to visit, share a cup of green tea, let them show me around a little. Japanese love to play host, and especially love to be the first ones to introduce something special about Japan.

Soon Berlitz students start requesting me, then later hint at private lessons. Such territory can be dangerous...I tread carefully. If teachers accept private offers then Berlitz loses business, and thus freelancers are fired. Yet in Japan nearly all foreigners give private lessons, regardless of institute rules. Apparently it requires only discretion. I start exchanging emails under the guise of following up on a lesson. Going the extra mile. They email me, I email them.

Later, I drop an invitation for tea. We meet near a temple or rock garden. Near the end of a rendezvous, I mention we might try private lessons, and they agree quickly, as if that's what they had in mind all along. I start building a lucrative business of private students at $50 an hour. I'm able to reduce my hours at Berlitz, which are killing me anyhow (50 plus teaching hours with a schedule that changes weekly).

At the expat bars, other foreigners love to hear my stories of private students. They toast me. "That's our edge," they say. "That's to make up for all the BS rules, the isolation, the long hours with little vacation." I think about the coin-operated shower adjacent to my apartment building, the squat toilets, hitting my head on all the doorways.

Side note: Finding good housing is extremely difficult for foreigners. First, the Japanese are kind to foreigners but it's often on the surface, and they want to keep you at a certain distance from their culture. They think (often accurately) that we are not as clean and harmonious, and more liable to destroy property, or at least leave property far more damaged than a Japanese would, especially since we are just "passing through." We don't have the same sense of Confucian shame that would keep us in line. On top of this, even for Japanese, securing housing is far more difficult than in America. You are required to pay "key money," like a deposit but often five or six times the amount of a usual American/Western deposit. Even more, you are required to have a kind of co-signor, someone who will take all responsibility if you fail in your rental duties. Combine all these factors—and foreigners are stuck in shoddy housing.

One of my Berlitz students, a doctor, proposes a Saturday lesson in his hospital with three other doctors. They pay me $250 for two hours and bow to me before and after. They laugh with me and work hard at all my lessons. It's so easy I feel guilty. But then again, I'm the one who moved to Japan, uprooted and replanted myself here. I miss home, I miss friends, I miss family. Maybe I should capitalize all I can, save up money for back in the states. Another private student teaches Science at a technical college, and we arrange a deal in which I instruct a class of twenty freshman for three hours a week. I enjoy teaching, enjoy the students, enjoy swimming in these friendly tides of Japanese culture.

With my newfound wealth, I can comfortably date and later maintain a Japanese girlfriend, Toa (pronounced 'toe-aye'). In Japan, men are expected to pay for everything without question. Toa is quick-witted, charismatic, and speaks English well, having lived in the U.S. four years. Toa looks more Chinese or Filipino than Japanese, with slightly darker skin and dark eyes. She's average height for a Japanese girl, 5'2, but unlike most Japanese women, has a substantial bosom.

I bike all over Kyoto, and meet her while biking home one night. I pedal slowly past two women on a cobblestone walkway, in a covered market, and turn my head and smile. They smile back. I am a little tipsy from just sharing sake with Japanese coworkers after work. Twenty feet later, I turn and smile again, wave goodbye. One girl says "Hey!" and I pedal back. I hop off, introduce myself, and walk with them awhile, invite the outgoing one who said "hey" and who speaks the best English—Toa—to an Irish bar up the street. I'm part Irish, I say, and have always wanted to try out this bar, The Hill of Tara. (True, not an impromptu line.)

She understands the West, my Japan impressions and frustrations. And I understand her. Apparently her living in San Diego for four years, and then returning to Japan, has created a cultural gulf. She turned a little Western; I'm turning a little Asian. Even more, we are the same age. We forget the people and environment around us; we could have been in any setting.

It felt like a magical night, in a foreign country, the future wide open, two strangers becoming intimate. We drink, we talk and talk. She touches my shoulder occasionally. I forget everything else in my life. All that matters is her dark mystical eyes, her quick wit, her youthful exotic skin dotted with adorable freckles, her magnificent large breasts.

I walk her home, she invites me up for a cup of green tea. Inside we soon kiss, she puts on Lenny Kravitz, the clothes fall away, we make love. A small earthquake shakes the room. Around 4:30 a.m. she serves Miso soup, then we have sex again. Another earthquake. I steal a

Hemingway line from *For Whom the Bell Tolls* and say: "Whenever we are together, the Earth moves." She is quiet for a moment, then pulls me close. She tells me she has a Japanese boyfriend, but likes me, too. Three weeks later, I bring her a handful of cherry blossoms, picked from alongside the *Kamo-Gawa* (Kamo River) while riding my bike to her downtown apartment. She breaks up with the other guy.

Toa lives two blocks from Berlitz. Twice a week I can skip the long bike ride into work. It's actually a lovely ride down two rivers and lots of narrow streets with interesting neighborhoods, but since it's summer, hot and humid, I relish avoiding the heat and shouldering a backpack stuffed with dress clothes. I'm feeling better about Japan, more grounded, a more comfortable work setup. My coworkers seem to notice my confidence and engage me more. Make fun of Montana now, I think. To boot, I land a small acting role in a provincial TV commercial, then work two days as a model for Universal Studios Japan, located in nearby Osaka. Some aspects of Japan still bring me down—the tight, crowded spaces, lower level of healthcare and services, narrow-minded homogenous views—but I seem to have built a comfortable life.

◆◆◆

I step into class for my 7:10 lesson: free-talking night. In a Japanese language school, free-talking night often translates into forty minutes of painful silence, and could double as spiritual training for Buddhist monks. I look around the classroom and see five ordinary stone-faced women. No, wait, one older lady stands out. She wears bright red, has large black eyes, meets my gaze instead of looking shyly to the side. She has long black curly hair. I notice a large ugly mole between her eyebrows. The woman in red, Yoshiko, starts the group off by chatting about recent politics. I feel grateful. As the forty minutes tick by, however, she continually and unabashedly hogs my attention, while I do my best to balance out the English conversation amidst all the students. I can't help thinking she might be an excellent candidate for private tutoring. And she appears wealthy, flaunts it in her dress and jewelry.

I see an opportunity to exchange emails at the end but hold back because of other alert or listening students. I must be careful, patient. Perhaps like bamboo, my ethics in Japan have become strong yet flexible. Lately I've been pondering how Japanese people bend the rules, and as long as they stay discreet and keep the surface of human relations clean and harmonious, no one seems to mind. Looking straight into Yoshiko's eyes, pausing a beat, I bid her a polite farewell until the next lesson. Securing lucrative private lessons in Japan—and in fact most Japanese business deals—resembles a careful courtship, and I find its rhythms intriguing.

◆ ◆ ◆

Three weeks later we run into each other on Teramachi Street, a large tunnel-like pavilion that sells market goods and traditional crafts. I'm heading to a movie but have an hour to spare. Her mole stands out, I feel bad noticing it, and try not to look at it. We duck into an underground eatery with a bar. She plays the consummate host, orders wine and snacks, then asks me all about Montana. Other Japanese around us stare, envious of her English, envious of her having a foreign friend. I feel a little like an accessory. I know the opportunity for private lessons approaches and prepare myself for an appropriate price. Perhaps I should raise my rates? To my surprise, she, too, has patience. "I have a proposal for you, Brendan, but not here. Have you ever had dinner at the Kyoto Hotel? They have wonderful dining on the top floor, overlooking the two Kyoto rivers and surrounding mountains. A fine night view. Shall we have dinner next Wednesday evening?" She tries to deliver these sentences naturally, but as an English teacher, I can tell they were scripted, studied, and practiced. I agree to dinner.

I sit in the movie theater alone and wonder how much money Yoshiko will offer. The surrounding Japanese are deathly quiet. I fear eating popcorn for the noise it might make. How long will the lessons be? Perhaps I can further reduce my hours at Berlitz? I felt comfortable in Japan now, and yet, it was hard to know when to stop.

The next week we dine on the top floor of the Kyoto Hotel. I soak up the tall ceilings, spacious doorways, plush carpets, elegant furniture, bright chandeliers, hyper-attentive service, and a long buffet overflowing with seafood, meats, soups, and breads. I feel Western again. In fact, I feel upper-class Western. The waiter brings a bottle of wine, insists I taste it first, for approval. I'm nervous, don't know the routine, go through a few motions, smell the wine and pretend to look at it carefully, taste it, then tell him it's fine.

Out the window and far below, the Kamo Gawa, or Kamo River, flashes silver and gold in the fading sunset. Geisha, maiko, and samurai once walked along this river, escorting imperial caravans. The Kamo Gawa runs alongside the famous Gion area, where narrow cobblestone streets wind their way through craft shops, markets, and traditional temples. The 1600 wooden temples in Kyoto were built without a single nail. Pressed up against this setting, modern buildings cast a shadow over the ancient past.

I look over at Yoshiko. She wears a high-cut silk blouse and flowing green silk skirt that ends at her ankles. She holds herself in a distinguished manner, sitting erect, poised, calm. The white purse alongside her chair has gold and silver speckles. An old lady purse, I think, but ritzy. The large mole between her eyebrows, sitting slightly more towards the right eyebrow, looks heavily powdered and less noticeable.

As if she senses my fixation on her mole, she speaks to break the spell. "Do you like this atmosphere? Atmosphere is important to me, especially now that I am getting older. I always want to have a beautiful atmosphere around me. Sometimes in life we must create this."

"It's wonderful, Yoshiko. And thank you for inviting me this evening."

"It is my pleasure. It will always be my pleasure, Brendan. You see, Kyoto has many splendid sights to visit and I would like to be your tour guide." She pulls out a piece of paper and studies it. "Forgive me, but I wrote all these sentences down, to communicate better. I tried to memorize them but it is difficult. Ah, here. In exchange for my hosting, please help me with my English, especially conversation. After a few years, I will move to New York City and live with my son, an architect. Therefore, I need good American English, and your speaking voice is quite clear, and you have a nice, deep voice. I find it relaxing. Can you do this for me?"

She looks up from her paper, steady; her eyes and mole seem to pierce my innermost being. However, I have prepared for this. And part of my mind can't help but think, cha-ching! Japanese yen would soon be flowing towards me like the Kamo Gawa in flood season.

"I would be honored, Yoshiko." I offer a small bow from across the table. "Kyoto is an amazing, magnificent city, and I count myself extremely fortunate to have you as a host. Also, I will use all my skills from Berlitz and my university education to improve your English mastery and prepare you for New York." I have grown accustomed to using over-the-top language in this country, as such phrasing fits well into the Japan idea of appeasing the ego and, as always, saving face. Also, I know not to speak of money until the end of any negotiation—another important custom.

Yoshiko smiles. We eat slowly and enjoy the surroundings. I have learned to be patient with Japanese people, giving them plenty of time to answer my questions or remaining silent between conversations, so they can choose appropriate vocabulary and form sentences. Such patience and respect have won me many invitations, drinks, and friends. Most Japanese people want you to be their special American friend; they wish to dazzle you with their country and culture. Sometimes they like to wear you on their arm like a shiny bracelet or badge, as if to say, "Look at this! I have an American friend, I can speak English, and we have overcome the barriers between our countries to form a beautiful relationship!"

While spooning vanilla ice cream, Yoshiko asks about my hourly fee for private lessons. I tell her 5,000 yen, roughly fifty dollars an hour. She nods, then asks if there will be a discount for five hours straight, since we will visit temples all over Kyoto and then dine out. She will pay all expenses, including the taxis around the city, which are expensive in Japan, as everything else. Our lessons will be casual. In Japanese style, once two people finish bartering or negotiating, the subject will not be addressed again. I nod and mentally weigh my words carefully. Sure, the expensive feast and plush environment of the Kyoto Hotel softened me up, but even before the dinner, I decided to keep my standards and price high, as I felt my education and American citizenship constituted valuable commodities. Plus, I have already weathered a year of Japan, negotiating culture shock, difficult living conditions, and a lonely social setting. I deserve to be well paid. Yet again, I also remember an article I'd read about children from broken and troubled homes; sometimes these children, the psychologist suggested, feel something was stolen from them, and therefore as adults are more apt to exploit other people or situations under the premise that the world still owes them something. And just where is the line between smart business and greedy exploitation, I wonder.

"I understand, Yoshiko. Your offer is wonderful. And, to accommodate your lesson time I should give up a day's work at Berlitz, and, in fact, one other private lesson with a university professor. I want to be fresh for our lessons and devote the day to you. Therefore, I must request the full hourly fee." She acts politely and says she must think about it for a few days, though I notice a fleeting wrinkle of anger alter her face, the tiniest betrayal of Japanese harmony, but the frown evaporates just as quickly, making me wonder if it was ever there. I try to keep my face polite and calm, while a part of me can't help but think, I'm a greedy bastard. And I have no intention of giving up the university professor but will simply switch him to another night.

On the way out of the restaurant, several Japanese staff stop us, ask me questions, then speak to Yoshiko in Japanese. She tells me that they think my height and blue eyes are wonderful, and I seem very kind. She tells me they envy her a great deal, having an American friend like myself, and that her English must be good. By the time I bid Yoshiko goodnight, a new aura of happiness dances over her aging countenance. I know she will pay the full amount. And so it begins.

◆◆◆

I teach private English lessons to Yoshiko on Wednesdays. She knocks on my door at 3 p.m., usually bearing a small snack or gift. She gives me a traditional teapot with cups so we can enjoy green tea or other herb teas that she brings. Another time she hands me a used but expensive silk scarf, which belonged to her husband when he was alive. I learn that he was a scientist who worked both in Japan and America, then died of cancer. She has four children: three daughters and the son in New York.

After a little chat, we take a taxi to a famous temple, such as *Kiyomizu Dera*. This large wooden structure rests at the base of a small mountain and its deck overlooks

Gion Village, sunlight or moonlight hitting reflective paper lanterns hanging below steeply-slanted roofs. Little streams run alongside *Kiyomizu Dera*, carrying tree leaves in the fall and cherry blossoms in the spring, trickling down hills until they disappear into the stone water ducts running through Gion. The rooms inside have floors of tatami, woven straw and rice, and picturesque screens depicting nature or royalty. The architectural design stretches out from side-to-side, rather than top-to-bottom, as American/Western buildings. Yoshiko and I walk slowly through the temples, and around the wide courtyard, while she explains the history, and I correct or assist her English.

We pass a three-story pagoda, *Koyasu-no-to,* which houses and protects a statue of the goddess of newborn infants. On the famous high deck, we drink hot ceremonial green tea and look down upon Gion. I try to imagine the legendary ninja who in the pure blackness of night scaled the wooden pillars, crept across cold floors, and assassinated high-ranking officials. Walking down steep stone stairs, Yoshiko takes my arm for balance. As we reach ground level, she continues to hold my arm. Eventually I withdraw, feeling a little strange, asking politely, "Are you alright now?" She pulls her arm back but says sometimes she will need my arm and body for assistance. I wonder if she is looking for excuses to touch me; touching is rare in Japan. But how can I say no to an elderly lady?

We always finish with four- or five-star dining. My first few months in Japan I hated sushi and other raw fish delicacies—much to the shock and dishonor of my hosts—but now I love it and try many kinds, provided I can still eat a good steak once in a while. Yoshiko always asks what I prefer to eat and offers a selection of appropriate restaurants. Together we enjoy sashimi, sushi, tempura, mochi, sekihan, tofu, donburi, takoyaki, yakatori, and okinori. This translates to octopus, yellowtail, eel, grilled chicken with soy sauce, raw whipped eggs, rice cakes, fish cakes, prawns, squid, and seaweed. Occasionally I insist we try a Western place for hamburgers, spaghetti, or sandwiches, but these are hard to find. We usually take 90 minutes or more for dinner, at first discussing popular English phrases or idioms, then turning to stories of her life or mine. After she hears of my fragmented childhood, including an alcoholic mother who married and divorced four times then later joined a strange religion considered by many a cult—she is even sweeter, and sometimes tries to mother me. Later, she frequently tells me that as an artist, whether I succeed in acting or writing, I should experience everything. "Everything, Brendan." She reiterates with an idiom I recently defined for her, "Brendan, you should leave no stone unturned." Her dark brown eyes flash brightly. I shift uncomfortably in my seat. I know she is hinting towards romance but of course I wish to sidestep this fantasy. She tells me that she taught and played piano most of her life. She, too, is an artist, and she says she therefore understands the wild, unique passions of artistic people.

After five months, I have visited over fifty historical sites in Japan's most revered city, thanks to Yoshiko. Sometimes while teaching at Berlitz other Japanese students will exclaim, "Wow! You have seen more of Kyoto than I have!" At $250 per lesson, I have made over $6K in cash. With Yoshiko dropping an additional $250 per lesson on taxi fare, activities, and dinner, she has spent approximately $12,000. I now work a reduced schedule at Berlitz, a light schedule at the Kyoto Biocollege, and have a lush array of private lessons. In addition to Yoshiko, I teach the group of doctors on Saturdays for $250 cash per two-hour session; I also meet a university professor once a week, two hours, $100 cash. They are fun to teach, too, though sometimes students cancel due to their busy schedules. Yoshiko never misses a lesson.

After Wednesday lessons with Yoshiko, I bike twenty-five minutes alongside the *Katsura Gawa* and *Kamo Gawa* rivers, then veer downtown to Toa's apartment. Toa and I are serious now. Her parents own a teapot company and Toa travels and sells for them part-time. In her free time, she practices flower-arrangement, calligraphy, and studies English. A few nights a week we drink sake, exchange details of the day, watch TV or a movie, make love. Various flowers and vases fill her apartment—experiments from her classes. I try to always spend Wednesday late nights with Toa. Although my time with Yoshiko is pleasant in many ways, and profitable, I feel a need to sweep away her oldness and gloom; as she once joked to me herself, she sometimes seems a vampire trying to suck my youth away while paying me well for it. Also, people stare at Yoshiko and me in public. She appears to like this. I don't. The way she dresses, touches me, and talks softly to me hints at a relationship beyond a private English teacher. Yoshiko knows about Toa but never discusses her; whenever I mention Toa, she quickly changes the subject.

About six months into our lessons, by happenstance we have dinner near Toa's apartment. I drink several cups of hot sake along with grilled meat and vegetables. Yoshiko encourages me to drink more. I start getting a little tipsy. I start thinking about Toa, her warmth, her touch, her naked body, making love. Rather than take a taxi 20 minutes home, then bike 30 minutes back to Toa's, I want to walk to her place from here. Usually after our dinners, Yoshiko hails me a cab, pays for it, and gives the driver directions. Tonight I tell her I don't need a taxi; I say I want to drop by Berlitz, also nearby, and get something from my teaching locker. I know it is best not to mention that I will instead walk two blocks to Toa's place.

The following Wednesday, Yoshiko seems unusually distant, albeit polite. Then suddenly at dinner she lambasts me: "You disrespected me last Wednesday! How could you do such a thing? I pay for an outing and lovely dinner, and then you spend the night with Toa! You must never do that again. I have a woman's intuition. I know what happened. From now on, Wednesdays are for me and me only. If you don't agree I will quit our lessons!"

I stop eating, take a shot of sake. "What do you mean? I..."

"You were a little drunk last Wednesday. Why would you step into Berlitz during work hours in such condition? You are too professional for that. And, I saw your face, you were thinking about another woman at the end of our dinner. You were thinking about Toa. I saw the excitement in your eyes, something you rarely show for me."

I take another shot of sake. The thought of slinking back to Berlitz on Wednesdays, coupled with losing this comfortable lifestyle I took so long to build, speeds up my thinking. I try to acquiesce without admitting the obvious truth that she has brought to the surface. "Well, Yoshiko, I know we have talked about my writing a book on Kyoto. Perhaps after your wonderful hosting on Wednesdays, I should focus only on this project, rather than pursuing other activities with friends. I should take notes, write down details while fresh in my memory, and organize temple pictures."

She takes a piece of sashimi, chews carefully, swallows. She clears her throat. "Yes, Wednesdays should be for me and your art. Your memory may forget things easily. You must take notes on the places we visit, and start putting together your book, week by week." She looks more relaxed now. "I am helping you write a beautiful book on Kyoto and Japan. Often Westerners do not understand or appreciate the richness of our history. You can show them."

I smile. I've become more Japanese, sweeping a difficult thing under the carpet and putting up a false harmonious front. I take another shot of sake. I'm a sellout, I think. An inner voice says, *Always take the taxi back to your apartment. Then you can ride your bike down the river and through the side streets as usual to Toa's. Yoshiko will never know.* This Japanese self goes on: *You can still take notes and write the book in your spare time. She is not controlling you, you are just letting her believe she is controlling you. Anyway, give her this gesture, she is an old lady who has treated you well. Let her have her fantasies. And, if you want to keep up these private lessons, don't make another mistake like that one!*

I think about the many Japanese husbands and "salary men", who visit prostitutes while traveling on business, and even close to home. What lies do they weave to their wives and selves? Or is this just accepted, considered natural in society, provided one stays discreet? I feel I am using Yoshiko, but isn't she also using me? At least we are still speaking and discussing English in the lessons.

Later that night I ride my bike down the river and through tiny backstreets to Toa's. I tell Toa everything. First she reacts with anger and demands I quit the lessons. Later, as I reveal other details, Yoshiko's small flirtations and attempts at old style courtship, she grows intrigued, amazed that an elderly Japanese lady would do such things. You know, she says, that is a lot of money to give up. And Yoshiko is very interesting. Try it a little longer, Brendan. Let's see what happens.

In my own mind, the truth I had tried to avoid could no longer be avoided: Yoshiko is trying to seduce me. The question is, how long could I sidestep this seduction and continue with the profitable arrangement? And, if possible, could I transform this energy back into a working friendship that benefits us both? I do gain satisfaction and joy from teaching, from having students learn well and appreciate my efforts, and it makes me feel as though I'm doing some good in the world. I don't want to lose these positive attributes.

At seven months, Yoshiko invites me to her house. Nearly all Japanese entertain outside of the home, and only good friends and relatives ever receive in-house invitations. I meet her mother-in-law, the reason she is "stuck in Japan." When her husband died, it became her cultural duty to look after her. When the mother-in-law dies, Yoshiko can move to New York and live with her son. The mother-in-law doesn't speak English; she looks old, but fit and happy. When I inquire about the mother-in-law, Yoshiko says with a sigh, "She is very healthy today, as always."

Yoshiko shows me around her house. High ceilings, lots of plants, clean, elegant. She takes me to her bedroom, which she calls the "Queen's Room," then points to three large pictures propped up on a bookshelf. She had spoken of her admiration for Sean Connery, and I see his image in the left-hand picture. Brad Pitt is framed in the right-hand picture. And the middle photograph? There I am, smiling back at me. Several weeks back, Yoshiko took this shot of me by a five-story pagoda, then blew it up to 8x10 and inserted my image in a silver pewter frame. It's an honor, I say, while I feel both proud (next to two titans) and panicked (maybe this has already gone too far?). I quickly ask to see her flower garden, which she has told me much about, and she takes my arm and leads me outside. Wait until Toa hears about this, I think.

Later, Yoshiko takes me to *Ryoan-ji*, Japan's most revered Zen rock garden. Several large rocks rest in a large oblong area of white sand. Islands in the ocean, an English translation reads, our souls amidst the world. Yoshiko translates an inscription on a stone water basin nearby: "I learn only to be contented." Today, Yoshiko's face matches the speckled shine of sunlight upon sand.

◆◆◆

Eight months into our lessons, Yoshiko shows up in a bright red silk dress, low-cut. She has a light, enthusiastic quality surrounding her. I sense she will make a move and must prepare. I have tried to keep her at bay for weeks now, dropping hints like, "You are like a wonderful Japanese aunt to me" and "You are a unique, special friend." Admittedly, I still want the lessons to continue as long as possible. She has brought dinner to my apartment tonight, and we are to stay in and watch a movie. Often she has told me I resemble Tyrone Powers, a famous American actor from the 1940s, and she wants us to watch one of his films, which she owns. She lights candles, we eat dinner, start the movie. Halfway through, she stops the movie and sets up dessert, Japanese plums, encircled by fragrant pink flowers. The plums and flowers create a light sweet scent that lingers in the air. She sits across my rectangular, wooden table. Outside we hear the croaking of thousands of frogs whooping it up for mating season in the myriad rice paddies nearby.

"Brendan, I can contain myself no longer. You see, I married very young, and simply followed my duty. But I didn't feel passion for my husband. In my heart, and regarding true love, I am still a young girl..."

"Yoshiko, I..."

"Stop. Let me finish. I am not a fool, Brendan. I know you better than you think. I watch you very closely every

Wednesday. I live for Wednesdays! We have something, Brendan, we have a special world, you and me. But you need a young woman's body. I know this. I want to show you something. I still have a young woman's body. Just watch."

She unbuttons her red blouse, peels it away from her shoulders, exposing her upper body and dark purple bra. Her hands reach behind her back and start unfastening the bra. I don't look closely at her body; I am too busy trying to stop this car crash while still saving face. How did it get to this? A sixty-four-year-old woman undressing for me and proclaiming her affection? I'm less than half her age.

"Yoshiko, no, I am sorry. Please don't do that. We have something special, yes, but it is friendship only." She stops, her hands still poised to unhook her bra. "Please don't, Yoshiko! It is better if we stay friends. I think of you as a wonderful family member."

Her hands drop to her sides. She grows quiet, puts her blouse back on, puts her head down. She starts crying. Now I feel guilty. And I know she has gravely crossed the line as a traditional Japanese woman. She is losing face.

"Yoshiko, please. Listen, I admire your bravado, your wild artistic spirit. It must take a great deal of courage and passion to try something like this. I respect you so much, and I appreciate our friendship. But I don't feel the same way sexually. I am sorry." What I say is true. What I leave out, however, is that I also feel nauseous, angry, and slightly violated. But if I express these feeling she will be devastated, as well as quit the lessons. Also, in many ways, she has grown on me as a friend, and I don't like hurting people. And I want to believe that I am valuable enough as a friend and English teacher for her to still want our lessons. Sometimes people, relationships, and cultures get so complex it's hard to see them clearly.

"I understand. Maybe I should quit your lessons. I can't take this. It is torture for me."

"Well, why don't we think things over for a while? I believe we can still be friends. We can do this, Yoshiko. I need your help on my Japan book. And someday you will travel to New York. You need good American English. It's okay. Let's see how things go."

She collects herself. "Okay, Brendan. We will see. We will try. I should go now."

She places the envelope with 25,000 yen on the desk. She leaves. I stare at the envelope for long while, not touching it. Later I take out the bills and count them. I want to continue buying nice dinners for Toa, saving money for graduate school back in America, purchasing traditional gifts to send family and friends back home. I want to continue visiting historical sites so that I can take notes for stories. Am I immoral to want this? Have I gone too far? What have I become? Whose morals and ethics do I follow, America's or Japan's?

I begin to see that each person has to construct their own moral universe, regardless of their environment, their family, their culture, their country. But most choose the easier path—simply following what they grew up around. The moral universe of my father and mother were strikingly different, which was confusing enough. But now, as I had started to find my place in my late twenties and early thirties, being intensely and intimately exposed to another culture's moral universe clouded my perspective. Again, I had to ultimately decide—and own—all my choices.

Toa listens to tonight's episode with rapt attention while we recline on her bed. I prepare myself for an outburst of anger and lecturing. Suddenly she laughs. "You should just sleep with her, Brendan. She has paid you so much money! Don't tease her like this." She laughs and pulls out her electronic dictionary. "Here it is—gigolo—that's what you can be." I laugh but also wince inwardly. Toa has a witty way of looking at life in an unadorned perspective and cutting to the chase. I tell her maybe I wouldn't mind a gigolo lifestyle if all my clients would be as foxy and beautiful as her.

Two weeks later, Yoshiko appears dignified as we resume the lessons. The following week, she brings a cutout from a fashion magazine. The wedding picture displays a Western man and woman side-by-side, beaming with happiness. Japanese advertisements often feature foreigners, Western and European models. Yoshiko has superimposed a photograph of my head—cut out from one of the pictures she took—on the man. "What do you think?" she asks. I am quiet. She says that I belong with Western women, my own culture and race. Toa is probably a decent girl, she continues, but I should break up with her before I go back home. Then some day when I marry I should send Yoshiko my wedding pictures. Trying to change the subject, I tell her I may leave this summer, anyway, and I am not sure what will happen between Toa and me. But I catch her meaning: if she can't have me, no Japanese woman should have me, and perhaps part of my turning her down should be related to culture, a rationalization that comforts her.

The ten-month marker. She sits in my room with that look again, like a mischievous young girl about to kiss a boy. She lifts her purse to the table and digs through it.

"Brendan, I have something to show you. I took some pictures with my Polaroid camera. You must understand, these pictures are art, not pornography." She finds the wad of pictures and pulls them out; a rubber band holds fifteen or twenty photos. I know they are naked pictures of her in some fashion.

I lift my forearms and cross them, making a large X, a common gesture in Japan that means "stop" or "forbidden."

"Please, Yoshiko, I shouldn't see those! If we are to keep our friendship, I shouldn't look at those pictures."

She stares at the pack of pictures, holding them in her hands for a few moments. Then she shoves them back into her purse. She drops her head down. Without looking at me she says, "Maybe it is better that you leave Japan this summer. I can't take this anymore."

"Yes, I will leave in July. That is two more months. Why don't we finish our time together as friends, and that will make a whole year, four seasons in Kyoto, a nice ending to our experience. You have a strong spirit, Yoshiko, you can do it." I had decided to leave that summer for various reasons, although none have to do with her. I have plenty on my mind: I'm thirty years old and still trying to cobble together a life and career. She has led her life, she has four grown children, she has traveled the world, she has her health and money. Soon she will move to New York with her successful son. I feel like I'm just another prize for her already full and luxurious life. Why should I worry about her so much?

The next week Yoshiko brings another movie, "Harold and Maude." The plot follows a relationship between a young man, 19, and a woman 79. They eventually have sex (not shown but inferred) and both are happy. Maude commits suicide at the end of the movie after her 80th birthday, since she believes 80 is the proper age to die. The movie ends with an oddly upbeat feeling. I'm not too concerned about Yoshiko following the same fate, though, since Japanese seem to love the theme of unrequited love, and they sometimes revel in the sweet sorrow it brings.

I prepare to leave Japan. Students give me fans, mini-screens, boxes of green tea, bamboo crafts; coworkers and friends buy me drinks. With tears and self-doubt, I break up with Toa. It's either that or plan to live together in America, and it doesn't feel right to me overall. Many foreigners talk about the two-year marker in Japan...either lay down roots or time to head home. And I remember vividly a recent dream: I am walking the streets of Kyoto, feel a strong wind at my back, run away from the wind half-heartedly, then it scoops me up, carries me a long way until I land in a green mountain meadow somewhere in Montana. I wake up refreshed.

Yoshiko and I meet for our last Wednesday. I have a million other things on my mind and am behind in packing. I try to act upbeat. I review our many positive outings, long interesting discussions, all the English learned. She carries herself with dignity, but a certain darkness betrays her, like a prisoner smiling while walking to the electric chair. The week previous, for a few moments, I had entertained the idea of sleeping with her, as a gift, but those thoughts only made me sick to my stomach. When the lesson ends, she cries a little. We hug. I kiss her cheek. With surprising strength, she suddenly pulls my lips to hers and holds them there, trying to engage me in a deep kiss. I grab her shoulders and gently push her face and body away, then lightly peck her cheek again, lead her out the door.

Walking down the street to the taxi I feel twice as heavy, as if I am carrying her. A taxi stops, we say goodbye, she climbs in. After a few seconds, while walking back across the street, I look back towards the departing taxi. She has turned around to watch me, our eyes meet briefly, then she is gone.

I must stay up all night Thursday to pack for next morning's flight and clean my apartment. Around 5 a.m. I finish. A hundred thoughts and emotions cram my head. I feel very strange. A thunderous excitement for America and Montana grows in me, yet something feels broken, too. Some aspects of Japan and its people I dearly love. And I loved Toa. Why am I leaving her? And what was Yoshiko to me? I partly conquered the foreign terrain of Japan, but in some ways, still feel a foreigner to myself. When I left American life, I believed the time away might offer some newfound clarity on my family and myself. But Japanese life has been so dense, with so many new experiences and alternate perspectives, my mind and heart feel rather more layered and complex.

The train from Kyoto to the airport takes one hour. Then I ride a shuttle bus to the plane. The loudspeaker announces various stops in Japanese, Chinese, Korean, French, and English.

America here I come. On the plane I take out my cell phone to turn it off. There is one message. I listen to it. "Brendan, this is Yoshiko. I just want to say, I love you."

CHAPTER 7, SOUTH KOREA
JOURNAL HIGHLIGHTS

Jan 15th, 2003: Jeonju, South Korea. The Big Picture: To be fair, one should note that the Korean Peninsula has had a rocky history at best. With respect to the various wars, foreign occupations, and for the last half century a reclusive and sinister northern regime, South Korea has come a long way on several fronts. Their economy has grown remarkably in the last few decades. Their co-hosting the 2002 World Cup was a positive step towards diversity. Generally speaking, however, for those of us used to Western affluence and international standards, South Korea is dirty, crowded, polluted, under-developed, xenophobic, socially narrow-minded, and politically ill-informed. To top things off, there is the occasional underlying feeling that America is White Satan, and North Korea is a powerful yet delightful country that could be congenially reunited with, if only America would get out of the way. However, economic growth, English education, and physical appearance seem extremely important to South Korea as well, and for these reasons, as an educated English teacher whose countenance is not entirely disagreeable, I am treated tolerably. In addition, I can say it is very interesting—and at times very exciting—to experience another new country. Finally, once one has negotiated the mentioned vexations, South Korea does have certain charms. The thought of returning to Japan has crossed my mind more than once, but for now I'm giving it some time.

Fast forwards in italics: True enough, Japan appreciates foreigners more and is more developed. But what Japan has taught you: give new countries a chance, give them some allowances, give it time to appreciate their perspective.

February 21st, 2003: Having taught in Japan for two years, the culture shock has been considerably reduced but is by no means absent. Once again I feel thrust down an Asian rabbit hole. The Korean language is more difficult to pronounce than Japanese, at least for Americans. Korean sounds a bit sing-songy with various melodic grunts and squeals thrown in. It comes across "whiny". Once again I walk through a sea of people that to my untrained eye look incredibly similar, and of course I stick out like a lumberjack on Wall Street. The underdevelopment and intense pollution of Korea make most places look like, upon first glance, a well-maintained garbage dump. A few weeks back, I saw the movie "8-Mile", and in the first few minutes the camera pans through some rough and impoverished Detroit neighborhoods, old decrepit buildings, garbage-strewn sidewalks, hazy air from nearby factories. You know the scenes. The audience is led to feel compassion for those growing up in hardscrabble conditions. Yet, my very first thought was, "Hey that looks like Korea."

Hardscrabble conditions exist in numerous countries around the globe. Americans are indeed spoiled compared to the global community.

<u>February 22nd, 2003:</u> The pollution in Korea is far worse than I had read. My guess is Jeonju, population 600,000, has similar air quality to Los Angeles, though LA is cleaner and greener and far more modern. Yet on the Internet Koreans tout Jeonju as a "clean," "beautiful," and "quaint" city! A good joke, but I'm not really laughing. When I ask locals about Jeonju's constant murkiness—a murkiness that makes a westerner wonder if someone was lighting oil trenches over here—they usually say, "Oh, it's just a little cloudy," or "Yes, it's a bit overcast today." Well, that's like saying the crowds of Tokyo are "just a busy day."

That said, when you have time to roam around, and can look closer at things, the artificial details are colorful. Various buildings, signs, street vendors, kiddie parks, cars, vans, and even construction tractors have more reds, blues, yellows, oranges, pinks, and purples than any western city. Imagine looking at old building walls in a ghetto--cracked and dirty and rust-stained--that also display giant abstract expressionist paintings and vibrant nature scenes. Or, imagine walking through a run-down yet colorful amusement park that the owners are working hard to rebuild.

One potential parallel: Think of how Asians always asked you about the high crime and murder rates in America, and you always brushed it off as the norm--just something society lives with. Perhaps normal is what we are used to, hence the definition, then relative from there. You know now that many cultures—especially Asia—live with incredibly-low crime rates, and how much safer, insulated, and more comfortable you felt there.

February 24th, 2003: A weird charm—all the kidlets you see out playing and adventuring by themselves. When school is out, my suburban area looks like a giant McDonald's playland. Elementary students cover the sidewalks and crosswalks like ants, zipping along on rollerblades, scooters, and even three-wheelers. You won't see that in LA.

Safer indeed.

March 1st, 2003: Another strange charm is how affectionate Koreans can be once they've gotten to know you and like you after a few short hours, or once they've been well-greased with alcohol. I've had guys touch or rub my arms and shoulders, girls rest their hands on my lap or be shoulder to shoulder, all in a casual and friendly way. Feel like a few drinks in the swarming university area or the vibrant downtown? It is less like a chain of bars and more like one giant party where are all invited and everyone is bound to get extremely drunk. Or a colorful, safe garbage dump with lots of bars and hair salons thrown in. Yet, mixed in is the occasional Korean giving you a cruel cold stare, or telling you, "We don't like Americans here."

As you hinted at before, the country was indeed flattened and a complete wreck after WWII. Imagine in your mind's eye Jeonju after bombs, tanks, Japanese colonization, dead bodies in the streets, and extreme poverty. And then fifty years later, this. Not as bad when judged on its own terms and history.

<u>March 4th, 2003:</u> I teach at a private English institute called "Speed Up." In South Korea, most students go to various private academies or institutes after public school, usually until 9:00 or 10:00 pm. This is the thrust of their quantitative educational whip-cracking. I work Monday to Friday, 3:15-10:15, teaching elementary, junior high, and a few high school students. There is a 5-minute break between the 45-minute classes, and teachers get a whopping 10 minutes for dinner to gobble down the free rice, kimchi, and other assorted things that try to pass for food. There is one female Korean math teacher, three

female Korean English teachers, and one Native English teacher (some vagabond from Montana). It gets a bit lonely and mind-rattling not speaking fluent English every day, though working alongside four kind women is comforting.

The conditions were difficult, but again, judging it on their terms, you were spoiled by the four women teachers. They helped with shopping and logistics, took you to temples and mountains, tolerated your first-world USA complaining, and one even dated you secretly, despite facing cultural and workplace shame if the relationship was revealed.

<u>March 5th, 2003:</u> My school-provided living quarters are tolerable, save my apartment's miniature hot water tank that couldn't give a proper shower to a mouse. Even washing dishes is done mostly in cold water. The first few weeks I showered in shivering increments, thirty seconds of lukewarm water and five minutes of waiting, but this does little for one's morning mood. For the last few weeks, the local gym and community bathhouse have found me a dedicated patron.

Welcome to third-world conditions. Many countries have this as a standard.

<u>March 7th, 2003:</u> The students seem a cauldron of contradictions. One minute they act prim, proper, and shy, working hard to mimic my pronunciation or scratching

away at my writing assignment, the next minute they flip each other off (not something I taught them, thank you very much), or check their cell phones as if they are in an urban cafe. Sometimes they bow and apologize if I scold them, displaying remorse equal to a repentant murderer, while other times they roll their eyes or laugh it off, then exchange sneaky words with their classmates. Generally, though, they seem to respond well. They say they like my tall height and blue eyes. They also enjoy my growing bag of teaching tricks, which now include theatrical games, riddles and puzzles, foreign bills & coins, card tricks, American pop music, and vivid pictures of Montana, Japan, and Thailand.

Americans are a cauldron of contradictions as well. For all our emphasis on fitness, we have the worst obesity; for all our trumpeting of freedom, we have a staggeringly-high violence and incarceration rate. Perhaps each culture has their set of incoherencies. The children are indeed a future map of the country, and it's cool you helped draft that map.

March 10th, 2003: I am thoroughly unimpressed with the food. At least once a week my stomach does circus flips after a school dinner or eating out, and remember I just finished living in Japan for two years. I am plenty acclimated to raw fish and seafood. Jeonju is supposed to be famous for its incredible Korean food, yet I find myself living off bakery bread and the local gym's whey protein drinks. Kimchi you ask? I would choose fresh produce over crushed, old, spiced-up vegetables any day. The poor food quality probably stems from the intense pollution, which includes the ever-wafting "yellow dust" from China.

Ha. Do you remember Japan and sushi? First you hated it. Then after three months, suddenly you not only got used to it, but loved it. Well, kimchi took a little longer, but you ended up loving that too, when it wasn't polluted. Yes, it is far more polluted in South Korea, so stomach problems are common. Yet you learned to like many of their foods and adapt.

<u>April 4th, 2003:</u> South Korea, like Japan, is roughly 80% mountainous, one factor in my choosing it. I often head for the small mountains around Jeonju, discovering temples, workout stations, and even an occasional mountain aerobics class led by a hearty Korean with her boombox playing sped-up dance music. The mountains are usually gritty—lots of dirt, sand, dryness, large rocks—and the hiking seems more like bouldering. But they offer up a bit of nature and exercise. Korean adults often avoid me, startled to see a foreigner and not sure how to react; they follow their social default—stone-faced expression and silence. Children, on the other hand, practically attack me, trying out their English: "How are you?", "Do you like pizza?", and "What's your favorite color?" They want to know how tall I am, feel my muscles, race me up the hill.

Yes, the new roadmap...you were in a unique, powerful position to make a lasting and positive Western impression. Perhaps you did.

<u>May 15th, 2003:</u> South Korea has few hot springs, but they compensate with *jjimjilbang*. These public bathhouses in Korea resemble Japanese bathhouses, and cost three dollars. After scrubbing yourself down with soap and pleasantly-abrasive washcloths, you can choose between several different hot pools varying in temperature and massage jets. After hot soaking, you can hop into a small cold pool or walk over stone pebble gardens that massage your feet. There are several saunas to choose from, some traditional wood and others with stone stumps atop pebbled floors. Amethyst and quartz are abundant in South Korea, so many saunas are beautifully-walled with these stones. *Jjimjilbang* also have, depending on their size, a gym, internet café, and movie room. If you are on higher ground in the city, gazing out over the lights and buildings, you can spot *jjimjilbang* by wisps of steam rising from roofs.

<u>June 9th, 2003:</u> I visited Jeju Island, the Hawaii of South Korea, to hike their highest mountain, *Halla-San*. I always enjoy gaining altitude and hiking the highest peak wherever I'm residing. *Halla-San* proved a formidable ascent, requiring five hours of steady climbing and some

light bouldering. The apex sits next to a dormant volcanic crater. At the summit I walked around puffy-chested—thinking my experience with Montana mountains gave me an edge over Asian trekkers—until I saw the throngs of Koreans in their fifties holding hiking sticks and watching their grandchildren skip alongside. I would be thrilled to be in such condition as a grandparent. Koreans often throw themselves wholeheartedly into whatever they pursue, thus outdoor enthusiasts were super fit.

July 7th, 2003: Korean culture has a strong group mentality, akin to Japan, though with considerably less organization. Walking down sidewalks—or hiking through crowds on a mountain—people just jumble together and walk crisscross. Foreigners like me curse under their breath. I want to pull out a loudspeaker and say in perfect Korean, "Listen up, folks, I have a new idea! How about everyone moving this direction walk on the right, and everyone moving the other direction walk on the left!"

July 21st, 2003: Finally made it to Seoul. "Nothing special" was my honest first reaction. It doesn't have that big city beat, that international feeling, that certain *je ne sais quoi*. But I will visit it a few more times and see what unfolds; perhaps Seoul is in the details. I kicked around a couple of downtown areas, went to the foreigner district called Itaewon (rather small and slummy), and took in some temples. Whenever riding the subway I feel a bit anxious, given that recently there was a major disaster in a Daegu subway--a fire killed nearly 200 people.

A South Korean might consider Bozeman or Whitefish (Montana) beautiful, clean, and full of open spaces, however, they might also find it incredibly devoid of heritage, culture, and rituals that link the past thousand years to the present day.

<u>August 10th, 2003:</u>   Seoul got better with more exploration. A favorite subway stop in Seoul: *Gyeongbokgung*, The Grand Palace, holding a large collection of temples, ponds, and historical artifacts. I also learned more about Japan's imperialistic past, as practically every South Korean temple has a paragraph going something like this: "Constructed by the Chin Dynasty in 1458, burned down by Japanese invaders in 1512; reconstructed by the Lee Dynasty in 1560, burned down by Japanese warriors in 1625; constructed by the Kim Royal Family in 1740, demolished by Japanese army in 1840," and so forth.

You should give credit to South Koreans for their persistence and fortitude. And perhaps be more understanding of their cultural anger towards Japan.

<u>August 19th, 2003:</u> Online gaming is huge over here. On weeknights and weekends, Koreans of all ages perch

themselves in Internet cafes and play, play, play. No use trying to do emails unless I bring my earplugs, and, since smoking seems a national pastime, a good air mask. As already mentioned, general Internet use is heavy among young kids, too, and you can imagine my surprise at how many elementary students can sing songs and relay life details of Christina Aguilera, Eminem, or Norah Jones.

August 27th, 2003: In my local neighborhood I'm a minor celebrity. From a block away I can see children and teenagers preparing some English to try on me for when we pass. After we exchange a few words, they usually cheer aloud and skip away. It's hard to maintain my bitterness about Korea after a few of these encounters.

Sept 20th, 2003: Regarding my teaching contract and school director, well, by Korean standards it is a reasonable job and probably better than most. By American or international standards, though, they have blatantly lied on some points and twisted the truth on others. One early disgruntlement was their having told me that Jeonju was a large and developed city, matching other ones I was considering. They said it had all basic goods and services as well as more liberal attitudes and something of an international feeling. This is clearly not the case; Jeonju is rather small-minded and limited. They simply did not want to lose me to a bigger city. And the Canadian teacher that I replaced, who praised the school so much...well, it turns out he didn't have a BA and was working there illegally. I have discovered several discrepancies through my new mole—the cute Korean coworker I am dating.

By their standards, Jeonju is international, more liberal, and has more goods and services. It wasn't all a lie; you simply have a larger and better perspective. If an Asian wanted a culturally-rich city in America, you might point them to Boston or Philadelphia, since they have documented history and older architecture than the American West; but in terms of Asian culture, their few hundred years pale to Asia's few thousand years.

Oct 24th, 2003: I've changed employers for my next year here. The school's name is "The Giving Tree," like the book by Shel Silverstein. My new bosses, a husband and wife team, lived in America for about seven years. They speak English well and they understand Western norms. Their schools are considered among the best in Jeonju, and I know several other foreigners who work for them. I've recently moved into a new apartment (the schools usually provide teacher accommodations), and, finally, I have air conditioning and other perks considered standard issue back home. I've already taught a few classes for them and start full-time in September.

My last school and two bosses—two brothers in their late thirties, with whom I've labored 10 months—turned out to be only slightly above the rank of dirty thieves. They cheated me out of about a grand (some of my airfare home and last paycheck), and tried to kick me out of my apartment (the school apartment) at 11pm one rainy night, several days before I was due to exit. Apparently they wanted me to move all my furniture and belongings outside and sleep on the street. It came down to three small but stocky Korean guys and me. This, after 10 months of supporting their institute and teaching the owner's daughter every day. They did a fair job of insulting my Korean girlfriend, Julia, who finally went back into the apartment at my direction as I argued with them on the street. It is the closest I've come to physical confrontation since my one and only fight in this life, an 8th grade bully when I was in the 7th grade at Whitefish Junior High. They didn't succeed in ejecting me from the apartment, and no blows were exchanged, but I felt sick and bitter about the whole thing and, as I said, they owe me money.

One of my good Korean friends, "Dr. No" as I've nick-named him, is a large, stocky, powerful judo instructor and acupuncturist who likes foreigners and seems to really like me. He also has a few connections to the Korean underworld. Dr. No offered to have "a little chat" with my former employers at Speed Up. I was tempted but ultimately declined. If I start something like that, perhaps my ex-bosses would sooner or later find a way to retaliate, and I didn't want to always be looking over my shoulder.

Yes, they are corrupt, but not really common thieves, and most institutes across Korea have issues like this. They treated you well for their standard of living. Many Koreans do not believe people change, that you must simply accept people as they are and act accordingly. So perhaps when you thought everything was going perfectly, they were actually frustrated but quietly accepting of you.

November 18th, 2003: I landed a small speaking part in a Korean movie. The movie premiered this spring, becoming famous all over Korea; the main actor is one of the most famous actors in the country. My fifteen minutes of Korean fame, or, actually, two minutes. Later when it comes out on video I'll buy a copy for folks back home. The movie, "*Hyojaw Dong Ilbalsa,*" or "President's Barber," is a dark comedy. One of the main characters goes to fight in the Vietnam War, and I play an American soldier that he meets.

January 24th, 2004: Korean society is quite conservative. (Though strangely, they have the highest prostitution rate in the world.) Many Koreans despise the fact that Western blood is "contaminating" their long history of cultural pureness. In this respect I sometimes wish my serious Korean girlfriend were Japanese. (Japan's bloodline is quite pure, too, but they are far more open to Western influence, even welcome it). Sometimes I feel like an American Indian might have felt trying to date a white woman sixty years ago. Occasionally we get cold stares and rude remarks, and part of me has become ever-prepared for confrontation. It is not a good feeling. But Korea is changing rapidly, and I know that most of my students will be more accepting, having grown up with far more exposure to foreigners. My girlfriend's family is traditional and conservative--yet have always had a few wild hairs in their ancestry. Her three older sisters are all married and living the traditional life in Korea, so her parents have apparently accepted that their fourth daughter will probably follow a more unique and alternative path.

On the flip side, Asian families do have some benefits over American ones. They are very close and committed to each other, including extended family. They always share holidays, and as most know, they take grandparents into their homes (rather than nursing homes) as they get older. Everyone chips in if someone is in trouble, financially or otherwise. Their familial unity seems diametrically opposed to the fragmentation I experienced.

February 19th, 2004: More on Dr. No. His actual last name is Noh, pronounced "No," and as mentioned he is both judo instructor and acupuncturist that dons a white medical jacket. Further, he looks quite similar to the thick and stock Asian character "Odd Job" of the Bond Film, the one where they try to destroy the gold in Fort Knox and Odd Job has a razor-sharp hat that he throws to kill people. But this Dr. No has a big smile and is very funny and friendly—unless you cross him—and truly his biceps are the size of my thighs. He needed someone to practice English with, and I needed a free private doctor and trainer, with all my various Korean illnesses and an old shoulder injury. The rest is history. Generally, the acupuncture has helped me considerably, and has been interesting to go through. On the down side, he isn't that experienced, and having a green acupuncturist who speaks very little English can have occasionally painful moments. He has probably tangled up a few of my "meridians," but by and large, all the parts seem to be working better than before. He also claims that acupuncture can revive people's body parts up to 72 hours after death, ha, and freaky. He wants to show me sometime.

March 20th, 2004: It's a good thing I have Dr. Noh along with a few other positive Korean families who have "taken me in." This helps balance out the darkness I have felt here. Two weeks ago, something dark did happen, and I'm struggling with how to deal with it. I should relay a few other events for better context.

In short, I often hear South Korean men beating their wives. Apartment walls are thin, and it's a common problem here. Typical of most Asian cultures, you are not supposed to interfere. The police rarely do anything, either, unless a person is severely injured or killed. In my first apartment, my neighbor immediately above me did it often, and finally one night I couldn't take any more. It was 2a.m., my Korean girlfriend was spending the night, and we woke up to the wife crying, yelling, and whimpering, with lots of banging. I went upstairs and knocked loud on the door, blood going, nervous, angry, worried about confrontation, but upset and fed up. The guy swore at me through the door, banged hard on his own door, but never opened it. No one else in the building came out. We finally went back downstairs. We didn't hear anything for the next month, then moved shortly thereafter.

My second apartment is comfortable but located in a seedy part of town, lots of call-girl "singing rooms" (karaoke and sex), and "love hotels," where you can rent a room by the hour. It's not like there were murders or theft, per se, just seedy characters and seedy activities involving misdemeanors, as far as I could tell. Besides all the singing and lovemaking, guys often stumbled around drunk, clothes disheveled, throwing up or throwing bottles, looking like they were up to something. However, I still felt safe, as a man anyway, and no violent crime ever occurred that I knew of, except all this wife-beating.

So two nights ago, sleeping alone, I awake to the most blood-curdling scream I have ever heard in my life. Half-asleep, I first thought an animal was being beaten or attacked, fighting for its life. I had never heard anything so horrible. I quickly comprehended it was a woman being beaten by a man. It was sickening and frightening. I listened for another minute to make sure, my heart racing, and then called the police. They barely understood me, and, anyway, I knew they wouldn't do much. I called back several times and demanded someone come out. The beating and screaming continued. My apartment building was full of tenants, and as usual not a single soul was doing anything. In the past, as mentioned, I had never witnessed or heard a Korean person intervene. I think Dr. Noh would, however, and maybe a few other Korean friends, especially the twenty-somethings.

I grabbed my baseball bat and walked up a floor to the apartment door. I was frightened there might be more men in the apartment, or perhaps the event gang-related; also, everyone within a mile radius knew exactly where I lived, and my lease was for another nine months in this apartment. But I had to do something! It was less of an intellectual reaction and more of a primal emotional one. I pounded on the door and yelled several times. The man yelled back. I pounded on the door again. Finally he opened the door. He was short, stocky, and had a heavily-pocked face, and he scowled at me. If he knew any kind of martial art, I figured he could take me. Plus he looked far crueler than me. I'm large and strong, but not trained as a fighter and not mean-spirited, which often goes a long way in a fight. My left hand with the baseball bat was visibly shaking. I was scared but also very angry. Oddly enough, I was nearly in tears, too. Even if I were to win this fight, I did not want to beat someone up with a baseball bat, but neither did I want the man to continue beating the woman. All these months in Korea listening to women cry and scream in pain. Something had to be done. With as much courage and meanness as I could muster, I told him, through words and body language, the police were coming, and he better not touch the woman any more. I could see the woman cowering in the corner of the tiny kitchen. She looked badly hurt, though I couldn't tell precisely how, just crouched over and disfigured. I wanted her to come out but she wouldn't move. The man didn't seem that scared of me, just pissed off, and a little confused as to what to do. It was as if no one had ever asked—or demanded—that he not beat up his girl. I again conveyed to him to not touch the woman, police are coming. I looked him in the eye. And then I walked back downstairs, sweating. I didn't hear any more noise or screaming. The police took ninety minutes, no joke. After the police talked to him, they came to my door. They apologized to me, thanked me, and tried to brush it off as a family matter. They said I had nothing to worry about. No arrest was made.

This event haunts me. I worry it will happen again. I also worry the man upstairs might do something to me. But equally disturbing, I don't know how to move forward. I felt I did what was right, but most other Koreans just brush it off when I tell them. Dr. Noh and a few other Korean friends look sad, and sigh, and say yes, that is very unfortunate. But they don't explain or offer a solution. Most of the foreigners understand—they are sick of all the wife- and woman-beating, too. But other foreigners say, that was stupid, why risk bodily harm for them? Their culture mostly ignores it anyway. You're fighting the whole damn country. Perhaps I was…but that time I was also fighting for one woman.

Thankfully, nothing more did happen. But I will never forget that scream. Maybe it was stupid to intervene, and not my culture, but I would probably do the same thing again. Some ethics must transcend cultural relativism.

July 26th, 2018: *Well, those journal entries ended on a dark note. But I did appreciate my time in South Korea. Considering all the entries from there and Japan, dear reader, it is such a strange thing in this life to progress in some ways and stay stationary in others. One becomes educated and more experienced, yet more entrenched in their own patterns and psychological framework. It is true that travel often broadens your mind and enlightens you. But it is not always a pretty or perfect picture. Sometimes travel, and especially living abroad, further confuses you, offers you additional religions, additional perspectives, additional morals and ethics, deepens your bewilderment at the great wide world and how to find a path. Sometimes it is easier to choose when we have fewer choices; but living in multiple countries gives you myriad possibilities. Indeed, I saw foreigners who transcended their challenging experiences to become wiser, more cultural pluralistic, and more secure in their own beliefs; I also saw many foreigners who became bitter, more confused, losing an ethical compass and exploiting Asian culture; and then I saw those who fell into a mix of both, perhaps like me.*

CHAPTER 8, YELLOW DUST

Yellow dust originates in the deserts of Mongolia where surface winds kick up dense clouds of dry, fine soil. Yellow dust drifts over industrialized parts of China and mixes with heavy pollution. Seasonal winds carry this mixture over the Yellow Sea to the Korean Peninsula. The Yellow Sea gets its name from the ancient Yellow River, which carries fine-grained calcareous silt and deposits it into the ocean, turning the waters golden. For years clouds of these dust particles have dropped into the sea on their way to Korea and intensified the yellow haze. When the yellow dust reaches South Korea, it throws a dirty yellowish spider web over the country, polluting the air, soil, and lakes. Many Koreans develop serious lung infections, while others battle lifelong respiratory problems. Yet most Koreans ignore, have grown accustomed to, or deny its damage.

Having grown up in the western United States, I'm reminded of our history of fool's gold, gold dust, gambling, and the Dead Man's Hand.

I started playing poker for money during my third year of teaching English in South Korea. The poker boom in America, namely Texas Hold'em, wafted over the Pacific Ocean and settled quickly in Asia. Soon it infected the 90 foreigners living in Jeonju, a gritty traditional city of 600,000 Koreans. Like Japan, we were allowed only knee-deep into Korean culture. Westerners formed a makeshift community in our own enclave. Most of us—Americans, Canadians, Australians, New Zealanders, British, and a few Irish—drank and partied every week. South Korean cities are brimming with bars and function perfectly for non-stop entertainment: Lounges are equipped with large comfortable sofas for hours of drinking, eating, and conversation. Sure, there were Korean temples to visit, interesting restaurants to dine in, and a few liberal Koreans to welcome you into their homes, but these opportunities were exhausted in a few months. Once you hunkered down into Korea for a year or more of teaching, you needed to dig into the local expat nightlife to have any kind of community and connection to the West.

I resisted this as long as I could. I explored various hidden temples in the prefecture and climbed challenging exotic mountains. Later, I became a gym rat, an old pastime. Besides, I was 32 when most of the expat crowd ranged from 21 to 27, and hanging out with them meant backpedaling to conversations and mindsets I had already explored and exhausted. Even more, I just didn't want to party that much. I had drunk plenty in Japan, and felt too old for such activity.

Then a Canadian named Liam started poker nights at the foreigner bar, Deep Inn. Liam was short, portly, charismatic, and a politician at heart. He had secured a cushy university position, worked part-time, rarely shaved or ironed his dress shirts. Yet he knew Korean culture well, played by the rules, bought Korean bosses and coworkers bottles of soju, bowed and kept quiet at the right times, and thus had a nice little life going and didn't plan to leave anytime soon. Other foreigners called him the unofficial mayor of Jeonju. He had an angelic dedicated Korean girlfriend as well as a slutty girl on the side, classic Korean style. He drank copious amounts and stayed out late, teaching only afternoon classes at the university. A better poker captain we could not have found. He had followed the Texas Hold'em boom in the United States, bought two heavy cases of chips and cards, and set up a weekly game a with detailed tournament structure alongside cash games.

Soon the Sunday games had thirty-plus foreigners filling the tables of Deep Inn, and even some foreign women came out to see the action. Gambling is illegal in South Korea, but then so is prostitution, and the country has the largest prostitution business in the world. (Every day I tore down fast-food flyers and call-girl flyers from my apartment door.) The Korean owner of Deep Inn appreciated the business that poker brought in, and knew we were stray sheep in his culture, so he let us continue gambling.

In some ways I was the opposite of Liam. I stood 6'3, lean, athletic, and often chose a good book or scrabble game over a night on the town, unless there were dancing involved. Plus I was getting older, and I didn't plan on making a life in South Korea. I was a transient like most of the foreigners—a nomad who had found a temporary home. But I had liked card games since childhood, ever since my grandparents taught me gin rummy and cribbage. I especially loved poker.

Yellow dust becomes the worst in springtime. It clogs the air, seeps into apartments, falls lightly onto furniture. Sometimes one can taste a thin film on the food like a gritty seasoning, as if someone sprinkled fine sand on your *kimchi* and *calbee*. During occasional air alerts in spring, you are advised to wear a surgical mask outside; strenuous exercise should be avoided. If yellow dust were gold dust Korea would have been filthy rich.

Yes, I've always had a knack—and intensity for—board games and card games, including chess, scrabble, cribbage, gin rummy, and now poker. Danny Baur, a next-door neighbor, taught me how to play poker when I was 9 years old. My parents were divorced, my single mother rarely home. Danny was 11 and bigger than I, which made him all the more frustrated when I started winning his quarters and dimes. One day I won fifteen dollars, cleaning out his change jars. His father found out and banned us from playing. A few years later, when visiting my father during the summer, I started a marathon game with a good friend, Jim Bercu. We started after dinner, played till 4 a.m., then got up at 7 a.m. to continue into Sunday morning. His mother wanted to take us to breakfast at a fancy golf course forty-five minutes away. We played in the suburban on the way to the restaurant, then during the drive back; the poker chips rattled with every turn or stop. Jim had recently visited Hawaii and brought back various souvenirs. I won them all, plus $25 dollars in cash. Jim didn't tell his mother, but I was proud, and wanted my father to applaud my success. But he made me give it all back.

Perhaps I was skilled at the probability and mental exercises involved in poker, various statistics, implied odds, remaining outs, poker theorems, etc. My mind could lose itself like a mathematician buried in theories, quotients, and ratios. Strangely enough, poker's math relaxed me. Perhaps it offered a structured escape from childhood, where I couldn't figure the odds of anything. Further, I was a natural actor, playing out many strange identities in my youth—and people rarely knew if I was bluffing. But life got busy after high school, as I moved from my small Montana town to Los Angeles to work in film production, so I rarely played poker. I had neither time nor money. Occasionally a film shoot would take us through Vegas, and I felt the irresistible pull from casinos like hotel-sized magnets drawing me in. But again, I didn't have the freedom or funds to spend more than an hour at the tables.

When Liam started the weekly games at Deep Inn, I imagined participating once a month. I hated the cigarette smoke and got bored with the conversation; the wooden chairs were stiff and uncomfortable. But then I started winning, a hundred here, two hundred there. It felt like an easy part-time job. Other foreigners gave me props for my skills. They trumpeted me as a highly-intuitive player who made great reads on people. Whereas before I felt like an outsider to this ragged bunch of transient foreigners, I now felt appreciated and, oddly enough, almost home.

Previously my main outlet had been playing Ultimate Frisbee. A few of us started in late summer, battling the Korean sun and intense humidity, playing on small, bumpy, dirt fields with concrete bleachers nearby. It was dangerous for skin and joints, and our clothes were sweat-soaked after an hour, but it was fun. This slowly evolved into about thirty foreigners meeting every Sunday afternoon on a plush grass field belonging to a Korean university campus. Later the fall weather fit perfectly with our games: dry blue skies, a slight chill in the air, the padding of fallen leaves underfoot. Even foreigners who didn't play Ultimate Frisbee started coming to hang out, have a picnic, cheer us on. As I sprinted down the field, chasing a floating disc, my other worries seemed to evaporate in the autumn air--cramped, dirty classrooms; unruly students; substandard living conditions; and the occasional heckling of Americans. The hardcore half of us played throughout winter, donning ski hats and goggles, our black cleats crunching the snow, and we loved diving for touchdown catches knowing we could land unharmed. All the Jeonju foreigners made big plans for our games when the snow melted in March, waiting for the communion, the camaraderie, the release, the picnics.

When spring finally came we encountered continual difficulty securing a field. First we fought soccer teams or scores of undisciplined children who wouldn't share the space. Then university officials tried to kick us off, even though several of the players worked as teachers at the university and should have been allowed full access to the fields. Next came the monsoons, soaking us head to foot and making the grass fields as slippery as mudslides. Still we met, we played, we fought the elements, the cultural differences, the prejudice. But in late spring came the worst of the yellow dust. The sunrises and sunsets looked stunning—streaks of gold like a treasure chest of coins scattered across the sky—but all else felt like a plague. The dust turned our eyes red and scratchy, slipped down our throats, worked on our lungs like fine sandpaper. We tried to wear surgical masks while playing but these only worked when you remained stationary or moved slowly; they weren't made for running, jumping, and diving. Global warming had supposedly increased the yellow dust. Yellow dust was the final contaminant that killed our sporting games, pushed us inside, back to the bars and nightlife. Liam stepped in with poker on Sunday evenings.

My Korean girlfriend, Seo-yeon, didn't like my playing poker; South Koreans consider it equal to or worse than prostitution. She also didn't like my hanging out at the bar for six or seven hours straight, which was something very new and unusual in my life. Nor did she like my irritability and mood swings when I occasionally lost, how I was pissed off for days. She tried to pull me away from it, tried to get me back in the gym, back to reading, writing, hiking, preparing for graduate school in America. Obviously she had good intentions—and part of me heartily agreed with her—so I cut back to every other week at Deep Inn. But it wasn't just about poker, it was also about community, something I lacked in Korea.

Coworkers are extremely important in Korean culture. Koreans work long and hard, like the Japanese, and thus your coworkers become a second family. Husbands will often use this as an excuse for drinking and debauchery, telling their wives they must go out with their colleagues and support them because of a work issue or personal problem. As it turns out, four of my fellow teachers, all Canadians, loved Texas Hold'em. We all lived in two apartment buildings four block away from each other, and soon developed a weekly Thursday night "home game." By now, gambling had worked its way into my brain and body like yellow dust, changed my consciousness, and influenced my decisions. I used the collegial and coworker aspect of Korean culture to persuade Seo-yeon to tolerate my Thursday night home game. My fellow teachers and I needed to commiserate, blow off steam, and bond, which was not entirely untrue. Now I had the weekly game with my coworkers and the biweekly game at Deep Inn. And, as my skills grew, I usually won money at both games.

Thomas, one of my poker-playing workmates, came from Newfoundland. He weighed a little over 300 pounds and had a high IQ. He used to lift weights a lot until he broke his foot in five places, stepping into a gutter in Japan one night while walking home drunk from the bars. He used to read and write a lot, too, until he started playing online poker. Thomas introduced me to online play. First I considered it a scam. Moreover, playing with other people you couldn't see seemed weird and isolating. But Thomas had cashed-out with over a grand a few times, and he said you could chat with people from all over the world while playing. So I tried it.

Now I could sit in the comfort of my own apartment, after work, settle into a cushioned office chair, enjoy a smoke-free space, and play a few hands of Hold'em. Ten minutes led to twenty, then a few hours would slip by. I ordered pizza, drank some soju. I completely forgot about missing home, missing Montana, missing my longtime friends, missing my culture, missing a good steak dinner, missing speaking fluent English on a daily basis. And when I won, I heard the animated sounds of the chips clinking their way to my online stack. It felt good. (And perhaps this resembled the Korean gamers sitting in Internet cafes.) Poker engaged mental faculties while stimulating emotion and adrenaline, a whole-body experience. Further, a strange process started. The more money I won, the more strange gaps from childhood seemed to fill in. I once read in a psychology book that people who steal or gamble are often trying to win back what was stolen from them in childhood. The adrenaline rush I got from gambling and winning felt better than sex sometimes, and that scared me. But it kept me coming back for more.

With the boom of Texas Hold'em in America, the online craze soon followed. Internet studies reported online gambling as three times more popular than porn. There are dozens of online sites to choose from. Most use financial middle brokers located in exotic or shady places with few legal limitations, like the Caribbean or Isle of Man or

Aruba. You can play penny games all the way up to tables where you buy in for fifty grand. You can play heads-up, six-person or ten-person tables, or tourneys that have hundreds or thousands of people. Every Sunday you can buy into large online tournaments for $250, then compete against six thousand other players, with a first-place payout of $200K.

◆◆◆

When I first learned about yellow dust in South Korea, and started experiencing it, I remember the denial from locals. The skies would appear murky and the air would feel gritty, yet they would say, "It's only cloudy today," or "It's overcast and humid from nearby monsoons." I don't think they had ever experienced true blue skies and clean air like my home state of Montana. Some Koreans might acknowledge the presence of yellow dust but downplay its effects and adjust to its presence. They cooked special foods to combat its toxins. Worst of all, a pair of local hikers told me that yellow dust helped clear out the lungs while others said it purified the air, a necessary scouring of sorts. Clearly the golden particles had polluted the Korean mindset. They rationalized or denied the yellow dust.

◆◆◆

Soon I cut gym time in half and played poker nearly every night after work. No more weekly hikes, either, as the yellow dust grew worse. I didn't tell Seo-yeon, and white-lied to her when she called to ask what I was doing. Sometimes I wouldn't even pick up the phone, making an excuse later. Hours would slip by. Sometimes I skipped the Deep Inn game to play online since I could win more money and take in less smoke. One weekend I won $1800 and finally told Seo-yeon. She liked my winning but was extremely concerned, and urged me to stop. Also, I wondered sometimes, what if I did win a fortune? What did I want to be known for—earning money from other people's misfortune and addiction? Or writing a best-selling book about the cultural differences between America, South Korea, and Japan? Even Thomas seemed a little concerned and said he regretted getting me started. He worried I would give up writing like he had. And that eventually the hammer would drop and I would lose big.

Seo-yeon was a sweet and special woman, and most other foreigners called her "the prettiest girl in Jeonju," yet the cultural differences wore me down. Sometimes I felt sick of South Korea, stuck and isolated. I felt too old to be here, believing I was capable of much more, but couldn't seem to cobble together a career back home. A future with graduate school, writing, and teaching was the dream that kept me going, yet this dream kept slipping further and further back. My older brother was the classic breadwinner, a computer programmer and manager making six figures; my younger half-brother, who grew up in a secure and stable environment (i.e., not a broken home as me), worked as an engineer for Boeing in Seattle, making airplane wings lightning-proof. Most of my high school and college friends already had families, careers, houses, and "normal" lives. What the fuck was wrong with me?

Perhaps the poker dream was to make enough money to take six months or a year off. I could read, write, exercise, and prep for graduate school. I could also clear my head once and for all. In this respect, I often felt as if I needed some kind of cocoon to change my consciousness and transcend the past. Maybe if I could win thirty or forty grand in a tourney, this cocoon could happen.

Not long after, on a winter evening in Jeonju, I was playing online and winning. I sat at the virtual table with five other players and had a chip stack of $600. Suddenly I "flopped the nuts," which means I was dealt the best possible hand at the table early in the betting. I kept restraint, slow-played the hand, and another player went all-in for his last $700. I called him, took down the pot, and doubled up. Now my chip stack was $1200. Soon I was dealt another "monster hand," pocket kings, meaning two kings. The first three face-up cards were K-8-8. I had a full house and the second-best possible hand. I made a large bet, and another player went all-in with $1400. I called, thinking he was bluffing and I would double up again to $2400. But the other player had pocket 8s—two eights—and thus his quads (four-of-a-kind) beat my full house. I lost $1200 in one hand. The odds of his hitting quads on the flop were incredibly low—maybe two thousand to one—and the odds that I would have such a good hand to justify calling his all-in were equally low. Truly the hand was a "cooler" and a "bad beat," and now I was on full "tilt," meaning I was emotionally off-keel, extremely upset, and liable to make bad decisions. And I did.

I kept playing at high stake tables outside of my comfort range, hoping to quickly win back what I had just lost. Two hours later I had drained both my checking and savings accounts and lost about five grand. That was a half year of savings from South Korea, thousands of English lessons. When I finally quit—as I had nothing left—it was one of the lowest points I had ever experienced. I jumped onto the bed and pounded my fists into the mattress. I cried tears of rage and disbelief. I kept thinking it must be a bad dream from which I would awake. I felt ashamed and crazy inside. Gambling, and especially online gambling, was the first real addiction I had ever experienced in my life. Before I had inwardly scoffed at those in AA or those with drug problems—they were losers who lacked self-control, and such a thing would never happen to me. But here I was, a loser, and very addicted.

In shock, I lay on my bed and stared at the ceiling for an hour. I opened the windows to let the cold air hit me; a light breeze pushed in the icy chill. The wind also carried in yellow dust—I could taste it, feel the particles all around me, settling on the furniture, scratching my throat. My mind was churning. Part of me felt relieved, it was finally over; another part of me started imagining how I could win it back. I could get an advance from work, wire the money home, deposit it into my poker site, Ultimate Bet, and play again in a week. Suddenly I grew scared. I was fighting myself—and became terrified of losing.

I got back online and sent an email to my bank, First Interstate. I told them I had a serious gambling problem, listed the sites I had played on and the financial middle brokers I had used, and asked them to please halt any future transactions dealing with these institutions. I called a First Interstate bank officer and left a similar message on her answering machine. Then I started an email to one of my good friends, and with tears dripping down my face, wrote him all that had happened and that I was seeking help.

Around 3 a.m. I went outside for a long walk. Litter covered the streets as usual. I got away from street lights—glowing with yellow halos—and found a small polluted river to walk alongside. Like in Japan, people threw anything into rivers, including old vacuum cleaners and electric heaters. Ice and snow still lined the banks. I tested the water with my hand and enjoyed its freezing bite. I still couldn't believe all that had happened. How could I have been such an idiot? I wanted to lie down in the river, let the cold water numb my body and end everything.

Deep down, I had always felt like something defective and discarded. If I just lay down with the rest of the junk in the river, it would all be over. No more pain, no more struggle, no more suffering. Nevermore.

Then another voice inside rose up. *You are truly okay inside, and always have been. You have a right to exist, and a right to make mistakes.* I sat down on the bank, shivering, crying. Eventually I stumbled home as if sleepwalking.

Poker wasn't the same after that. I felt dark, hollow, as if a piece of me had been carved out. I told Seo-yeon about it. She yelled at me, then cried, tried to help me. I didn't tell my coworkers, but they sensed that something had happened. Thomas knew intuitively. He had had big losses before, too, and knew the feeling. He apologized for getting me started with online play. Seo-yeon wanted me to quit altogether, but I still resisted, saying I needed live play to hang out with other foreigners. Maybe that much was true.

I also wanted to finish the league my coworkers and I had started—we accumulated points for each weekly win, and at the end of the school year, the person with the most points would win a separate, large kitty of about six hundred dollars.

In the end, just before departing South Korea, I won this kitty, far ahead of everyone else.

◆ ◆ ◆

In 2006, the official "Gamblers Anonymous Website" posed twenty questions regarding the behavior and effects of gambling. It stated that most compulsive gamblers will answer yes to at least seven of their questions. I answered yes to all twenty. This concerned me. That said, I noticed many of these answers depended on the mindset and condition I was in. If drunk or emotionally upset, I was more vulnerable and a willing participant.

◆ ◆ ◆

Yellow Dust waxes and wanes in South Korea. From my research, it contains carbon monoxide, ash, soot, sulfur, and other toxic pollutants including heavy metals (including mercury, cadmium, chromium, arsenic, lead, zinc, copper) and other carcinogens. Plus there are pesticides, asbestos, viruses, fungi, bacteria, herbicides, plastic, combustion products as well as hormone-mimicking phthalates.

Sometimes during the year, yellow dust would seem to disappear. But then it drifted back in depending on climate, wind, industrial activity, and other seasonal factors.

◆ ◆ ◆

After I left Asia, my relationship to poker improved. I attended and finished graduate school, tackled professional projects, and embarked on many interesting adventures. But there have been occasional dark days and setbacks. To be sure, there is enough material for "Yellow Dust II." After grad school, I moved to Las Vegas for five years, started a website about cool activities around town, and covered the World Series of Poker for four years as a writer/media correspondent. I've met many famous and professional players--as well as witnessed widespread addiction. Thankfully, I have great passion for many things in this life, including literature and writing, fitness and outdoors, travel and teaching, and this perhaps has saved me.

If I had to put in monetary terms what I think my addiction to and passion for poker has taken from me, considering my health, career, relationships, time consumed, and so forth, I would want to win at least a half million to feel redeemed. Obviously, this will probably never come to pass. I might as well dive back into the polluted Yellow Sea, searching for golden treasure beneath its sparkling chemical waves, and drown myself in yellow dust.

CHAPTER 9, WOUNDED TIGERS

The tiger is often a legendary symbol in Asia, especially for China and the two Koreas.

When I first started teaching English in South Korea, I posted a map of the Korean Peninsula in the classroom, a purchase from a Barnes & Noble bookstore back in America. The map clearly denoted North and South Korea, the DMZ (demilitarized zone separating North and South), and the body of water on the east side of the peninsula as "The Sea of Japan." I've always liked maps, and thought it gave us a good visual to work from. Tell me what cities or mountains you've visited, I would ask. Students hated the map, and as days went by, I found out why. They secretly made changes with hasty writing and various markers; they crossed out the words "North" and "South" and wrote one big "Korea." They crossed out the DMZ line. They crossed out "The Sea of Japan" and wrote "Korean Sea." They labeled a small island between Japan and South Korea as "Dokdo, Korean Land." Eventually I took the map down out of frustration. Any time I tried discussing these issues with them—and I strove to be an objective, outside party—they either said absolutely nothing or started lengthy rants (in broken English) clearly taught to them by parents and school teachers.

At my second school, I sometimes played a circle game in the classroom where each student passed a tennis ball around, and when the ball is in your hand, you have to say a word that fits the game's topic. Subjects included things like foods, sports, and jobs. Whenever I chose the topic of countries, the students would say "Korea," and look perplexed when I mentioned North Korea and South Korea. Some older students reacted angrily, as if I was trying to separate their country or trying to prevent reunification. They again launched into rants. I experienced the same reaction when I tried to use a new National Geographic map of North and South Korea for a lesson.

As you've probably guessed, no Korean person in South Korea says, "South Korea." They always say "Korea." And I have yet to see a Korean map that differentiates North and South; it is always shown as one country. Even the DMZ line, marked on most modern maps around the world, is rarely shown on a Korean map.

Between 2003-2006 I taught English in Jeonju. Through private academies, public schools, and private lessons, I came to know students of all ages. Through coworker relations, public bathhouses, playing soccer, hiking, drinking, dancing, dating, festivals, and daily Korean activities, I came to know Korean people of all walks of life. The biggest factor of these would have to be drinking, for although South Koreans start with a stone face, once they start downing soju they start spilling their hearts. Further, I have befriended a great many foreigners living in South Korea, and we often swap stories and talk politics. Of course, I am an outsider here, and can't know what it feels like to be born of Korean blood and on Korean soil. But perhaps from the above experiences, I can offer some observations regarding South Koreans and their mindset on North Korea and reunification.

Although South Koreans differ on ways to reunite with the North, and how much they would personally invest or sacrifice to do so, they all want reunification deep in their hearts. Korean history is roughly 5,000 years old, and it hasn't been easy. They have been invaded, conquered, broken-up, bullied, and colonized several times, primarily by the Japanese and sometimes by China. They see themselves as victims and underdogs trying to make a stand. More importantly, they see the division of Korea as relatively recent and only a temporary state that will eventually be remedied. The attacks on their culture have left deep scars. Korean social self-esteem is quite low, and they commonly hide flaws. They overcompensate for feelings of inadequacy by infecting themselves and their youth with hubris. It continually amazes me how my students think all countries know myriad minor details about Korea and its history, and even believe that Korean TV stars and singers have fans all over the world. Most adults, upon my first outing with them, will sound off a list of credits of Korean culture, from the "brave and brilliant"

Lee Soon Shin, who invented ironclad ships and thwarted the Japanese for a short time, to the amazing properties of kimchi, a dish that can "fight off all kinds of flus and diseases, including SARS." A sad truth regarding modern kimchi: despite its many health properties and the chef's good intentions, the environment in South Korea is so polluted and the cooking conditions so unclean that food poisoning, stomach ulcers, and gastrointestinal viruses are common. Further, like someone who has had something stolen from them or something terrible happen to them in their youth, Koreans often think the world owes them something. And on various levels they act accordingly. (Yes, I can relate, as I've been guilty of this.)

The older generation generally distrusts the North and still holds some respect for America because they remember the Korean War firsthand. Many secretly hope "Bush will attack" the North (I was there when George W. Bush held the presidency,) the U.S. and U.N. will then step in to fund rebuilding and redeveloping, and Korea will eventually become strong and whole.

The middle generation largely dislikes or hates America. They want reunification but worry about who will pick up the reunification tab, and hope America or the United Nations can. However, they loathe the idea of America attacking North Korea and then becoming further intertwined with South Korea. They really want America out of South Korea and hate feeling any kind of indebtedness towards America due to national pride and the Korean inferiority complex. To be fair, the American government and American soldiers haven't always been on their best behavior in South Korea, which amplified this attitude.

Looking at South Korean youth, they fervently want to reunite with North Korea and, just as the middle generation, generally dislike or despise America. Both ideas have been taught to them by their parents, and reunification seems equally a dream within their hearts as well as a fad to pursue. Many secretly fantasize about America's downfall while dreaming of Korea becoming a world superpower. Some students even say they don't want North Korea to give up its nuclear weapons in order to help fulfill this dream. This nuclear-armed, superpower fantasy has been the topic of numerous junior high and high school student essays in my classes.

To further complicate the situation, the middle and younger generations greatly envy America and the West, though they will rarely admit it. A tidal wave of Western movies, music, and English is sweeping over Asia with all kinds of ramifications. For example, plastic surgery to make one's eyes appear bigger and more open, and the sockets more sunken like a Western eye, is extremely popular with people from 12 to 60. Further, they copy American and Western art and technology unabashedly, including movies, computer programs, fashion, architecture, and especially music. A Korean singer acting like a black gangster rapper and dressed in hip hop clothes is both comical and telling.

Take a walk down a busy city street in South Korea. You will see English splashed everywhere, mixed with Korean. Most businesses and employees don't know any more English than what is written on their storefront; it is simply in fashion and an illusion of being international. Look also at the various billboards and advertisements—you will see mostly Western faces, Western bodies, Western clothes, even though the stores don't carry Western sizes. Listen to the music pumping from store speakers—you will hear Korean pop with all kinds of 70s and 80s Western backbeats or original songs mixed in. Peruse the cafes or restaurants—you will find McDonalds, Baskin Robbins, or Starbuck's imitations next to traditional Korean eateries. South Korea is becoming Westernized, as fast as their Northern counterpart becomes reclusive. The dream of reunifying is far sweeter than the bitter reality.

From a Western viewpoint, there is an elephant in the living room. Just what is happening in North Korea? How can South Korea want to interact with such a regime given its nefarious actions? But I understand now, they view them as family, whatever happens. Most South Koreans could spend all evening degrading the U.S. or Japan, but never utter a negative word about North Korea.

Several years back, near Seoul, a very unfortunate accident occurred with the U.S. military. A tank killed two Korean schoolgirls on a suburban road. All South Korea was whipped into a frenzy, and the widespread fallout lasted two years. Many students cursed their foreign teachers (regardless of nationality), many taxis and restaurants wouldn't serve foreigners, and the media continually ran pictures of the girls and their families. When students tried to relate the details to me, they either shut down with anger or shed tears. However, I never heard clear details of the story, only the strong insinuation that the "American soldiers were happy or thrilled to take the lives of two innocent Korean girls." That seems ludicrous. Who wants to crush two young girls with a tank? It should be noted here that Korean children run across the street in a very haphazard and foolhardy fashion; in my city alone there have been several deaths involving children hit by cars. And a military tank isn't the quickest and quietest vehicle out there. Isn't it easy to hear clanking metal treads coming up behind you?

Even if America was clearly to blame, I'm sure it was not intentional. And the reaction was extreme. To compare, let us look at the two to three million people reported dead due to famine and poverty in North Korea over the last few decades, while the government spent most of its money building a military and preserving an isolationist stance against the outside world. In three years of living and working in South Korea, not once have I heard a reference to this tragic situation. Not a single sentence. I kid you not. And if I bring it up delicately, the conversation is quickly changed.

For this past year, the hot issue on the Korean mind has been Dokdo, an island located between South Korea and Japan, with both countries claiming ownership. The small rocky island has little value save fishing rights, and the primary fight seems to be the principle—don't let Japan take any more land from Korea. An understandable principle given Japan's past brutal actions against Korea, the years of colonization, "comfort women," and centuries of burning down their sacred temples. However, as usual, the reaction seems extreme and overblown. In the classroom students gave me ongoing lessons regarding Dokdo and the evils of Japan; students came in wearing shirts and socks that said, "Dokdo—Korean territory." Yet, did any students or adults know about North Korean concentration camps or mention the present terrible plight of North Korean people? They refuse to dig deeper.

I concluded that many South Koreans are ignorant about North Korea's atrocities. South Korean media tends to spotlight American and Japanese "evils," and hide Korean problems, especially North Korean issues. Those who are not ignorant about North Korea seem to feel a deep shame regarding these matters, and do not want to discuss further, as perhaps it wounds their pride. Yet, they are always ready to criticize America and Japan for hours with a few glasses of soju or Korean beer in hand. Even my Korean fiancée of two years, an educated and bright person, tended toward this pattern. I recognize that America and the West are not without major scandals and biased media, but the amount of propaganda I have seen here feels staggering.

Reunification will happen eventually because almost all South Koreans want it and North Koreans need it, though I am not sure how it will take place or the struggle it will involve. South Korea seems to view North Korea as a troublesome sibling whom they will always love and defend—despite crimes committed and vulgarities exchanged—and with whom a reunion is always sought. However, they are not sure how much of their bankbook, lifestyle, and self-worth they want to risk for such a reunion. If the Korean people can step out of their "sunshine stance" (which seem more like "sunshine trance"), and step up to the reunification plate by themselves—financially, emotionally, responsibly—perhaps it can happen.

July 15th, 2018: _I haven't been to South Korea for 12 years. I wonder, what are Koreans thinking today? I am happy the two countries recently held a historic summit, and it appears the beginning steps of reunification have occurred. I had my frustrations with South Korea, but I also feel some "jeong," a strong connection and sentiment based on shared experiences. I wish all Koreans the best._

CHAPTER 10,
ADIEU AND HOME ANEW

*And the end of all our exploring/ will be to arrive
where we started/ and know the place for the
first time. –T.S. Eliot*

*I'm sitting in the railway station, got a ticket to
my destination. On a tour of one-night stands, my
suitcase and guitar in hand, every stop is neatly
planned for a poet and a one-man band.
Homeward bound – I wish I was – homeward
bound.
–Simon & Garfunkel*

Thrice I came home after Asian adventures. The first
time was after two years in Japan, the second after
two years in South Korea, then a third and final
homecoming after a total of five years in Northeast Asia.

The first return felt magical. My oldest brother picked
me up at the Seattle Airport on a summer afternoon. As
much as I enjoyed Japan--and I truly did overall--I could
have kissed the concrete floor in customs. I had always
associated my home with various cities or areas, Missoula

or Whitefish, Paradise Valley or Flathead Valley, Glacier National Park or Yellowstone National Park, or my beloved state of Montana, but now in a grander scope, I saw America as home.

I could speak fluent English and people understood me! Body language and basic customs were second nature, no need for second guessing or feeling perplexed! And space, lo and behold, I had space!

Looking around Seattle and its outskirts, the vast spaciousness overwhelmed me. Wider streets, bigger buildings, bigger parks, fewer people, and inside a restaurant, taller ceilings, larger chairs, larger tables, and larger silverware.

My soul stretched out. I stood taller, walked faster, breathed easier.

My brother must have chuckled inside, seeing me so wide-eyed and astonished at a city I had already seen a hundred times.

The other detail that shocked me: most Americans are fat, relative to the rest of the world. Everywhere I looked, fat fat and more fat. Tall people, short people, old people, young people, a sea of fatness. And the food--massive sizes and portions. Now I knew why Asians and Europeans often joked about fat Americans.

Missoula, Montana felt twice the fantasy land. Clean, green, extremely spacious, big sky overhead, river running through it, friendly casual people. I slipped back in the "Garden City" like wearing a favorite old coat.

The first few months were fantastic, as I saw family, friends, and partook in all my favorite Montana activities. Yet, sometimes I got very quiet, and didn't want to see anyone. Occasionally a reverse culture shock came over me, and I sequestered myself. And a few friends remarked that I acted too polite, smiled too much, and spoke a little like a car salesman. Residue from Japan, I guessed.

Then another odd thing happened. As I pondered graduate school applications, I suddenly craved more travel. I craved another adventure. I saw a few ads at my alma mater for teaching English in South Korea. I had heard you could make good money there, and in Japan had met a few foreigners who said it was great. Plus I knew the foreign drill and had more teaching experience. After six months back home, I again found myself flying to Asia.

Fast-forward two years, and I'm returning to Montana for the summer, with a Korean fiancée. Again I loved being back, and soaked up the exotic rush of bouncing between two very different worlds. My ability to transition back and forth improved.

Two years in South Korea would have been plenty, and in fact, it may have been too long, as I enjoyed Japan more. But love makes us do lots of things, as it should, and I agreed to one more year in Jeonju for my fiancée. As mentioned earlier, that would eventually unravel and we would never marry, but I'm still very grateful. I experienced many interesting and wonderful days in South Korea and with my first fiancée.

After that third year in South Korea, my third homecoming was without question a final one. I was grateful for all my time there, but a bit in a daze and worn out, wondering how a total of six years had went by since my first leaving for Japan. I needed to resume an American life, and especially, some sort of career.

Yet again, I now felt a citizen of the world, not just a citizen of America. I had forged friendships with individuals around the world, Europe to the Middle East, Australia and New Zealand, and of course throughout Asia. I had weathered a total of five years on foreign soil. I felt bigger and stronger, deeper and wiser. My time there seemed like two other lifetimes.

If you read travel books, you may often hear claims like this, and they're probably accurate. But let me tell you something you may not often read: Extensive travel can also confuse and complicate you. It's not always a Zen rock garden, as you've read here. It blurs your cultural habits, your ethics, your spirituality (or non-spirituality), your perspective on the world. Sometimes while trekking forward, you're also spiraling back, picking up long lost pieces of yourself to carry to the present. You have to dig deep, and decide your true north, not only what your country and culture have taught you.

I recommend travel without reservation, and it is now an ongoing love of my life. Extended travel requires a bold voyage both outward and inward. Be brave!

Brendan

EPILOGUE (12 YEARS LATER)

I've undertaken three new adventures since Asian travels.

First, I started graduate school at age 34, later obtaining an MFA in Creative Writing Nonfiction. The one-horse, high-altitude town of Laramie, Wyoming proved a striking contrast to my overseas adventures, albeit fairly akin to Montana.

Second, I later moved to Las Vegas and started a company called Global Top Picks, Inc. The flagship website is LasVegasTopPicks.com, where I feature top picks around the city, including dining, shows, events, nightclubs, poker (of course), and hotels, plus nearby hiking and unique attractions. Through this I meet a variety of interesting characters and celebrities. I'm slowly expanding these "Top Picks" websites to other famous cities and worthwhile destinations, including LA, NYC, Montana, Europe, and Russia.

Third, I married a Russian. She's my first wife (and if I know what's good for me, also my last). We've known each other five years and have been married two and a half. She's a travel enthusiast, fitness lover, and book nerd like me; she's both a fierce patriot and fierce critic of her own country, also like me. I've explored Russia extensively, especially St. Petersburg (aka Leningrad 1924-1991) and Moscow, and have drank vodka with many a Russian. I absolutely love St. Pete--a cultural, historical, and geographical gem. Russians, like Asians, know much more about us than we know of them, and lately they're a hot topic, full of intrigue and drama. I have much to report! But that's another story...

If I haven't bored you entirely, please watch for my next eBook: *Blue River in a Red Forest, The Russian Chronicles.*

Brendan Magone, September 8, 2018

Made in United States
North Haven, CT
23 October 2022

25832154R00093

"Beautifully portrayed in poignant narrative, *Lilia* is a heart-wrenching coming of age set amidst the cruelties of a fascist Italy allied with the Nazis during WWII. Month after month and tragedy after tragedy, the plight of Lilia's family worsens. Ganzini brilliantly depicts the turmoil and upheaval of a family caught in the crosshairs of the partisan/fascist conflict. But Lilia's tender heart, broken time and time again by the betrayals and bloodshed of war, and a mother irreparably broken by loss, refuses to succumb, clinging fiercely to her dreams of finding true love and everlasting happiness. *Lilia* will possess your heart and linger on in your mind long after you finish the final chapter."

ROXI HARMS, *Author of The Upside of Hunger*

"The indignities, atrocities, and terrors visited on a poor family in a tiny Northern Italian village during WWII place in stark relief the human toll war takes on those the history books never document. Told with deep emotion and love, Lilia's story steals your breath at the misery and hardship visited on a young girl forced to grow up far too fast in a world torn apart by the greed for power in fascist Italy. Yet there are rare moments of beautiful joy too. Through it all, Lilia's incredible well of resilience never runs dry. Ganzini's poetic prose renders this story both a warning about the slide into fascism in modern times and a beacon of hope for the strength of the human spirit. Read it now."

TAM DERUDDER JACKSON, *Author of The Talisman Series*

"*Lilia* is a labor of love, and it shows. The amount of detail, emotional nuance, and attention to the unfolding story of a family held together by love and hope lends itself to an exquisite and heartfelt narrative. Linda Ganzini has created a work that reflects the cruel realities of the past and heralds a clarion call to the time we currently find ourselves. Like Lilia and her family members, we can choose resilience and allow our personal stories to become beacons for our collective human journey. This is an important book for a transformative moment in our history."

NIRMALA NATARAJ, *Writer, Editor, and Author*

"*Lilia* is a timely and must-read book. The author's powerfully evocative and descriptive writing transported me back in time to a world of uncertainty, where innocent people were stripped of their humanity, dignity and faith. And a time where bonds were strengthened to survive the unthinkable. My thanks to Linda Ganzini for allowing readers to connect to her family's past trials and tribulations in Northern Italy during WWII—events few know and talk about, especially our younger generation."

ELSA ZAMPARELLI, *Oscar-Nominated, and Award-Winning Costume Designer*

"Linda's story of her mother's determined resistance to the tyranny of fascism is as heartwarming as it is heart-tugging. It is a story of the human spirit's strength and resilience, even as it prevails over the cruelest monstrosities of hate, fear, and oppression. Lilia's journey is an important life-affirming lesson for us all."

VALERY SATTERWHITE, *Author*

LILIA

ISBN: 978-1-7776073-1-9

This work is based on actual events in the life of the author's mother and depicted
as truthfully as recollection permits. However, this book is creative nonfiction and
is not historical biography. Historical references are from the author's research,
and all photos are from the author's family collection.

Cover and interior design by Linda Ganzini

LILIA

A TRUE STORY OF LOVE, COURAGE, AND
SURVIVAL IN THE SHADOW OF WAR.

LINDA GANZINI

"Memories of war and a stolen childhood still burn in my heart and tear at my soul. I was a young girl who was made to endure the unthinkable. During the occupation, German soldiers invaded our village—a known hideout for partisans. Spies acted as friends by day and informants to the Nazis by night. Unable to trust anyone, we lived in silence so deafening it was torture. The darkest day of my life came when the Nazis took my brother. I felt helpless as the war tore our family apart. His last words to my mother: 'Mama, if I don't go now, they will kill us all.' I saw the pain in my mother's eyes. I felt her heart cry words she could never speak. Haunted by death, I prayed: *God, let me grow up before I die.* Like the war, my life was senseless."

❧ ❧

LILIA GANZINI

Lilia
Giovanni
Riccardo
Bruno

Virginia Lilia Maria Eliseo
Riccardo Bruno

Family Home

Arturo

Lilia

Erminio

LILIA'S STORY
1939 to 1952

Lilia & Maria

Lilia & Ermides

Lilia, Cornelia, Ermides

Forever in our *Hearts*

Class of 1964-1965

Renzo ~ Prince Charming

Maria & Virginio

Dina

Ermides

Nonno Giovanni

To my beloved mother, Lilia,
Thank you for believing in me and seeing me through the writing
of this heart-driven book. You taught me to trust myself and
connect with my inner compass. I am honored to have journeyed
this passage with you and together tell your story.

To my sister, Cosetta,
Thank you for being my second pair of eyes when I was too tired
to see, my cheerleader when I struggled through heart-wrenching
scenes—you were my grounding force, my Obi-Wan Kenobi.

To my friends and family,
Without your continued love and support, the making of this
book would not have been possible—you are the wind beneath
my wings.

To my social media tribe of fabulous authors and supporters,
Thank you for strengthening my belief there is an essential place
for my book in the world. You have become more than my
writing community, teachers and friends—you are family.

A special thank you to Yolanda Phelps from The Simply Rustic
Home on Etsy for hand-crafting the four-leaf clover. And to
Karen Merrilees at XO Memories for the legacy memorial
photo collage—both are beautiful additions to this book.

For my mother, Lilia
May this legacy give you eternal life and honor the lives
of our loved ones, so they will never be forgotten.
I can feel your luminous spirit shine through this book—
you are an extraordinary woman and an inextricable part
of my soul. With all my heart, I will love you forever.

ℰℴ My name is Lilia. This book tells my story—the journey of my soul. I am so grateful to and proud of my daughter, Linda, for giving birth to this book. Years ago, when she first asked me to write about my life growing up during the war, I couldn't do it—the memories were too painful. After some time and thought, I decided to share my story. I hope it will not only inspire others but become a legacy to my parents and siblings, those still here and those who have passed on.

As we journeyed back to my childhood, I cried, struggling to open the door to a harrowing past, and my daughter cried, listening to me as I returned to a part of my life I had buried deep within—now poured on to the pages of this book, a book she has written through her tears. In reliving these heart-rending memories, what also surfaced were beautiful memories that had been masked by pain yet yearned to be remembered.

To the girls of today: You are fortunate to have opportunities and the chance to make your own choices and follow your dreams. I never had time for mine, as I was always helping others through times of poverty and the horrors of war. Despite all the darkness, I never gave up believing . . . in me. Life is too short. Strive to make the best of it. Stay in close contact with your parents and siblings and be happy.

To the parents of today: Be kind to your children. Honor and respect them. We have power in how we shape their lives and how they see themselves. Be selfless in your choice of words and actions so your children may fly freely and feel loved.

I hope in reading this book, you will connect with my story and know that our past does not dictate our future. I am proud of my accomplishments, and although growing up was a challenge for me, the love of my three children makes up for all that had been longing in me for so long.

Twelve years ago, I lost the love of my life to cancer. One day, I will reunite with my sweetheart, my Prince Charming, but until then, we have more life to live. I am thankful for mine.

God bless you all,

"What is done cannot be undone, but one can prevent it happening again."

ANNE FRANK, *The Diary of a Young Girl*

May 1944

1 | MAMA!

Italy 1939

"We are not asking for the opinion of the world,
but we want the world to be informed—"

ℬ "Mama? Papa? Mussolini is on the radio. He's giving a speech in Rome!" hollered sixteen-year-old Ermides from the front door of the house, arms akimbo as she waited for her parents to respond. Known for her bossy behavior and stern, no-nonsense demeanor, Ermides insisted on always having the upper hand.

Fifty feet away, her mother, Maria, slowly worked her way down the ladder that rose to the hayloft above the old yellow brick barn. Her clothes smelled of musty old straw. While brushing away the dry stalks from her black dress and apron, she looked up to see her third oldest child motioning for her and Virginio to go inside.

Maria flung her right arm up in the air as she set foot on the ground. "Ahhh, dear daughter of mine," she said, shaking her head disdainfully, "why should I care what Mussolini has to say? I have better things to do with my time." She turned her back on Ermides and pulled open the russet-painted barn door. Its tired hinges creaked, serving to irritate Maria even further. She proceeded to sweep the wooden plank floor as her aggravation grew. Unfazed by her mother's reaction, Ermides rolled her eyes and went back into the house.

Maria's husband, Virginio, had spent the morning sitting at his workbench inside the barn, laboring away on the finishing touches for a pair of wooden clogs for one of the locals. Virginio observed his wife as he sharpened his tools. He removed his glasses and let out a long, deep breath. "I don't trust him any more than you do, but we have to keep our strong opinions to ourselves."

Maria flipped her hand up and scoffed.

"Maria, Mussons is a *small* village. There are eyes and ears around every corner. I don't think a week goes by without one of the *Camicie Nere* asking me, 'Why are you not wearing a black shirt?' Because I'm not a fascist and don't want to support that treacherous, tyrannical man!" Virginio moaned contemptuously at the present state of the world as he flung his tools on the workbench. "Maria, I barely survived the trenches in the Great War—my lungs were never the same after inhaling that damn mustard gas! Every day I'm grateful that part of my life is over, but the world is changing again—we need to watch our words and keep our thoughts to ourselves. The air is thick with whispers."

Maria bit her tongue and swept more vigorously, squinting her eyes in consternation. Already perplexed by a myriad of thoughts, another one dawned on her. Her eyes flew open. She turned to Virginio with a puzzled and suspicious look.

"When, and *how*, did we buy . . . a radio?"

Virginio shrugged. "I made Silvano a pair of shoes. He had an old, used radio at the store. He gave it to me in trade."

"Mother of God! We don't need a radio. We need money for food! Why didn't you tell me?"

"I'm sorry. You're right." Virginio raised his hands as if to appease his quick-tempered and irritable wife. "I thought the kids would enjoy it."

"Yes, and now they have Mussolini in their ears to enjoy!" Annoyed, she threw down the large straw broom and exited the barn, startling the chickens into a round of squawking hysterics.

A simple man in his early forties, Virginio lived an honest life. His pale-blue eyes were infused with kindness and understanding, as though filled with God's light. Calm and never combative, he smiled often and relished telling joy-filled stories. He gave in to Maria most days because his compassion for her had grown stronger than his wariness of her nagging. Despite Maria's stoic exterior, Virginio intimately knew the sadness in her heart, the vulnerability and powerlessness she desperately tried to mask. He only ever wanted to soothe her pain, culled from years of despair, and fill the dark memories with his love.

Virginio held the honor as the one stable force in Maria's life and the heart of Mussons—a small farming community of mostly peasant workers nestled by the Tagliamento River in North-eastern Italy. From carpenter to blacksmith, barber, butcher, and sexton, Virginio mastered every craft. His skills and labor were in constant demand among the villagers, and true to his nature, he eagerly enrolled himself to help. Against Maria's wishes, he frequently worked for free, sympathizing with those who could not afford to pay him when he had little more than the shirt on his back.

Irritated, Maria went about her chores. She yanked every piece of dry clothing off the clothesline while mumbling under her breath, suppressing her anger and frustration.

Day in and day out, Maria twisted her long black hair back into a neat bun, carefully tying it with a black headscarf. Between the kitchen, barn, and garden, she worked from dawn until dusk. When not maintaining the family home and tending to her children, Maria nursed the locals. She administered injections to the elderly, cooked for them, and acted as a midwife for expectant mothers. She even sold her beautiful raven locks to the wealthy, who used them to make wigs—one of the many sacrifices made for the ones she loved. And although Maria had a sharp tongue, she never once used it to complain about the cards she'd been dealt.

Maria usually remained silent until pushed past her limits. A strong, self-reliant woman, she fiercely protected her family. Although close-knit, Mussons still had its fair share of gossip, bullies, and people with malicious intent. Maria trusted no one. Over time she believed more in the barricades she'd built for herself.

A typically slim, firm woman in her late thirties, she often seemed older—hardened and made sturdy by decades as a farmworker. Her dark clothing rarely changed from day to day—a symbol of respect and grief for the children she'd lost in childbearing. In the past ten years, Maria suffered three miscarriages and one stillborn. She lost twin boys at the age of two from enteritis and a daughter of six months from pneumonia. The irreparable loss had left its imprint forever. She felt beaten down by the storms of life, believing everything was as it should be—and that she would lose every time.

Back in the house, young voices escalated in the kitchen. Four siblings sat around the table, staring down at the radio, waiting with ears cocked for clear reception.

"Turn it up!" Seventeen-year-old Erminio shouted in excitement as a radio station broke through the static.

Erminio reigned quietly as Maria's favorite child and struggled as the sensitive and delicate one of his siblings. He had spent more than half his life battling a multitude of health issues, from rheumatic fever to countless bouts of pneumonia—illnesses that could have taken a turn for the worse and even resulted in death. His suffering amplified Maria's protective maternal instincts.

Despite his sensitive nature and fragile constitution, Erminio landed himself on an undeniable ground of popularity with the girls who swooned at the sight of him. From his tousled dark hair to his penetrating brown eyes, he bore a striking resemblance to the great film actor Rudolph Valentino. Erminio embraced this perk by ensuring he maintained his reputation for being impeccably dressed, always prepared for the unexpected. He had luscious full lips that curved into an irresistible smile, almost as if he had a secret to tell. Naturally, with young girls from around the village falling at his feet, he often avoided his chores while attending to his throng of admirers. Unlike his courageous older brother, Arturo, who was more responsible and level-headed, the idea of being drafted into war sent him into a panic, stirring his nerves.

"Relax, impatient one," laughed Arturo as he fiddled with the tuner. "I'm trying to get the signal back."

At nineteen, Arturo led the clan as the eldest of his siblings. Four months into his eighteen-month compulsory military training in Udine, a city in the neighboring province between the Adriatic Sea and the Alps, he had claimed a weekend pass to return home. Tall in stature, Arturo ducked his head when entering a room. His blonde hair framed blue eyes, the color of the sea—eyes filled with softness and honesty. His smile was gentle, like the sound of his voice. His most profound beauty came from deep within—his thoughtfulness, selflessness, and kindness. Unlike his younger brother, Arturo took pride in being an introvert and not one for drinking or flirting with women. He preferred solitude to crowds as he drew his energy from quiet, reflective moments and found peace in the company of his family.

Maria and Virginio's second-oldest daughter, fourteen-year-old Dina, hovered over her brothers at the table and scoffed at the radio.

"That sure is a rickety old thing."

An artist with a cheeky sense of humor, Dina livened up every occasion and relished pulling no punches with her words. Her parents proclaimed that, no sooner had she been born, she grasped a pencil in her hand. Throughout her youth, she took small pieces of coal from the fireplace and drew elaborate pictures on the white kitchen wall. With every drawing, Maria became more and more frustrated and instructed Virginio to paint over it. As soon as Dina's artistic spirit emerged on the wall, her father reluctantly erased all traces of her creative expression. Still, Dina stood in her truth with relentless determination, and the paint buckets continued to require refilling.

"Dina, at least we *have* a radio," Ermides scolded her sister. "Papa worked hard to give it to us when he could have taken money for his work instead. Show some respect!"

"The signal's back again!" Arturo raised a victorious smile with his announcement. "Listen, listen!"

> "—We don't want to hear any more about brotherhood, sisterhood, or cousinhood, or any other similar bastard relationships."

"That *bastard* took my wedding band!" Maria bellowed as she charged into the kitchen, her anger getting the best of her. Virginio trailed behind her and tried to soothe his wife by rubbing her shoulder.

"Maria, please, calm down—that was a long time ago. The neighbors will hear you!"

"I made coffee!" Dina interjected quickly, hoping to diffuse the tension. "Anyone?" She passed a cup and spoon to her father and gave him a sympathetic look. Arturo, Erminio, and Ermides ignored their mother's outburst, trying to focus on the Prime Minister's speech.

"What? I don't care about the neighbors! It's true! I remember it as if it were yesterday," Maria huffed in irritation. "Four years ago, that idiot was desperate, but smart too, like a fox. It wasn't our fault the country was losing money. We were stupid and ignorant to give up our wedding bands, and for what? For some patriotic ring made of steel! Gold to the homeland? Did women think a metal ring inscribed with these lies was a fair trade? You gave me that ring!" She turned to her husband, and her blazing eyes were not only filled with anger, but sadness, too.

"I know, Maria, I know," Virginio nodded, demonstrating his sympathy. He lowered his gaze and let out a deep exhale, and the steam from his coffee rose in swirls mingling with his breath until both disappeared.

"I remember the soldier at our front gate, encouraging me to give up my gold, *my* jewelery." Maria pulled back the sleeves of her black sweater, revealing her bare wrist, and stuck out her bare neck. "What jewelery? Do you *see* jewelery? That ring was all I had—and the rosary in my pocket." Maria pointed through the kitchen window that looked out on to the street and front gate of their home. "He stood right there, arrogant, with a smug smile. I wanted to slap it off his face! 'The queen laid down *her* wedding ring,' he said to me, like I cared about the queen! She probably had ten more where *that* came from!"

"Well, you *did* throw the steel ring back at him, Mama. I remember *that* like it was yesterday," Dina leaned back in her chair laughing.

"You laugh, but don't be fooled by Mussolini. Women should be ashamed of being forced to give up what was rightly theirs."

"Shh! Mama!" Arturo whispered as he raised the volume on the radio.

```
    "This is your day, your great day with
   your courage, with your sacrifice, with your
    faith, you have given a mighty impulse
             to the wheel of history."
```

"You begging bandit!" Maria blurted.
"Shhhh," the children hissed with annoyance.

```
     "Now I'm asking you . . . I'm asking you:
Do you want honors? Rewards? A comfortable life?
         Does the impossible exist for you?"
```

"Thief!" Maria shouted, shaking her fist at the radio.
Ermides shot Maria a withering look. "Mama, enough, no?"

```
     "What are the three words forming our dogma?
                Believe. Obey. Fight.
   Well, comrades, in these three words it was,
               it is, and it will be
            the secret of every victory!"
```

The roaring Roman crowd burst into applause, which crackled on the old radio.

"Mark my words," Maria declared, motioning to the ground, "Rome can honor him all they want, but he's manipulating all of Italy. Mussolini's an actor on a stage. He promises us that fascism will replace democracy, and the war will be over. It won't be over. It will never be over. Your mother may be a poor peasant woman, but I wasn't born yesterday." Her eyes gleamed with pride as she raised her finger in the air, "*And*, he's not even Catholic. He's an atheist!"

Erminio turned off the radio. The room grew quiet. The children felt pinned to their seats by their mother's wave of emotion.

Maria turned to her boys. "Why do you think you had to wear black shirts, caps, and gray socks all through school? And you two, I had to make you both black dresses with white collars. Why? I'll tell you why—because those are Mussolini's fascist colors. We have to dress like him, pray to him, *be* like him. He's becoming Hitler!" "Enough, Maria, enough now," Virginio spoke softly but firmly, before taking a soothing sip of his coffee.

Maria gave her husband an exasperated look and charged out of the kitchen.

"Where are you going?"

"To wake up our other three mouths to feed! The sun's coming up. Enjoy your *radio!*"

Dina rolled her eyes and whispered. "I know teenage daughters always find their mothers annoying, but she *really* is!" Her brothers giggled, while Ermides gave her sister an annoyed sidelong glance.

"I heard that!" spat Maria from the great room.

"Those mood swings can make one's life a living hell. It's a good thing we're leaving soon," Dina winked and smiled wryly at her sister.

Virginio and Maria had sent their girls far from home to work as maids at the ages of ten and twelve, which was customary for children in poor peasant families. Nonetheless, as parents, it tore them up inside.

"I heard that, too!" grumbled Maria as she pounded her way up the stairs.

The children shook their heads incredulously.

"Yes, yes, sometimes she is overly passionate, but your mother's right," Virginio sighed as he stirred his cup and took a seat at the table. "The war is costing Italy a lot of money, and we are a poor country. Mussolini took thirty-five tons of gold from his people. We will never get that back."

"Our military isn't as strong as the French and British, Papa. I'm not confident this war will end well." Arturo's worried tone triggered anxiety around the table.

"I'm scared of this war," Erminio's fear made it difficult for him to accept how his life could change if he were a soldier. "If I get drafted, I don't want to go."

"Yes, the *girls* need you here," Arturo winked at him in an attempt to add levity to the dark moment.

Virginio looked earnestly at his children, and his eyes settled on Erminio, "Son, we can't let fear run our lives. I'm proud of you for being who you are, but not proud of what is happening in this war. If we can't be loyal to ourselves and this country, we lose our self-respect—our dignity."

He looked around the table and clapped his hands, as if to end the conversation. "All right, no more talk about war today. Come on, help your mama by making breakfast. Lilia, Giovanni, and Riccardo will be down soon." Virginio tapped the murky surface of his now-cold cup of coffee and swirled it around before taking the last swig. He rose from the table and pushed in his chair. At the doorway, Virginio paused and looked back at his children. "You know, behind that prickly shell, your mother has a good heart. She's endured more hardship in her lifetime than any woman I know. Be kind to her."

The children bowed their heads in shame for not being more understanding. As difficult as their mother could be, they knew their father was right.

"Papa?"

"Yes, Ermides?"

"Dina and I are leaving to go back to work in a few days. I don't think we'll be able to come back for at least another six months." She sighed, jutting her bottom lip out, the air fanning her bangs. "I wish things were different. Sometimes, I wish I had been born a boy."

Her words struck Virginio hard. Tears filled his eyes at the thought of his two daughters leaving again, and all for the sake of supporting the family and taking on their expected roles as young women. Mussolini wanted a nation of warriors. While boys were taught to be the soldiers of the future, girls were groomed to farm, serve as maids, and eventually, become mothers to fascist sons. Children were taught at a young age that Mussolini was the only man who would make Italy great again. 'War is to the male what childbearing is to the female' was one of the many fascist slogans.

"We see so little of you girls year after year," Virginio lamented. "Your mother and I wanted to give all of you so much more. Until last year, Mussolini promised families higher welfare and healthcare benefits to increase Italy's population and grow a stronger country. His plan failed, and the little money he gave us never made much of a difference. It couldn't save the children we lost, and now here you both are, having to scrub other people's floors. I'm so sorry to put this burden on you."

"It's fine, Papa," Ermides went over to her father to comfort him. "In this family, we help each other."

Virginio beamed at his daughter and looked lovingly at each of his children. "We may not have much in the way of material comforts, but we have love—and that counts for everything. And although we're in the middle of a war, no one can beat us if we never give up."

☙ ❧

Upstairs, Maria gathered the next pile of clothing and linens that needed washing before waking up four-year-old Lilia, two-year-old Giovanni, and Riccardo, who was nearly one year old.

As the rooster crowed and the bells of Santa Osvaldo Church rang their last chime on the hour, Maria swung open the old green wooden shutters to bring in the daybreak. Slivers of golden light danced across the room. Exhausted from her morning episode, she breathed in the crisp air, her face warmed by the sun rising behind the church steeple. She was tickled by the sounds of baby chicks chirping in the courtyard, craning their necks and waiting to be fed.

"Sleepyhead! Time to get up! Come for breakfast, and then you can help me feed the chicks. Hurry now. You're the last one. Your brothers are coming downstairs with me." Maria left the room and headed downstairs, holding Riccardo in one arm and laundry in the other, while Giovanni trailed behind.

Wide brown eyes slowly caught the rays of brightness as ten little toes rose up from under the sheets. Lilia blinked a few times to adjust to the sun that had kissed her awake. She peered over her feet to the empty beds around her and smiled, excited to see her family. *They can't have fun without me!* Lilia thought as she slid off her mattress. She rubbed the sleep from her lids and, still in her pink nightie, scurried down the long narrow hallway, hopping over patches of sunlight that streamed through the window and on to the hardwood floor. Her long chestnut braid flew behind her. She halted at the landing and held on to the walls as she descended the steep stairs. On the first step, her foot caught on the edge of her nightie, and she tripped down the flight of stairs. Lilia tumbled and twirled, and with nothing to grab on to, she felt her body spinning in slow motion as if she were floating through a surreal and scary dream.

On the last step, Lilia bounced on her bottom and landed on her stomach, screaming loud enough to drain the faces of her family as they rushed forward.

"Mamaaaaaa!" Lilia cried, as she looked down at her scraped-up hands and knees. Tears streamed down her reddened face.

"Liliutti, did you hurt yourself? Where does it hurt?" Maria swiftly checked her daughter's arms and legs.

With a quivering lip, Lilia looked up at her concerned parents and siblings, who now stood all around her. Despite her throbbing pain, for that brief moment, she felt her world would always be safe. Lilia's frown quickly broke into a smile, and everyone smiled back in relief. Arturo carried her to the kitchen. Lilia wrapped her arms tightly around him and whimpered on his shoulder, secretly glad for the attention. Arturo was Lilia's favorite brother.

"You silly girl. Don't scare me like that again. What would I do without you?"

Being the youngest girl made Lilia feel special, like she could melt away the darkest cloud that loomed over her family. In her siblings' eyes, she was a ray of light whose innocence and old-soul wisdom brought them hope; she was pure happiness growing in a world where, day by day, the sun seemed to fade into gray.

As her wounds were patched and kissed, she observed her family one by one, taking in the unique love each of them had for her. A warmth came over Lilia. She knew this was a moment to be treasured. Too young to understand the impending conflict of wartime, she was mostly lost in daydreaming and playing with her younger brothers. Lilia dreamed of becoming a fairy princess, like the ones in the stories her father read to her. She imagined herself growing up and traveling the world, adventuring far and wide. Yet, something in the air felt heavy, and she perceived that life as she knew it would never be the same. Her childlike days would soon be over.

৵ଡ଼ ୭৵

By October 1940, Germany had invaded Poland, and Great Britain and France had declared war on Adolf Hitler and his Nazi regime. Warsaw surrendered to the Nazis, Germany bombed and entered Paris, and Italy invaded Greece.

Like the chill of October, the war had settled over the rural countryside and village of Mussons. It pressed through the misty fog, resounding doom and disaster. As the days grew shorter and the nights longer, and as the cold dark weeks rolled on, songs of fear lingered in the air. A war that once seemed safely distant was now becoming all too real.

The streets of Mussons lay empty and bare. Villagers were at the mercy of winter and drenched by sheets of frigid rain. The brown meadows, falling chestnuts, frost-covered grass, and scent of burning wood ushered in a time of change—not merely a change of season, but a change in people's hope, as they were now uncertain of what their future held.

While resting her chin in her cupped hands, Lilia looked out the bedroom window and lowered her gaze to the falling rain as it bounced off the courtyard. She listened to the dull rumble on the clay roof tiles and found herself longing for the pleasure and sounds of summer. However, the cold shadows did have a silver lining. Lilia's mother brought her eleventh child into the world, a baby boy named Bruno.

With one more child to feed and little money to spare, Maria and Virginio had no means to afford a car. Whether hauling a wagon by bicycle, pushing a wheelbarrow, or lugging a yoke, they couldn't travel far. Maria was discharged from the nearest hospital in San Vito, fifteen kilometers from Mussons. Alone, with her bundled newborn in her arms, she took the bus to the town of Morsano, the last stop on the route, four kilometers from home. Upon arriving, she plodded a few blocks to the center square and sat on the only bench, where she waited for Erminio and Lilia to take her and Bruno back to Mussons.

Although exhausted, Maria sank into the welcoming thought she would soon be home. "Here we are, just me and you," she smiled down to her newborn boy, enjoying these few quiet moments with him. "For all your hopes and dreams to come, I pray God promises you a good life." Maria closed her eyes not only in prayer but to rest her weary mind as well.

In the meantime, Erminio and Lilia's four-kilometer journey of great anticipation commenced. He rode his father's bicycle while she sat in the attached open wagon, giddy with excitement to meet her new baby brother.

"Erminio, pedal faster!" Lilia pleaded, laughing as her voice jumped scales with every bump in the gravel road.

"Hang on, Liliutti. We're turning a corner!" Erminio looked back, laughing as his sister—who barely weighed more than a sack of potatoes—toggle from side to side.

Aware the air was growing colder by the moment, he pedaled harder and faster. As they arrived in Morsano, Lilia could see her mother on the bench, and the repose on her face as she bowed over the bundle in her arms.

For the last twenty years of being a mother, Maria had tried to make peace with the life God had given her. Despite having birthed ten other children and being well accustomed to the relentless routine—sleepless nights, rocking, pacing, nursing—worry consumed her. Maria now had one more body to care for, one more mouth to feed.

She gazed down at her baby and offered yet another prayer. "God, I pray for strength, for grace, and that I'm not too tired to be a good mother. I trust that you will only ever give me what I can handle."

"Mama, Mama!" Maria was stirred out of her thoughts by the sweet sound of Lilia's cries of joy. Passers-by stopped to watch the beautiful little girl as she flew across the street with open arms and bright eyes, her shoes nearly slapping her bottom as she ran towards her mother. Catching a glimpse of the baby's face, Lilia paused in wonderment. She tiptoed closer to her tiny baby brother as if she'd magically and unexpectedly stumbled upon a treasure chest. Overcome with awe, Lilia retreated a few steps and looked to her mother for a sign of what to do next.

Maria beckoned her daughter over with a nod. "Come hold your new baby brother."

Lilia stretched out her arms to receive him with a pounding heart and sweaty palms, while Erminio stood back smiling with complete adoration. She pulled Bruno close to her heart, gazing into his eyes as they stared back intensely into hers.

"I'm your big sister, Lilia. I'm going to take care of you." The baby gurgled softly in agreement. Although Lilia already had two younger brothers, she didn't remember their births—this moment was precious.

As they endured the long ride home, Lilia remained transfixed on little Bruno's small features and bewildered stare. Her eyes softened as he cooed and smiled. She wanted nothing more than to protect him.

To Maria, the journey seemed endless. She pulled the wool blanket over her chilled bone and curled up to the side of the wagon, trying to withstand the bumps in the uneven road. She eagerly awaited Virginio's embrace, seeing her family, and collapsing into the comfort of her warm bed.

It was midday, and there was barely a sound sailing on the breeze. People had scampered indoors for *riposo*, their regular mid-day rest. The smell of burning wood wafted from the chimneys of nearby homes, and row upon row of corn and wheat fields lined the gravel street for as long as the eye could see. As the cool breeze blew over the pastures, the straw waved hello in streams of gold—a sight that nearly lulled Maria to sleep. All the while, Lilia hoped the ride would last longer so she could have Bruno to herself.

Nearing their home on Via della Chiesa, in the heart of Mussons, Erminio proudly rang his bicycle bell in celebration—dring-dring! A succession of ringing sounds echoed throughout the streets, summoning neighbors to welcome baby Bruno's arrival. Cycling past La Bottega, the village bar, patrons shouted, "*Cincin*! Cheers Maria! Congratulations!" as they raised a glass in the Meneguzzis' honor. Shutters flew open to waving hands and delighted faces. An inaudible sigh of relief was felt throughout the village. Baby Bruno was here! And hopefully, he would restore joy and excitement to a family that had suffered the extremes of heartache and loss.

Lilia could see the church up ahead, which meant they were close to home. After pulling up to the wooden gate of their two-story, white, brick house, Maria and Lilia poured out of the wagon. Virginio was anxiously waiting and rushed out to greet them. Arturo and Ermides followed. Giovanni clung to his father's pant leg, while Dina held Riccardo in her arms. Arturo had been granted another weekend pass, and the girls had returned home for a few days to help prepare for Bruno's arrival.

"Look, kids—look what Mama brought home from the store!" Virginio's pride shone as ripples of joy warmed his heart.

Giovanni poked his head between the wooden bars of the gate, reaching his hands out to his mother. "Mama, Mama!"

"Maria, let me look at you." Virginio tenderly cupped his wife's face and kissed her forehead. Seeing how the day drained her strength away, he lifted his infant son out of Maria's arms and cradled him in his. "You must be exhausted."

"Humph!" Maria grunted in an undertone. "Right now? All I want is quiet, and to lie down and rest."

Virginio felt a sudden pang of regret. He paused, waiting for Maria's inevitable reaction.

Maria dragged her tired feet into the front courtyard, leading her trailing clan behind her. She breathed a sigh of relief to be home at last. As she opened the door, her eyes widened in shock—she was welcomed by an overwhelming barrage of friends, all of whom were shouting one on top of the other, each raising a glass. Maria turned back to Virginio and gave him a seething look. He pretended not to notice.

"Welcome back, Maria!"

"Maria! You brought home a boy!"

"Look, a boy!"

"Maria, what a beautiful, baby boy!"

"Congratulations!"

Maria wanted to disappear. It took all of her strength to maintain her composure and a pleasant smile. Everyone was pushing through for a closer look at Bruno until Maria was practically shoved into the corner of the dining area in the great room. Fatigued, and now irritated, she spied Virginio through the boisterous crowd and raised her brow in discontent. Catching Maria's disapproval from across the room, he shrugged, jiggled Bruno in his arms, and smiled, mouthing the words, "We had a baby!"

Maria laughed for a minute, and then the corners of her mouth drooped as she thought to herself, *No, I had a baby*!

She looked around the room. The white plaster walls were stacked high with fresh corn from the fields, ready for shucking. It was customary for locals to come together and help each other with an abundant harvest. The cleanest shells were being saved and piled in the barn. Virginio used them for kindling, to refill mattresses, weave baskets, and make shoes. Everyone celebrated Bruno's homecoming by peeling husks, eating roasted chestnuts, drinking Virginio's homemade wine and grappa, and feasting on a table of hot food, the smell of which wafted in the air.

Traditional, Alpine home-cooking graced the dining-room table. Family friends brought cutting boards of local cheese and homemade salami, a pot of minestrone, vegetable platters prepared with oil and vinegar, risotto, a roasted chicken, pasta dishes, and a copper pot of polenta, sausage, turnips, and grape skins. Seeing the food made Maria's mouth water.

Lilia ran behind her mother to avoid all the grown-ups fussing over Bruno and the random neighbors who intermittently stopped to coo over her and pinch her cheeks. She caught the glow of a silver candelabra gleaming across luxurious Parisian table settings. The display had been causing a stir among the women as they gawked openly at the fine china and whispered among themselves.

"Maria! Where did you get these beautiful settings?" gushed Maria's neighbor, Carlotta, from the other end of the long table.

"Uh, one minute, Carlotta!" Maria was flushed with embarrassment, as she had no idea how the place settings had made their way into this humble abode. She discreetly waved her daughters over and whispered to them in a low, irritated voice.

"Ermides, Dina, where did you get these plates? Did you steal them?!" Quietly, the girls huddled at their mother's side.

"Mama, relax," Ermides clucked her tongue and rolled her eyes. "The family in Rome gave me the dishes as a gift for you."

"And the Milanese gave me the candelabra," Dina replied with a proud smile. "I didn't *steal* it! I wouldn't steal a needle if it fell on their floor. Would you believe they keep leaving pennies everywhere to see what I'll do? I mean, do I *look* like a thief?" Dina rolled her eyes, too. "Mama, please, *enjoy* the gifts!"

As Maria wordlessly marveled over the elegant offerings, Dina added, "Mama, everything is old or damaged. They buy new things and give the old away." She pointed to a plate on the table. "Look, you see? This one is chipped, and that one has a crack in it."

Lilia couldn't help but run her fingers over the fancy plates rimmed with gold. The Eiffel Tower was painted in the center. *They're the plates of kings and queens*, she thought in admiration.

"Lilia! Don't touch!" Maria swatted her little hand away. "Girls, before you both go back, help me write a letter to thank them." Maria wistfully held one of the plates in her hands. "The good life belongs to the wealthy, not poor people like us. I never see my daughters, but I have gold-rimmed plates." She shook her head at the unfairness of life.

"Carlotta, the girls brought them back from Rome and Milan—a gift from their employers," Having to raise her voice above the noise, Maria satisfied her nosy neighbor.

"Ah, *il baston da la veciaia*!" replied Carlotta.

"What is she saying?" confused, Dina looked up to her older sister.

"It's an old saying in the villages," Ermides proceeded to explain. "You know, how boys get the right to go to school and have a career, while we're born and raised to work the fields, or in our case, be maids. We get married, have babies, and care for our husbands. Then, one day, our aging parents. In essence, we become il baston da la veciaia, *the walking stick of the elderly*."

"This can't be all there is," Dina moaned at the thought. "One day I'll leave this country, and everything will be different."

In contrast, Lilia was still admiring the fine china, imagining what a privilege it would be to become a maid like her sisters, surrounded by all these riches.

At that moment, Maria passed a hand over her tired eyes, as she was beginning to see double. She waved Virginio over, giving him a signal that she had tolerated enough of the boisterousness.

"Hey, everybody," Virginio announced to their friends, "Thank you for coming and welcoming our son. It's been a long day for both Maria and Bruno, and they need their rest." Still celebrating the newborn's arrival, the villagers lowered their voices, emptied their glasses of wine, and scanned the table for any leftovers they could scavenge.

"Yes, it was lovely to see you—and thank you for all the offerings," Maria waved and forced a gracious smile despite not even having sampled the food. As the crowd thinned out, Maria grabbed Bruno from her husband and immediately whisked the baby and Lilia upstairs while Ermides and Dina cleaned up after the party. It would be a quiet Saturday night for them, as they had to pack their bags for a next-day departure. However, Erminio and Arturo had other plans.

"Papa, there's a party at Padovan's barn tonight. Pierino's bringing his accordion. Can Arturo and I go?" Erminio was sharply dressed in a gray, wool suit and burgundy tie. His wavy black hair shone like glass.

Arturo chuckled and teased, "A little too much *olive oil* there?"

Erminio half-smiled at his brother's comment, unfazed, "Well, *girls* like it."

"Go on, have fun," Virginio grinned at the brotherly banter. "Here's some coins for each of you. Erminio, go buy a girl a Coca Cola." He nudged Erminio, shooting him a wink. Arturo smiled. He was happy to see his brother enjoying his last year at home before going off to military training. Unlike Erminio, Arturo felt loud parties and drinking were a giant waste of time.

"Papa, is that all you have?" Erminio was clearly disappointed as he looked down at the few coins in his hand.

"You know if I could, I would give you more." He lovingly reached out to rub his son's head, but Erminio dodged his father's attempt.

"Not the hair, Papa! Never. Touch. The hair."

Virginio quickly withdrew his hands and offered his son a slight apologetic bow, but his eyes were dancing with laughter. "Don't be home too late." He tapped his eye with his index finger, tacitly advising his sons to behave.

"Here, Erminio, take my coins," Arturo handed them to his brother. "I'm not going."

"Why not? It'll be fun!" Erminio grimaced in irritation. He couldn't believe his brother was bowing out. "Where are *you* off to?"

"To see Angelina."

"Oooh, she's a hot number, all right!"

"Stop. She's special. She's my girl."

Arturo was a modest, unassuming gentleman whose strength and good looks had women across the village pining for him. However, he only had eyes for one woman: Angelina Pizzolitto.

Angelina was a tall, confident blonde whose spellbinding gaze and thinly arched brows demanded attention. Her golden hair fell in loose curls that bounced as she walked, and the clicking of her heels was like music to Arturo's ears. Angelina was the most beautiful and vivacious woman he had ever seen. At the age of nineteen, she lived with her parents and teenage sisters, while her older brother ran a Catholic parish on the other side of the river. Now and again, Angelina's best friend, Frida, gifted her velvet and silk fabrics in stunning colors. Frida's aunt shipped them from Florence. Although they were both peasant girls who had never left Mussons, Angelina and Frida dressed like the bourgeoisie—and because of this, they were the kind of women men desired, and women loved to hate. As for Angelina, she didn't care; in her mind, she would one day live comfortably, as the upper classes did.

Such glamorous thoughts were far from the minds of the Meneguzzi women. Upstairs, on the bed, Maria was teaching Lilia how to change a cloth diaper and swaddle Bruno before she lay down to rest her weary body after an overly stressful day.

"Do you see what I'm doing here?"

"Yes, Mama," Lilia obediently responded. It was obvious to her this was no easy task to remember.

"I made these cloths by hand. Some are square, some rectangular, and they have these long ties at the corners. The important thing is to make sure Bruno's bottom is sitting in the middle. Pay close attention because you'll be doing this tomorrow."

Maria proceeded to show Lilia how to wrap the edges and tie the diaper in place. Resting her chin on her hands at the side of the bed, Lilia looked on intently during the process, trying not to miss a step.

"Now we swaddle him tight, making sure we keep his legs together. You'll be doing this for the next few months."

Lilia was confused. To her, being in a tight bundle looked like it was extremely uncomfortable. Bruno whimpered, fussed and kicked his legs, clearly wanting to be free.

"Mama, it looks like you're wrapping him too tightly, like a salami. What if he doesn't like it?" Lilia's eyes filled with genuine concern.

"Lilia, if he grows up with crooked legs, I will look like an unfit mother. He's fine!"

"He doesn't like it, Mama," Lilia insisted, raising both brows.

"He will sleep better and cry less. That means *I* will sleep better and cry less!"

"I don't know, Mama. If I couldn't move all night, I would *probably* die."

"All right, get ready for bed," Maria snapped, tired from the day's events. "Tomorrow you can ask Bruno how he liked it."

For the next six months, day in and day out, Lilia carried Bruno across her hip while enduring the drudgery of caring for her two other brothers—her hands were full.

One Saturday afternoon, while Maria was in the garden pulling weeds under the stifling spring heat, Virginio took Giovanni and Riccardo with him on his errands, and Lilia agonized over her brother Bruno's constant fussing.

"Bruno, you cry non-stop. I can't put you down for one minute!"

Bruno kept crying.

"I'm sorry, but I can't keep carrying you. You're too heavy, and my back hurts. You may be too young to walk, but today, you are going to learn to crawl!"

Lilia's parents couldn't afford a stroller, so she was determined to give him his freedom—and to claim her own. "Bruno, sit right here." Lilia leaned her brother up against the kitchen wall. "Now, come to me. Come on. You can do it!" She got on his level, opened her arms, and gave him an encouraging smile.

Bruno rolled, rocked and squirmed in his first attempt to creep and crawl to his sister. He repeatedly plopped his bottom to the ground. Relentless, Lilia propped him back up again.

"You are going to do this! Come to me!" Lilia placed a spoon on either side of Bruno, slightly out of reach, encouraging him to twist and turn to reach them. She put all the excitement she had in her voice to motivate him to crawl and let him know how happy she was.

Bruno's little hands and legs wobbled to and fro as he tentatively made yet another unsteady attempt. Giggling and babbling, he plopped back down. To his surprise, he sat up on his own and smiled. His arms wildly gyrated and grasped the air as he let out joyful cries, his chubby cheeks jiggling—he was halfway there.

With eyes as wide as saucers, Bruno barreled ahead, crawling to his sister. Filled with pride, he fell into Lilia's arms and screeched with delight, as if he'd achieved the most remarkable feat.

"Mama!" Lilia hollered to her mother, eager to share the news. "Bruno is crawling!"

But Maria was too out of range to hear.

"Bravo! You did it! I'm so proud of you!"

Still bouncing with joy, Bruno beamed a smile of infant adoration at Lilia. "Mama!" he lovingly called out to his older sister.

2 | COME BACK

6 April 1941

೨ಂ೨ It was Palm Sunday. Adolf Hitler's German forces bombed Belgrade and invaded Yugoslavia. People from neighboring towns and villages had gathered for services in the capital port city. Thousands of civilians were killed—the most significant number of casualties since the war had begun.

Europe was in a state of what felt like irreversible upheaval. Despite Italy being one of Germany's allies, the families of Mussons no longer felt shielded from war.

Maria, Virginio, and their children were preparing for church. Arturo came home to help his brother Erminio, who had reached military age, and was about to commence his mandatory eighteen -month training in Udine.

"Here, put this on," insisted Maria, giving Lilia a light sweater to cover her bare shoulders.

"Uffa, Mama, I'm too hot!" Lilia whined, as she pouted, furrowed her brow, and crossed her arms in protest.

Maria pulled them apart. "Put it on! Padre won't allow sleeveless women into the church, not even in the streets, and that goes for six-year-old girls too." Maria snatched her daughter by the arm. "Remember what happened to your cousin Speme? She learned the hard way. Padre called her up to the front of the church and slapped her face in front of the entire congregation. Is that what you want?"

"No, Mama." Lilia shook her head without following her mother's orders.

"Ignorant priest," Maria scoffed, making a gesture with her chin. Padre was a controlling tyrant who dominated the village. "Don't make me angry—put it on."

Reluctantly, Lilia agreed. "Yes, Mama." Flustered with her daughter, Maria shook off the moment and her sharp contention with the priest, and hurried to the kitchen to prepare breakfast for her family.

Maria set out caffè latte for the adults, hot milk for the children, and rolls with butter and homemade marmalade. "It's ready!" hollered Maria. "Come eat." Virginio, Lilia, and the young boys sat down to breakfast. While Lilia was still fussing with her sweater, the kitchen door sprang wide open. Arturo stood there with a look of concern verging on panic. Startled, Maria and Virginio turned to each other and leaped out of their chairs. A sense of alarm enveloped them. They had never seen their son with anything except a calm demeanor.

"Arturo? What happened?"

"Papa, Hitler bombed Belgrade today!"

"Oh my God!" Maria eased back in her chair, raising one hand to her heart while clamping on to the rosary in her skirt pocket with the other. "On Palm Sunday!" Covering her mouth in disbelief, she closed her eyes and sent the victims a silent prayer.

"Tens of thousands of civilians died. They bombed Piraeus in Greece, too. They're stationing me in Yugoslavia soon after I return to Udine tomorrow."

A thud sounded. Arturo whipped around to see Erminio standing at the foot of the stairs with a heavy army bag at his feet, pale-faced. His brother's fingers twitched nervously.

"What, what's going to happen . . . to me?" Erminio stuttered as beads of sweat formed on his brow.

Arturo ran over to him and grabbed his shoulders. "You'll be fine! Udine is safe, and you're too young. The army won't put you on the field. In eighteen months, you'll be home." Arturo knew there were no guarantees, but he was familiar with his brother's anxiety, as well as his fear of guns and war. He had to reassure Erminio and keep him calm.

Looking up at Virginio, Maria shook her head incredulously. Her husband's mood turned serious, something she had not seen in many years. Aware that her young children were present, she tried to remain calm and silence the loop of worrisome thoughts that played out in her head; at the least, Maria needed to conceal her fears.

ೂ⊚ ⊙ಎ

Not fully understanding the darkness that had fallen upon her family, Lilia nervously removed the uncomfortable sweater and watched her father as he paced the kitchen, rubbing his temples. Everyone watched him, waiting for him to say something.

Virginio abruptly stopped. "We're going to church, as a family. Tomorrow is tomorrow. Today, we pray." He hoped the house of God would provide them with peace and calm.

"Do I have to put my sweater back on?"

Irritated, Maria snapped, "Yes, Lilia!"

Palm Sunday marked the beginning of Holy Week—an important celebration in the village, second only to Christmas. The days leading up to Easter were marked with rituals of penance and daily masses. The family joined in the yearly traditional procession as it passed by their home. Padre Munnini led the trailing crowd towards the church. He was dressed in a long red robe buttoned up to his neck, his shiny black boots peeking out from below the hem. He held a chalice of holy water, which he used to bless the palm leaves each of his patrons carried. The palms were a symbol of victory signaling the end of conflict, but the announcement of deployment sent a somber hush over what was usually a jovial assembly.

The villagers quietly shuffled into the church. As she sat in the pew between her older brothers, Lilia peered around to see her neighbors. She noticed her cousin Speme was wearing a long-sleeved sweater. Lilia was glad to be wearing hers, too. As Lilia continued to look around, she noticed scattered tears and forlorn faces, which troubled her.

As Padre Munnini entered the chapel and rose his hands in the air, the congregation stood. "Let us pray," he said, and the mass began. Lilia placed her palm frond on the seat behind her and grabbed Arturo and Erminio's hands, squeezing them tight. Sensing the heaviness around her, Lilia felt protected knowing her big brothers were there.

Arriving home from the service, Virginio strung the palms together and hung them in the house.

"Papa?" Lilia looked up at the palms on the great room's wall above the dining table. "Why are we keeping them?"

"Palms are a symbol of peace, protection, and good luck. And right now, we need *all* three." Virginio pinched the tip of her nose playfully. Lilia gave him a half-smile as she watched sadness creep into her father's eyes.

The hours passed wearily for the entire family. During their midday rest, Lilia sat awake in her room, while her little brothers napped in the beds next to her. In the larger bedroom at the end of the hall, Arturo and Erminio lay awake chatting. Although they didn't invite Lilia into the conversation, she enjoyed their deep resonating voices and the sweet sound of their laughter, signaling the comfort of home and family. Like music to her ears, she listened for a while and soothed herself to sleep.

Two hours later, Lilia was stirred awake by her mother's announcement dinner was ready.

"Everyone downstairs and hurry! The table is set, and the food will get cold."

Racing each other down the stairs, the children quickly gathered around the kitchen table to feast on their favorite dish—their mother's polenta and stew.

Virginio arrived with his wicker-covered green wine flask. He sat down and patted his stomach, wearing a proud smile. "Nobody cooks like Mama!" He bowed his head in prayer while everyone held hands. "Dear Lord, bless these gifts we are about to receive and protect my boys with the shield of your strength. Surround them with your angels and keep them safe from harm. May the power of your love bring them home to all of us who love them—"

"It's getting cold! For the love of God, eat, drink, and whatever you do, don't let yourselves get hurt. Amen!" interrupted Maria, throwing her arms up in irritation.

A unanimous "Amen" quietly circled around the table. Then, everyone shifted their eyes and attention to Maria.

"What? Why are you all looking at *me*?" Maria mumbled incoherently as she stuck her fork in the polenta and hastily drove the tines into her mouth. It didn't taste right. Nothing did. All she felt was a rush of nausea. She threw her fork down and abruptly left the table.

Concerned, Virginio stood up from his chair, "Maria, where are you going?"

"I need some air. Eat!" Maria grabbed her basket and gardening knife and stormed out the front door, slamming it behind her—the sound of her voice still bouncing off the walls.

Lilia's eyes wandered over the table. "Mama needs some air," she said, in all seriousness. "Eat!" Her family broke into laughter.

Soon, it was dusk. The children were immersed in their own tasks as Virginio and Maria sat at the dining table discussing their sons' imminent departure. Maria couldn't take her eyes off the green army bags parked by the front door. It reminded her of the Great War, when her beloved Virginio had been drafted. She remembered the feelings of despair and uncertainty, and how so few of those good men returned.

"Virginio, what's going to happen to our boys?"

Virginio shook his head and rubbed his eyes. "I don't know, Maria, I don't know."

"Have mercy on us!" Maria lamented, fearing her family's future and questioning her own faith. "What if they don't return?" A whimper escaped her as she nervously fiddled with her apron, still eying the bags. She tightened her jaw as her emotions threatened to burst.

⁊₢₢ ₲₢₢

Virginio fought to keep his chin from quivering as his shoulders dropped in resignation. Clenching his fist, he slammed it on the table. "Damn it! Woman, if I could take their place, you know I would." He grabbed Maria's fidgety hands. "Look at me." She raised her eyes, now filled with tears, but she wouldn't let a single one fall. These were not tears of sadness but of hatred for the people and forces that were taking her sons from her.

"Arturo is strong, Maria. He's stronger than me—and smarter. He will return. The military won't be easy for Erminio, but we knew this was coming. We have to believe he'll get through it."

Maria lost the battle, letting a single tear rush down her cheek.

"Erminio is *not* strong enough to endure this. His body is not *healthy* enough. I prayed day and night he wouldn't pass the physical. Cruel fate has taken enough from us. I won't let God take my boys, too!"

"It's not God, Maria," Virginio sighed deeply at the unpleasant facts of humanity. "It's people—people with too much ego who feed off power and control. And like our sons, good men are condemned to risk their lives for the soulless."

Breaking her hands free, Maria looked around, searching for her sons. "Where are they?" Panic rushed over her like a tidal wave. They would be gone all too soon.

"I told Erminio he could go see his friends. He needs a distraction to take his mind elsewhere. Arturo left to see that girl, Angelina."

"Ah, I see." Maria couldn't help but feel upset that her sons had chosen not to be home with their mother.

Virginio could sense his wife's unrest. "Maria, Arturo's in love. Let him have this time. The love of a woman is powerful. It's what makes us men fight to come home." He winked at his wife. "You kept me alive some twenty years ago." He searched her face for some semblance of a smile, but there was none. "Now, go to bed. I'll wait up for them."

Exhausted by the day's events and all its accompanying emotions, Maria retired to her bed. Upstairs in her room, she watched as Bruno lay fast asleep in the open top drawer of her wooden dresser. The moonlight swept over his tiny features, and his chest rose and fell with ease.

"My dearest treasure, your mother brought you into a war." The waves of sadness were so strong, she could taste her sorrow. "Dear God, watch over my sons—over us all."

Maria crawled into bed. Her tired limbs had become a constant in her life, but this night, her mind was distracted by worry. The sheets felt heavy and crisp as the evening chill spilled into the air. The shutters were open to a sky that was black as ink, with not one visible star. Maria held her rosary in both hands and closed her eyes. "Hail Mary, full of grace—" Her hopelessness had no other outlet. With every word of prayer, emotions welled inside her and tears flowed faster than her heart could beat.

Fifty yards from home, in the center square, Arturo and Angelina sat side by side on the steps of La Bottega. It was Palm Sunday, and the bar had closed early. Arturo watched as the soft glow of the moon caressed Angelina's face. He felt himself drowning in the depths of her piercing green eyes, as he had been many times before. He couldn't fathom how someone like Angelina could love him, but his words spilled out before he could stop them.

"Angelina, my beautiful Angelina." Arturo brushed the hair from her eyes. He smiled at her with adoration. "I whisper to you every night I am away. No one can hear me but the midnight sky. I always hope my words will find you."

Angelina blushed and gave him a coy smile. "You do that?" Her eyes danced with light as the pink flush grew on her cheeks.

"I'd do anything for you." Arturo cradled her face. "Angelina, I know you like pretty things, and although I have nothing to give you now, one day I will give you the world. You are my life!" He ran his hands through her silky blonde hair, squeezing the strands through his fingers. Gazing upon her angelic features, tracing them with his eyes, he pulled Angelina closer to kiss her.

"*Ti vuei ben*, I love you," he whispered. She could feel the heat of his breath on her ear. "You're like a fire in my soul. I'd go crazy without you! Marry me, Angelina. Marry me before I go! Come to Udine with me tomorrow, and we'll go to City Hall before I'm transferred!" Arturo searched her face for an answer.

Angelina paused. She pulled away from his hold. "I . . . I can't, Arturo. It's too fast. And what if you don't come back? What will I do then?" The moonlight illuminated her face as her eyes filled with tears.

Bewildered by her response, Arturo was taken over by a passionate need to prove himself to her. Nothing was stronger than his love for Angelina...not even this damn war. He promptly got down on his knees. "I'm coming back! I promise you. I'm coming back! Marry me!"

"No, Arturo. It's better that we wait."

"Promise me!" he insisted.

Angelina was overcome by the power of his emotions. She succumbed, "Yes, *yes*! I promise. My brother's a priest. He can marry us when you come back!" She smiled and kissed him, as if to alleviate his doubts. "Now, walk me home, you incorrigible man!"

Arturo saw Angelina to her front door, where they shared one last kiss.

"When the wind blows through our windows, I'll speak your name and blow it your way," he proclaimed.

"And I'll catch it and hold on to it until you return. Now, go already! And *please* be careful!"

Midway down the street, Arturo turned and yelled, "Do you hear the music?"

"What music?"

He put his hand to his ear. "Shhh, listen." Arturo flung his arms up in the air and belted out verses from a popular love song:

> *E nell'estasi di una musica io ti mormoro*
> And in the ecstasy of music, I'll whisper to you
> *Senti il cuor quello che ti dice*
> Hear the heart and what it tells you
> *Treman le mie labbra allor parlano d'amor*
> My lips tremble and speak of love
> *Ba . . . ba . . . baciami piccina*
> Ki . . . ki . . . kiss me, little one
> *Sulla bo . . . bo . . . bocca piccolina*

On the mou . . . mou . . . mouth, little one
Dammi tan tan tanti baci in quantita
Give me ma . . . ma . . . many kisses in quantity
Tu . . . tu . . . tu sei birichina
You . . . you . . . you are mischievous
Ma sei ta . . . ta . . . tanto deliziosa
But you are s . . . s . . . so delicious

Still glowing, Angelina shook her head, unable to stop the giddy laugh that bubbled up as a result of her lover's serenade. She turned and closed the door behind her.

Arturo danced home smiling and singing to the starless sky. "*Ba . . . ba . . . baciami piccina.*" He was happier than he'd ever been.

Arturo was still floating on air as he neared the front gate of his home, where he spotted his brother coming from the opposite direction.

"Hey! How was your night?"

"It was fine. Almost all my friends are leaving for Udine, too." Erminio was clearly out of sorts—his mind overrun with many questions and no promising answers. "Why are *you* in such a *good* mood?" He looked suspiciously at Arturo, seeing no reason for joy or celebration.

"I asked Angelina, and she said yes! She's going to marry me when I return."

"Well, that's great! I'm happy for you." Buried in his own thoughts, Erminio turned away from his brother and entered the gate. He tried his best to sound enthused, but he was consumed by fear and doubt. He had hoped Arturo would be stationed in Udine with him. And now he would be facing this turning point alone, without his big brother to protect him. He couldn't help but feel angry, and even jealous, at

Arturo's unwavering strength. And although it was out of Arturo's control, Erminio felt deserted. He turned to face his brother.

"How does it feel to never be afraid?" A note of resentment and envy crept into Erminio's words. Head down, he shuffled halfheartedly towards the front door and into the house.

Left feeling stunned at the gate, Arturo looked wordlessly after his brother. He understood why Erminio couldn't share his happiness, but he didn't know what more he could do or say to reassure him of his future. Watching his brother unravel before him, Arturo felt he had little power over either of their lives. For the first time, he was left with the reality of an uncertain future. His only salvation now was his vision of Angelina. It was burned into his heart. For him, she was the way back home.

"Erminio?" Virginio called out from his seat at the dining table. "Did you have a good night with your friends?"

"Papa, I didn't see you. What are you doing sitting in the dark?"

"Where's your brother?"

Arturo ducked under the doorway.

"I'm right here, Papa."

Virginio put his shot glass down on the table and lit the lantern on the buffet. "I've been sitting here for hours thinking about you both and remembering my days on the front lines." He brushed his hand across his mouth to wipe the grappa from his lips. "Sons, history keeps repeating, and yet we don't seem to learn anything. The same mistakes are made over and over again. People don't change."

"What if history didn't repeat itself?" Arturo pulled a chair out from the table to join his father. "Would we do anything to make this world better? It seems people only wake up when their lives or livelihood are threatened."

"It's the government making the mistakes," Erminio piped in, "and it's poor people like us who suffer."

Virginio patted an empty seat next to him, beckoning Erminio to take it. The three of them sat in silence, each attempting to process their thoughts. A few precious hours were left, and none of them knew what to say.

"How's Mama?" Erminio knew the depth of her love and concern for him.

"Oh, you know your mother, tough as nails. She's worried, of course—it's her job. I'm sure she's upstairs wearing out the rosary."

"Papa, I have some news!" Arturo's chest filled with pride as he remembered there was a reason to be joyful despite the heaviness of the day.

"Do you both mind if I go to bed?" Erminio was far too distressed to shift his mood into one of celebration.

"Go ahead, get your rest. We'll see you in the morning." Virginio watched his son trudge up the stairs, wearing a long and drawn face. "I'm worried about him, Arturo. He's not made for the military."

"No one is, Papa."

Seeing Arturo's trepidation, Virginio rattled his son's arm as if to drive any negative thoughts from his mind. "Now, what's this good news?"

"I asked Angelina to marry me." Arturo half raised his eyes, hoping for his father's approval, as he knew his mother didn't like her.

"That's wonderful. Congratulations!" Virginio slapped Arturo's shoulder, then pulled him into a hug. "I'd offer you a grappa to commemorate this fine moment, but you don't drink, so I'll have one for you!" He smiled as he poured himself another shot of his homemade brew.

"When I come home and Angelina and I marry, maybe then I'll have a swig of that gasoline."

Virginio threw his head back and chuckled from his belly.

"Well then, we'll have yet another reason to celebrate—my eldest son drinking with his old man."

"I don't think Mama cares for Angelina," Arturo sighed, "I know when I break the news to Mama, she won't be so quick to break out a celebratory drink."

"Ah! Your mother doesn't like anybody," Virginio smirked at his own jest, then realized Arturo was probably right. "She'll come around," he consoled his son.

"I'm sure," Arturo nodded in agreement. "Goodnight, Papa. I'm going to bed. I love you."

"I love you too. Good night." Virginio smoothed his hand over Arturo's face, giving him a gentle tap, "I'm proud of you. Both your mother and I have always been proud of you. You're a saint of a man."

Arturo slid his chair in and rested his hand on his father's shoulder. "I'll do whatever I can to help Erminio's transition to Udine. For as much time as I will have there, I will help him."

Virginio nodded and patted Arturo's hand. He poured another shot. "Cincin to that! Sleep well, my boy."

Virginio leaned back as the empty room stared him in the face. He blinked back a tear. He didn't want to give in to his worst thoughts, but Virginio had an angst in his heart that his sons would never fill this home again.

⁖

The following morning, the house was bursting with the sound of children running and the aroma of caffé latte and biscotti. Giovanni and Riccardo had abandoned their shoes and were chasing each other barefoot, back and forth from the garden, dragging dirt into the house. They were too young to comprehend the gravity of the day. In a way, their obliviousness gave Virginio a momentary reprieve from his sorrow.

Maria, however, awoke with a short fuse, her nerves on edge. She had lain awake most of the night, tormented by the harsh realities of war. Once again, she was fighting the devil. Her life felt like a poisonous weed overtaking her precious garden—her family.

"Good God, Lilia!" hollered Maria from the front door, seeing her sons traipsing dirt on to the clean floor of the great room. "Get those boys' shoes on! And wash their feet at the water pump."

"Yes, Mama." Lilia exhaled sharply, exasperated with the daily drudgery of caring for her younger siblings. With Bruno in her arms, she hauled her brothers across the street to the water pump, the only source of drinking water on Via della Chiesa. Giovanni and Riccardo fussed and whined until their feet were dry and back in their shoes.

Lilia went into the kitchen and sat Bruno down on the rustic brick floor to wash and dry her hands. It was early, and she was already feeling drained.

"Lilia!" her mother hollered again.

"Yes, Mama?" Lilia rolled her eyes in frustration.

"Turn around." Maria was holding out a broom and staring down at the dirty floor in disappointment.

Lilia turned to see her brothers' shoes scattered about the front door once again, and four bare black feet tracking dirt back into the house. Lilia felt defeated. Arturo arrived downstairs and caught his little sister's frown.

"Lilia! Are you going to do anything?" Maria motioned to the boys with her broom.

"Mama, relax!" Arturo gestured with his hands. "Let them play. Where's the harm? It's a little dirt, and they're happy."

Maria's face flushed with embarrassment. She stumbled over the shoes on her way back into the kitchen. She knew her son was right, especially in light of the day's circumstances. Her motherly fears had driven her wild, and perhaps there was no need for that kind of harshness now. At a loss for words, she distracted herself by preparing packs of food for her sons to take on the road.

Lilia turned towards the sound of Arturo's voice and immediately ran to her big brother.

"Hey, little one!" Arturo scooped Lilia into his arms. "How's my favorite girl?" He carried Lilia outside and sat her down on one of the soft grass patches under the fig tree. He sat next to her, clasping his arms around his knees.

"The sun feels soothing, doesn't it?" Arturo gazed up at the infinite blue sky as he inhaled deeply. "Do you smell that? Hmmm, I love the scent of Mama's roses, don't you? Come on, put your head back like me, close your eyes, listen to the sounds, and feel the breeze on your skin. If you lay real still, you can almost hear butterflies flutter."

"You're leaving me again, aren't you?" Lilia felt a rush of sadness knowing Arturo's time at home was coming to an end. Each time he went away, Lilia's sense of abandonment and emptiness grew. She didn't understand why he couldn't simply stay with her.

"Well, I'm not leaving you, but yes, I am leaving."

"Are you coming back?" Lilia dropped her head against his shoulder. "What if I slept here forever? Would you still leave?"

He pulled her hair gently. "Well, I guess if you did, then I wouldn't go. How could I ever wake Sleeping Beauty?"

Lilia smiled despite herself.

"When I get back, we'll have a party, just you and me. Does that sound good?"

"I won't sleep until you get home." Lilia sniffled. Arturo looked away; he, too, felt tears creeping out of the corners of his eyes.

Arturo grabbed and shook Lilia's hand, "It's a deal. I won't sleep, either." Together they walked into the house to find Erminio sitting restlessly in a kitchen chair, his knee bouncing up and down, the boys spinning pennies on the floor as Bruno watched on, and Virginio joining Maria to help wrap up the last of the food packs.

"So, when do they arrive?" Virginio frowned when he looked at his sons.

"Our ride should be here any minute, Papa," Arturo gave his father an assuring nod. "Ready, brother?"

"Um, yeah." Erminio peered down at his feet, at the stylish black loafers he would soon be trading in for army boots.

Erminio stood up next to his big brother. Maria nervously rubbed her hands on her apron.

"My sweet boys," Maria's voice cracked and caught in her throat, "your father and I packed some things for you to take. Panini, biscotti, water. There's even a rosary—one for each of you." Tears were in her eyes, but she bravely attempted to be light with her words. "Don't be heroes. Are you listening? You come back to me, both of you. I'll be here waiting and praying."

Maria felt a rush of pure affection and profound adoration— something only a mother could understand. Flashes of their childhood flooded her memory. How Maria wished she could turn back time and rewrite the future . . . but she was powerless. Her sons now belonged to this grueling war, which seemed to be the sole determinant of her family's fate. It was devastating to think she had no control over any of it. Maria had little faith left in the world, knowing this might be the last time she'd set eyes upon her two beloved sons—the last time she might feel the warmth and aliveness of their skin and bodies.

Arturo tried to remain calm and composed, but his mind was tangled in thoughts. Maria could sense his discomfort and could no longer hold back. Her armor collapsed. Brick by brick, Maria's walls crumbled as she fell sobbing into his arms.

Arturo's heart ached to see his mother's sudden display of emotion. "Don't worry, Mama. Nothing, not even this war, will keep me away from my family!"

Erminio tried to follow his brother's lead. "Arturo's right, Mama, don't worry." He swallowed hard and clenched his teeth to keep his panic at bay. "In eighteen months, I'll be home." His voice trembled, "I'm sure they'll give me a pass to come back and visit soon."

Maria pulled Erminio into a tight embrace. "Don't get sick, you hear me? You take care of yourself out there and be strong!" She leaned close and whispered in his ear, "My sweet boy. I always loved you the most because I worried about you the most. I'd move heaven and earth for you." Erminio felt cocooned in his mother's arms as he bathed in her warmth. Afraid to give into more emotions and the fact her delicate boy was leaving for war, Maria released him from her arms as if to deny the reality of what was at stake.

All the while, Virginio stood back in silence. His throat tightened with every breath. He remembered all too well his own wartime history and the horrors he'd witnessed. He knew the road ahead for his sons . . . what they would face, what they would be exposed to. Virginio took in the sight of his boys, his strong-willed Arturo, and his sensitive Erminio. Both to be robbed of their innocence all too soon. He embraced them both, resting his forehead against each of theirs. There was little need for words. The brothers nodded, absorbing their father's energy, strength, and courage.

"My boys, I love you with all my heart."

"We love you too, Papa."

The sound of a horn broke upon the air. The army truck had arrived. Like a cruel laugh, they were summoned away from their farewell. Walking through the great room, they turned around to give their home one last look. Arturo blew it a kiss, "See you soon."

Lilia was standing by the green duffel bags at the front door, her three little brothers huddled under her arms. Every memory she had of Arturo and Erminio rushed back into her head as sadness engulfed her entire body. In trying to speak, Lilia's lips quivered. What if she never saw her brothers again?

Her voice sounded like it was made of gravel when she finally found the words, "Please don't leave me." Her tears felt cold as they slid down her face.

"Liliutti, my favorite girl in the entire world," Arturo brushed his hand against her cheek.

"More favorite than Angelina?"

"Hey, how did you know about Angelina?"

"I know *everything* about you," she said proudly.

A smile spread across his face. "*You* are my number one!" Arturo kissed Lilia on the forehead, then kneeled and rubbed his little brothers' heads.

"Boys, be good to your sister, Mama, and Papa, too. Listen to what they tell you." Giovanni, and Riccardo looked confused but nodded at their big brother's wishes, while Bruno was too young to understand what was going on in the world around him.

Erminio gave his siblings a warm hug, kissing each one of them. He was afraid to let them go, but he tried to remain strong. "Hey, don't you be riding in that wagon without me!" Erminio winked at Lilia. "I'll take you out on a long bike ride soon!"

The two young men made their way to the front gate.

"Wait!" Lilia cried out as she ran after them, throwing her arms around her brothers one final time. She felt a terrible dread come over her. What if this truly was the last time she would see them? "I love you. I will love you forever. Don't forget me."

"Liliutti, we'll be back soon," Erminio winked at Lilia and gave her the most confident and assured look he could muster before mounting the jeep.

"Save me a spot under the tree, Piccina!" Arturo gave Lilia one last kiss before releasing her and joining Erminio.

Soon, the vehicle shifted gears and started rolling away. Maria and Virginio ran outside as Arturo and Erminio sat in the open back of the truck, waving goodbye to their family, to their home.

"Come back! Come back! I'll be waiting for you!" Like a river escaping a dam, tears spilled over Maria's face as she ran after the moving truck, waving her white dishcloth. "Arturo! Erminio!"

Virginio sank back against the wall of his house. He lowered his head and gave out a quiet sob. He could hear the dull pang in his heart, which sounded like a drum in his ears. He had been through it all—war, the fear of death, the memories of bloodshed and suffering etched into his soul. His insides burned. He knew that his sons would be stripped of their identities and innocence. Even if they came home alive, war changed men forever.

Lilia found herself in the middle of the street, watching her big brothers as they drove away. The world closed in around her. She felt her body shrink and sink into the earth. Falling to her knees, she stretched her arms out to them, still seeing their faces long after they had faded into the horizon. For what seemed like ages, Lilia cried out in a soft, fragile voice, "Come back."

3 | ARE YOU LONELY TOO?

September 1941

◈ After the April bombing of the Greek port city of Piraeus, tens of thousands of civilians died, and the Jewish population was deported to Auschwitz and Treblinka. Survivors remained in hiding or joined the resistance.

In June of that year, Hitler launched a surprise attack on the Soviet Union, killing masses of Soviet soldiers. His plan was to eradicate all extremists, communists, political dissidents, and anyone considered dangerous. This encompassed all Jews. By the early fall, entire Jewish communities were killed by the SS and police, marking the beginning of what would become Hitler's 'Final Solution'—the annihilation of all Jews.

Five months had passed since Arturo was stationed in Yugoslavia. Unable to stop the bombardments and ground forces, the Yugoslav Army surrendered. With no sign of Arturo's whereabouts and no telegrams from Erminio in Udine, Virginio kept an ever-vigilant ear on news from other families. Word filtered through the village that Arturo's comrades had been transported to Montenegro and Greece.

The war was engulfing the whole of Europe, and the darkness gradually came to enfold the entire village of Mussons.

A silent agony tore through Maria. She could hardly fathom how one day her sons had been safe at home . . . and the next, they were gone without a trace in a world dominated by terror. She felt as if her courage was being tested, and she was powerless. Unable to do anything, she raised her armor once again.

Since her brothers' departure, Lilia battled their absence—a void that nothing could fill. She had grown numb, confused, and distressed. Everyone she loved seemed to be leaving her.

Day after day, Lilia felt seized by despair. Bruno, who had yet to walk on his own, became too heavy for her little body to carry. Shifting him from side to side caused Lilia's hips to misalign. She rubbed the small of her back to relieve the pain that had settled there, but to no avail. Lilia struggled to juggle her chores and tend to her three brothers, until her once-radiant light succumbed to shadows. She had grown thin, pale, and drawn.

It pained Virginio to witness his little girl being robbed so cruelly of her joy. To alleviate some of the pressure, he built her a little red wagon in which she could transport Bruno as she went about her routine. Lilia was grateful to her father, but she yearned to return to her old life, free of responsibilities. Lilia felt her childhood was over before it could even begin—like a wilting rose, her days had lost their color.

Despite the war still raging, life in Mussons carried on. Wishing for anything more felt like a road to nowhere, but Lilia and her family plodded on and looked forward with hope.

Nearby neighbors, Louigia Padovan and her husband Tony, the village caretaker, were hosting a casual gathering in their barn—an evening of bonding between the local women. Virginio knew how much Lilia missed her brothers and sensed the melancholy that settled over her.

Virginio found his wife in the kitchen, making him borage tea for his asthma. "Maria, why don't you take Lilia with you to Padovan's? Our little girl's spirit is breaking. She's young and sensitive, and she hasn't been doing well since the boys left."

"And *I'm* doing well?" replied Maria, feeling overlooked.

"Maria," Virginio pleaded, "she's six years old."

"Bah! I raised *nine* children by myself growing up. She needs to toughen up because as sad as it is, life is like this. And I have no desire to go tonight. I'm tired and not in the mood for laughter and women's useless chatter."

"Maria!" Virginio gave her an imploring look. "It's one night, and it will do you both some good. I'll put the boys to bed."

Maria sighed and nodded. Despite having lost her enthusiasm for previously enjoyable gatherings, she was too tired to argue.

Without the helping hands of his eldest sons, Virginio worked extra-long hours throughout the harvest. Weary to the bone, he retired early. His face was drawn and pale from exhaustion, and his asthma was rearing its ugly head again.

Maria looked at him with concern. "Are you sure you're all right?"

He nodded.

"Fine then, we'll be back in a few hours. I'll be up before you leave tomorrow morning. Don't forget to drink the tea!"

Maria had grown the delicate, purple-flowered plant in her garden. The needle-like spines on the stems made the borage hard to handle, but when the petals were dried and steeped in hot water, they soothed Virginio's spasming lungs.

Virginio wheezed as he shuffled up the stairs with his steaming cup of tea. Despite his exhaustion and discomfort, he smiled, relieved his daughter was enjoying a night out, distracted from all the troubled thoughts occupying her heart and mind. Accustomed to his evening routine, Virginio seldom needed to light the way to his bedroom or open his drooping eyes. The dreaded thought of having to wake before the rooster's crow at daybreak weighed heavily on his soul. Before he could surrender to the few hours of sleep ahead of him, Virginio made his way to the boy's room to tuck them in.

"It's time for shut-eye." Virginio pulled up the boy's blankets and stroked their brow.

"Papa," whispered Giovanni. "Where's Lilia?"

"She went to Padovan's barn with Mama."

"Can I go?"

"Don't worry. You're not missing anything. It's a bunch of gossiping hens knitting. Now close your eyes. Good night, Giovanni."

"Good night, Papa."

Before Virginio melted into his bed, he prayed, "Dear Lord, help soften Maria's heart. Give her the strength to show her children who she is, and the endurance to get through this war. And help me be a better father, so my children . . ." sapped of his energy, Virginio sank into his pillow, his eyes beginning to close, ". . . grow up feeling we had some good times, too."

As night descended, the chill of the air passed over the village, and the dwellings and street noise died down. Maria and Lilia walked the long stretch of dirt road for half a mile, until they saw lights through the trees and the barn up ahead. Lilia was content to be spending time with her mother and partaking in something other than chores.

"Mama? What are we going to do at Padovan's?"

"Oh, we'll probably snack on something, sit together, and talk, knit, and sew."

"Talk about what?"

"Silly things that silly women talk about."

"Well, if they're silly, why are we going?"

Maria broke out into a chuckle, "That's a good question. I wish I had the answer."

As they approached the barn, Lilia looked up at her mother with wondering eyes, "What do you think Arturo and Erminio are doing right now?"

When Maria saw her daughter's innocent, inquiring eyes, she didn't know how to respond. Maria breathed a heavy sigh. "Let's go inside."

As they entered the barn, Lilia rubbed her nose frantically, assaulted by the stench of manure. Caught off guard, Lilia tripped over the shovel that leaned up against the stall and landed on all fours on the dirty barn floor. The prickly straw scratched her bare legs and stuck to her hands and knees as she pulled herself up.

"Lilia! Watch where you're going!" Flustered, Maria slapped the chaff and straw from Lilia's hair and freshly washed dress. "I should have left you at home!"

Lilia felt herself withdraw into her safe and numb place as she heard her mother's harsh words. She wished Arturo was there. He always made her feel better, especially in those moments when Maria was a little too sharp.

"Hello, Maria!" Louigia welcomed her in with a rough hug, nearly knocking Maria over. Maria hugged back for a second or two, then released her hold. Lilia saw Louigia's chubby fingers coming at her cheeks. She flinched and pulled away like a cat avoiding a pat on the head.

"Come over here where it's warm. Sit. Eat."

Maria and Lilia sat comfortably on a woolen blanket thrown over the haystack, as cows and sheep rested close by. The barn was modest and rimmed with stacked buckets, pitchforks, and pails of seed and grain. Lanterns lay scattered about, flickering their light and illuminating the spiderwebs that stretched across the rafters. Soon enough, the wafting dust, hay, and sweet roasted chestnuts masked the more unpleasant smells.

A tight circle of half a dozen women busily knitting sweaters, embroidering linens, and losing themselves in age-old fables and small-town folklore quickly formed over the course of the evening. Their voices and laughter grew louder as each woman tried to outdo the other in revealing their most gossip-worthy stories. In contrast, the sound of the chickens cooing was far more soothing to Lilia's ears.

Arturo would hate this, she thought, releasing a deep sigh and rolling her eyes.

"Did *you* hear about Ana's son?" one woman asked. Her eyes darted furtively as she whispered, "That boy got some girl *pregnant.*"

"I heard it was the Baldini family's daughter, from Poiana," replied another, with an affirmative nod.

"Hmmm, I don't think it was her," said yet another woman as she leaned into the circle, drawing everyone closer. "*I* heard he got *Aradia* pregnant!"

"No!" The women pulled back and covered their mouths, stunned at the news.

"Mama?" whispered Lilia, tugging on her mother's skirt. "Who's Aradia?"

Not one for gossip, Maria's eyes stayed focused on her knitting. "She's a local girl. These women think she's a witch," Maria whispered back. "Pay them no attention."

As Maria looked disapprovingly at the women, she thought, *our boys are out there fighting in a war, and all they can do is stick their noses where they don't belong!*

The clacking of Maria's needles sped up as she knitted faster and faster, growing more irritated by the minute. *Knit one, purl one. Knit one, purl one.* This repetitive mantra helped Maria press her lips together and hold back the words she was bursting to fling at them.

"Lilia!" piped up Louigia, fluttering her eyes. "Do you want to hear about the witches in Mussons?"

Lilia's body stiffened as she held her breath. She nodded yes, but she meant no.

Louigia widened her eyes. "There are three sisters—Julia, Aradia, and Pasquina. They are all witches. If they cast envious thoughts or their malevolent stare upon you, it can cause you harm and make you ill, plaguing you with *Malocchio*, the curse of the evil eye. Envy is a dangerous emotion and has negative power. You must never brag about yourself or others. If the witches become jealous, they will bring you dreadful luck."

Lilia's mouth went dry. She clutched her mother's skirt for comfort. Maria swatted Lilia's hand away and gave her a ball of yarn to keep her occupied. "Here, wind this up for me." Transfixed on Louigia's face as she continued, Lilia wound the yarn at a snail's pace.

"Once a month beneath the full moon, the witches meet in the town square," Louigia threw up her hands dramatically. Lilia swallowed hard, and her heartbeat quickened. Maria raised a brow at Louigia, ready to throw a ball of yarn at her.

"With hands clasped, the sisters dance and chant their evil spells. Sometimes, they startle the neighbors awake. Everyone runs to their windows to peek through the shutter cracks so as not to be seen. They wait and watch in silence. Sometimes, the witches take flight and fly high above the rooftops. Afraid of the curse, people hide under their covers and cross their index fingers for protection. Should you ever encounter these sisters, you must *never* make eye contact."

Lilia's voice trembled as she spoke, "What do we do if we have the curse?"

Louigia beckoned Lilia closer to demonstrate the process. "Fill a plate with water. Then dip your finger into a cup of olive oil and let four drops fall into the water, making the sign of the cross. If the oil does not move, you are not cursed. But if the oil forms into the shape of an eye, this is a sign the curse is present—and the witches saw you and bewitched you!"

"And then what happens?" The hair rose on the back of Lilia's neck.

"Well, you must speak the Holy Trinity out loud, of course! In the name of the Father, the Son, and the Holy Spirit. May all evil be gone!" Louigia leaned in close and whispered, "Do not underestimate the powers of Malocchio."

Maria was primed to whack her knitting needles over Louigia's head. From behind the stall where Tony was working, he overheard his wife's tall tales and noticed the effect Louigia was having on Lilia, and how Maria's patience had worn thin. Tony quickly sauntered over to the circle and pulled Lilia up on to his lap, all the while raising a disapproving brow at his wife.

"Lilia, let *me* tell you a story. Once upon a time in a tiny village, there lived a good king and queen who had a kind daughter named Lilia. She was the most beautiful princess anyone had ever seen. All the men in the kingdom wanted to marry her but were too afraid to approach this fair young maiden. One day, a handsome prince heard Lilia singing in the castle tower. He knew then, by the sound of her magical voice, he had found his future bride."

Lilia smiled at Tony's predictable little story; as much as she loved storytelling, she preferred reading her books—the children's fairy tales her sisters sent from the big city. Many nights after her bedtime and unbeknownst to her mother, Lilia spent the wee hours getting lost in her fantasy world. Cinderella, Snow White, and Sleeping Beauty were her escape—it was the only time she felt free when everyone in her world was sound asleep.

Superstitions and fears aside, Lilia *did* believe one day her prince would come. Like the princesses in her books, she too would wait for the knight in shining armor to rescue her from the evil clutches of doom and change her life forever.

Darkness fell, and the breeze picked up as midnight came upon them. It was hours past Lilia's bedtime. Maria and Lilia said goodbye to the women. Walking home under a clouded moon, Maria held her knitting basket in one hand and Lilia's tightening grip in the other.

Lilia's senses were heightened and in a flurry from the evening's fables. She kept looking over her shoulder for fear a witch might appear through the thick of the night and grab her. Every sound magnified as it came alive in the pitch black surrounding her. The gravel crunching under Lilia's shuffling feet, the wind screeching through the trees, bat wings fluttering as they swooped high and low, all echoed like thunder in her head.

"Lilia! Slow down, you're pulling me!" Maria wrenched her hand free and shook Lilia's arm. "Why are you so afraid? There is no one here but you and me!" Maria grumbled all the way home. "That *damn* Louigia!"

Upon arrival, Maria ordered Lilia straight to bed while she put away her knitting and preoccupied herself with the loose ends of the day, which, despite Virginio's best efforts, hadn't been tied up neatly. Wrapping up the borage, Maria paused and looked through the kitchen window out into the moonlit street. She blinked away a tear. "Where are you, my sons?" Her voice cracked with emotion as she searched the night sky. "Where are you?"

Meanwhile, the thought of climbing the narrow staircase alone sent shivers down Lilia's spine. What was waiting for her up there? She froze, unable to move forward and lift her foot on to the first step.

"Lilia! What did I say? Go to bed!" Maria had little time for such things as remembering what it was like to be a frightened six-year-old girl.

Startled, Lilia ran up the stairs as fast as she could, afraid to look back. She feared not only evil spirits floating out of the darkness, up the steps, and snatching her ankles, but also her mother's wrath. Catching her breath on the landing, Lilia braced herself for the long walk towards her bed. Despite the chill in the air, her clothes were soaked with sweat. Her lips drawn tight and limbs trembling, hardly daring to breathe, Lilia crept one inch, then another, down the dimly lit hallway.

A mere sliver of light from the clouded moon trickled through the window and cast an ominous blue-white glow on the paint-chipped walls. The shadows lengthened and crept up to the ceiling, where they hovered like huge spiders. Her hands grew clammy as they clung to the wall, feeling her way to the bedroom. Lilia kept her focus on the door while battling the voices in her head. *Is there something behind me? Shh! Don't turn around! You're almost there!*

The creaking floorboards were drowned by the thunder of Lilia's beating heart. Her pulse skipped with every step. As she turned the knob and pushed open the door, the squeaky hinges whined, sending Lilia into yet another flurry of panic. Dirty dress and all, she leaped to the safety of her bed and quickly tucked up her feet, as monsters were surely waiting to grab them! Lilia hauled the sheets up to her neck and listened, willing the sounds to fade and die.

A sudden wind rattled the shutters as a mist of light filtered through the wooden slats and slithered across the room. Lilia watched the door creak slowly, and the lock abruptly click back into place. Imagining a hulking body standing in the open armoire and witches circling above her head, Lilia buried herself under her woolen blanket. She squeezed her eyes shut, crossed her index fingers, and recited the Holy Trinity over and over until she fell into a fitful sleep.

ഐ ഇ

Days passed, and Lilia had long forgotten about witches and evil eye spells. It was Sunday. Maria and Virginio retreated to their bedroom for their midday riposo, right in time for Lilia to plan her escape. Now and again, without waking the boys, Lilia snuck out of the house while her parents were sleeping. With so many demands on her, Lilia had little time to play with other children. Those few afternoon hours were the only precious moments Lilia could steal away from her mother's watchful eye.

Neighborhood girls gathered on the weekends for a game of Buttons. Lilia and her friends would form a circle around the game leader and extend their hands out, palms together. The leader took a button, and one by one, put their hands in the other players' hands until they chose where to drop the button; only the giver and receiver knew where it was. The girls in the circle then called out, "Button, button, who has the button?" Whoever guessed where it was won the leader's position. After the game, the girls played Show and Tell and traded their collection of buttons.

Lilia wanted to play with her friends but was visibly embarrassed every time she showed up with the same old small white buttons. The other girls brought fancier pearlescent and colorful ones—pink, blue, and yellow. Lilia folded her arms on the windowsill and gazed out into the courtyard, pondering what to do. "Do I sneak out and risk being caught by Mama or stay home and nap?" While watching the linen bedding her mother had hung to dry early that morning sway back and forth in the gentle breeze, Lilia's eyes grew wide and twinkled with pride at her brilliant idea. She instantly perked up: "Mama's buttons!"

Lilia closed her bedroom door softly behind her so as not to wake her brothers. Treading lightly on her tiptoes, she crept down the hall holding her breath, listening for her mother's inevitable call, but it never came. Lilia controlled her steps, slow and steady until she victoriously made her way outside, and her feet touched the grass. Lilia quickly rummaged through her father's workbench in the barn, looking for something to remove the buttons. She skimmed the wooden shelves, and her eyes landed on a pair of scissors hanging on a rusty nail. Lilia's eyes lit up at her timely find. With the cleavers in hand, Lilia balanced on her mother's garden stool, reached up to the clothesline, and cut off all the large gold-engraved pearl buttons from each lace-edged pillowcase. Lilia admired the buttons as she held them up to the sunlight, excited to show them off to her friends.

"Lilia!"

At the sound of her name, Lilia lost her balance and tumbled off the stool on to the ground. The scissors flew through the air, but she kept the buttons gripped tightly in her hand. Ermides swung through the gate, announcing her arrival.

"Hello? Mama! Papa! It's me, Ermides! Wake up!" Ermides put down a large box and ran over to help pull her little sister up from her fall. "What were you doing up there?" Before Lilia could reply, she looked up to see her mother standing at the front door.

Maria picked up the scissors that had landed by her foot and gave Lilia a suspicious look. "Yes, what *were* you doing?" Her gaze quickly moved over to Ermides. "And what are you doing here?" Surprised to see her eldest daughter, Maria gathered her in a tight but fast embrace.

Her gaze boomeranged quickly back to Lilia, letting her know that she wasn't off the hook.

Thrilled to see his daughter, Virginio came running out of the house. His delight quickly turned to concern. "Ermides! Why didn't you write us to say you were coming? Is everything all right?"

"Yes, yes, I'm fine!" Ermides smiled at her father and hugged him. "It's a quick trip, I'm afraid. I'm headed to Venice in the morning to meet up with the Zamparellis for a few weeks. They have a vacation home there. I have to watch their children and tend to my usual duties while they do whatever socialites do. And I wanted to bring *this*!" Ermides picked up the large box and winked at her little sister.

Lilia was still rubbing off the sand and pebbles that stuck to her hand and legs from the fall. Maria squinted at her. "What were you doing with these scissors, and what's in your hand?"

Ignoring Maria, Lilia squealed with excitement to see her big sister and ran over to her. She was doubly thankful for the perfectly timed distraction against the ticking time-bomb that was her mother.

"Everybody inside!" Virginio's voice brimmed with joy. He folded his arm into his daughter's, and escorted her into the kitchen.

"Not so fast, young lady!" Maria halted Lilia with the back of her hand.

"But . . . Ermides is here, and—"

"What's in your hand?"

Lilia opened her left hand to reveal nothing.

"The *other* hand!" Maria grabbed Lilia's hand and pried her fingers open. "Where did you get these buttons?" Looking at the scissors in her hand and the stool toppled over on the ground, Maria put two and two together. She pulled the linen bedding off the line to find gaping holes everywhere. Furious, Maria rattled Lilia's arms while shaking the pillowcases in her face. "Look what you did! Who taught you to do these things? Dina sent these from Milan. They are expensive! Why did you do this?"

"I wanted pretty buttons to show my friends." Lilia felt her cheeks turn red as her lips quivered.

"*Friends*? You don't have time for friends. When your sister leaves, you're going to sew all those buttons back on and make sure they look better than they did before you cut them off! Now, go inside." Maria spanked Lilia's bottom and followed her into the house.

After her own grueling years at the helm, Ermides was fully aware of the intensity of her mother's reprimand. "Lilia! What's the matter?" Lilia bent her head to hide the deep flush slowly spreading over her face.

Ermides attempted to comfort her sister. "Come here—look at what I brought you: a gift from Rome!"

A *gift*? Lilia thought, never having received one before.

"Open it!" Ermides handed Lilia a tall box wrapped in shiny, gold-colored paper. Slowly, Lilia's fingers tore one corner at a time. "Rip it, like this!" Ermides laughed at how nervous her sister was. Assisting Lilia, she wildly tore the paper off to reveal a porcelain doll, brand new in its box.

Lilia gasped at first, then put her hands to her face and stared in awe. "For *me*? She's *mine*?"

"She's one-of-a-kind, like you, and cost me a pretty penny—so take good care of her."

Lilia never could have imagined anything so precious. She felt maybe her eyes were deceiving her. She was afraid to touch the doll. "A real doll!" Lilia's eyes widened in disbelief.

Ermides gave her a side hug. "She belongs to *you*."

Standing upright, the doll was half Lilia's height. Her brilliant blue eyes and long lashes opened and closed when Lilia picked her up. She had a sprinkling of freckles across her nose, rosy cheeks, and pink lips—and she wore a blue-and-gold silk brocade dress and lace socks in little white satin shoes. Her long golden hair was braided and tied with sapphire-blue ribbons. Lilia hugged her new doll tightly to her chest. Virginio flashed Ermides a grateful smile, happy to see the joy restored to his little girl.

Threatened by the fear of her mother's reprisal, Lilia slowly raised her eyes to meet Maria's. "Mama? Can I go play with her?"

"Not now. Later." Maria grabbed the doll from Lilia's hands, mumbling to herself as she took it upstairs on her way to wake the boys, "I can't believe she spent all this money on a toy."

Hearing her mother's words, Lilia's eyes grew sad and a frown curled across her lips. She looked to her sister and father for some comfort, but it seemed no one had heard—or they simply didn't care.

Ermides promptly turned her attention to Virginio. "Papa, any news from Arturo and Erminio?"

"No, I'm afraid. We're without any word from either of them. All we heard was Arturo might be in Montenegro or Greece. Your mother doesn't sleep. She bursts into tirades for no reason, or she's in deep silence, buried in her thoughts. I pray we hear something soon."

"Me too, Papa, me too."

Giovanni, Riccardo, and Bruno stormed into the kitchen, breaking the quiet conversation. Shouts of happiness erupted from all three boys as their eldest sister pulled them in for a hug. "Everyone, come sit!" ordered Ermides. "I want to tell you about the movie I saw!"

Fascinated, the family gathered around the table.

"I went to the theatre to see a film a few months ago!" Ermides announced.

"*Theatre?*" asked Lilia, perplexed. "A *film?* What is that?"

"A *film*, Lilia, yes! The theatre is a dark room the size of a church. At the far wall is a big white screen made out of material like canvas, and tall as the wall of the altar. People gather there to watch stories come to life—like a play with real people but projected on the screen."

Lilia and Giovanni looked at each other, their eyes bulging with intrigue. Virginio sat with his arms crossed. He leaned into the table, nodding but not knowing what to say, as he was also confused. All the while, Maria—who was still upset with Lilia for stripping the pillowcases of their buttons and with Ermides for indulging Lilia with a foolish doll—pretended not to care.

"Ah! It all sounds a little stupid to me! When I was your age, I was married with a baby."

"Maria, let Ermides tell her story," pleaded Virginio, wanting to embrace this brief and special visit.

"What film did you see?" asked Virginio.

"*The Adventures of Robin Hood.*"

"Ah, I'm an old man from another time. This modern culture is beyond me." Virginio laughed at himself, taken aback by a world he knew nothing about. At the same time, he had an appreciation for learning new things and was eager to hear more.

"It's a film with famous American actors. It's about a man turned outlaw. The actor's name is Errol Flynn. He's handsome, with blue eyes, dark hair, and a mustache—like you, Papa! He wears a green beret with a feather in it. He and his tribe of men rob from the rich to give to the poor."

With every detail of Ermides's experience, her family's curiosity increased. They were left both baffled and delighted. Maria cast her gaze across the table at Ermides and back down in her apron—her eyes dull with disinterest and carrying a hint of jealousy.

"This Robin Hood sounds like an Alpini soldier from deep in the mountain forest!" Virginio left the room, and in minutes, returned, wearing his Alpini beret with the black raven feather. He danced around the kitchen, pretending to steal a loaf of bread. With animated eyes, he scanned the room left and right to ensure the coast was clear before quickly breaking the bread into pieces and sharing it with his family. Virginio was proud to have served as an Alpini soldier and amused his daughter thought he resembled some famous actor—but mostly, he felt elated he could make his family laugh.

"See, I can be Robin Hood! Maybe the Americans can put me in a film."

The children burst into laughter, and their sound filled the room with a warmth that had been long overdue.

"Please, don't encourage him." Maria shook her head but smiled despite herself. "I married a crazy man!"

Early the next morning, Ermides was ready to catch the early train east. Before parting, she took the doll from her mother's room and laid her next to Lilia in her bed. She gazed lovingly at her little sister, reflecting in wonderment on the years that had passed. Ermides gently stroked Lilia's hair, careful not to wake her. "We have too many years between us, little one. I'm sorry I can't be here for you—to change things, to make them easier. I hope, in some way, you'll one day live a better life than the rest of us."

Soon after her sister left, Lilia woke to see a pair of twinkly blue eyes staring at her. A smile spread across her face. "I'm happy you're here," she said to the doll. "I bet you were lonely in that box, weren't you? I feel like I live in a box, too, and no one can see me. Sometimes, I get scared I'll never get out."

Lilia ran her fingers over the doll's golden hair; she was immediately reminded of Sleeping Beauty. "You are beautiful. I'm going to name you Little Rose. One day our prince will find us, and when he does, he will set us free with a kiss." Lilia raised her hands to her lips, kissed her fingers, and lightly placed the kiss on the doll's cheek. "You're *my* little daughter now."

Little Rose quickly became Lilia's confidant and the gatekeeper of all her secrets and fears. "You're a good girl—special and important. I love you with all my heart." In many ways, the tender words that Lilia shared with Little Rose were the ones she longed to hear from her mother.

A few weeks later, before having to surrender to her morning chores, and attend her first-grade class in school, Lilia embraced precious moments with her doll. While playing with Little Rose, Lilia accidentally pulled on the blue ribbons from her hair, unraveling Little Rose's long golden braids. All her efforts to twist the strands back into place failed. Knowing how upset her mother would be, she panicked and cried in earnest.

Maria heard her daughter's tears and called up from the bottom of the stairs, "Lilia, what happened?"

No answer.

She called again in a sharper tone, "Lilia!"

Lilia didn't make a sound. Now worried, Maria scurried up to her daughter's room to find Lilia with her head down and her fists clenched. "Mama . . . I'm sorry. I broke her braids!" Lilia lifted her face and cried without ceasing.

"Ahhh, silly girl, give her to me. I can fix that." Maria quickly brushed out the doll's long hair and redid the braids. "See? She looks brand-new again."

Lilia's tears quickly dried up. As she reached her arms up to take back her Little Rose, Maria gave Lilia a scornful look. "Well, you don't think you're going to *play* with her again, do you?"

Lilia's face went pale. She didn't understand what was happening.

"I'll sit the doll up on my chest of drawers, where she'll keep safe." Maria felt it was best to preserve such an expensive doll as a relic and not a child's toy. Lilia sat dumbfounded on her bed, feeling her heart break into a million pieces. Like Little Rose, she was once again trapped in a box, all alone and with no way out. She burst into silent tears.

Lilia tried to bury her tragic morning, get through her usual chores, and prepare for school. Before leaving for class, Lilia peeked into her parents' bedroom. Her doll was high up and out of reach. She wondered if Little Rose was sad and lonely, too. *What is a girl without her mother?* Lilia thought. She looked forlornly at her doll. "Little Rose? Never forget, *your* mommy loves you."

Lilia strode along Via della Chiesa, with her head down, heading to her first-grade class. The grit of the pavement scuffed the already-worn soles of her clog sandals. Lilia stared at her feet. She could almost imagine a new pair of shoes. She squinted down the road, and her school appeared to blur, vanishing into the trees that lined the street.

Lilia drifted into a daydream. Like her school, she wished she, too, could disappear. She wasn't looking forward to another round of religious studies. "I miss you Little Rose."

Behind the wooden-fenced playground stood the elementary school, on Piazza IV November 11, a stone's throw from Lilia's front door. Rising two stories in the center of the piazza, the school was flanked by the only clothing and fabric store to the right, and the bar to the left. Lilia uttered a familiar sigh of discontent as she walked into her first-floor classroom.

Catechism was mandatory for the children of Mussons. Before regular studies, Padre Muninni led the class, teaching fundamental doctrine with questions and answers about God, the commandments, mortal sin, penance, prayer, and salvation—a challenging experience to sit through for a group of six-year-olds.

"Who made you? Does God exist in other people? What does every sin deserve?" he asked. The room turned cold, and nervous tension rose. The children fiddled in their seats, fearing the priest. Should they disobey him or incorrectly answer a question, he abused them with a hard slap in the face or smacked their hands with his wooden ruler. Driven by ego and arrogance, Padre had flexed his stern religious beliefs and used his power to force his twisted discipline on to the children and families of Mussons. Padre's beatings were routine. Although afraid, the children felt they deserved his punishment, and the children's parents viewed Padre as a god among men.

Lilia drew her thoughts and attention inward as she rested her cheek on her fist. It was easy for her to tune out the priest's sermon until all she could hear was a muffled sound. Lilia chipped away at layers of green and yellow paint on her desk as she prayed for time to pass—but the hands on the clock seemed to stand still.

"Lilia, how can you glorify God?" Padre was malignant in his tone.

Caught off guard, Lilia jolted her head up and blurted out, "Ah, I . . . I don't know, Padre."

He grabbed Lilia by her white collar and shook her from her dazed state. "Had you been listening, you would know the answer!"

Lilia rubbed her sweaty palms on her black dress and trembled in her seat. Padre raised his ruler and circled the room, fixing his menacing eyes on his students. The children shrank into their seats, hiding their hands from his sight. Padre filled his chest with air and raised his head, signaling his superiority. He swirled his ruler above the class and dictated, "*You* shall *love* me and the Lord your God with all your *heart*, and with all your *soul*, and with all your *mind*."

Consumed by guilt, fear, humiliation, helplessness, and shame, the children bowed their heads, resigned to his commands.

"As you are to God, so shall you be to me!"

Lilia quickly drifted off, daydreaming out the open window, wishing to escape this compulsory hell. At the foot of her dead-end street, Saint Osvaldo, the village parish, reminded Lilia of the powers that be. She breathed another sigh. Caught between worlds—the control of her mother and the authority of the church—Lilia felt small, oppressed, and insignificant. She couldn't understand why God had put her here, but Lilia knew she had to find a way out.

4 | FOUR FEET DEEP

வ It was late fall 1941. In Germany, and throughout Nazi-occupied Europe, Jewish shops were marked with a yellow star. Jewish men, women, and children were ordered to wear a badge in the shape of the star to mark their identity, which made it easier for the Nazis to transport them to concentration camps. During the experimental use of gas chambers at Auschwitz, hundreds of Polish prisoners were killed; the construction of mobile gas vans and crematoriums were in full effect throughout camps in Poland.

In the face of the ever-increasing horrors across Europe, the villagers of Mussons struggled to find peace and understanding. How could their innermost beings accept the inexplicable tragedy of war? As they suffered through months of bleakness and despair, the church became their means of hope and salvation; in God's house, they felt their earnest prayers could be heard.

"Let us pray. May the Lord light the way home for our beloved and keep them safe from harm. In the name of the Father, the Son, and the Holy Spirit. The mass is ended. Go in peace to love and serve the Lord."

Those words were a double-edged sword that pierced Maria's heart. Since her boys left, Padre's sermons and final blessings had taken on a different meaning for her. As the choir led the congregation outside with their closing hymn, Maria lit a candle and knelt at the altar.

She spoke in a quiet voice, beseeching her unseen God: "Go in *peace*? My sons were pushed out of our home to *serve*, but serve *who*?

Is this *love*—giving life to my sons so evil hands can use my flesh and blood to fight *their* battles? Where is there peace in a savage war?"

Maria no longer drew the same nourishment from the white walls of her church. In her mind, they ran red. "This war will devour us all," she whimpered to herself.

Patterns of light filtered through the stained-glass windows, casting colorful beams across Maria's praying hands. Holding her rosary, she bowed and poured her heart into her Hail Marys, her soft cadence floating through the church. A warm glow bathed the stations of the cross hanging on the walls, and the fragrant smell of incense filled the air—a sign of reverence. Maria lifted her eyes to the statue of Mary cradling baby Jesus; a golden aura surrounded His body, emanating beams of divine light. Enraptured by His radiance, Maria raised her hands, imploring the Mother of God. "Would you not have given up your life for your child—the only cause worth dying for? Saint Mary, Mother of God, take me and bring my sons home!"

Maria made the sign of the cross, kissed her rosary, and wiped away a sorrowful tear. She felt exhausted and empty as she pulled her aching body up from the wooden planks that spanned the church. She turned and shuffled to the open door and squinted against the morning light, the weight of the world on her shoulders. Throughout her life, she had an intense desire to be understood, but today, all Maria wanted was to be heard.

As she walked home in the middle of the dusty road, Maria's tired body struggled to move; her worrisome thoughts trailed behind her, hovering like a shadow. She imagined her sons' faces, their smiles, and the sound of their voices.

"Good morning, Maria!" a neighbor called out, waving as Maria passed by.

No answer. Maria didn't want to taint the moment.

While rinsing and ringing out the newly washed laundry at the street water pump, Lilia spotted Maria up ahead. She lay the clothing in her straw basket, leaving it inside the gate, and ran over to join her mother. She could feel and sense Maria's mood like a cat could feel tremors in the earth. "Mama, what's wrong?"

Maria opened her eyes and smiled slightly, but the smile wasn't for Lilia.

"Did you finish your chores?" she said curtly as she looked down at her daughter.

"No, Mama."

"Then what are you *doing* here?"

Lilia dropped her head and plodded back home. Guilt swept over Maria, but she wanted to slip back into her thoughts and be alone.

In the months that followed her brothers' absence, six-year-old Lilia had been left to raise her three younger brothers alone while her parents worked day and night to survive the war. Supporting their family was becoming increasingly challenging. As her eldest sibling left, Lilia felt it was up to her to be the glue that held everyone together.

Early one morning before leaving for school, Lilia helped her brothers get dressed, changed the sheets, made their beds, and hand-washed a pile of laundry, all in time for breakfast.

"Lilia!" Maria hollered from the kitchen. "Run to the dairy before all the milk is gone! Tell Franco to fill up the pail."

Heeding her mother's urgent request, Lilia scrambled out the door. At the end of her street, she saw a large crowd forming. The window of the dairy was open. Women raised their pails above their heads, trying to squeeze their way through to the front of the line. Panic gripped Lilia as chatter rose impatiently from the crowd.

"Excuse me. Excuse me?" Lilia's tiny voice raised barely above a whisper. "Please, can you let me in, too?" As hard as she tried to push past the tide of adults, she was shoved aside. Lilia finally reached the window and stretched out her pail. Rushing to load his wagon with the empty stainless-steel containers, Franco stopped when he saw the defeat in Lilia's big brown eyes. It broke his heart.

"I'm sorry, Lilia, but the milk is all gone. The Germans took half the truck's supply before it arrived here. Try to come earlier tomorrow."

Lilia nodded and shrugged her shoulders. On her way home, she dropped her head in despair. As her eyes moved in rhythm with the swinging pail, the echo of the empty can, and thoughts of her little brothers overwhelmed her. Lilia didn't want to disappoint anyone, especially her mother. She wished she had left for the dairy sooner.

Gigi, an elderly neighbor, was riding his wobbly bicycle past Lilia when he noticed her walking home and wearing a deep frown.

"Lilia? Why the long face?"

"Franco ran out of milk, and now we have nothing for my brothers." Lilia promptly broke into tears.

"Oh, there, there now. Don't cry. Come here—hop on." Gigi tapped his hand on the handlebars. "Come with me." Lilia hopped on to the bars, and in minutes, arrived at Gigi's front door.

"Wait here." The old man shuffled into his kitchen.

Lilia sat on the gravel walkway and waited patiently; she wasn't entirely sure why she was there, but it was better than going home empty-handed. Lilia imagined her mother's reaction. She could see the tendons in Maria's neck tighten upon finding out about the milk. This caused Lilia to weep some more in silence.

"Here, Lilia, take this."

Lilia rose to attention at Gigi's arrival. His wrinkled hands shook as he kindly poured half his liter of milk into her pail. "Shh! Don't tell my wife," he said, chuckling and giving Lilia a wink. "Take this to your mama and keep your chin up!"

Lilia smiled through her tears, dried her eyes on her sleeve, and nodded. "Thank you."

Gigi tipped his worn fedora and smiled back.

Week after week, war was like a tempest sweeping from village to village, bringing with it the inevitable rationing. Despite the system put in place by the wartime government, food was scarce for the rural community of Mussons. Bread and rice trucks arrived every two weeks. Those with a ration badge would have the first pick—those without were left empty-handed. If trucks transporting supplies were not bombed, they were confiscated by Germans. Each person was allowed one bread bun, which was hardly enough to satisfy the six members of the Meneguzzi family. Virginio cycled for miles in search of cornmeal, their main sustenance. When the bread ran out, Maria diced roasted polenta or boiled potatoes into bowls of warm milk for breakfast. Those fortunate to grow wheat or raise stock had bartering power. Virginio and Maria raised chickens, rabbits, and ducks, all of which they sold to the villagers and sometimes traded for a bar of soap made from pig fat. When not using the soap to clean themselves, they washed their clothing and linens in the river or in the washboard basin in their courtyard. The family lived off the live-stock they raised, along with gatherings from the garden and heaping spoonfuls of polenta cooked over the fire in their cast-iron cauldron.

As time went by, the shortage of money and food became more severe. Maria and Virginio grew weary of a war from which they could find no relief. Night after night, Lilia listened as her mother prayed in the quiet hours asking for help.

Countless Our Fathers and Hail Marys later, a light of hope

graced their family. It was late October. Virginio was piling up firewood inside the barn for the impending winter.

"Good morning, Virginio! Need some help?" a voice bellowed from behind the gate. Eliseo, the village tailor, was a jolly little man in his late sixties, and like Virginio, was a staple in Mussons. As the village tailor, he'd built close relationships with many of the locals and a deep friendship with Virginio over the years.

"Hello! Come in, come in." Virginio wiped his hands on his pants and excitedly ran over to greet Eliseo, pulling him in for a one-armed hug. Virginio loved company and someone to share a drink with. "How's the day? What can I get you? Coffee? Maria made some fresh this morning."

Eliseo gave a knowing wink. "Coffee? Hmm, wine is better, no?"

"Always better!" Virginio whisked into the cantina and returned with his straw-covered flask of homemade wine and two glasses.

"Come. Sit with me in the barn."

Eliseo pulled up a stool against the workbench as Virginio poured two glasses, each four fingers high.

"Maria and I have been thinking about you since Mariutta passed away. How's the family? How are you managing?"

Eliseo shrugged his shoulders and let out a sigh of lamentation. "Twenty years of marriage, and my beloved's heart gives out. Mariutta was washing *my* dirty clothes when it happened." He made a gesture of self-disgust. "And where was I? At the bar. I should have been home." Eliseo removed his spectacles and rubbed his eyes. Virginio could clearly see the heavy weight of guilt that burdened his friend. He reached over and put a sympathetic hand on Eliseo's shoulder.

"It's not your fault. It was her time. We *all* have our time, and she's with God now."

"Virginio, our kids—well, Mariutta's kids—want me out of the house." The harsh sentiment was difficult for Eliseo to repeat. "I married a war bride with four children, and no matter how hard I tried, they never took to me. Thank God Mariutta and I had Pio and Mateo; otherwise, I'd be without a family." Eliseo gulped his wine and Virginio refilled his glass. "With the boys now grown and gone, I have nowhere to go." Embarrassed, Eliseo held his words for a moment, but Virginio understood.

"Eliseo, my friend, if you need a place to stay, we have the empty room upstairs."

Close to tears, Eliseo put his hands together and scrunched his eyes closed. "Thank you, Virginio! I'll pay you for the room, and for a space to cut and sew, if you have it. How much do you want? Whatever you need!"

"If we weren't in the middle of a war with all these little mouths to feed, I'd give you the room for free. You know that." Virginio took Eliseo's shoulders in his hands and gave him a little shake. "You'll be good here. We need to stick together, and the kids will love having you around."

Virginio smiled and clinked Eliseo's glass. "Lay aside your cares now and finish that wine. I'll help you get your things, and we'll bring you home. *Salût*! Cheers! my friend."

⁘⁘⁘

One month had passed. Virginio and Maria had taken in Eliseo and converted a portion of their great room into a sewing space. The rent money became a welcome blessing, as did Eliseo's light-hearted company and his helping hand.

A crisp, sunny, November afternoon was followed by a week of rain. The streets of Mussons lay quiet and bare as villagers retreated indoors for their riposo. They had yet to see the first signs of snowfall.

"Children! Up to your room—and lie there quietly. I don't want to hear a peep!" ordered Maria. Maria and Virginio also climbed into their bed and closed their tired eyes for a spell. Eliseo, however, spent his Saturday afternoon with the patrons of the bar, playing a few rounds of Briscola and Scopa, the usual card games, over drinks.

Little did his parents know Giovanni was spying through the open crack of their bedroom door. Convinced they had finally fallen asleep, he slinked back down the hall to his room and reached over to his sister in bed. Giovanni tapped Lilia on the shoulder. "Psst, are you awake?"

"Shhh! Yes, I'm awake," Lilia whispered, not wanting to wake the other boys, especially Bruno—once he was up, he cried and fussed, and it was impossible to get him back to sleep.

"I want to show you something. Come see what I found yesterday!"

"Where?"

"At the river dike."

"Giovanni, we have to be quiet or Mama will kill us!"

"She won't even know we're gone!" Giovanni's bright blue eyes sparkled with excitement. He rubbed his hands together, smiling mischievously.

Lilia rolled her eyes. "All right, show me, but we *must* be quiet!"

Giovanni had been waiting all morning to share his findings with his big sister. The two grabbed their shoes and tiptoed barefoot down the hallway. Lilia knew where the floorboards creaked, so she led the way, placing each light step with caution. A plethora of thoughts rattled Lilia's brain. *If Mama hears us, she's going to scold him, but she'll punish me!*

Like most mothers, Maria had elephant ears and eyes in the back of her head, but she sank into a deep slumber from utter exhaustion this day. Lilia and Giovanni continued down the flight of stairs and successfully darted out the front door, sharing a victorious grin.

Children of all ages in Mussons spent much of their spring and summer months by the dike, sliding down the muddy embankment, swimming in the Tagliamento, and lying out on the river rocks. With the weather now turned colder, the noises from the vast open playground had grown quiet.

Stomping through the grassy, tree-filled farmland and open woodland, Lilia and her brother reached their destination. The flood bank rose some thirty feet above the river, which backed on to bush and willow branches that loomed over the waterway. The shore was covered with gravel and small white stones, mixed with coarse salt-and-pepper sand. The landscape was mute and desolate, apart from squawking seagulls that reeled in the sky and swooped into the river. The chill in the air penetrated Lilia's bones, prompting her to rush her brother to speed up his revelation. "So, what did you want to show me?"

"Follow me." Giovanni led his sister towards a grove. "Up there!"

Lilia lifted her head; towering above her was a majestic poplar tree. The sunlight danced through the leaves as they fell, tugged loose by the autumn breeze. Giovanni proceeded to climb the tree. "Come up and look what I found yesterday!"

Lilia followed. Halfway up the tree, she heard a pleasant little chirp, then another. The sound was sweet to her ears; it lit her face up as she listened. "Oh, Giovanni, a bird's nest! Look at the babies!" Two tiny brown nestlings were bobbing, twitching and vibrating their wings. They looked up at Lilia and cried piteously for attention and food. "Giovanni, it's too cold, and they need to eat. Let's take them home!"

As Lilia drew near, the nestlings tilted their heads sharply upward, letting out their cries of distress. "I know what it is to feel neglected and alone. Don't be scared. I'll keep you safe. I promise." Lilia climbed down first, cradling the nest in her dress. "Hurry, Giovanni! We need to go home and hide the babies before Mama wakes up!"

The two siblings walked home at a brisk pace, careful not to stress the nestlings.

"Lilia, where should we hide them? In the garden? The barn?"

"Hmmm, no, because Mama will find them in the garden, and Papa is always in the barn. What if we hide them on the roof behind the chimney? I think they'll like the shade there."

"Yes! Let's do that!"

Lilia and Giovanni made their way up to their bedroom without a sound. Even the nestlings were quiet. "Giovanni," whispered Lilia. "As soon as Mama and Papa wake up and go downstairs, we'll bring the nest up to the chimney."

"Good idea!" he nodded enthusiastically.

Not moments later, there was movement in the hallway. "Children?" hollered Maria. "Get up and come downstairs!"

Giovanni kept a watchful eye. Once his parents left, he motioned Lilia over. "Now! Let's go!"

The window in the hallway led to an open-air terrace stacked with corn husks, laid out to dry. Lilia got on her hands and knees to give Giovanni a boost out the window. He put the nest on the terrace and pulled Lilia up. A five-step ladder leaned against the wall. Lilia and her brother climbed up to the terracotta roof and hid the nest in the shade behind the chimney.

"Lilia, they look hungry. What do we feed them?"

Lilia searched her brother's face for a moment before her eyes lit up with delight. "I know the perfect thing!"

Each morning, Lilia watched her mother prepare the feed for their ducklings—a mixture of shredded radicchio, diced beets, and corn. Lilia decided this would be suitable for the nestlings. While Maria was harvesting vegetables and planting bulbs in the garden, Lilia snuck into the kitchen to grab a handful of the duck feed. Giovanni stood guard as Lilia painstakingly shredded the feed into tiny slivers. In the days that followed, they repeated the process and fed the nestlings morning, noon, and night, figuring the baby chick's mealtimes were similar to that of humans. Lilia dropped the feed one pinch at a time into the hungry mouths of the chirping birds, whose little tongues eagerly wagged. She followed with drops of water, thinking it would quench their thirst.

Days later, Lilia and Giovanni sat back on the terrace amid the stacks of corn and took a moment to reflect.

"We saved their lives, Giovanni." Lilia shook her head, her face serious. "How could their mother leave her babies alone?"

"I don't know, but we didn't get caught!" Giovanni looked up at his sister and smiled broadly, feeling proud of their accomplishment, "Can you imagine what Mama would do if she knew?" On his climb down from the window, Giovanni's feet slipped under him, and he fell to the floor with a painful-sounding thud causing Lilia to yelp.

Maria had heard her children running up and down the stairs, and took notice of the stretches of silence in between. Naturally, she became suspicious when she heard the shriek. "What are you two doing up there?"

"Nothing, Mama," they replied as Giovanni helped his sister down from the window.

One week later, what had initially been a great and revered victory had turned to horror when Lilia and Giovanni discovered the nestlings—dead.

Giovanni peered into the nest and exchanged a look of confusion with his sister. "Are they sleeping?" He reached his finger out to poke the birds. "They're not moving!"

Lilia gasped and quickly brushed her hand over the babies' bodies—they felt cold. She recoiled and stepped back. Her face flushed in disbelief. "It's not fair. It's not *fair*! What happened?" Their heads sank in despair as they gazed back into the nest.

Giovanni breathed a deep sigh. "What do we do with them now?"

"Bury them, I guess."

"Where?"

"Past the garden, in Papa's vineyard. Mama won't find them there—we have to move, and fast!"

Lilia and Giovanni wrapped the nestlings ever so gently in a tea towel, and together, laid their babies to rest in the soil. Broken-hearted, they wore long, sad faces and moped throughout the day.

"What's wrong with you two?" asked Maria, her suspicion triggered once again. "You look like somebody died."

Lilia and Giovanni looked at each other. Their eyes widened at their mother's choice of words. Giovanni shot his sister a look that implored her not to say anything. On the verge of tears, Lilia held a stiff lip. "Nothing's wrong." They scampered upstairs to drown their sorrows in bed.

Lilia lay restless throughout the night. She missed the chirping sounds that had filled her with so much joy. She felt guilty for the birds' short lives. *It was wrong of me to take them,* she thought. *Babies need their mothers, and mothers need their babies.* With Little Rose taken from her, and the war that had stolen Arturo and Erminio from their mother, Lilia began to make sense of the wrong she had done. She threw her face onto her pillow and cried herself to sleep.

The following morning, Lilia paid the nestlings a solemn visit to ask for forgiveness. As she approached the grapevines, she saw what appeared to be a cross jutting up from the ground. Two small willow branches were bound together with twine to mark the gravesite. Lilia's heart plummeted. She realized Maria had uncovered her and Giovanni's secret.

"Lilia!" her mother called out. "Come inside and help me make the barn feed."

Lilia approached the kitchen at a snail's pace. Afraid to look up and catch the disappointment in her mother's eyes, Lilia's gaze remained fixed on her feet, which fidgeted nervously.

To her surprise, Maria didn't even look up but continued shredding radicchio and corn on the table. "Lilia, see the beets in the bowl on the counter? Bring them here and chop them up small for me so I can feed the ducklings. And be careful—beets have a way of catching you by surprise. They will leave your hands stained for days."

Lilia stood motionless and swallowed back her fear. She raised her hands in front of her, palms up—they were stained red. Lilia shot her hands down to her sides and waited for her mother to turn around and reprimand her, but Maria never did.

"Lilia? What are you waiting for?"

"Ah, yes, Mama."

Lilia spent the day working alongside her mother in the garden. She occasionally cast a forlorn glance at the cross and a confused one at Maria, still expecting to be interrogated. Maria never mentioned the nestlings. At that moment, Lilia understood her mother—and she understood the cross. Overwhelmed with emotion, Lilia threw her arms around her mother, catching Maria off guard.

"I love you, Mama." Lilia squeezed her mother tight. Maria didn't flinch or respond. Her hands remained gripped around her gardening tools. Misty-eyed, she dropped her head and kept digging and planting.

⚬⚘ ⚘⚬

Weeks rolled by, and the weather turned frigid. As the days grew progressively shorter, Eliseo's memories of his late wife grew more inaccessible, as if veiled by winter's fog. To numb his overwhelming grief, he frequented La Bottega and several other bars in nearby villages. On countless nights, he stumbled home in a drunken stupor.

Over the last couple of months that Eliseo stayed with them, Maria and Virginio had embraced him as a part of their family, so they excused his behavior out of pity. They appreciated Eliseo's kind nature and supportive hand with the children, which far outshone his vices. On some afternoons, he took Bruno off Lilia's hands to give her a respite from her little tribe of siblings. Eliseo's childlike qualities captivated the boys, especially Bruno. Eliseo had a knack for concocting stories that kept their attention and created a warm and cheerful atmosphere. Bruno idolized him, hanging on his every word and following him everywhere.

"Hey, little drunkard, come with me," Eliseo said to Bruno one day, reaching for his hand. "Let's go!"

Elated, Bruno ran towards him with a giggle so infectious Eliseo could not help but join in. Hand in hand, they playfully weaved their way down the street to the bar.

"You homeless alcoholic, what are you doing taking my youngest boy to the bar? Are you teaching him the ropes?" Maria hollered in jest from the front gate.

"Yes!" Eliseo chuckled, smiling back as he waved his arm in a wide arc. "He's keeping me company, *and* he's keeping me out of trouble!"

Maria couldn't complain too much. At least Bruno was content with his new companion. Eliseo had a special gift for drawing laughter out of Bruno—a child who fussed constantly and always seemed to be launching into fits of tears. While Eliseo played cards and bocce ball with the other men, Bruno drew an adoring crowd, which made him beam a giddy grin that stretched ear-to-ear.

⚬◦ℓ℮ ℮ℓ◦⚬

It was a crisp night in January. Eliseo's breath rose in visible puffs against the moonlit sky, and the chill in the air brought a crispness to the sparkling snow that glittered on the rooftops and crunched beneath his heavy feet.

After spending hours at the bar, Eliseo staggered home sluggishly, swaying left and right as snowflakes gracefully floated to the ground. With every other step, he startled himself awake by his own stumbling, forcing his eyes to flash open. Eliseo rubbed his cold, reddened ears with his stiffening fingers, and his teeth chattered while he let out a silent groan. "Ugh, I can't control my damn w-whiskey anymore!"

Eliseo managed to pass through the front gate when his bladder grew full and his stomach ached, both howling for relief. The milky moon kindly illuminated the courtyard and guided a muddled Eliseo safely towards the outhouse—a two-foot hole cut out of plywood that rested atop a four-foot-deep foundation. The toilet stood past the barn by the entrance to the garden. Each time he took a deep breath, Eliseo's lungs filled with a sharp coldness, and dampness crept into his body. Still, in his drunken state, he was lured away from the numbing sensation and launched into serenading the night sky with his incoherent songs. While Eliseo pulled down his pants and crouched over the hole, his singing grew louder and louder until he lost his balance, plummeting four feet into the pit. "Ahhhh, dammit!" At first, he was angry at his misfortune—and then, he panicked. Eliseo kicked and flailed his arms as he unsuccessfully tried to pull himself out. "Help! Help! Somebody! I'm s-stuck and I c-can't get out!"

The ever-vigilant mother, Maria's eyes sprung open as she lifted her head from the pillow. Scanning the room, she thought, *Are those my children? Wait . . . what is that?* Maria keened her ears and made out a faint cry from outside her bedroom window. Jumping to her feet, Maria pushed open the shutters to a snow-sprinkled ground, star-filled sky, and the sound of Eliseo crying out for help. She threw on her robe and slippers and ran outside to see what the ruckus was about. When she found Eliseo, Maria threw her hands up in the air, shaking her head in disbelief.

"Oh, my God! Eliseo, what did you do? Stay there. Don't move!"

"Moooove? Wheeeere d'you think I'm going? H-h-h-heeey! Get me out of here!" Eliseo slurred. "Heeelp me up!"

Maria ran back to the house and called out to her husband from under their bedroom window. "Virginio! Come outside—quick, quick!"

Virginio leaped out of bed and looked out the window to see Maria waving her arms. "What happened?"

"Eliseo fell in the toilet! He's drunk!"

Virginio ran outside in his pajamas. Nearing the outhouse, he could not believe his eyes.

"Saint Mary, Mother of God! Eliseo! I see you found yourself in some deep shit!" Virginio couldn't stifle his laughter, which also sent Maria into a fit of giggles. They tried to suppress their eruption when Eliseo gave them a dirty look.

"Wha . . . what the heck are you two laughing at? H-help me out already!" Eliseo continued to moan incoherently.

Virginio and Maria's laughter quickly turned into grimaces. Both held their breath as they heaved Eliseo out of the hell hole. Free at last of his predicament, Eliseo stood drenched head to toe in sludge and excrement. "Mariutta, call my Mariutta!" he mumbled.

Grabbing hold of his arms, Virginio and Maria patiently walked their grunting, limp-bodied friend back inside the house.

"Virginio, take his clothes off and toss them outside. I'll boil some water."

Eliseo stood trembling naked by the fireplace in the great room while Maria bathed him. All she could think about was the mess waiting for her to clean up before the children awoke to witness this ridiculous event. "Don't move a muscle, you hear me? Let's try and keep this sludge in one place, shall we?" Disgusted by the smell, now permeating all her senses, Maria bravely plodded on in the spirit of kindness. Eliseo was too far out into oblivion to notice the awkward situation he put her in. Upstairs, Lilia could hear the commotion from her bedroom window. Running to the top of the landing, she called down, "Mama? Papa? What's going on?"

"Nothing! Go back to bed!" Maria shuddered at the thought of her children witnessing this debacle.

Eliseo teetered in circles, barely able to keep his eyes open. He groaned again. "Ugh! What stinks?" He was soon dressed in his pajamas and accompanied to his room. Exhausted from the night's episode, Maria and Virginio crawled back into bed.

Distressed for his friend, Virginio turned to his wife with a compassionate gaze. "Poor soul. He's had a rough go of it these past years. It broke my heart when he called out for his beloved Mariutta."

"Well, if the drinking doesn't get him, something will, and he'll be seeing his beloved before he knows it." Maria rested her head onto

Virginio's chest and caressed his shoulder. "We're lucky to have each other. I don't know what I would do without you."

The following afternoon, Eliseo's memory was foggy at best as he tried to piece together scenes from the night before. With a pounding headache, queasy stomach, and on shaky legs, he drifted to the front door of the house and noticed his garments had been washed and hung to dry outside. Maria was pulling them off the line. He lingered a few moments as he watched her fold his clothes, confused as to what had happened.

"Good afternoon!" Virginio sauntered out from the kitchen and greeted Eliseo with a slap on the back. "How are we feeling today?"

"I don't want to talk about it," Eliseo snapped, as he rubbed his temples and the back of his neck.

Not moments later, Maria piped into the conversation as she met the men at the doorway. "Well, sometimes you need to fall hard to learn how to stand on your feet." She handed Eliseo his clean clothes, neatly stacked. Looking at the underwear in his hands, he closed his eyes. Like a jolt of coffee, his memory jarred him enough to leave him unquestionably embarrassed.

"Look on the bright side," Maria said sympathetically.

Eliseo looked at Maria sideways. "There's a *bright* side?"

"Thank your lucky stars you're over four feet tall!" Maria giggled as she walked into the kitchen.

"Come on, old friend." Virginio shot Eliseo an encouraging wink. "Let's go grab a pick-me-up at the bar."

⋘⚬⚬⋙

The occasional amusement of Eliseo's antics were balanced against the growing burden of Lilia's daily responsibilities. But a surprise had been brewing over the months, leading up to what would become an unexpected special occasion.

It was a midsummer morning in July. Lilia was seven years old.

"I almost forgot. You're one year older today!" remarked Maria, without wishing her daughter a happy birthday. "I want to see all your chores done when I get home—and keep your brothers out of trouble, understood?"

"Yes, Mama."

Maria left for Morsano to run errands for the day. Virginio had been up at the crack of dawn, busily working on a project in his barn. He excitedly called his daughter over.

"Lilia! Boys! Come outside. There's something I want to show you."

Lilia and her little brothers ran out to the courtyard to find their father holding up four wooden poles of different heights. The children looked at each other, bewildered. "What are those?" Lilia asked.

"You walk with them, like this!" Virginio stepped up on the footrests and proceeded to parade around the courtyard on the wooden stilts he'd made. "Look at me! I'm a giant, as tall as a tree!" Virginio pulled figs from the top branches and tossed them to his children.

Their jaws dropped in amazement at this magical invention. The courtyard livened up as Lilia, Giovanni, Riccardo, and Bruno swarmed around their father, tugging at his pant legs, begging to get on the stilts.

"Can I try?"

"Me, too!"

"And me?"

"Me, three!"

Virginio tried to steady himself by holding on to a tree branch but lost his grip and cascaded to the ground, taking his little army with him. Splashes of laughter rose up in the air. The children's pulses raced as they took turns. They were awkward and shaky at first but eventually managed to balance themselves on the stilts and adjust to their new legs. Up and down Via della Chiesa, to the church and back, they beamed with pride. Waving to nearby neighbors, they shouted in triumph, making their presence known:

"I'm a giraffe!"

"I'm the Eiffel Tower!"

"I'm Jack in the Beanstalk!"

"I'm a giant!"

Giggles and songs filtered through the air—a day unlike any other. Lilia loved being one of the boys. She felt tall and strong, as if she could conquer the world. Virginio's smile grew as he watched Lilia and the boys happy and free—as children should be.

In the late afternoon, Maria neared the piazza of Mussons when she saw children in the distance prancing around on wooden pegs. She shook her head disapprovingly.

Mercy me! What irresponsible parents would allow such a thing! she thought, appalled at the display. Nearing the front gate, Maria squinted and looked more closely. Blinking in disbelief, she squinted again. Sure enough, they were *her* children! In a split second, her disapproval turned to fear.

Raising her hands to her head, she cried out, "Dear God! Virginio! Have you gone insane!? Letting those kids out there like that? And that's not a game for girls. Lilia's wearing a dress! Have you no sense of decency? What if they fall? Get them inside!"

"Ah, woman, they're fine! Let them play. Look at those faces. Tears make more noise than laughter." Virginio smiled at his wife, searching for kindness and understanding.

Oblivious to her husband's good intentions, Maria burst through the gate, grabbed her willow branch, and ran out into the middle of the street, waving an angry fist in the air. "Get inside right now! If you fall and crack your heads open, I'll kill you all! Do you hear me?" Nearby neighbors' antennas went up immediately as they retreated back into their homes. Maria was at it again, like a drill sergeant surveying her troops.

Caught off guard, Lilia lost her confidence—and her balance. Before her father could catch her fall, Lilia's legs flailed, and she toppled to the ground. Her dress tumbled over her head. Maria covered her outraged face.

Embarrassed, Lilia hobbled home with scraped knees and elbows, and her brothers trailed close behind, afraid of their mother's wrath. Maria stood at the gate, arms crossed, staring them down one by one as they walked past her.

"Lose your head today?" Maria swatted Virginio on the back of his neck. "And you! You should know better! What if something had happened to your brothers?" Maria slapped Lilia's legs with the willow branch. "Get in the house—all of you!"

Reluctantly, Lilia looked up at her father, expecting to see his disappointment. She felt that had she not fallen, he wouldn't also be in trouble. Virginio saw her sad brown eyes and winked to assure Lilia everything was fine. He scanned to see if the coast was clear, leaned in, and whispered, "Tell me, though—it *was* fun, wasn't it? Happy birthday!"

Lilia's frown bloomed into a smile. In that moment, her world was perfect. She felt like a princess, because her father was a king.

5 | HEAVEN CAN WAIT

September 1942

Eliseo blinked in the gray morning light as it streamed into the great room's sewing area, where he sat hunkered over his tailoring table, which was layered with lengths of fabric, spools of thread, shears, and a coal-heated iron. He was late with another deadline. His sewing machine whirred at a breathless speed as he pushed the foot treadle and sped the needle through the dark-brown wool fabric.

"Eliseo? There is a man at the gate asking if his pants are ready yet." Lilia's sweet voice rose above the sound of the chugging machine. Eliseo broke free from his frenzied state, paused the pedal, and looked up to see Lilia's body silhouetted in the doorway, the light pouring out around her.

"Ugh!" Irritated, Eliseo put his head back down and continued sewing. He brushed his hand through the air like he was flicking away dust. "Tell Mr. Impatient to come back tomorrow. He'll get his pants then!"

"Mr. Impatient? He said to come back tomorrow," Lilia innocently told the customer.

Eliseo chuckled slightly and smiled as he fed the fabric under the needle. "That'll teach him," he mumbled to himself.

Over a year had passed since his wife's death. With the rejection of his stepchildren, the struggles of war, and his lingering grief over losing Mariutta, Eliseo's passion for tailoring had waned. Clients frequently left empty-handed and dissatisfied. No amount of money could fill the ever-growing hole in Eliseo's heart. His orders were continually laid aside as he spent more afternoons and nights in the bar and fewer at his table.

"Late again I see?" Maria asked, overhearing the exchange between him and her daughter.

Working the pedals, Eliseo revved the sewing machine at full speed. "My machine didn't like your comment, Maria."

Maria merely shrugged off his remark as she passed him on her way to the kitchen. Grabbing her woven straw basket and pruning knife, she headed for the garden. Three rows of vegetable plants lined the far end of the property, past the barn on the right and the outhouse on the left. "Lilia, watch your brothers and sweep out the front walkway. Later, you can help me wash the radicchio."

"Yes, Mama."

While the boys sat quietly playing in the courtyard, Lilia swept the autumn leaves that had accumulated in small drifts around the house. Moments later, the sound of her brothers' voices cut into the calm of the morning.

"Hey, Giovanni, Bruno. Look!" Four-year-old Riccardo had magically discovered that inserting a bean into his ear and then tilting his head would cause the bean to roll back into his hand. "See? Magic! I have beans coming out of my head!" he exclaimed, proud of his ingenuity. The trio fell into hysterics and bobbing and weaving their heads like owls. Back and forth, side to side, they made beans vanish and reappear.

"Good morning, boys!" a familiar voice called out from behind the gate. It was Berto, the village postman. He peered over the gate's wooden bars into the courtyard and smiled at the sound of the children's giggling. Berto also laughed and winked at Lilia. "Watch yourselves, you might grow a beanstalk in your ears!"

"Noooo!" they snickered and continued with their game.

"Boys!" Lilia shook her head at her brothers' antics and rolled her eyes. She turned to meet Berto at the gate.

"Lilia, I have a letter here from Udine. Get this to your mama right away." He tapped her chin and waved goodbye to the boys. "Have fun but be careful now!"

"Ciaooo, Bertooooo!" they replied, still bobbing their heads.

Lilia saw Erminio's name on the envelope and was immediately curious. She raised it to the light and squinted, hoping to make out its contents.

"Mama!" Lilia hollered. "A letter arrived from Udine!"

Maria froze between garden rows as her heart leaped wildly at the news. Her face blanched. "My boys!" Maria jumped and released her basket, scattering vegetables everywhere. She raced back to the house. Out of breath, she pulled the envelope out of Lilia's hand, nearly knocking her over. Eliseo stood unseen in the shadow of the doorway—he was nervous, too. Maria ripped open the envelope and read the brief note. The pounding of her heart drowned out any other sound.

Mama, I was in the hospital with pneumonia,
but I'm fine now. They are sending us to Russia tomorrow.
All my love, Erminio

Closing her eyes, Maria pressed the paper to her chest. She controlled her breathing but wanted to scream with fury.

"Mama?" Lilia gently pulled on her mother's apron. "What's wrong? What does it say?"

"Erminio is going to Russia." A whimper escaped her lips. "I'll never see him again." Maria pushed through the front door, inadvertently shoving Eliseo to the side on her way into the kitchen.

"Maria?" Eliseo reached out to console her, but she wiggled out of his reach.

"I want to be left alone." Maria closed the kitchen door behind her.

Lilia's face flushed red, and her eyes glazed with blinding tears. In the background, she could still hear her brothers' laughter. "W-we're never going to see Erminio again?"

Eliseo felt crushed by the force of her little-girl panic. He removed his glasses, looked at the pile of fabric and orders on his table, and rubbed his neck and head. "Lilia, where is your papa?"

"He's at Pietro's butchering a pig."

Eliseo grabbed his fedora and dashed through the gate. In between tending to her chores and little brothers, Lilia nervously watched her mother's silhouette through the linen curtain behind the kitchen door. Time passed, and Maria didn't move.

After what felt like an eternity, Lilia heard the front door opening. "Liliutti?" At the sound of her father's voice, a wave of tears erupted. Lilia buried her face in her father's shoulder, soaking his already-drenched shirt.

"Papa! Berto delivered a letter . . . and Mama . . . Mama said that—"

"Shh, shh, it's all right. I know everything." Virginio gently patted her back, as he was covered in dirt from head to toe and his clothes were stained with blood. "Go outside with the boys and let me talk to Mama."

Sensing the rising angst in the room, Eliseo quietly excused himself and took his sewing upstairs, offering the family space.

Virginio tapped the door. "Maria? It's me."

Maria didn't respond. He tapped harder and the door gave way, opening to his wife sitting at the kitchen table—fixated on the letter in her hands. There was an emptiness in her eyes. It was as if her soul had wilted.

"Maria, our son is not dead. He's at war."

"He's in Russia," she replied in a monotone voice, never lifting her eyes from the table.

"Maria—"

"He's in Russia!" she bellowed, shaking the letter at him.

"Maria, this happens. Divisions get transferred—"

"I don't care! He is in Russia. *Russia*! He will never survive that winter. He's not strong enough. Erminio is weak. My Erminio is never coming home!" Maria's hands quivered as she stroked the cursive handwriting on the page, every swish and every curl. "These are the last words I will ever read from him. His last words . . . to me."

Virginio felt withered himself and had nothing left to say. Deep down, he knew Maria was right, but he clung to undying hope, for it was all he had left.

Lilia sat on the walkway under the kitchen window, hearing her parents' every word. Erminio promised he'd be home soon and take her out on a long bike ride, but Lilia knew that day would never come. Her beloved big brother would never return.

Three weeks had passed without any further news from her sons. Maria wished she could steal away to some dark corner of the Earth and let herself feel the anguish she had suppressed for so long. But her younger children needed their mother—and her husband needed his wife.

It was early October. Maria was heating another cauldron of water in the fireplace to fill the shallow oval-shaped wooden tub in the kitchen for Lilia to bathe the boys—their weekly Saturday night ritual. Lilia would wash later, once the boys were put to bed.

"Boys! In the tub," ordered Maria. Undressing the trio was a small affair but having them sit still to wash was another story. Giovanni, Riccardo, and Bruno splashed one another, making waves. Lilia sighed, lamenting over the puddles of water pooling on the kitchen floor, which she would soon need to mop up. Like Cinderella, she felt her life was one long list of chores.

"Ow! You hit me!" yelled Riccardo, rubbing the side of his head.

"I didn't hit you!" Giovanni shrugged his shoulders, feeling he was wrongfully accused.

"Then stop touching my ear—it hurts!" Riccardo elbowed Giovanni away.

"I didn't!" Giovanni elbowed him back.

Trapped between the pushing and shoving, a blast of fear stiffened little Bruno's body. His wide eyes shifted side to side as he watched his brothers fight. His lips quivered and contorted into a pout before he burst into a fit of uncontrollable tears.

"Will you all please stop crying?" Exasperated, Maria dropped the cauldron to the floor. Her nerves had reached their breaking point.

Lilia quickly lifted Bruno out of the tub and into her arms to calm him while Maria towel-dried the other two. She noticed Riccardo twitching his head and sticking his finger in his ear. Maria swatted his hand away and proceeded to wipe him.

"Oweee! Stop, that hurts!" yelped Riccardo as tears coursed down his face.

"What hurts?"

"My ear! My ear hurts!"

Maria drew closer to see what the fuss was all about. "Turn your head this way so I can get a better look." She peered into Riccardo's ear, where she could vaguely make out a foreign object. "Jesus almighty, what did you stick in your ear?!"

Lilia quickly dressed Bruno and helped pull down the flannel pajama top over Giovanni's arms raised high above his head. With a proud smile on his lips, he said, "We put beans in our ears, Mama! Beans from the garden!"

"Why in God's name would you do that?! Riccardo, what did you do? You children are going to kill me!" After further inspection, Maria could see what looked to be a tiny white sprout lodged deep inside Riccardo's ear canal—too far for her to reach. She had no choice but to get him to the doctor. "Don't I have enough things to worry about, and now I have to deal with this, too?" Maria mumbled to herself, chagrined by the night's events. "Maybe I should shake you upside down until the damn thing falls out! That will teach you never to do this again."

At that moment, Virginio sauntered into the kitchen. Seeing the look on his children's faces which signaled that something had gone awry, he asked, "What's going on?"

"What's going on? Your intelligent son put a bean in his ear, that's what. And now, it's sprouted!"

Shielding his mouth, Virginio was torn between concern and laughter.

"Virginio!" Maria darted a deadly look at him.

"I'll take him to Morsano first thing in the morning. Come on, little buddy, come to bed and we'll go see the doctor tomorrow."

The following day, Virginio sat Riccardo on top of his handlebars, and together, they cycled four kilometers to the doctor's office. Upon inspection, the doctor confirmed that the bean had indeed sprouted and come to life inside Riccardo's ear canal. Sniffling back his tears, the four-year-old magician tried to be brave as the doctor tilted his head, and with forceps and a flush of water, removed the bean. The pressure and pain were gone instantly.

"Thank you, doctor—thank you for everything and for taking us right away."

"Not to worry! Children have been putting strange things in their mouths, noses, and ears since the beginning of time. Over the years, I have fished, flushed, and extracted many objects from pencils to toys, coins, and even stones . . . and now—a sprouting bean! Children are born curious and get bored easily, it seems."

"Oh yes, Maria and I know all about that. Lilia once swallowed a twenty-five-cent coin. When she passed it days later, she washed and saved that well-traveled coin for the gelato truck that same afternoon!" Virginio and the doctor both shared a laugh. In a way, Riccardo's shenanigans had brought some levity to a somber few weeks.

The doctor turned to Riccardo. "My dear boy, you are lucky your eardrum wasn't ruptured. Your ears are for listening, and nothing more." Riccardo bowed his head in shame and nodded.

"Thank you again!" Virginio grabbed the doctor's hand with both of his. "Next time you come to Mussons, I'll have a whole chicken ready for you, but for now," Virginio winked, "here's a twenty-five-cent coin tip."

⊷⊙⊚ ⊚⊙⊷

One week passed. It was morning, and Maria was tending to the flower bed in the courtyard. Looking up to the sky, she felt an eerie sensation deep in her bones. A faint light glowed on the horizon.

Clouds had rolled over Mussons during the night, and a dark vapor seemed to be suspended over her house. She could smell the rain. Lilia remained in the kitchen, feeding bowls of warm milk with bread to the boys, while Virginio lay resting in bed, once again suffering from a bout of asthma. At the end of the hall, Eliseo rattled the foundation of the house with his thunderous snoring.

"*Posta*! Mail! Meneguuuuzzi, you have mail!" panted Berto, as he weaved and wobbled his ancient creaking bicycle to the weathered and worn wooden gate.

Maria swung her head up to the sound of Berto trundling up the road. She called out while making her way to the gate, some half-forgotten azaleas in hand.

"Berto, *Bundì*! Good morning! Heavy bag today. You should come inside, take a rest. I have a fresh pot of coffee keeping warm."

"Bundì, Maria! Yes, too heavy," he wheezed. "I have a telegram here from City Hall." Berto paused. "Perhaps one of your boys wrote?" Pausing again, he looked at her apologetically, as her breathing had audibly quickened. "Maria, I could smell the wondrous aroma of your coffee from down the street, but I'm late on my rounds. Give my love to Virginio. Next time for sure. *Mandi*, Bye, Mariiiiaaaa." Waving goodbye, Berto's voice trailed off as he freewheeled his bicycle, which careened with the weight of his mailbag, up the street.

"Ah. Yes. Right. Mandi, Berto." she mumbled, distracted by the envelope in her hands. Maria broke free from her daze, looked up, and waved goodbye to the ever-diminishing mailman as he sped away.

She held the envelope for a beat. Her fingers trembled and fumbled as she tore open the sealed flap, hoping to find positive news from one of her sons. The telegram was from the Italian Military Forces. As Maria scanned the message, words seemed to magnify and ink appeared to grow darker, blending letters, bleeding through the paper and on to her skin. Chills rippled through her body. The light grew dim. Her heart raced. Her arms tingled. She felt weak and unsteady. The earth became a vortex beneath her feet. Maria lost her balance and sank into the gate. She looked up at the vacant sky as the first icy droplet of rain fell and pierced her skin. The telegram slipped from her hands and floated to the ground, landing on the already-scattered azaleas.

Maria clenched the wooden gate and cried out, "Virginio!"

Lilia heard her mother's wail from inside the kitchen, and immediately called out, "Papa!" She pressed her hands and face to the window and saw her mother leaning like a rag doll propped up by the gate. Virginio burst through his bedroom door and scrambled down the stairs.

"Papa, something's wrong with Mama!"

"Stay inside with the boys," he commanded.

Virginio dashed out the front door of the house in a blind panic to the gate, barking, "Maria! Maria! What happened? Did you hurt yourself?"

Maria was leaning against the gate, holding on to the wooden slats for support. Words eluded her, and she could only give her husband a resigned look, which made him feel even more panicked. She pointed to the telegram on the ground as a steady rain began to fall.

Virginio took a deep breath, reached for the telegram, and mentally prepared himself for traumatizing news about one or both of his sons. Battling hope and fear, Virginio closed his eyes for a moment in prayer. "God, let them be alive. Anything. I'll do . . . or give you anything—please let them be alive." Smoothing the hair from his eyes and looking skyward, he allowed his words to marinate the moment.

As he scanned the telegram, a few direful lines glared at him, while the rest receded from view. He read, then blinked hard in disbelief.

Virginio Meneguzzi.
In accordance with the National Service Act,
you are called upon for service in the Royal Italian Army
and are required to present yourself on
Wednesday, 11 November 1942, between 9 a.m. and 12 noon,
or as soon as possible thereafter on that day, to Istria.

The words gripped his head like a vice. He stopped reading. Light and love drained from his face. The raging fire of anger took over. Feeling his soul shift in and out of his body, Virginio dropped to his knees and pulled Maria into his arms. She buried herself into him in silent agony, as if she could meld herself into his core, and that might stop the pain.

Lilia watched from the kitchen window, witnessing her parents' silent dissolution. Her own heart went cold, and a black pit grew in her stomach. She knew what was happening as she watched her parents through the window. Her world was crumbling. One by one, everyone she loved was being ripped from her life.

◦◦◎◎◎◦◦

It was the evening before Virginio's departure. The house echoed silence for the entire day. Even the street noise grew quiet, as if everyone sensed the darkness scattering. Maria vacillated between bitter sadness and wearing a brave face for her children. Resting into a chair against the wall by the kitchen window, she distracted herself by mending the family's clothing. The stark gray light filtered on to Maria's face as she sobbed quietly, the tears seeping through her fingers. She felt as if she were hovering in another world.

Lilia stood back in the doorway as bitter cries fell on her ears. Maria raised a despairing voice to the heavens: "God, what did I do to you? You bring me so much agony. So much pain. This war has my flesh and blood—and now my husband! What more do you want from me?"

Thunder erupted, tearing the sky apart, making Lilia wince. She could not bear to see her mother suffer. *What can I do? How can I take away the pain and make her feel better?* Lilia moved gingerly towards the window. The rain trickled down the glass as tears rolled down Maria's pale face. Lilia could hear her own anxious breathing as her slow steps approached her mother. Kneeling by her side, Lilia stroked her mother's hands.

"Mama don't worry. Papa said not to be scared, that he will be home soon. He said God has a plan and we need to trust in Him."

Unable to turn away from the window, Maria remained fixed on the dark clouds as they mirrored the pain in her soul. "I don't want to talk right now, Lilia. Get the boys ready for bed." The fear of losing Virginio crippled her ability to embrace her family's love.

Lilia cast a forlorn look on her mother, closed her eyes, and bowed her head. "Yes, Mama." Tears leaked from the corners of Lilia's eyes as she shuffled across the great room to the stairs. She felt numb. She knew her father might never return.

What if something happens to Mama? Will I be alone? An orphan? Will I die, too?

In the barn, Virginio was busy carving a piece of basswood, lost in thought over this war and the war that had preceded it. Adrenaline flooded his body. His eyes shuttered as his mind spilled with memories of the first war.

"Virginio!" Eliseo was running towards him, a newspaper over his head and a bottle of wine and two glasses in his free hand. "As it's your last night, how about a drink? You and me! And then I'll leave you to your family."

"Thank you, friend. I need something to calm my nerves. I've been preparing for tomorrow's departure for the last few weeks, but the day has finally come. Sit with me. Pull up a stool." Virginio let out a deep, shaky sigh as his friend poured them both a glass of wine. "Eliseo, I'm forty-four years old . . . forty-four! This country is on the brink of military disaster; otherwise, they wouldn't be calling up men like me. Mussolini is a weak leader and an incompetent—if I could deny this order, I would."

"Yes, but then you'd be a deserter. You won't be any good to your family in prison."

Virginio nodded in agreement as he looked into his glass. He swirled the red wine with a gentle motion of his wrist, revisiting his past and pondering what was to come. Virginio shot back the wine. "Again!" he exclaimed, as he slammed the empty glass upside on his workbench. "I still have visions of the horrid trenches, Eliseo . . . the thick mud, rats, and bitter cold . . . the night-time raids and the stench of death. I thought those memories were long-distant nightmares, and now they're back to taunt me."

"I'm sorry," replied Eliseo as he squeezed Virginio's left arm. "Life can be unfair, Virginio. It rarely makes sense, and it probably never will until we're called back home, back to the *other* side."

Virginio tapped his friend's face and smiled. "I was driven to the brink of insanity once, and I vow not to let this war take me there again. Maria needs me. My children need hope. Watch over them when I'm gone, Eliseo."

"Go be with your family. *Buine gnot*, Good night, Virginio." The two friends embraced for what might have been the last time. Eliseo left Virginio to his thoughts and turned in for the evening.

Buffered by the storm, Virginio peered through sheets of rain to see Maria staring at him from behind the window. He could feel her pain. He knew how much she'd suffered through years of grief and loss. Virginio was guilt-ridden, aware of the torment and mental anguish she would endure without him.

Dashing for the front door, he cut through the pelting rain and into the great room. He was nearly drenched, and a small puddle of water soon pooled by his shoes. The expression in Maria's eyes changed from hurt to anger.

"Maria? My love?" There was no response. "Maria?"

She turned away from him.

"What?" she retorted abruptly.

"I'm going to say goodbye—" he paused, "—good night to our children."

Maria remained silent. With a heavy heart, Virginio climbed the stairway. Step upon step, he wondered how he would protect his children, give them strength, and ease their fear in such an unpredictable time.

Upstairs, Lilia quickly slid on her nightgown and lingered in the hallway, waiting for her father to come and tuck her into bed. She felt more alone than ever. The cold floorboards under her bare feet caused her to shiver and rub her goose-pimpled arms, but outside, the storm was passing. Drawn to the window, Lilia stood high on her tiptoes to gaze at the sky. As clouds parted, her thoughts became lost in the mystery of her ever-changing world.

"God? Why do you let bad people live? And why do you take good people away? Can you not take Hitler and let my papa stay?"

A soft whistle broke the silence and stole her attention.

"Papa!"

Virginio approached his daughter and gave her the biggest smile he could muster. "My little treasure of gold," he smoothed his fingers down her braids "Are the four of you ready for bed?"

Lilia swept her father's wet hair off his face. "Yes, we are." Lilia paused as fear filled her eyes. "Papa, stay! Don't go! Why can't we all run away tonight, and never come back? We can hide in the mountains!"

Virginio knelt and cupped her face in his hands.

"Liliutti, look at me."

She raised her big brown eyes.

"Trust me when I say I will come home." Virginio wiped his daughter's tears away in an attempt to also brush away her concern and his own doubts. "How could I ever miss watching my favorite girl grow up and marry her Prince Charming."

Lilia managed a half smile and fell into her father's protective arms. Peace enveloped her. The rain dwindled, and the moon streamed through the window, casting an aura of calm on their embrace. God's light was present and palpable.

"Come, let's get you to bed."

Virginio watched his children snuggled beneath the covers; their innocent faces pierced his heart. How would they manage in his absence? *What if this is the last time I see and hold my babies?* The dreadful thought looped in his mind—a noise that felt impossible to erase.

"Is everyone ready for a bedtime story?"

"Yes!" they exclaimed in unison.

"All right then, close your eyes and imagine a blue sky, the color of a robin's egg. The hot sun peeking out from behind the clouds. In front of you is a white bridge over a narrow river. Across the bridge, you see a green meadow. The meadow blooms with wildflowers of every color leading up to a hilltop in the distance. Perched on the hill is a graceful weeping willow. Its delicate branches hang low, drifting in the breeze as though they are dancing to a summer song. Leading up to the bridge is a long and winding country road lined with hundreds and hundreds of fluffy, white sheep. One by one, the sheep must cross the bridge to take shelter in the shade under the tree. Every night before you fall asleep, close your eyes and count each little sheep. One sheep, two sheep, three sheep. When they have all crossed and are resting under the tree, Papa will be home to finish telling the story."

Their lids grew heavy. In a sleepy haze, the boys struggled to keep them open so as not to lose sight of their father's loving face. Lulled by Virginio's kind and gentle voice, his sons sank into their pillows and drifted off to dream of fluffy, white sheep. Virginio brushed a kiss on their foreheads one last time.

"How blessed I am to have this precious gift," he whispered. "What good must I have done in this life to deserve this family. God, if you can hear me, protect them, and let your faithfulness be my guide. I will walk with your full armor, stand against this evil war, and return here, where I belong. Should I fall, carry me home, so I may love them a little more while I still can."

Virginio slowly gathered himself and quietly left the room. Unable to sleep, Lilia propped herself up in the bed and with a quivering tone, called out to her father. "Papa?"

Virginio could hear the worry in her voice and turned back. He gently lifted Lilia on to his lap. "Look here—look what Papa has for you." Reaching into his vest pocket, Virginio pulled out a hand-carved four-leaf clover, strung on to a leather cord. "I've been waiting to give this to you, and now seems like the right time." He placed it around Lilia's neck. "Do you remember the day we went snail-picking together by the river, and you found that four-leaf clover?"

"Yes, Papa, I was so sad when I lost it."

"Well, I carved this one for you. Each one of these petals has a special meaning; faith, hope, love, and luck—it's the symbol of the cross." Virginio paused. "You see, Eve brought a four-leaf clover with her when she was expelled from paradise, so anyone lucky enough to wear one has a piece of heaven with them. It will protect you."

Virginio rocked Lilia in a blanket in his arms. Her embrace softened the chill from his damp clothes, while her tears felt warm against his skin. Lilia didn't care that her father was wet. She was where she wanted to be. "Always remember how important and special you are. Never give up on your dreams, for one day you will be blessed with everything you want and deserve. I promise you."

He pressed a tender kiss on her head to silence her sadness. Lilia placed her hand on her father's heart.

"Papa, wherever you are, if you get scared, think of me. I will be right here."

Virginio did all he could to hold back his tears. He held her little hand tight against his chest before tucking her into bed.

Virginio pushed open the shutters a crack and listened to the night wind as it howled, seeming to mimic the turmoil in his mind. How things can change in an instant, he thought. Virginio looked back as the silvery moon cast its light upon his children. The boys lay sound asleep, unaware of their father's plight. Lilia's eyes remained fixed on her father as she sent him silent messages of hope. *Don't die. Come back. I need you.* Virginio's chest rose and fell as he took in his reason for being one last time.

Virginio shuffled down the hallway and heard his wife's soft cries. He peered into their bedroom to see Maria curled up against his pillow, a rosary entwined in her fingers. Overwhelmed with sadness, he bowed his head, kept walking, and crept downstairs.

As he walked through the great room, impending doom consumed his every thought, and the past horrors of war blurred his vision of the future. He lit his lantern, and the soft glow of light brushed over family photos on the walls and buffet, bringing a lump to his throat. Pulling paper out from the buffet drawer, Virginio sat his tired body at the table. He hovered over the blank sheet with quill in hand, put on his wire-rimmed spectacles, and began to write his daughters.

10 November 1942

Dear Ermides,

By this time tomorrow, I will be deployed to Istria. It was sudden and unexpected. Mussolini is enlisting everyone. We've heard no word from your brothers, and now with my leaving, I don't know how your mother will cope. As a husband and father to all my beautiful children, I feel powerless. You are old enough now to understand the brutal realities of war. I have been praying for God's hand to protect me and our family should I not return.

I want you to know how sorry I am your mother and I could never provide you with the life you deserve. Sending you away so young has always been one of my greatest regrets, but perhaps life turned out better where you are. Soon we will need to send Lilia away, too. When the time comes, watch over her. I sometimes feel like I have failed you all.

My beloved daughter, if something should happen to me, be there for your mother. She acts strong and fearless, but at her core, she is frightened, and her shoulders get heavier with each passing moment. If not for Eliseo and your little sister, I don't know how we would survive the days. Write to your mother as often as you can. She loves her children more than life itself and needs your strength. When this war is over, the world will be calm again. We must keep believing and never lose hope.

I want you to know how proud I am of you, and for all you sacrificed in the name of family. We Meneguzzis are strong. Never forget that. May God grant my safe return and bring us all together again.

With all my heart and soul, I love you.

Papa

With one more letter left to write, Virginio stared at his words and the profound reality that he might be facing death shook him to his core. *There is no greater teacher to remind me how precious the wonder of my life is,* he thought. *There is no greater test of the meaning of family.* Maria was at the forefront of his mind: how much he loved her, through all the layers. Even after years of her unwillingness to let go and be vulnerable, and after all her chastising and withholding of affection, he still needed her. More than that, Virginio wanted her. Shortly after he lovingly signed the last of what could be his final letters to his daughters, he made his way back up the stairs. He yearned to hold his wife, soothe her fears, and escape his own.

Virginio found Maria leaned up against her pillow, gazing out the window, and lost in the full moon. He listened as she pleaded for guidance.

"You give, and then you take away? Why do I pray to you if you don't hear me? Help me understand and find the strength to endure."

The moon beamed through scattered clouds in sharp blades of light, illuminating the emptiness in Maria's eyes. Darkness spread through her body. Her thoughts smoldered with despair. She felt the hole in her chest expand as she tried to breathe through the pain. Heavy-hearted, Virginio watched as time and his wife dissolved before him. Maria's strength had always been something he admired, and the reason he had fallen in love with her. With the weight of the years and Virginio's imminent departure, the spark inside Maria was dimming, and it showed. Virginio approached the bed.

"My love, how are you feeling?"

Maria revealed her tear-stained face. It was mixed with emotions; the anger melded with worry. "Virginio, where have you been?"

"I was writing the girls a letter. They need to know what is happening." Drained by the million thoughts circling his brain, Virginio removed his glasses and rubbed his tired eyes. "This war, Maria. Damn this war!"

Maria clenched her lids shut. "Our family is falling apart. What am I to do?"

Her begging for an answer broke Virginio's heart. *I can't save her; I can't protect my children.* He pulled Maria to his chest and held her tight.

"Virginio, how do I do this without you?" Maria drew her face upward, her eyes wide with fear.

"Maria, you won't have to."

"If you don't come back, I'll die without you." Maria swallowed the sadness that welled in her throat as she ran her fingers over his lips. The veneer of hardness, the armor that she was so accustomed to bearing was quickly slipping off her body. "Virginio, tell me this isn't the end."

The intensity of his gaze grew. He wanted her to see everything—his love, his soul. "It's not the end, Maria. Our love? This big love? It will guide me home, back to you, back to our children and us."

Maria inched closer. Parting her lips, she whispered, "Take me away from this hell. Far away. Help me forget, even if just for tonight."

He heard the tremor in Maria's voice and knew he couldn't erase her pain. Tears stung his eyes and fell from his face, mingling with hers. He untied the ribbon from Maria's white nightgown and slipped it off her shoulders, revealing her delicate silhouette. "You're beautiful to me," he breathed against her lips.

Moving his hand through her hair, he removed her pins one by one. Maria's dark silken strands tumbled over her pale skin. Virginio brushed the locks from her face, leaned in, and melted away the sorrow in her heart with his kisses.

Virginio caressed every detail of Maria's body. He pulled her into him—he took in her essence. Several long moments seemed to last an eternity, as they slipped into a universe of their own. Their old, familiar passion swept over them. Maria's inhibitions fell away as they both surrendered to the rhythm and intensity of their love. For a moment, the cave in her heart filled with light, and they swirled among the stars. Maria shuddered in the safety of her husband's arms. She clutched him as tightly as she could, wishing she could hold him in her embrace forever. "Come back to me soon."

"Look there." Virginio pointed out the window. "Wherever we are, that is *our* moon. We will find each other there. Your light and our love will guide me home. We *must* have faith in that."

Maria buried her head in his chest. Soothed by Virginio's words, warmth, and the beating of his heart, she regained hope. Virginio stroked Maria's hair, lulling his beloved into a peaceful sleep.

He himself lay awake until the wee hours, reflecting on his life and all that was at stake. He prayed in silence. *God, only you know my future and that of my sons. Our destiny lies in your hands. Show us the way out of this darkness and back to our family. We need each other. We are not whole without one another.*

The morning finally broke. The stark light filled the room with shadows, drawing attention to the harsh reality of what was to come—the uncertainty of Virginio's fate.

"Maria?" Virginio nudged her back. "Are you awake?"

"Yes, did you sleep?"

"No, but I'm glad you were able to rest. Maria, we don't have much time. I want to keep this morning as normal as possible so as not to frighten the children."

"I was thinking the same."

Virginio was deep in thought, reflecting on whether he'd been a good father, whether he could have done things differently.

"Kids!" hollered Virginio. "Everybody on Mama and Papa's bed!"

"What happened to a *normal* morning?" Maria gave him a sarcastic look.

"I changed my mind." Virginio's response caused a smile to flutter over his wife's lips, despite the heaviness in her heart.

Laughter and loud conversation buzzed in the hallway. Virginio felt overcome by his children's joy. His sorrow was momentarily lifted by the love that resounded in his heart: His family made life sacred, something to be cherished and loved. War was unnatural and pathetic compared to what he knew to be true. He folded his fingers into Maria's and squeezed tight. "I'm a lucky man."

Giovanni, Riccardo, and Bruno skidded to a halt behind their sister, whose arms blocked their entry to their parents' doorway. Lilia stepped one tentative foot into the room, leaned her head in, and looked to her mother for approval. "Mama? Can we?"

Maria looked at Virginio. He squeezed her hand again. "Yes, yes, everybody up on the bed."

The children quickly ran in to snuggle between their parents—a rare and special occurrence.

Virginio glanced at Maria, squeezing her hand yet again. "Try to stay positive while Papa is gone. Take whatever happiness from this life you can and make the best of each moment, knowing you can make the next day even better." Virginio pulled his family into a warm embrace. "You are my world, my strength, my everything."

The morning was beautiful, but it couldn't erase the fact that he was leaving. Soon enough, he was at the gate, prepared to say his goodbyes.

"Come here, my boys." Giovanni, Riccardo, and Bruno rushed into their father's arms. Virginio managed a smile as he hugged them tightly. "Be good to Mama and your sister. And when you've finished counting the sheep, you know I'll be home."

Virginio turned to Maria and grasped her hands. They were clammy, and he could feel her trembling. "Maria, I've loved you for twenty-two years. You and I will be walking the long road together. I know this in my heart."

Tears rained down Maria's face, and her lips quivered. "I will stay strong. For our children."

Virginio caressed Maria's face delicately and kissed her goodbye. "Remember *our* moon. I'll be waiting for you there."

Virginio spied Lilia at the front door, knelt, and beckoned her over. He knew this was hard for her. It was hard for him. Lilia ran to her father and threw her arms around his neck, her shoulders shaking as she wept. Virginio swooped her into a warm hug.

"Remember everything I told you last night."

"Don't leave me!" Lilia blurted through her sobs.

Virginio released his daughter's arms and gave her an assuring smile, "No more tears, right? I'll see you soon." He strapped his army bag across his back and began the long walk towards Morsano to catch the train. Down the road, he turned to capture the image of his family, all huddled together waving from the gate. He wanted their shining light to leave a lasting impression.

"Papa, wait!" Lilia darted towards her father.

"What is it, sweetheart?"

"I almost forgot!" Lilia lifted the four-leaf clover necklace from her neck and placed it around her father's as he bent down before her. "For you, Papa. To protect you, if you get in trouble. I want you to have my faith, hope, and luck—you will always have my love. You need a piece of heaven, too. Papa, I believe every life matters, but yours matters to me most."

Virginio was overcome by emotion as he hugged his daughter one last time and watched her run back to her mother and brothers. He then turned around in the village square giving Mussons a final farewell. Neighboring women and children waved from their windows, and men saluted silently by raising a glass from the bar. In a way, the villagers were delivering him the strength to survive the coming days, and hopefully, make it back to Mussons.

Virginio walked the long dirt road for four kilometers, confident his journey would not end in war. He breathed in, filling his lungs with courage, letting out his fear. He professed to himself, "Heaven can wait. I'll find my way back home."

6 | I WISH I WERE DEAD

೨ಲ Lilia uncovered her eyes from beneath the covers. It was dawn, and she could hear the early morning rapture of chirping sparrows. She rose to her feet, pushed open the shutters, and peered over the ledge to catch their melody. To her ears, their music throbbed with sadness. The ground looked cold and somber, as days of November rain had plastered the courtyard with sodden leaves in muted fall colors. As the drizzle died off, the gray clouds parted, a silver mist hovered, and an occasional spear of sunlight struggled to break through.

With each new daybreak, Lilia felt her brothers' and father's absence that much more. How she wished she could erase time or push it forward! But there was no arguing with Mother Nature, or the unfairness of war.

In the kitchen, Maria sat by the window watching the light bleed through the rain-spattered panes. Over the past days, her sadness had grown heavy like the wet earth. A few of Maria's neighbors were gathered around the table, offering their support and counsel.

"What if Virginio never comes back?" Maria's question silenced the room. "What will I do alone with this house and four small children?" She rubbed her cold, clammy hands as her eyes skimmed the floor. The women watched Maria, and her desperate anguish washed over them.

"I think about him every day—where he is and if he's safe. I promised Virginio I wouldn't lose hope, but this war is becoming greater than even I can bear. God knows I can't go on if he doesn't return. And Arturo? My Erminio?" Her chin trembled, but she quickly willed herself back to steadiness. She refused to expose her raw pain. She needed her walls to be stronger than they'd ever been, now that Virginio was gone.

One of the women pulled her chair close and wrapped her arm around Maria. "They didn't have a choice. You can't change that, but you can choose to keep hope alive. They need you to be strong for them. Your young children need you, too."

A single tear slid down Maria's cheek. When she thought she had no choice but to surrender to her emotions, a little voice called out from the front door, jolting Maria back to reality.

"Hello? Signora Meneguzzi? It's Solidea. Is Lilia home?"

Solidea was Lilia's closest friend—a pretty girl with pale skin, long wavy black hair, and large blue eyes. Lilia mostly saw her at school or when she snuck away to play a game of buttons.

Maria wiped the tear off her face with her apron, quickly pulled herself together, and met Solidea at the entryway. "Good morning, Solidea."

"Good morning, Signora. Is Lilia here?"

"Lilia!" Maria hollered up to her daughter's bedroom. "Your friend is here."

Lilia's hair did a lively dance as she ran excitedly down the stairs. The two girls embraced, and Lilia's grin widened by the second. Finally, a diversion from her sad, lonely thoughts!

"Mama? Can I go play with Solidea in the courtyard?"

"Not now. Carlotta asked me if you would herd their geese to the farm this morning, and they'll herd them back to the pens later. After that, you and I are going to chop and collect wood by the river." Turning on her heel, Maria stalked back into the kitchen, closing the door behind her.

Lilia's shoulders slumped, and a pout formed on her lips. Although unsurprised by her mother's orders, she flashed Solidea a mournful gaze as she scuffed her shoe against the floor. "Mama, can she come with me?" Lilia shouted through the door while looking at her friend.

Solidea nodded and smiled, and her freckled nose crinkled as she whispered, "Yes!"

"All right, but do a good job. We're getting paid for this. Don't lose a goose!"

"I won't, Mama!" Lilia felt less unhappy knowing she wouldn't be alone. "Solidea, come with me to the barn. That's where Papa keeps the pole with the palm-leaf brush. We use that to keep the geese from running away."

As she entered the barn, Lilia was strongly aware of her father's gentle presence. She felt him in everything, from the stool to his hanging tools, which she lovingly ran her hands over. Strands of leather and shavings of basswood lay scattered across the workbench—remnants from the necklace her father had made her. Lilia's eyes quickly glazed over with tears.

"I miss him, Solidea. I miss my papa." Lilia looked up at the sky as tears dripped from her chin. "I'm glad it's an ugly gray day. It would be mean for the sun to come out when he's not here."

Eager to distract her friend from her sadness, Solidea reached over and grabbed Lilia's hand. "Honk! Honk!" she said, as she crossed her eyes, flapped her arms, and ran in circles. The two girls instantaneously burst into laughter.

Down the meandering long and narrow dirt road, Solidea trailed beside Lilia for the one kilometer walk to the edge of Mussons, helping to herd the geese until they reached Carlotta's farm.

"So, what will Carlotta do once she gets these birds?"

"She'll fatten them up. It takes about two hours of them feeding until their necks fill up. That's how they get meaty before Carlotta turns them into Christmas dinner."

"That's so unfair," murmured Solidea, ruminating over the geese's short lives.

A few of the geese drifted off track. "That's life. It's always unfair," replied Lilia as she ran after the fowl and gently thrashed them back in line with her palm leaf.

"They look like an army of soldiers marching." Solidea laughed at the rows of squawking geese.

"At least they're not soldiers marching off to war," Lilia sighed, as dread weighed heavily on her mind.

Feeling her friend's heartache once more, Solidea tried to cheer her up. She waddled behind the geese in imitation, rocking her feet from side to side. "Look, Lilia! Do I look like a goose?"

"Yes, you *are* a goose!" Lilia giggled, appreciating Solidea's attempt to distract her.

At that moment, a villager rode his bicycle up the dusty road, ringing his bell. He frightened the flock of geese into a panic-stricken flurry, forcing them to break rank. They honked, cocked their necks, flailed their wings, and scattered in all directions. Lilia and Solidea frantically halted the wanderers by waving their arms and the palm brush and shouting goose calls. Eventually, they corralled them back into formation and into the field to graze on the winter wheat.

A few hours passed and Lilia was back home preparing for a new experience, one that would soon become her most trying duty. With Virginio gone, Maria's workload had doubled, and Lilia was next on the pecking order when it came to handling the household responsibilities.

Lilia was a child who worked tirelessly. Hauling heavy bags of flour, balancing yokes with pails of water, hand-washing laundry on the washboard basin, scrubbing floors, cooking, and carrying Bruno since she was a young child herself had all but permanently displaced

Lilia's right hip and shoulder. Still, she received no respite from the onslaught of chores that needed to be done.

With the cold, winter months soon approaching, the fireplace was the family's only source of heat to warm the house and boil water for bathing and cooking. In the fall, heavy rains sent floodwater and tree branches surging down the hills into the Tagliamento River. As the branches washed up on the riverbed and dried along the muddy embankment, the locals chopped and fetched wood, carrying them home on their backs. On this gloomy day, Lilia accompanied Maria for the first time.

"Here, wear these in your shoes." Maria tossed Lilia a thick pair of long woolen socks that Lilia pulled up to her knees. She slid back into her wooden clogs and anchored her feet with the wrap-around leather straps.

"Why do I have to wear these? I don't like them—they're itchy!" Lilia whined in discomfort.

"You'll scrape and cut your feet if you don't! We'll be walking through thorny fields while gathering dry wood. Keep them on until I tell you to take them off."

Lilia had already prepared herself for increasingly difficult responsibilities during her father's absence. Still, she was excited to help her mother on what felt like a new adventure. It gave Lilia a reprieve from household chores and tending to her brothers, who on this occasion, were under the watchful eye of Eliseo. Lilia hoped that if she could take on a typical man's work and do it well, she'd finally earn Maria's love. After all, a mother's love had to be earned. But it was all to no avail; time and again, no matter what Lilia did, she felt rejected and unappreciated—her efforts went unnoticed.

Maybe I'll never be good enough for her, Lilia often thought to herself. But as discouraged as she felt, she never gave up attempting to please her mother.

Maria gave Lilia the small axe with the shorter handle—the one Virginio used to chop kindling. Within several hours, they dragged and trimmed branches and chopped them into manageable-sized firewood while seagulls hovered overhead in pursuit of sardines in the river.

"Mama, what do we do with all these pieces of wood now?"

"We're going to tie them together and carry the bundles on our backs. Once we leave the field, take off your socks and clogs, or you'll lose your balance."

As she walked barefoot from the grass to the main road, Lilia felt the cold, wet mud gurgle and squelch between her toes. She used the wool socks to tie her clogs to the bundle, and Maria placed a layer of burlap over Lilia's shoulders to keep her bones from breaking. Together, they trudged for three kilometers until they made it home.

Little did Lilia know she would be fetching and carrying wood bundles alone twice a day on foot until snow covered the ground. She strived to bring more than the required firewood back for the winter months, always with the hope of making her mother proud. On the rarest of occasions, she would hear Maria say, "You see? Look what a good girl you are." Those magical words were enough to motivate Lilia to push far beyond what any child her age should have been expected to.

From time to time, Lilia's chores surfaced unexpected—and unwanted—encounters. One in particular haunted her for weeks and months to come.

On one of her treks, Lilia carried heavy bags of flour on foot to the only bakery in the nearby town of St Paulo, three kilometers away. The flour was weighed and traded for fresh loaves of bread she brought back to the family. Walking towards home, Lilia noticed a scruffy, unkempt, shriveled homeless man. He had a scraggly beard and a tangled lion-like mop of hair, and he was urinating on the side of the road. She could smell his pungent stench as it wafted in the breeze. She screwed up her nose in automatic disgust. Still, she was curious, and paused to take in this strange vision for as long as she dared look. She was full of questions. *What is he doing? Why is he so dirty? Who is he?* The befuddled man appeared drunk, He stood there swaying and singing through mumbled laughter. When he managed to zip his pants, he noticed Lilia and shuffled towards her on unsteady legs. A toothless smile formed on his grimy, wrinkled face.

"Heeeeeeey, little girl," he slurred. "How about some of that bread . . . or some of this?" Without shame, he removed his pants and exposed himself.

Lilia's eyes bulged with shock and terror, and adrenaline rushed through her veins. She felt as if she could neither breathe nor move a muscle. A scream barely escaped her throat. And she knew there was no one around to hear or save her. Bags dropped from her arms, sending one of the loaves of fresh, warm bread rolling out on to the ground. Terrified by the encounter, all thoughts of her mother punishing her for losing an entire loaf of bread were non-existent. In the flurry of the moment, she wobbled backwards, nearly tripping over herself and on to the gravel road. Lilia grabbed the bag of remaining bread and ran for home as fast as her legs would take her. All she could feel and hear was her feet pounding the ground, the racing of her heart, and the fading sounds of the old man's cackle.

She took a final backward glance and saw him kneeling in the middle of the street, ravaging the bread like a wild animal. "Thank you!" he called out. "You're a good and kind girl."

Lilia's lashes blinked heavy with tears all the way home as his words echoed in her thoughts. The words that should have come from her mother and not the mouth of a roaming derelict.

৩ঙ ঙৎ

It was January 5, the day before the Feast of the Three Kings: the Epiphany. Italians celebrated the Epiphany with *La Befana*—the Christmas witch. As the legend was told, La Befana was a witch who flew the skies on her tattered broomstick, swooping down chimneys to deliver sweets to children, hiding them in their shoes while they slept. If children were well-behaved, they received cookies, candies, nuts, and fruit, while naughty children were given lumps of coal—typically in the form of dark-colored candy. The witch had been an Italian tradition since the eighth century, long before St Nicholas was even a twinkle in his mother's eye.

Year after year, by the crack of dawn, Lilia and her siblings would make a mad dash for their parents' bedroom, dump their shoes on the bed, and count their treasures, sharing what the witch had brought them.

With Virginio gone, Maria's father, Giovanni, came to spend a few days with his daughter and grandchildren. Maria typically visited him a few times per month in Romans, a village that was an hour's walk away, across the Tagliamento. On occasion, Lilia joined her mother.

"Nonno! Nonno's coming!" Lilia hollered from the front gate to alert her family as she watched her grandfather pedaling his way up Via della Chiesa on his bicycle, ringing his bell. The front door burst open as the boys came running outside and Maria trailed behind. It was the first time Maria had seen her father since Virginio was called to war.

Giovanni made friends everywhere he went and kept them with ease. His blue eyes twinkled in the sunlight, and his bushy black brows rose high above his silver wire-rimmed glasses when he smiled. The villagers welcomed his arrival with open arms, as he always drew out the best in people with his kindness, generosity, and willingness to listen.

A man in his seventh decade, Giovanni had earned his wrinkles from raising nine children alone. His wife, Dina, died at the age of forty-seven from appendicitis when Maria was giving birth to her firstborn at the age of nineteen. For Maria, the loss of her mother and the added burden of helping to raise her siblings as well as her own children left a bitter taste in her mouth. Any dreams she'd even remotely had vanished altogether.

"Hey, look at all those beautiful faces! It's a good thing it hasn't snowed yet, otherwise your ol' grandpa may not have made it," Giovanni laughed at the limitations and losses that accompany old age as he carefully dismounted his bicycle.

"What did you bring us?"

"Yes! What did you bring?"

"Did you bring something for me, too?"

"Chocolate?"

"That's enough! Don't be so greedy. Let Nonno get through the gate!" Maria scolded her children. "Go inside, and Nonno and I will come in shortly." The children retreated into the kitchen, waiting patiently as their mother had a moment with her father.

"Let's put your bike in the barn," Maria offered.

Giovanni's back hunched in fatigue, and he grimaced with each step. "I'm getting too old to ride," he chuckled, scratching the fringe of white hair on his balding scalp. "Life at my age is not as forgiving as it once was. My aches are becoming my constant companions."

Giovanni gave his daughter his arm and leaned on her as he walked his bicycle through the courtyard. He leaned it up against a haystack in the barn. "How are you, my dear? It's been weeks since I've seen you." The tight grip she routinely kept on her emotions had always concerned him, but now more than ever.

Maria raised her eyes to her father. "My man. My boys. They're all gone, and I'm terrified. I feel abandoned and beaten by life. This *miserable* life."

Sadness filled his heart as he heard the pain and bitterness in his daughter's voice. Giovanni brushed his hand over her hair, and for the first time in years, he saw the frail and vulnerable parts of Maria. Not one who was given to words, he pulled Maria into his arms, offering her head a soft, safe place to land. A tide of emotions swept over her, and in the loving warmth of her father's arms, she wept tears the rest of the world would never see.

Minutes passed, and the children called out for their grandfather. "Come on, Nera," he said, using the fond nickname he'd always called his raven-haired daughter. "Dry up that face. I have a pocket full of chocolate about to melt to my toes." Giovanni gently grabbed her by the chin and lifted her face. "You have a little army in there that still needs you. Don't forget that."

Maria broke eye contact with her father, unwilling to accept any potential maternal failings on her part.

"They should feel lucky and grateful," Maria shot back. "Life is hard, and like me, they have to learn to deal with it. The sooner, the better—it'll prepare them to be strong for future difficulties."

The children rushed to the front door eager to see what their grandfather had brought them.

"Let's see, what do I have here?" Giovanni reached deep into his pocket and pulled out four bars of chocolate. "And they're still in one piece!"

The look of surprise on the children's faces was priceless. Grateful for the gift, they thanked their grandfather and tore off to huddle in the far corner of the great room. The children excitedly ripped open the wrappers, shoving the chocolate in their mouths. Luscious, rich cocoa swirled over their tongues, a sensation they would not soon forget.

"Now, don't eat too much of that chocolate, otherwise La Befana won't leave any treats in your shoes tonight!" Maria warned from across the room.

"Yes, Mama!" replied the boys, staring at each other anxiously, the chocolate already smudged across their lips. Lilia nodded back at her mother, sealing her lips together, hiding her chocolate-smeared fingers behind her back.

Close to bedtime, Lilia and her siblings set out the traditional glass of red wine and a plate of food on the fireplace hearth, grateful for La Befana's long-anticipated arrival. The children soon rushed upstairs and put on their pajamas, but not before each placed one of their shoes on the open windowsill of their parents' bedroom, ready to count the hours like sheep until morning when their mother would wake them with the news: "La Befana came! Go see what she left in your shoes!" Giovanni escorted his grandchildren to their rooms and watched as they scurried under the covers.

"Nonno?" asked Lilia. "Will you tell us the story of La Befana? Papa always does, but . . ." her voice trailed off.

"Yes, of course. I'd be happy to. Come, sit close to me." The children threw off their blankets and clustered around their grandfather as he told the tale they all loved so much.

"Nearing the Epiphany, the Three Wise Men—Gaspar, Balthasar, and Melchior—knocked on La Befana's door asking for directions to Bethlehem. They were searching for a bright star, which was believed to lead them to the newborn king. The Wise Men wanted to pay homage and offer gifts. They invited La Befana to join them.

Never having heard of Bethlehem, she rejected their invitation. Days later, La Befana noticed an unusually bright star. Its energy filled her with warmth and love. Curious, she decided to follow it. Filling her basket with freshly baked cookies, candies, nuts, and fruit, she traveled to village after village after village. La Befana could not find Bethlehem, nor the King.

To this day, La Befana is still searching. Year after year, on the Epiphany, she flies across the sky on her broom, filling children's shoes with sweets, hoping to one day find the Baby King of Bethlehem. But remember, she only comes when children are asleep in their beds until morning! Now, crawl into bed and sleep tight!"

Giovanni gave them a light pat on their backs. "Goodnight, you four."

"Goodnight, Nonno!" The children crawled back into their beds, content to feel the warm and comforting presence of their grandfather, which added a much-needed air of celebration to their home.

The boys soon succumbed to the call of sleep, but Lilia tossed and turned, unable to resist the temptation to see La Befana for herself. On a typical night, between finishing homework and reading her fairy tales, sleeplessness tormented her. This night, while her brothers counted fluffy white sheep, Lilia was determined to spy on La Befana.

Thinking she heard footsteps on the roof, Lilia's heart thumped in her chest.

La Befana is here!

Envisioning the witch flying her broom through the chimney and up the stairs to fill her shoes made Lilia breathless with excitement and a little fear.

I shouldn't be scared. After all, La Befana is a good witch. And I'm a good girl, so my shoes will be full of sweets!

When she made sure the coast was clear, Lilia tiptoed down the hallway, careful not to make a sound. With a moonless sky and little light filtering through the window, the corridor was swathed in darkness. As she flitted to her parents' room, she saw the door was slightly ajar. Cautiously, Lilia peered through the crack. To her surprise and dismay, she witnessed her mother filling everyone's shoes with treats. Lilia touched her fingers to her lips, let out a gasp, jumped back, and flattened herself against the wall.

La Befana was nothing but a myth, after all!

Lilia tried to inch her way back to her room while escaping detection. Although she felt sad to discover the ruse, she also felt guilty for spying on her mother. She hunched over and crept slowly along.

"Lilia! What are you doing?"

Lilia froze, trapped. She had no choice but to turn around and face the *real* Befana.

Maria stood tall in the middle of the dark hallway, her fists on her waist. Lilia could only see the slight glow of her mother's white apron and the gleam in her eyes.

She swallowed back her fear. "I—I couldn't sleep."

"Come here!"

Lilia sheepishly dragged herself over to her mother. Maria grabbed Lilia by the arm and pulled her into the room.

"Now, since you misbehaved and did precisely what your grandfather told you *not* to do, you're going to help me fill these shoes. And you can forget about putting your shoes out ever again. This year is your last, young lady."

Lilia felt her cheeks flush as she gulped back her tears. Instead of distributing candies, nuts, and fruit into her brother's shoes, she wished she could be safe in her room, counting fluffy white sheep. She missed her papa so much.

⁓⌾⌾⁓

Weeks passed, and for Maria, almost every night was filled with nightmares. Her sleep was tormented by visions of Virginio and her sons at war. They were running towards her in spite of their injuries, screaming her name. Each time she tried to reach out to touch them, they sank farther away, back into a tunnel of darkness. Maria cried out to them, but her voice carried no weight, no sound. Her cries woke her up. She was soaked in sweat that reeked of fear. She felt sick to her stomach as she pushed open the shutters to a thick, opaque fog that blotted out her view. The clouds lay low, and she wondered if she were still in her dream, floating somewhere between heaven and hell.

Maria hung her head out the window and tried to breathe out her anxiety. It was February 19: the birthday of both Maria and her son Erminio, who would be twenty-one today. "Happy birthday, my son," she whispered, praying he could somehow hear her silent wishes.

Every memory of Erminio played like a song in Maria's head. An integral piece of her heart couldn't find its beat without him. To Maria, he was everything beautiful in this miserable world.

"I miss you," she breathed a heavy sigh.

Moments later, a faint yellow light bled through the fog, and Maria could barely make out a green vehicle parked outside her home. She quickly threw her clothes on and ran outside. The court-yard was veiled in a heavy mist as her eyes traveled to the gate. The cool, damp, morning air seeped through her clothes and gripped her bones. She could make out the figure of a man in uniform as she drew closer. Her heart raced with hope, and then dread. Maria opened the gate to an officer from the Italian Army.

"Maria Meneguzzi?"

"Yes, yes, what is it?"

"I have an important message to deliver from the Secretary of the Army. May we go inside?"

"Yes, of course."

Upon entering the front door, the officer hesitated before saying, "It's best you be seated."

Maria stood tall, unflinching. "I prefer to stand." She already knew by his demeanor he was delivering grim news.

He pulled out an official document from the war office and proceeded to read. "The Secretary of the Alpine Troops Command has entrusted me to express his deepest regret that your son, Private Erminio Meneguzzi, is presumed to have been killed in action. This presumption was made under the Missing Persons Act in Stalingrad on 2 February 1943. The Secretary extends his deepest sympathy to you and your family for your loss."

Maria swallowed hard, her black hair now framing a deathly pale face. "Missing person? *Missing person*! What does that mean?"

"He's missing in action, Signora Meneguzzi. The Soviet troops launched an offensive attack on Stalingrad in early January. Your son was on the front lines. The attack ended with Germany surrendering, and your son's body was never found. I'm sorry, Signora."

"Then he could still be alive!" she protested, shaking her head as if it could ward off the horrible truth in front of her.

"He is presumed to have been killed in action, Signora, but yes, he is declared missing in action."

Maria glared at the young man, wishing she could spit the venom that was in her heart at him. *Who are you? What makes you so special that you get to live, and my son doesn't? What do you know about being a mother? How dare you take away my hope!*

Maria turned her back and walked away from the soldier. Unsteady, she braced herself against the dining-room table and gazed longingly at the framed photo of Erminio on the buffet.

"Get out of my house," she said quietly.

"Is there another next of kin or adult in your home, Signora Meneguzzi?"

"Eliseo. He lives with us. He's upstairs with my children."

"Perhaps, you should ask him to join us. It will be best if someone is here with you."

"Get out of my house!" She couldn't bear to look at this young man, who seemed to her barely older than Erminio.

The young officer nodded, but his heart was full of unwept tears. He felt like the messenger of doom. Maria was the first of many mothers he had to visit that day, and this was a torment he hadn't been prepared for. He thought of his mother and how much she loved him. The young officer turned and walked away, disappearing into the fog from which he had come.

Eliseo, Lilia, and the boys had heard Maria's yelling. As they ran downstairs, their pace quickened. They found Maria in the courtyard walking around in circles, calling her son's name in the mist, over and over. "Erminio, where are you?"

Lilia immediately ran to her mother. She had already intuited the news, and her big little heart crackled like glass. Eliseo tried to hold the boys back at the door, but they broke free and ran to their mother. Eliseo felt drained by his sadness as he watched the cold white blanket of death swallow Maria and her children.

In the days that followed, neighbors arrived to leave food and offer their help, but Maria was inconsolable.

"Maria, he's missing in action. There's still hope!" said one of the women.

"My Erminio froze to death in the snow. He's never coming back." Maria touched the kitchen window with her hand, hoping Erminio could feel it and touch her back wherever he was.

"Don't lose hope, Maria."

"Thank you—all of you." Maria's back remained turned. "I want to be alone with the memory of my son."

Maria's grief had hollowed her, almost as if she didn't exist at all. Over the months of sleepless nights and compounded worry, she had aged profoundly. Her face was gaunt, and the luster had left her hair. Even her steps were more labored with each step she took. Her eyes had grown sullen and blazed with anger and disdain.

Later that day, as she sat on the edge of her parents' bed, Lilia held in an ocean of tears and released her despair to Little Rose. As usual, the doll was propped up against the far wall atop Maria's chest of drawers, perpetually out of reach.

"Arturo left, Papa is gone, and Erminio might be in God's hands now. And . . . I lost you, too." Lilia's bottom lip quivered. "I feel sad and scared all the time, Little Rose. Even when the sun comes out, it's dark and cold. I was happier when Papa was here."

Slowly but surely, Lilia's anger—which she'd held in for so long—bubbled up to the surface. She clenched her fists tightly by her sides as she swallowed her tears. "I try to be honest, good, and kind—I do whatever I'm told! I—I work *so* hard!" Lilia lifted her eyes to Little Rose, as if begging for answers. "Why is the world so *mean*? Why is God taking everyone away from me? I'm just a girl!"

Lilia threw herself on to the bed and smashed her face into the pillow, as if to hold back the tide of tears that threatened to drown her. As she wrapped her arms around her father's pillow, memories of him and her older brothers raced towards her, drenching her in even more sadness.

"My heart hurts every time I think of you. I miss talking and laughing the way we did. There's no one to hug me—no more good-night kisses. I don't matter to anybody any more!" Desolate sobs escaped her. She was drained of hope. She knew there was nobody to hear her, and nobody to respond. And Little Rose simply stared at Lilia with glassy, unfeeling blue eyes.

"I miss you so much it hurts."

ﻼﻻﻩﻭ

March 1943

Like a shallow wave, the first wash of spring awakened the sleeping winter giant in Mussons. Patches of snow melted throughout the courtyard and tiny blades of grass peeped up, struggling to rise a little higher. The sun was warm that day, and the light breeze rustled the blooming fig tree and the unfurling leaves of the hedges that bordered the fence and garden path where Maria was planting her root vegetables.

Lilia was upstairs pulling bedsheets off the beds, while Giovanni and Riccardo accompanied Eliseo on his client deliveries. Bruno was playing in the courtyard with his friend Pia, the neighbor's three-year-old daughter. She had wandered in barefoot from across the street. Pia's mother had ten illegitimate children, which she pawned off on others and neglected far too often. A quiet child, Pia's face and hands were grimy, her long blonde hair matted and straggly, and her once-white dress now tattered and gray.

Early that morning, Bruno had watched Lilia chop kindling on the wooden stump by the barn, which fascinated him. Bruno loved the motion of his sister's arm raising the small axe, the force of its downward swing, and the sound the wood made as it split. The splitting axe was left leaning up against the stump. As the sun danced along the length of the blade, the flashing light caught Bruno's eye, luring him to pick up the axe.

"Pia, want to help me chop wood?"

"Sure!" Pia grabbed a thin but long piece of wood. "Bruno, I hold it and you chop it?"

After each chop and before every swing of the axe, Pia moved her grip up. "Bruno, chop, chop!" As Bruno raised the axe high with both hands, down came the blade hard and fast, right on Pia's thumb, swiftly cutting it off. A fountain of bright-red blood surged everywhere, bleeding on to Pia's dress, gushing between Bruno's fingers, and mingling with the snow-covered ground.

From the force of the blade, Pia's thumb went flying over the adjoining chain-link fence and into the neighbor's garden. Shocked at the sight of the blood and her missing digit, Pia let out a primal scream, echoing her pain into the air. Terror filled Bruno as he saw Pia in hysterics, blood-spattered across her face. His cheeks turned beet red as he sat frozen in place, sobbing and shaking. Alarmed neighbors craned their necks to locate the raw cries.

Maria and Lilia ran towards the barn. "Oh my God, what did you do?!" Maria screamed in horror. Fear permeated Bruno, who was still gripping the axe tightly in his hand. Maria grabbed the axe and rushed Pia into the house.

Lilia held her little brother tightly and rubbed his back, desperately trying to calm him outside, while Maria bandaged Pia's bloody hand as best she could. A tide of fury coursed through her, leaving Maria no choice but to reach for her willow branch, the one she kept leaning in the corner by the front door, and run on to the street, calling out to Pia's mother.

"Giovanna! You ugly whore! Where the hell are you? Do you even know where all your children are? Pia is hurt! Get over here, *now*!" Maria's elevated voice carried up and down Via dell Chiesa—everyone could hear her outrage.

Giovanna dashed out of her house and across the street, still in her nightgown and robe. She was disheveled and stank of stale alcohol and sex. Giovanna followed Maria into the kitchen and, through confused, bleary eyes, stared at her daughter . . . and her dazed state soon gave way to shame and horror. She stood frozen, unsure of what to do.

"For the love of God!" Maria was ready to throttle her. "What are you *doing*? Get your daughter to the doctor! Take our bicycle!"

Giovanna blinked, as if to clear her shock. Without a word, she lifted her daughter on to the handlebars and quickly pedaled to Morsano and the nearest doctor.

After calming and putting Bruno to bed, Maria and Lilia immediately split up to search for Pia's lost thumb. High and low, on their hand and knees, they rummaged through every square inch of the snow-patched courtyard—but there was no sign of the appendage.

"But Mama, where could it be? How far could it have gone?"

"You're asking *me*? Where were *you* when this all happened?" Maria's eyes narrowed in irritation.

Cornelia, the neighbor's daughter, overheard the day's events and joined the search party. Moments later, as she bent over her mother's garden, Cornelia discovered Pia's small bloody thumb cradled in a crinkled cabbage leaf. "Maria, Maria! I found Pia's thumb!" She quickly wrapped the thumb in her handkerchief and passed it to Maria through the fence. "They probably can't reattach it, but I'm sure Giovanna will be happy to have it back!"

"Poor Bruno," Maria sighed. "This day will forever be imprinted in his memory."

"Well, maybe when Pia grows up—sadly, without a thumb—Bruno can repent for what he did and marry the girl," a wry chuckle escaped Cornelia's lips while Lilia stood quietly by the adjoining fence. Maria was too irritated to laugh. She was mostly angry at Lilia for not being more careful and attentive, and to that whore Giovanna for being such a terrible mother.

"Lilia! What were you doing while this mess was happening?" Maria questioned once again.

"Mama, it was an accident. And I was upstairs trying to—" Maria whacked her daughter across the head before she could continue to justify herself.

"What did I tell you about leaving tools outside the barn? Look what Bruno did because of your carelessness! Look what happened to that poor girl's finger!" She shook her daughter, who rattled around in her arms like a helpless rag doll.

Lilia couldn't take it any more. "It wasn't my fault! I carried the wood home from the river. I chopped the kindling like you asked me to. I'm tired of you hitting me. It was an accident! *You're* his mother—where were *you*?!" Lilia's tears flowed uncontrollably as the harsh words, which couldn't be taken back, erupted from her.

"With a mouth like that, you'd better run, young lady. Do you hear me?!" Maria remained unshaken by her daughter's boldness as she stood tall and unforgiving, hands on her hips.

Lilia felt like a wild stream had been let loose. "I hate you! I hate you!"

Maria grabbed her willow branch, and Lilia made a fast break. She burst through the gate and sprinted down the street while her mother thundered behind her.

"Get back here and wash that mouth out with soap!" Maria chased her daughter while waving her infamous willow branch all the way from Mussons and into the next village of Villanova.

Gasping for air, Lilia eventually doubled over. She was small and tough, but she knew she could no longer outrun her determined mother. *If I'm not punished now, I will be later.*

She stopped running and gave in to the force of her mother's frustration in silence. Lilia's only form of protection was to cover her head with her arms. She closed her eyes and prayed her punishment would soon be over. Unrelenting, Maria whipped Lilia's neck, shoulders, and legs until all her anger and strength were finally drained.

"You disrespectful child! I told you to behave! I gave you so many chances! But you never listen!"

Maria went on like that for several long moments, but as quickly as it had begun, the beating stopped. Lilia released her arms from her head and slowly turned around. Maria had walked away—her head was bowed, her hands clenched into tight fists by her side.

Over the following days, a wall of silence grew between them. The tension in the air was thick, and conversation was minimal. Lilia was unsure of how to react, so she measured her every word and obeyed Maria as best she could. She felt she had no choice but to resign herself to the awful truth: her mother hated her.

⁓ေ ၅⁓

It was mid-June, and with the school year nearing its end, Lilia's work doubled. Between her homework and the relentless duties in the house, Lilia frequently arrived late to class. Each night, Lilia collapsed into a deep slumber with her schoolbooks and pencil in hand. Many nights, Lilia traded her sleep to read her fairy-tale books—her escape from the drudgery and harshness of the real world . . . her world.

"Lilia! Go to sleep!" Maria could see a thin line of light under her daughter's door. It wasn't the first time.

"Yes, Mama."

Lilia played the waiting game. She blew out the lantern and patiently bided her time until the house fell silent. Anxious to return to her reading, Lilia crawled out of bed and laid towels on the floor to cover the gap beneath her door, cleverly preventing the light from seeping back into the hallway.

Lilia loved these enchanting stories of handsome knights and beautiful princesses. Lost in tales of old, Lilia dreamed of herself coming to life in the pages of her books. Since her existence mirrored Cinderella's, Lilia felt a temporary assurance that one day her prince would come to save her. It was the only ray of hope and fleeting joy that shone on to her life.

She read into the wee hours of the morning. As she finally closed her book, contentment washed over Lilia, and her heart slowed to a tranquil beat. Lilia was quietly lured into a peaceful sleep when she sprung awake, as if she'd been disrupted out of bed by an earthquake. And indeed, she had been—by her mother, the epicenter of Lilia's life.

"Lilia! Wake up! It's six o'clock." Maria stood impatiently waiting at the bottom of the stairs. "Hurry up! You have things to do! Hang the clothes I washed! And the boys are here waiting for their breakfast. Come on, quickly, before school!"

Barely conscious, Lilia nodded off again. Lost in a lucid dream, she imagined herself as the imprisoned girl from one of her books, trapped in a tower without doors. *Rapunzel, Rapunzel, let down your hair, so that I may climb thy golden stair.*

"Lilia!!"

Lilia's eyes sprung wide open again. Praying to steal a few more minutes of sleep, she stomped her feet loudly on the wood floor, alerting her mother that she was awake and in motion. Crawling back under the sheets, she pulled them over her head and wished the entire universe would disappear. Clinging to her pillow, she held on to precious time.

"Lilia! What are you doing? Move it!"

Lilia immediately leaped out of bed. Bleary-eyed and semi-conscious, she stared vacantly at pages of homework scattered on the floor. Still fuzzy, Lilia rubbed her eyes and sank into a momentary depression. Sitting at the edge of the bed, she watched as her pale, scrawny legs dangled. *The moment my feet touch the ground,* she thought, *I am no longer me, but whatever and whoever everyone else wants me to be.*

"I hate my life," Lilia mumbled aloud.

She quickly pulled herself together. As she pushed open the tall green shutters of her bedroom window, the sweet scent of red crown-of-thorn flowers wafted in from the courtyard and invigorated her. The flower was said to be a good omen that foretold the luck of those who grew it.

As the soft light of the morning sun rose on Lilia's face, she paused in prayer and lifted her tired eyes heavenward. "God? Are you there? Can you hear me? Why can't I be like other kids? Does Mama love me less than my brothers? Maybe if I were a boy, she would love me more." Her eyes glimmered with tears as she poured her heart out to God and the angels. "Sometimes, I think it would be better if I were dead. Day after day, I do whatever I can to listen to Mama, to be a good girl, but I don't know how much longer I can take it."

"Lilia! This warning is your last!"

"Coming, Mama!"

After plowing through her morning routine, Lilia gathered her stack of textbooks and papers and made the mad race off to school. As she sat quietly on the hard concrete steps of the building's entryway, Lilia fanned her homework out across her lap to study for the last few minutes before class started. She watched as her three closest friends—Solidea, Dolores, and Lydia—played skip rope and spun their hula hoops. It didn't seem fair that they were so happy when she felt like Cinderella, trapped with no escape. Lilia wished someone, anyone, could feel her pain.

Admiring the sea of pretty dresses twirling before her, their colors bright and cheerful, her eyes turned to the scuff marks on her old shoes and the faded blue on her hand-me-down smock. Her envy faded into sadness. She was glad her friends didn't have to live in her world and feel her loneliness. Their smiles and laughter simultaneously warmed and broke Lilia's heart. She continued with her lessons and swallowed the lump in her throat.

Lilia spent the morning studying mathematics and science—neither her best nor her favorite subjects. She loved literature and was frequently asked to stand up and read to her classmates, but this day, the lessons demanded too much of her attention. She drifted off into a daydream but quickly returned at the sound of the recess bell signaling the mid-morning half-hour break of their five-hour school day. The air filled with excitement as children burst through the classroom and raced for their spots on the playground. The girls played hopscotch while the boys gathered for a game of kickball.

"Hey, Lilia, come play with us!"

Lilia gave her friends a longing look. She desperately wanted to join in the fun but knew that she couldn't.

"Next time, I promise." Lilia masked her pain behind a smile. She knew a familiar piercing alarm of a different kind would soon steal any hard-earned moments of freedom.

"Lilia!" Maria waved her hands at the front gate where everyone could see her. Almost every recess, she waited for Lilia to return home and get through yet another series of chores.

Lilia's heavy lids closed as she gave a long, weary sigh.

I'll be old like Mama before I ever know what it feels like to be happy. Nobody sees me. I'm invisible.

She wished she could melt into the ground. Having her mother calling for her day after day was mortifying. She scurried home to avoid further embarrassment.

Lilia didn't understand why Maria was so mean to her. She seemed more like one of the wicked stepmothers from her fairy tales than a true mother . . . a mother who was warm, nurturing, kind . . . a mother who could easily fill a young girl's heart with joy and appreciation . . . a mother who could take away all her sorrows with a simple embrace and words of comfort.

Sapped of her energy, Lilia prepared to plod back to school after minding Bruno, while her mother took the other boys and tended to errands.

"Square those shoulders and stand up straight!" Maria scolded Lilia, swatting her back on her way out of the gate. "You'll grow crooked!"

"Yes, Mama."

"And when you get home from school, I need you to carry the bags of flour to the bakery before they close. Don't be late!"

"Yes, Mama." Lilia's eyes screwed shut with dread at her mother's request. She shivered with the thought of running back into the drunken vagrant who had made his disgusting gesture almost a year ago. Lilia felt defeated by a life that wasn't and never would be hers.

She sat ever so studiously at her desk that afternoon, concentrating on completing a math test before the end of class. Anxiety permeated the room as the teacher, Signore Maestro, kept a watchful eye over his students. "Fifteen more minutes," he said. The children watched the big hand on the clock leap ahead. "Pencils down. Turn your sheet over."

Silvano, a boy who sat behind Lilia, tapped her on the shoulder in a panic, hoping for the answer to a question. Lilia turned to offer her help. As Lilia turned back to her desk, she spotted the teacher's shiny black shoes before her. Her heart leaped to her throat.

"Lilia, give me your hands!" he commanded.

"No, Signore Maestro! Please, I was trying to help, and—"

The teacher forcibly stretched out both her hands on the wooden desk and struck them with his knotted walking cane. Paralyzed in their seats, the other children watched in horror.

"This will teach you to behave in class! That goes for all of you!"

Lilia's hands swelled and turned every shade of purple. She cried uncontrollably, barely able to catch her breath. This was the first time her teacher had punished her. Lilia jumped up, nearly knocking over her desk, and ran all the way home. She shook her hands, hoping to relieve the throbbing pain. As Lilia approached the gate, she cried out to her mother. Maria was sitting on a wooden chair outside the front door, her straw basket resting on her lap. She was nimbly snapping the tips off green beans. "Mama, Mama! My hands hurt!"

Alarmed by her daughter's frantic state, Maria sprung to her feet, putting the basket on the chair. "Lilia, what did you do?!"

"Signore Maestro hit me! Mama, I did nothing wrong! I promise! I was a good girl, Mama, I was good! I was helping Silvano."

Lilia heard her own raw sounds as they penetrated the air. For a moment, she searched her mother's eyes for any sign of comfort . . . but of course, Maria couldn't give her what she wanted. She took one look at Lilia's tear-filled face and her small, swollen, bruised hands— and without a word, directed Lilia into the house.

"Go to your room, lie down, and rest. You'll be fine by tomorrow," she said, after wrapping Lilia's hands in a tea towel filled with ice.

The day ended in silence, and although Lilia's tears were visible, she didn't utter a sound.

Lilia woke up early the next morning, disheartened and confused as she grudgingly shuffled back to school. She allowed herself to feel something she rarely did: anger and resentment. Lilia resented her mother for not letting her stay home today, and for casting her back into the arms of evil. How could she?

Moments into the class lesson, a bold knock sounded at the door. Signore Maestro answered the door to reveal Maria Meneguzzi in her usual black uniform—her hands clenched firmly at her waist and her eyes filled with determined rage.

"Maria, what are you doing here?"

Surprised to see her mother, Lilia watched with growing alarm. The children's eyes widened as they stared at one another in disbelief. Pinned to their seats, they covered their mouths and held their breaths, not knowing what was about to transpire.

With the presence and posture of a commanding war general, Maria raised her arm and pointed a stiff finger right into the teacher's face. "You—you little coward of a man. Don't you ever, *ever* touch my child again! Do you see what you did to my daughter? Look at those hands! You go home and beat *your* children, not *mine*!" Her words rang through the room, which fell into pin-drop silence Maria slammed the door and stormed off. Signore Maestro retired behind his desk in shock and embarrassment.

Pride rose within Lilia's heart, but she was careful to hide the smile on her face. She might not have received the hug she'd desired . . . the one that would have made such a difference on so many occasions . . . but at that moment, Lilia's mother was her hero.

7 | FOUR-LEAF CLOVER

July 1943

As Lilia and her family approached the summer months, the sun stopped being a source of joy. An unexpected turn of events blanketed Mussons in confusion and panic.

Rome was bombed—the first time the eternal city had suffered an attack during the war. Public opinion quickly turned against Mussolini, who became the most hated man in Italy. The monarchs fared no better. When the King of Italy, Victor Emmanuel III, paid his respects to the Romans, they blamed him for the war. The king's reputation had become tarnished due to his aligning with fascism, suppressing the basic freedom of the Italian people, and taking Italy into battle. With the threat of a revolution, the government voted Mussolini out of power. That same day, the king appointed General Pietro Badoglio as Mussolini's successor.

Although Mussolini's denouncement brought relief to the Italian people, it was unclear whether Italy would remain Germany's ally or surrender due to their failing military. The army was ill equipped, its soldiers poorly trained. Mussolini had led the country to the brink of disaster and humiliation. A twenty-one-year-long authoritarian regime was presumed to have ended, and people rejoiced by tearing down fascist symbols throughout the villages, towns, and cities.

Days later, in Mussons, a roar of excitement pierced the air as the news of Badoglio's rise to power swept through the village.

Lilia was crouched by the cold-water pump across the street, rinsing a bucket of soapy laundry, when she heard the clamor. Startled by the unusual outburst, Lilia followed the shouting that was coming from La Bottega.

As she walked towards the bar, she stopped to pluck off a square piece of paper stuck to her shoe. Lilia turned it over in her hand—it was a partially burned photograph of Mussolini. When she looked up, she noticed other randomly sized papers being tossed from nearby windows. One woman spat on a photo before releasing it with an abrupt gesture, sending a crumpled, defeated Mussolini floating to the ground. The energy of Mussons was explosive as villagers expressed years of resentment and deeply rooted anger. People embraced. Tears erupted.

"The end of fascism! Long live Badoglio! Long live the king!" Men and women cheered at the broadcast—and ripped every fascist emblem from the walls of the bar and the surrounding buildings.

The commotion drew Maria outside. Concerned, she signaled Lilia to come home. "What in the world is going on?"

Lilia shrugged. "I don't know. I think everybody is going crazy." Lilia rolled her eyes dramatically. "I heard a woman yelling swear words at Mussolini. She said, 'I hope they hang the fascist pi—'"

Maria covered Lilia's mouth. "Never repeat those words! Do you hear me?"

Lilia quickly nodded in agreement and handed her mother the damaged photo as if it were a hot potato. At that moment, Eliseo came running up the street shouting the news.

"Maria! I heard on the radio that Mussolini stepped down. General Pietro Badoglio is our new prime minister!"

"What does that mean?" Maria took a deep breath to calm herself. "Is the war over?" She clenched her teeth in a vain attempt to suppress the surge of emotions: anger, fear, astonishment, exhilaration. All she could focus on was her husband and sons. Despite what her heart already knew, some part of her secretly hoped that Erminio was still alive.

"I don't know, Maria, but Mussolini was running this country into the ground. After the broadcast, they played our national anthem, when they always played that fascist Genoese hymn before. Fascism is dead, so maybe that's a sign this damn war is coming to an end!"

"Maybe?" Maria's eyes turned hard and steely, pulling her back to the reality of who was still ruling the country. She watched the euphoric crowd and shook her head. "Do you truly believe the Germans will accept Italy pulling out of the war? People are celebrating far too soon. I didn't trust Mussolini, and I don't trust the king—neither did Virginio." Maria burst her own bubble with the truth. "Eliseo, please be careful what you say and whom you trust—the Camicie Nere are everywhere." She handed him the photo. "We haven't seen the worst yet. Mark my words."

She returned to the house, and Lilia trailed behind her. Eliseo was left standing in the middle of the street, befuddled by Maria's lack of enthusiasm. She had knocked the wind out of his sails. But as he watched the neighbors rejoice over what seemed a victory, determination arose in his heart. He had to fight for his beliefs! He yearned for what Italy had been before fascism—a country full of pride and integrity.

Even in the face of a hopeful nation, Badoglio still sported the fascist badge—and the fighting continued. The king announced there would be a less destructive but still fascist government. Italy would remain fighting alongside Germany. And, unbeknownst to the Italian people, little would change.

⁂

Despite the new prime minister maintaining relations with Germany and announcing his commitment to the alliance, Badoglio secretly negotiated the Armistice of Cassibile—a cease-fire agreement with the Allied forces. On September 8, the armistice was announced, with an immediate order to end all hostilities against the British and Americans. The next day, the king, Badoglio, and their subordinates fled the Allied lines—fearing for their safety and a German advance on Rome. They abandoned their beloved city and left the country without a ruling government—and in a state of complete chaos.

Confusion and panic quickly spread throughout the country and Europe's other occupied territories. The Italian people felt deflated and betrayed by their government after having been so hopeful weeks prior. The army was left without orders, dismantled and disarmed, leaving the whole of Italy at the mercy of Nazi Germany. By September 11, as far as Italy was concerned, the war was lost. Germany closed in and raided Rome—a now German-held territory. Hundreds of Jewish men, women, and children were captured by the Gestapo and deported to Auschwitz. The horror had begun.

With no superior orders at the helm, Italians were pitted against each other—it was every man for himself. The resistance had fought underground against Mussolini's regime for years, and with the fall of the government, these guerrilla fighters continued to grow in numbers and were now fighting against German fascism. Morale plummeted, and widespread panic had army units dismantling, with thousands of Italian soldiers deserting their posts and escaping back home to their families. Northern Italy was on high alert as Hitler's newly established SS were on a mission to capture and arrest every Jewish Italian, Jewish refugee, and partisan. Some individual Italian soldiers or whole units joined the local resistance movements. It was a perilous time for civilians, too. Hundreds of thousands were transported by train to internment prison camps before arriving at their final destination—to be exterminated.

ᴥᴥᴥ

At the same time, other atrocities were underway. Trieste became occupied by the Yugoslav resistance; this partisan group initiated the Foibe Massacres, also referred to as the Italian Holocaust. The foibes were sinkholes scattered throughout the hills of this port city. They dropped hundreds of meters into the earth and became a killing ground for the local Italian people.

An estimated 300,000 Italians living in Trieste, Gorizia, and the Istrian Peninsula were forced to flee the area. Thousands were tortured, shot, or thrown into these cavernous pits. Many of the prisoners were sympathizers of Mussolini's regime, while others were innocent civilians—men, women, and children. They were lined up on the edge of the chasms, chained together by their ankles, and machine-gunned; like dominoes, they were pushed to their death—some still alive and left to rot in the bowels of the earth. The Slavs believed Italy was a threat to the future of their communist state, and nothing would stop them from eradicating Yugoslavia of its Italian population.

Among the massive foibe killings, the highest SS commander, Odilo Globocnik, ran the SS concentration camp in Trieste, Italy—the Risiera De San Sabba prison. A feared Nazi leader, he was responsible for the atrocities in Warsaw, Poland, and headed the construction of extermination camps in Germany. Globocnik was on a rampage to persecute Jews, partisans, and Italian civilians, imprison them in the transit camp, and then deport them to Auschwitz. More than 25,000 civilians passed through San Sabba, and over 5,000 that remained were gassed to death.

The fear of being captured by Nazi soldiers and Yugoslav partisans haunted many Italian soldiers—which is why Virginio fled for his life.

Northern Italy was a war zone, and he feared if he did not escape Trieste before the border closed, he could be captured, interrogated, imprisoned, taken to a camp, or face death. Virginio's hatred for this war was cemented by the terror that surrounded him on all sides. He couldn't bear the chilling reality that both his sons were facing the same struggles . . . and the thought that he might never see them again. His love for his family gave him the strength and courage to stay alive.

In a dazed state of shock, Virginio wildly traipsed the streets of Trieste. He felt the world had come to an end—even the birds were silent. A port city that once burst with life was still and bare, with nothing but the wind to remind him that he was still alive. Smoke billowed up from the ground, where bombs had ruptured the earth and the air was pungent with the scent of the unburied dead. Homes were burned to the ground and farm animals roamed, lost and confused. People were too fear-stricken to dare leave their homes. Civilians were spotted scurrying between alleyways and fleeing into the unknown. German soldiers patrolled day and night.

When he saw the coast was clear, Virginio ran along the ridge, down the hillside, and into the woods. His brain still rattled with the echoes of agonized howls; the sights, sounds, and smells of war pierced him like jagged glass. Out of the corner of his eye, Virginio saw flashes of men darting between trees. Were they soldiers? Partisans? Germans? Bushes rattled as secret whistle calls lanced through the darkness. Virginio's eyes widened. His heart thudded like the pounding hooves of a runaway horse as he ran off into the turmoil of the night. He knew that he couldn't risk trusting anyone. In this war, everyone was now out for themselves.

The hours stretched as Virginio trudged through tangled branches and ground cover. His mind was a battlefield.

My legs, my back—I can't take this throbbing—It feels like nails are puncturing my insides. I've been in war before, but I don't know if I can make it out this time. I'm weak—my spirit is breaking.

His wincing amplified with every step. He was breathing, but he didn't feel fully alive.

I don't know what's worse—drowning in pain or dying from this hunger and thirst.

As his agony threatened to claim him, Virginio's heart raced wildly in his chest. *Maria, pray for me—my heart beats for you.*

It felt like the devil was crawling up his spine to his head, forcing his hands to cover his ears to dull the noise. He dragged one faltering foot in front of the other until he heard the rippling of running water as it permeated the silence of the ink-colored sky. Virginio followed the sound to a rail bridge over a shallow creek on a bed of lime-stone. He entered the arched tunnel, and the last trickle of moonlight snaked away as he trudged on. Virginio took refuge in a safe, dry corner where he sank his tired bones back against the cold stone wall.

Food had been scarce for days, and although hunger was a vicious and ruthless companion, he fought to ignore the gnawing pain in his stomach. Virginio plunged his cupped hands in the creek, bringing ice-cold water up to soothe his cracked lips and quench his parched, dry mouth. Virginio's last provision was a piece of stale bread buried in his pant pocket. He drew up his legs close for warmth, dropped his head to his knees, and wept.

Yesterday, I was fighting with the Germans, and tonight, I'm running for my life.

At that moment, Virginio's solemn face turned towards the sound of something rustling on the gravel next to him. He looked down to see a lean, gray rat scurrying around his leg. Virginio pulled out the bread from his pocket, and with his cramped, stiff fingers, ripped a piece off to offer to the scrawny rat.

"Here," he said feebly, his words barely forming a sound. "You deserve to live as much as I do."

Despite his weak condition, Virginio couldn't help but smile at the little creature. His smile became a grimace as pain shot through his lungs. He gradually quieted his breath and gave in to exhaustion. His arms went limp. He released his fingers and watched the bread roll away. His head lolled left, right, and then sank to his chest. As the rat nibbled on the generous offering, one sentence escaped Virginio's parched lips: "Maria . . . I love you." And then, he drifted into an abyss of sleep.

The late-night train howled like far-off thunder. Virginio's eyes sprung open. He didn't know if he'd been asleep for hours or days, but the rumble was a welcome reprieve from his tormented sleep. Bullet fire and the cries of wounded men echoed in his skull—the nightmare had come on strong and fast. He was desperate to erase these demons of panic and fear from his memory and focus on the shining light: his family. A cold wind swept under the bridge and permeated his limbs, which rippled with pain. The frozen ground sent chills through his body. Virginio's pale hands trembled as he opened them, one finger at a time.

The approaching train's forlorn whistle warned him that he needed to make his break—and fast. Virginio rose to his knees.

"Please, God," he begged with open hands. "Give me the strength to get home. I need you now more than ever."

In near darkness, Virginio made his way out to the entrance of the tunnel. He forced his body to run through shallow puddles that had formed from night rain. He was grateful for the moonlight. Determined to make the train, he scrambled up the muddy, tree-lined ridge, crawling like a serpent through tall, soggy whips of grass. He paused to catch his breath, scanning the coast left to right. The track was deserted. Virginio caught the headlights in the distance. Careful not to blind his night vision, he looked to his hands as they absorbed the vibration that rumbled beneath the ground.

Now! Go now! he urged himself, pulling his haggard, exhausted body over the ridge as he climbed to his feet. It was now or never. As the freight train accelerated, stock car by stock car flashed before him. His eyes bulged wide with fear. Virginio spotted an open car and ran like the devil was at his heels. His legs wobbled until he thought he might collapse, and his ankles would give way to the layers of granite ballast beneath him.

The pounding of his heart and the crunch of stones beneath his feet were drowned by the sound of cars rushing by on the metal rails. Virginio took one desperate leap towards the rail car, clamping both hands on to the latch of the wooden door. He held on with every ounce of strength he had left. As the train rounded a tree-lined corner, a tangle of gnarled branches reached out and grabbed Virginio, nearly pulling him to the ground.

He let out a deep cry. "Come on! Come on!"

Virginio hoisted his body through the door while the train moved at full speed, launching him deep into the car. Dazed and breathless, he found himself backed into a wooden crate—it was covered in urine-soaked hay. The car was filthy. A pail had fallen and spilled in the back corner. The stench of feces was unbearable. But sweet relief flooded him all the same. Heading West, he knew he wasn't much more than an hour from the border. Closer to freedom than he'd been in months.

He moved the crate aside and spotted a filthy doll on the floor. Her eyes were wide and round, as if she'd been frozen into permanent shock. She wore a checkered, red-and-white dress that was stained, tattered, and torn. Her matted black hair was braided and tied with old frayed red ribbon. Virginio scooped the small, cold doll into his hands and felt his strength drain from his body.

"Am I on a death train?" The doll was the one memory left of a little girl, taken to God only knew where. "Bless her soul."

He wiped the grime off the doll's face, wondering about the fate of the child who'd once treasured it. Images and memories of Lilia and his other children spun a hurricane of emotion in his mind. He gently lay the doll on the car floor so he could rest his tired bones and cease the stream of thought.

As the moonlight filtered into the car, Virginio gazed out at the passing landscape, bidding it goodbye. It would not be missed.

"See me through the night *bella luna*. See me through."

And with that, peace enveloped him, cradling his bruised, battered body in dreams of home.

ଏ⁓ ୨ଇ⁓

Close to the border, Virginio could feel the train slowing and creeping to a stop. The hiss of the brakes snapped him awake—he immediately stood up and pulled the car door closed. Outside, farther ahead, men spoke in urgent, angry German.

Through the broken wooden slats of the door, Virginio watched as the full moon cast its light on three German soldiers, who made their way down the track. The youngest was merely a boy, presumably enlisted in Hitler's youth brigade. Within minutes, Virginio heard shouting.

"Get out! Come down here. Now!"

Virginio gripped the wall as his eyes came to rest on a man and his son stepping off the train. The boy was in tears as he clung to his father.

"Come here! On your knees. On your knees, I said, both of you!" one of the officers shouted with fiery contempt.

"Please!" begged the man as he sank to his knees. "I beg you, let my son go. He's a child! I'll do anything you want—let him go!"

"Shut up, filthy vermin!" the officer sneered. He cracked his pistol over the man's head and knocked him to the ground. The boy froze, and his eyes remained fixed on his father. Two remorseless gunshots split the air. Virginio released his grip and sank to the car floor as he watched the man and his child fall to their deaths—the little boy's tears now turned to blood.

The German's devilish laughter broke the silence as he spat in disgust on the bodies. "Useless parasites." He gazed triumphantly on the young soldier, who looked stunned as he stared at the lifeless forms on the ground.

"You see that, boy?" The officer's lips curled into a smile. "When we eliminate the waste, we make Germany victorious!"

The young soldier failed to respond.

"What are you waiting for? Start at the end and check every car!"

The boy hesitated, afraid of what would now be expected of him if he came face-to-face with the enemy.

"Go!" the officer said sharply.

Reluctantly, the young soldier went to inspect the cars. Virginio stayed focused on the anxious young man. As he watched him head towards the end of the train, a flurry of dark thoughts circled his mind. Virginio's world stood still as he waited; the risk of capture was real. Although he had his orders, Virginio hoped by the young soldier seeing the man and his son fall to their death, unarmed and with desperation in their eyes, would have left him covered in shame. A wife had lost her husband—a mother, her child.

With each shuffle of the young soldier's boots, Virginio could only think of Erminio forced into battle, a war he wasn't ready to fight. Virginio believed, like all people, Germans were not all cut from the same cloth. He prayed this soldier's family didn't raise him to become one of Hitler's faithful, but a young man of peace and strength, like his boys, guided by kindness. But he was a German soldier—a title that forced him to raise a proud Nazi salute and obey his superiors' single-minded mandate. Virginio knew, refusal to comply was not an option for this young man and that he'd be prepared to stand or fall for his country.

Light filtered down the track as the soldier pointed his flashlight between the wooden slats, searching each compartment. Virginio swayed and lost his balance in the far corner, alerting the soldier to stop at Virginio's car. He slid the door open and climbed in—the stench permeated his senses. Virginio saw the soldier's nose wrinkle in disgust as his left hand rose instinctively to block the smell.

"Who—who's there?" Panic rose to the boy's face.

Virginio's heart was beating violently. Dread crept over him, his throat tightened, and perspiration ran in cold beads down the back of his neck. He covered his mouth to fight the rush of nausea. He willed himself into stillness.

Mother of God, what am I going to do? Is this how it's going to end?

The seconds felt like hours. Virginio held still, every tired muscle contracting in protest. Holding his breath, he curled his fingers into a fist. His leg twitched abruptly, jolting the crate and alerting the enemy to his presence.

"C-come out where I can see you," the soldier stammered.

There was no way out.

"All right, I'm coming out." Virginio pulled himself to his feet and shuffled slowly towards the soldier, his hands in the air. The boy seemed to him younger than Erminio. His heart ached as he imagined the atrocities the young soldier had lived through . . . and waged on others.

Virginio kept his eyes on the enemy and attempted to keep his voice and body calm and steady. "Son, put the gun down. You don't want to hurt anyone. You saw what they did out there. Is that who you want to be?"

"Stop talking, or I'll—I'll shoot!" The boy waved his hand around, motioning with the gun erratically.

"What's your name, son?"

"Stop talking, I said, or I'll shoot you!"

Virginio knew that the combination of the soldier's visible panic and the orders he'd been given by the officer left no room for idle chatter. Without thinking, he launched himself forward and grabbed hold of the gun barrel, twisting the young man's arm. He had to act fast. He wrenched the gun from the soldier's grip and forced him to the floor. In the struggle, Lilia's four-leaf clover necklace was yanked off Virginio's neck and landed next to the soldier. Pinning the boy with his knee, hand on his mouth and gun to his head, Virginio struggled. Panic clawed its way up his throat. The soldier was at Virginio's mercy.

If I shoot him, I die, too.

Virginio saw the fear in the young man's eyes, and in that moment, Arturo and Erminio flashed before him. The cold reality of this senseless war was inescapable. Darting his eyes to the clover, he heard his daughter's words: "Every life matters."

Virginio pulled the soldier up—the gun still pointed at his head.

"You're not one of them. I don't hate you because you're German. I hate this war. Anyone can be a soldier, but it takes a man of courage, honor, and conviction to be a great soldier. Fight for that. We are both walking out of here alive."

To Virginio's horror, he heard one of the officers nearing the end of the train. "Stupid boy, where are you?!"

Virginio released the soldier from his grip and placed the gun back in his hand. "Every life matters." Their eyes locked. "Mine and yours."

"I'm here!" shouted the young soldier. "I'm coming out now." He swallowed hard, turned quickly, and climbed out of the car.

"What were you doing in there?" the officer snapped.

Virginio's entire body was a silent prayer . . . a bated breath.

"I . . . I thought I heard something. There's nothing here. The train is clear." He closed the car door behind him.

Virginio held still until the Germans pulled away and the train was once again in motion. The wheels groaned as they started to roll. He reached for the necklace.

"Faith, hope, love, and good luck!" He kissed the clover, grateful for his daughter's invisible presence and gentle yet persistent belief in her father. A piece of heaven was with him.

"You only die once. Today is not the day," he whispered to himself. For a moment, he forgot his hunger. He forgot his pain. He felt his entire life in the grip of the miraculous. Although Virginio hated the enemy, he had witnessed hope for the future.

8 | BELLA CIAO

O partigiano, portarmi via
Oh partisan, carry me away
O bella, ciao, bella, ciao, bella, ciao, ciao, ciao
Oh beautiful, goodbye
O partigiano, portarmi via
Oh partisan, carry me away
Ché mi sento di morir
Because I feel I'm going to die

The anti-fascist hymn echoed throughout Mussons. Arm in arm, partisan men and women sang in solidarity as they walked the streets united. "Bella Ciao" was their anthem—Italy's hymn of freedom.

The music fell softly on the villagers' ears and penetrated their souls, filling them with pride. The villagers embraced these words in honor of all the brave soldiers who died fighting for a war they did not believe in. Despite the many casualties, despite the years of oppression, Italians fought for what they felt their country stood for.

E seppellire lassù in montagna
Bury me up in the mountain
O bella ciao, bella ciao, bella ciao, ciao, ciao
Oh beautiful, goodbye
E seppellire lassù in montagna
Bury me up in the mountain
Sotto l'ombra di un bel fior
Under the shade of a beautiful flower

Mussons was a sought-after hiding place for partisans. The guerrilla fighters numbered over 80,000 and were made up of peasant workers, disbanded soldiers, deserters, and escaped prisoners of war. During World War I, the Italian Resistance ran for safety in the trenches that were hidden within the banks of the Tagliamento. The trenches remained intact nearly twenty years later, providing escape for partisans or anyone hiding from the Nazis and fascist allies. Many young Italian men fled army enlistment and were recruited by the partisans. Women joined out of patriotism or political principle; they didn't rouse much suspicion, as the majority were granted the role of couriers who covertly delivered intelligence messages to resistance leaders.

A hush fell over Mussons as villagers observed in sullen silence from their windows; shutters opened wide enough to hear the words that were intoned with such respect. The riverbank had given the village of Mussons a dangerous reputation in Northern Italy, as it was frequented by Germans in search of anti-fascists and destitute Jews who'd fled to Italy in hopes of sanctuary. Many of the villagers feared displaying their patriotism too openly, as some of the locals had turned spies, pretending to be partisans while reporting back to the Nazis. These traitors believed in the fascist regime; to them, it restored order and made Italy stronger. They admired their former leader, while the majority of Italians believed that next to Hitler, Mussolini was the chief villain of this war.

Soon after the armistice, Nazi soldiers entered the village on a rampant search—the Camice Nere had informed them of the resistance's presence in and around Mussons. All true Italians were partisans at heart, and they were terrified. The villagers lived in constant fear, as their hamlet was now the hunted one.

It was early Sunday morning in the first week of October. The sound of the church bells rolled through Via della Chiesa, calling in the faithful to worship. The clanging echoed like distant thunder throughout Mussons, as if warning the villagers of the torment about to descend upon them.

Maria chose to forgo mass and tend to her chores with Lilia, while the boys were still asleep and dreaming in their beds. Her long-standing love for the church had waned, and her relationship with God had dwindled almost entirely. With each passing day, the bitterness of war tore at Maria's heart, leaving it fractured. To her, the world was broken, and God had left her side and failed her family. Maria's faith floated away like a dead autumn leaf on the wind.

"Lilia, take the radicchio and wash it at the pump. Make sure you get *all* the bugs out—they're tiny and hard to see. Otherwise, we'll all be eating them later, including you. Wash every leaf."

"Yes, Mama," Lilia sighed quietly so as not to upset her mother. It was yet another weekend of chores, but with the German occupation, the tension in the village had heightened and grew more palpable with each passing day.

Maria continued to hang the wet linen on the clothesline. She fulfilled her task absently, her thoughts abuzz with her men. She wondered when they would return. Visions of their eyes twinkling with laughter appeared as quickly as they left, flitting between the billowing sheets—nothing but a fleeting mirage in the breeze. Maria's longing always came in the quiet moments; everywhere she looked, Virginio and her sons were there, reminding her of the seemingly bottomless pain within her heart.

Now that the village seemed to be at the mercy of the partisans and the Germans, Maria felt helpless. She questioned the solidarity of her neighbors, as she knew well fascist spies lived among them. In Mussons, no one could share the stories that lived within their walls. Everyone was prisoner to a pervasive fear.

The fruit trees in the courtyard were nearly bare as shafts of sunlight danced through the branches, glinting off the colored leaves strewn on the ground. The fresh autumn air seemed to offer itself to Maria as a nudge towards aliveness, but her spirits were too heavy to be lifted. The Nazis had reared their ugly heads and wormed their way into the village. Maria knew that she needed to focus on protecting her children, to maintain her home under an umbrella of peace, to keep some semblance of hope alive.

Across the street, Lilia rested on her knees on the dirt road and ran the cold water over the radicchio. One by one, methodically, she washed each leaf in the colander, as her mother had ordered. Startled, her ears were alerted to the sound of German soldiers approaching. She knew who they were—even before hearing them speak or lifting her eyes. She knew by the firmness of their gait and the coarse odor of their black tobacco.

Lilia kept her head down until the sound of their boots and the harshness of their voices were far enough away. She drew in a nervous breath and let it out slowly as she raised her head. To Lilia's right, a military truck was driving away from the bar, leaving a trail of exhaust fumes that permeated the air; to her left, armed foot soldiers headed towards the church.

Maria spied the German intrusion and quickly called out, "Lilia! Come inside."

Without hesitation, Lilia pulled up the colander of radicchio, left the water pump, and ran into the courtyard, back to the safety of home. Her heart was beating hard and fast.

"Mama! I saw German soldiers walking towards the church. They have guns. What do they want?"

"They're looking for partisans," Maria explained, her calm demeanor belying her swirling thoughts. She scanned the street from the gate. "Go inside. You are not to speak to anyone—do you hear me? Not a German, not a partisan—no one. If someone asks you a question, say *nothing*. Trust no one but your mother."

Lilia's brow furrowed in confusion. "Mama, how do I know who the partisans are? And why are the Germans looking for them?"

Maria thought for a long moment as she looked at her daughter—a young child subjected to an unfair world far different from Maria's experience growing up. Although she'd been raised in poverty, Maria had always felt safe and secure. It was important that Lilia understand the reality of what lay before them. Maria needed to warn and protect her daughter, whose innocent, trusting nature could all too easily be betrayed.

"We don't always know who the partisans are," Maria admitted. "Some wear a red scarf around their neck, some green, while others dress like ex-military or even civilians. And like us, the Germans don't know either, so they question anyone who makes them feel suspicious. And they offer rewards in exchange for information. There are spies in our village, Lilia, which is why you must not talk to anyone."

"What do the Germans want?"

"The partisans are against Mussolini and Hitler's beliefs and will fight those who share in these beliefs, from Germans to poor peasants like us, and the Camice Nere. This is why Hitler wants to capture these men and women and take them away. For years, Mussolini and his followers have been watching what we do and controlling how we live our lives. We could never say or do what we wanted, and that hasn't changed. If we voice our opinions or speak our truth, we could face punishment."

"Like when Signore Maestro hit me?" Lilia cringed at the horrible memory. She could almost feel her hands stinging.

"Yes, Lilia, but much worse!" Maria replied, observing silently as her daughter's eyes watered and her body trembled.

Good, Maria thought. *These are uncertain times, and the more frightened Lilia is, the more careful and safer she'll be.*

"This life is not the one your father and I chose for our family, but we have no choice, so we obey the rules and pray things will change one day. Hitler is the devil himself, and now his soldiers are here in Mussons. This is why you must not trust anyone!" Maria gave her daughter a stern look. "We have to be quiet and invisible. Do you understand?"

With a faint nod of her head, Lilia handed her mother the colander of greens and went running into the house.

Maria wrapped the radicchio in a dishtowel and pulled all four corners of the towel together, twisting them to hold the leaves in place. She stood in the middle of the courtyard and repeatedly swung the radicchio over her head like a lasso to fling the water out. With each swing of her arm, she released some of the angst that had been building for weeks since the Germans infested the village.

"Hey! Woman!"

Startled by a man's shout, Maria lost her grip on the towel. Radicchio burst into a green explosion all around her and scattered on the ground. Her insides seemed to follow. A partisan stood at the front gate with a black Beretta in his hands while three of his comrades paced behind him. He appeared nervous as he stuttered his words and frantically waved the gun. He wore a faded jacket and a green scarf around his neck, signaling he was part of the Brigate Osoppo-Friuli, known to be Christian democrats—the Communist Garibaldi, in contrast, wore red scarves.

"Hide my gun!" The man threw the pistol at Maria's feet. "I'll come back for it!

"W-what are you doing!?" Maria cried out. "I have four children! They will kill us all!"

Maria stared with contempt at the gun that was thrown so hastily to the ground. She picked up the Beretta. The metal felt cold against her skin, and in that suspended moment, the knots in her stomach tightened. She was holding a weapon of death. How many lives had it taken? She gasped for air as every cell of her body filled with terror.

Maria gave him an incredulous look. "You can't leave this gun here! If the Germans find it . . . dear God, no!"

"Hide it. *Now!*" The gunman and two of the other men dressed in civilian clothing left running like frightened birds. They dispersed in opposite directions to avoid capture, while the fourth partisan burst through Maria's front gate, searching for a place to hide. He was a thin, unshaven man who wore a worn jacket, baggy pants, and torn shoes.

"The Germans are patrolling up ahead," he cried out. "They're waiting to question people, and if they find me, they'll kill me. You have to take me in!"

"No, no! Not in my house! I have four children!" Maria blocked the front door with her body, her fingers curled around the handle of the gun, but her grip was slackening. Maria's brain was bursting with conflicting thoughts. *What will the Germans do if they find out? I'm endangering my family! They'll burn my house! I don't know what to do!*

"I beg of you!" Her hands trembled as she held the heavy, loaded pistol. She feared she'd accidentally pull the trigger and sound off a cracking noise in the air, alerting the soldiers. Her thoughts spun as she tried to think of a suitable hiding place. Maria hated the Nazis as much as the partisans, but now she resented the latter for putting her and her family in danger.

Lilia stood shivering in fear behind her mother. She held her breath and swallowed her tears, afraid to make a sound. *What's happening? Who is this man? Is he going to hurt us? Why is Mama holding a gun?*

The partisan's concern for himself outweighed any empathy for Maria and her family's safety. Without a word, the partisan spotted the barn and sped up the wooden ladder leading to the second floor of the stall to mounds of hay. He burrowed a hole in the haystack and buried himself there.

Maria's thoughts quickly turned back to the heavy, loaded pistol in her trembling hands. *What do I do with this gun? Where do I hide it so the Germans don't find it?*

Lilia watched in confusion and alarm as her mother's panic reached a fever pitch. Maria ran in a flurry of circles around the house, as if caught in a windstorm.

"Mama, what is happening?"

"The partisans! We help them, and we pay with our lives!" The threat of arrest, or her family being dragged to the camps—or even worse, being shot—invaded Maria's entire being. Firing machine guns seemed to echo in her brain as fear surged through her veins. The more she pondered the ugly manner in which the Germans would surely choose to punish her, the more she was compelled to think—and act—fast.

In moments, Maria ran to the kitchen and hid the gun under the water pipe in the subfloor. Soaked in a nervous sweat, she paced for what felt like an eternity.

No, no! If the Germans invade my home, they will find it there!

She quickly removed the gun and frantically scanned every corner of the great room, kitchen, cantina, and fireplace, searching for a safe hideaway. Maria spotted a glassine bag sticking out of her sewing basket on a chair next to the buffet. She wrapped the weapon in the bag while Lilia stood back, pale-faced and fighting her impulse to scream.

"Lilia! Quick, get me the big red pail outside!"

Lilia ran like the wind to retrieve the pail, glad for a task that would momentarily keep the sick feeling of terror at bay.

"Here, Mama!" Lilia handed it to her mother. She stood waiting and watching at the front door as her mother placed the gun in the bucket, filled the pail with pig feed, and lugged it to the barn. Maria dumped the contents of the pail into the pig trough, praying it would be safe there.

"Lilia, you can *never* tell anyone about this, do you hear me? No one!"

"Why, Mama?"

Maria grabbed her daughter's shoulders and looked her square in the eye, her face hard and resolute. "No one can ever know we helped the partisans—not your friends, not the neighbors. We can't trust anyone. If the Germans find out, they will kill us all. Do you understand? If we survive this God-forsaken war, maybe one day you can tell the world what we went through, but now, we remain silent. Get inside and keep your brothers upstairs!"

Lilia ran to her room and pulled her brothers close.

"Lilia!" Giovanni cried out. "What's wrong?"

"You mustn't make a sound! Help me keep Bruno and Riccardo

quiet!" The four children huddled in silence, while Lilia kept an eye out for possible danger from the open crack in the shutters.

Maria sat on her wooden chair outside the front door, where she typically spent hours pruning vegetables. She tried to appear as unruffled as possible while keeping a sharp eye on the man in the barn and the street leading from the church, where the Germans were questioning villagers.

Maria's life flashed before her. Twenty long minutes had passed when she heard German soldiers approaching. She remained as calm as she could, all the while praying her children would stay quiet and out of sight. One of the soldiers extended his rifle and tapped the gate to get Maria's attention.

"You. Are there any men hiding in your house?"

"No, nobody. I haven't seen anyone."

"Why is there lettuce all over the ground?"

"My daughter is clumsy. You know how children are."

The soldiers conversed in German as she clenched her teeth and held her breath. The gate abruptly swung open, and Maria rose to her feet with unsteady legs. She was in the clutches of such a powerful fear that she felt she would lose control of her bowels. One of the soldiers pushed Maria aside to enter her home while two others made their way to the barn. Her heart leaped in terror, but there was nothing she could do. Frozen in place, Maria stood by the chair waiting. She felt her head cold and wet, the blood pumping in her brain, her mind racing.

Stay calm and give nothing away, she ordered herself.

The soldier quickly scanned the main floor of the house. "Are you alone? Anybody upstairs?"

"My four children, but they are sleeping. There is no one else here. My husband and sons are fighting in the war, and our tenant is away."

"If I find you are lying, we will take you all to Germany." The fear-inducing words spewed from the soldier's grimly set mouth. His face was impassive as his steely eyes bore coldly into hers.

"As God is my witness, and on the lives of my children, we are alone!" Maria rattled inside as the pit snowballed in her stomach. She felt as if she were being held hostage in her own home.

The soldier exited the house, while the other two climbed the ladder to the top of the barn. They repeatedly plunged a pitchfork into the hay. Maria could feel her world about to end as vomit rose into her throat. The sky spun, and the earth beneath her feet was quicksand. She put her hand on the back of the chair to steady herself.

A loud horn abruptly cut the air as an army truck pulled up to the side of the road. The red-faced driver yelled something in German. Satisfied with his search, the intimidating soldier ordered his comrades out of the barn. He looked at Maria, leaned his rifle up against her face, and slowly traced a path down to her breasts with the barrel. His pupils gleamed like living coal, and his lips twisted into an evil smile.

"Next time, I will have my way with you, and then I'll burn your house." He pushed Maria back into the chair. "Remember my face, because you'll be seeing it again."

The soldiers got into the vehicle and pulled away. Maria shuddered with relief as silent sobs racked her body. Startled, she saw the partisan climbing down from the barn. Fury spread through Maria's entire being as she sprang to her feet, knocking the chair over. Maria charged after him, her eyes blazing. She slapped his face with such a force that he stumbled backward.

"I swear to God, if you *ever* endanger my family again, I will kill you myself!"

The partisan's eyes widened in shock—her metal wedding band had cut his cheek. His lips tightened in anger, and a grimace came over his face. He struggled to sputter out words but couldn't say anything—Maria intimidated and frightened him, and the imminent threat of capture implored him to run. Frantic with despair, he darted out the gate and into the street, peering in all directions.

Lilia watched from her bedroom window. Now, she finally understood her mother's fear of the Nazis. The world felt like a monster with its jaws wide open, ready to swallow them all.

જાઉ ગ્રા

Nothing would ever be as it was. Like the other villagers, Maria and Lilia were afraid to leave their home during the day and lay awake at night, tormented by sleeplessness and distressing thoughts.

But even in war, life had to go on.

The Germans came to the villagers' doors to harass them on random unsuspecting nights, asking for proof of citizenship. If they were challenged, or felt they were being deceived, soldiers took men away to a holding camp for questioning, leaving wives, children, and the elderly alone to pray for their safe return. Each dusk, many of the men of Mussons and nearby villages left covertly, escaping to the fields until morning, regardless of whether they had legal papers or not. The risk of capture induced a palpable angst that swept over the town like a dark and angry cloud.

That evening, Eliseo had still not returned home from visiting his son, leaving Maria to feel that much more vulnerable. After the day's emotional and crippling events, she and the children retired to their beds, even though sleep seemed unfathomable now. From her window, Lilia watched groups of men carrying blankets and walking towards the fields. She wondered if her father and brother were also hiding somewhere—if they were safe. She turned to see her little brothers huddled together in one bed, frightened and confused. Always a protective older sister, she vowed to keep her ears tuned like antennas that night for as long as her tired body would allow.

At 6 am, gunfire cracked into the air, drowning out the other sounds of dawn. A single bullet ripped into the children's bedroom, and the noise reverberating above their heads beat upon their ears, throwing them into a fit of screams.

Everything around Maria felt like it was moving in slow motion as she barreled down the hallway.

"Get down! Get down on the floor!"

"Mama!" Lilia cried out. She had instinctively thrown her body over her three brothers, who trembled and whimpered beneath her.

Outside, one of Arturo's closest friends, Pietro, had been walking next to his cow-driven wagon, headed towards his family's farm. As an only child, he was exempt from military service. The village square was lined with jeeps and surrounded by SS and Gestapo officers. They'd received the alert that partisans had been spotted in high numbers. Upon seeing the men up ahead armed with machine guns, Pietro panicked, abandoned his wagon, and bolted across the street towards Maria's house. Although innocent, he was frightened by the Nazis, and barreled down her garden, hoping to hop the fence and run and hide.

Maria heard the gate rattle open. Germans shouted in the courtyard. More bullets fired overhead.

Maria's shrill cries echoed as she flew down the stairs, her arms flailing madly. "Oh, dear God, help us!" Maria threw the front door open, gasping for air. She watched in horror as the SS dragged the young man through the soil of her garden by his feet. The saliva thickened in Maria's throat as the soldiers beat the boy ruthlessly with the butts of their guns and kicked him repeatedly with their boots. Gore sprayed across his teeth and lips until he was unrecognizable. The cold-hearted SS knew Pietro was innocent. They took him anyway.

"Pietro!" Maria cried out to him. His hands clawed the earth in desperation, and his screams were choked by blood. His eyes pierced Maria's heart, and she knew that she would never forget them.

"Maria! Say goodbye to my mama. Tell her I love her," he managed to sputter out.

His wailing receded into a whimper as the Germans pulled him out into the street.

Maria sank to her knees as she watched the soldiers take her son's friend away. Shutters inched open as neighbors craned to watch the chaos unfold before them. What had been the terrain of nightmares was now a daily occurrence in this once-peaceful haven. And as horrified as the villagers were, there was nothing they could do about it.

"Why did you run?" Maria's weeping wouldn't cease as she asked the single question over and over again.

A silent scream inflated her body. It was for Pietro, for Arturo, for Erminio, for Virginio. For the tragic fate that had befallen so many innocent men and their families.

Later that afternoon, Mussons was free from the prison of roaming soldiers—a freedom that couldn't be controlled or predicted. The trucks had left, but the Germans had imprinted the streets with danger and shadows of fear. Maria and her children rested in the safe harbor of their kitchen, trying to settle their twisted stomachs with a light soup and some bread. Through the open window, Maria heard shuffling about the courtyard. She pulled back the curtain enough to see the man who had thrown his gun at her feet. Alarmed for her children, Maria ran outside and closed the door behind her.

"It's in the pig trough," Maria said, darting her eyes to the barn. "Get it yourself." She watched as the man plunged his arm into the feed and pulled out the bag. He emptied its contents and headed towards the gate, never offering a word of thanks or apology. Maria blocked his exit as rage hissed through her body. Her eyes narrowed, and her face turned red. Her words spewed out like the flames of a dragon.

"You're afraid of the Germans? Fear me more. You and your clan almost had my family killed! Show your face here again, and it will be the last thing you do. Run, before I turn you over to the Nazi scum!"

The partisan scanned the courtyard and quickly darted into the garden before hopping the fence.

Maria shook her fist skyward and roared her defiance. "What more do you want from me?!"

Primal, wordless screams racked Maria's body She screamed and screamed, until her throat was hoarse, and her body and spirit felt drained of all life.

9 | DAMN THIS WAR TO HELL

🙰 It was midday on a Saturday in October. Eliseo had returned from delivering a client's order and found Maria sitting in the kitchen, her lips mumbling the words of a letter as she read aloud. She wore a look of concern, and she absentmindedly smoothed the wrinkles from her brow with her hand.

"Maria?" Eliseo leaned his head in. "Is something wrong?"

"It's a letter from Dina. I've had no news from her or Ermides in months." Maria bit her lip, consumed with her own worst-case scenarios. She looked at him with an anxious frown. "There were bombings in Milan and the Gestapo entered Rome, arresting hundreds of Jews, men, women, and children—they deported them to Auschwitz. The world is falling apart. Why did she wait so long to write to me?"

"How are the girls? Are they safe?"

"Yes, thank God!" Maria tried to shake off the horrific thought of them in danger. "Dina has since moved to Udine to work for a pharmacist's family—she said it's safer there—and Ermides is protected where she is in Rome. Still . . . Eliseo, I don't understand what is happening! And why are the Germans still bombing? I thought our people were not supporting the war anymore!"

"Hitler's men are the terrors of Germany, out to destroy all of us who resist the Nazi rule. The British and Americans want Badoglio to surrender. But I don't think there will be any further bombings, Maria," Eliseo attempted to assure her.

"It's enough the Germans have now taken over our lives—and our families." Maria's eyes glazed over. "I need to soak in some much-needed peace and quiet. I'm going to lie down for a few hours. Surprisingly, the children are already upstairs in their beds. They've endured enough these last days—we all have."

"Yes, I could use a rest too. I'm heading up to my room soon after I finish hemming these pants. I'm gearing up for a game of Briscola tonight at the bar—maybe I'll place some winning bets." He winked and gave her a broad smile as he retreated into his workspace in the great room and cranked up his sewing machine. "Sleep well, Maria."

Maria gave him a doubtful shrug and a resigned sigh before getting up from the table and shuffling up the stairs to her bedroom.

The weather was overcast that day, and the streets were deserted. With no German soldiers in sight, shutters were drawn, and villagers lay down to sleep. An hour passed in perfect silence. Right as the church bells tolled two o'clock, a boom rumbled underground, shaking the Meneguzzi house and rattling the windows.

The neighboring town of Morsano had been bombed.

Maria was swept into a whirlpool of frightening thoughts. *They're bombing the village! They're bombing us!*

Panic-stricken, Eliseo and Maria tore out of their bedrooms and down the hall, calling out the children's names. Lilia turned white as a sheet as she emerged from her room. She stood trembling in the doorway. The boys huddled in a fetal position in their beds, their hands on their ears; unable to cry out, seized up in the grip of overwhelming fear. Eliseo pulled Bruno into his arms, and Lilia and Giovanni ran closely behind them. Afraid to move, Riccardo remained in the room, his hands clawing the bedpost. Maria peeled him free into her arms and barreled downstairs.

They fled the house and emerged on to the street, where neighbors were circling like a disturbed flock of pheasants.

"What was that?"

"Dear, God, what's going on?"

"What do we do?"

"Everybody, stay on the ground floor!"

Some villagers ran to the river for cover, while others retreated to their homes. Maria and Eliseo hauled two mattresses from upstairs and set up a sleeping zone in the kitchen.

Lilia and the boys could sense their mother's fear. The thought of her children being hit by a bomb terrified Maria, and although she did her best to mask her worry, the children remained frightened.

"Are we going to die?"

"Why do they want to bomb Mussons?"

"What if the roof falls?"

"I'm scared!"

The boys trembled, their eyes wild with terror as they lay sandwiched between their mother, sister, and Eliseo.

"As long as we stay together, we'll be safe!" Eliseo tried to comfort them. The family clung to each other desperately, huddled in prayer.

They spent the next week living and sleeping on the ground floor until word got out that the bombing in Morsano had been accidental. Although Italy was in a civil war, the knowledge that Morsano hadn't been a direct target was a relief among the villagers. The mattresses were placed back into their frames, and life plodded on as usual.

⟶◦◦⟵

After a night of rain, the afternoon sky broke free of clouds. The sunlight had burst through the morning mist, bathing the courtyard in warmth. Waves of anxiety still lingered from the torment of the last week, but as Lilia closed her eyes and basked in the rays, the fragrance of the autumnal earth filled her senses with calm. She was gathering fallen leaves and raking them into a massive mound. Giovanni helped his sister by loading the foliage into the wheelbarrow for their mother, who used it as mulch to protect the garden from early morning frost.

If Papa were here, Lilia thought, *we'd be jumping in these leaves.* She let out a deep sigh.

All at once, Lilia and her brother saw objects floating far up in the sky, glittering in the light. They were coming from the direction of the river.

"Mama, Come! Look!" Lilia beckoned her mother, pointing towards to sky. "Can we go see what it is?" Maria exited the barn and looked up.

"Fine, but stay together and don't be too long!" The village seemed relatively tranquil after days of fright and commotion. She felt whatever it was seemed harmless enough.

Lilia and Giovanni ran up the street, and other children excitedly joined in the quest. What were these twinkling things? Hightailing it past the church and skipping through the wheat fields, they witnessed what appeared to be long, silver, metal-like strips falling in hundreds to the ground, interspersed with larger sheets of paper. The children squealed as they ran in circles with their arms in the air, leaping up to grab handfuls of silver ribbons, which drifted around them like snowflakes.

"Giovanni! We can tie these strips together and weave them into belts and bracelets!" Lilia screamed with delight, her face aglow with enthusiasm.

"What about these bigger papers?" Giovanni held one in his hand—it was a yellowish color with writing printed on it.

"Nah, just the pretty silver ones!"

Giovanni released the paper to the ground with the others, leaving his muddy footprint on it as he ran off with Lilia to bring their newly found treasures home.

These were aerial leaflets being dropped from the air by American pilots to warn Italians of coming destruction. Within the manifesto's lengthy message were these words:

```
      "Why are you dying for Hitler?
No one asked you if you wanted this war.
       But they sent you to die.
They told you: 'Believe, obey, fight.'
     Why? For whom? For how long?
Germany will fight until the last Italian."
```

꧁꧂

As Maria and the children weathered the ever-changing face of war, Virginio continued his seemingly endless flight from the Nazis as Italian soldiers and civilians continued to be the objects of attack.

Between the wooden car slats, he watched the sunset and Trieste city's boundary recede into the distance. However, as time passed, his feelings of safety also fled. Virginio knew he could not risk further run-ins with German soldiers. Latisana was situated on the Tagliamento River, eight kilometers from Mussons. It was the closest town to get to by foot from the border.

I must get off this train and make my way to Latisana on foot, through the woods. I will be safe there.

Virginio slid the door open and waited for his car to clear the corner on the track before leaping off the train. He clutched his stomach and folded his body as he hit the ground, tumbling down the slope of the ridge and on to the forest floor. He let out a loud groan from the harsh landing. Disoriented, he shook his head several times to clear it and to regain his night vision. His hands grew cold as they pressed against the earth and a damp chill bled through his fatigues.

The air was cool and moist, and Virginio could smell a storm brewing, but he was grateful to no longer have his senses assaulted by the stench on the train. He lifted his head to the night sky and witnessed the moon fading behind the fast-moving clouds.

"That is our moon, Maria. I hope you can see me in there—your light and love are guiding me home," he whispered. Then he pulled himself up and ran, weaving through the trees in the hopes of beating the storm. His mind raced like the wind as it bade his tired limbs to keep moving.

Bright flashes appeared ahead, and within moments, a thunder-clap rolled overhead. Like a reflection of his own erratic thoughts, lightning forked across the sinister sky. Every step Virginio took was clipped by heavy rumbling, which echoed all around him. It sounded as though heaven were being torn apart.

God's angry at this war, too.

Thunder permeated the air as rain pelted his face.

I need to find shelter! I need food and water. Get me home!

Virginio's teeth clattered together as sheets of rain beat down relentlessly. He had nowhere to hide. His body wanted to give up and collapse. Still, he quickened his pace and prayed for a sign. He paused as the streaks of white filling the sky illuminated a rooftop up ahead. Without a second thought, Virginio pushed through his exhaustion, battling through a tangle of ferns. Thick, pasty mud clung to his body—it was cold like the hands of the dead weighing him down. The woods opened up to a field. His heart lifted on a wave of relief—at last, he had arrived in Latisana!

As he crept closer to the two-story farmhouse, a faint glow streamed through the ground-floor window. He peered in and saw a dwindling fire in the fireplace. Virginio's weak body craved warmth, his stomach howled with hunger, and his need for water dominated his every thought. His throat was parched—and he would do anything to quench this horrible thirst.

Virginio weakly raised the pane and slithered inside the house, dripping water on to the floor. His head throbbed as he blindly rummaged the shelves searching for food and anything containing liquid. As his eyes gradually adjusted to the dim light, he spotted a sealed bottle of milk and a wrapped bar of butter floating in a pail of water. He plunged his cupped hands into the container and gulped water until his chest spasmed.

The silence was abruptly pierced by loud gunfire. Virginio leaped out of his skin, slipped on the floor, and landed in the pool of water. Astonishment and a surge of adrenaline sharpened his senses. "My God, don't shoot!" He sprung to his feet and raised his hands high over his head as he shivered violently from the startling sound and the wetness that clung to his skin.

"Who are you? What do you want?" a woman's voice yelled from the entryway.

Virginio could make out her form, silhouetted against a vague backdrop of firelight. She appeared to be in her nightgown, and she was holding the biggest shotgun he'd ever seen. The long barrel was aimed at his face.

"I'm a soldier, Signora. I mean no harm! All I need is some food and water, and I'll be on my way." Virginio bowed to her in the hope that she would see he was not a robber, but a gentleman. "Please, I'm unarmed."

"Don't move, or I swear to God! I'm not afraid to use this!" The woman motioned Virginio to light the lantern on the table while she kept a tight grip on the gun. "Let me see your face!"

With the kitchen fully lit, Virginio could see the door swaying on its hinges.

"You're drenched and dripping on my clean floor," she said, clearly irritated. "It appears you were dragged through the mud, as well." Her face seemed to soften as she looked him over: covered in dirt, pale-faced, and shivering. She sighed. "Sit!" she motioned to the chair with her gun before lowering it. "What's your name?"

"Virginio, Signora, Virginio Meneguzzi." He removed his army beret and slowly lowered himself into the seat.

"Where are you from, soldier?"

"Mussons. I left Trieste days ago, Signora, and need to get home to my family."

Her face still immovable, she motioned him to the other room.

"There is a wash basin over by the fireplace. The water is not hot, but it's clean, and I will round up a change of clothes. You look to be my husband's size. I'm assuming you'll want to bury that uniform. The Germans are everywhere, soldier, but they stalk this place like watchdogs at night. It's best you leave at dawn. Take my husband's bicycle. It's leaning against the old barn in the back of our house."

"Signora, if I might ask, where is your husband?"

The woman ignored his question and went into the kitchen, taking the shotgun with her, before closing the door.

"Thank you, Signora," Virginio hoped she heard him—and she knew his gratitude was genuine.

Virginio quickly peeled off the damp, mud-sodden clothing—it was heavy as lead as he dropped it on the brick floor. He noticed a wood frame photo on the hearth—a man, flanked on one side by the woman and a young girl on the other. It leaned up against a sizable, tarnished mirror.

Virginio gazed beyond the photo, caught his reflection, and frowned; he looked old and beaten . . . a shell of the man he once was. And his eyes, which had always danced with life and joy, looked tired. He was tired—of everything.

Virginio leaned over the basin and squeezed the washcloth letting the lukewarm water roll down his back. It soothed his aching muscles, and the chill slowly faded from his bones. He heaved a sigh of relief.

Moments later, a soft ray of light glanced off the mirror. Virginio could see the woman watching him silently from the open crack of the door. Although the room was dark, the sorrow—and loneliness—in her eyes was clear as day.

"I have a beautiful daughter at home, too," he said softly, his back turned to her, "and three young boys and my wife, all waiting for me." In the mirror, he could see the woman quickly turn away.

"There is soup on the table with extra bread, as well as a flask of water. Take what you need." Virginio could hear her scurry away and then pause. "I'm sorry if I frightened you. You are lucky—your family . . ." her words trailed off on a quiet whimper. "Be careful on your way home—with your life." He heard her retreating footsteps as she went upstairs.

Virginio felt satiated although he hadn't eaten much. He was grateful for the bounty and the angel he'd happened upon this night. As gray dawn filtered into the room, he prepared for his journey. The rain continued to fall steadily, and the clouds kept the birds subdued, but streams of light were fighting to break through, as if searching for the sun.

Virginio pulled his beret back on to shield his head and made his way to the barn to retrieve the bicycle. A persimmon tree graced the pathway, struggling to hold on. Virginio observed its branches, weighed down with rotten fruit, and yellow, red, and orange leaves that glistened with raindrops. He noticed two wooden crosses, one of them smaller, white, and weathered; they had been planted without gravestones under the protective canopy. While he wasn't certain if this was the woman's family, he remembered the grief in her eyes . . . and he knew that look all too well. Perhaps part of her had died along with them, but her kind heart kept beating. He knew she kept breathing, like Maria, because she had to.

⁓ﻌ ℘℘ﻌ⁓

The bicycle chain creaked with every slow turn of the old wheels as Virginio pressed down on the rusted pedals. His legs weakened and his muscles twitched. Dark images of war continued to flash and burn within Virginio, threatening to cloud his thoughts as he pedaled down what seemed to be a never-ending road.

Despite the many months he'd been away braving the unthinkable, Virginio couldn't help but imagine the gaping hole he had left in his family for nearly a year. *What they must have endured without me.* Still, he managed to muster a smile as he entertained the thought of his children parading the street on stilts, laughing; he heard their voices cry out, "Papa!" as they ran into his arms. He could almost feel Maria's welcoming embrace, and the delectable flavors of a home-cooked meal. His memories fueled him with bliss.

Would he see Arturo and Erminio? And the girls? Were they safe? With many questions and no answers, he put his faith in God.

The anticipation of the last leg of his journey coming to an end invigorated him and filled him with his last reserves of energy. The power of love gave Virginio the strength he needed to keep going, and momentarily, the unflagging memories of grisly death were overtaken by memories of his family.

An hour and a half later, the rain had stopped. The sun peeked out to welcome Virginio back from his hopelessness and to reunite him with his loved ones. Elated the sky had opened up and grateful for the warm light permeating every pore of his body, he looked up to see a familiar sign on the side of the road. Was it a mirage, or was it a word that had now become the most precious to his heart, one that he had never read with such enthusiasm before?

Mussons.

Tears escaped the corners of his eyes and blew dry on his face the faster he pedaled. His relief felt impossible to contain. *I'm almost home!*

Virginio's pulse raced as he entered Via della Chiesa. He was in a flutter of nervous excitement at the sight of his house—and his precious Lilia, who was crouched at the water pump filling a bucket of water. Virginio pressed his hand over the clover necklace beneath his flannel shirt.

"Papa?" Lilia thought her eyes were deceiving her. "Papa!!" She dropped her bucket spilling water down the street and ran to her father, her shoes pounding the dirt road. "Mama! Mama! Papa is home!"

Lilia's little brothers flew out the gate, trailing behind her, their eyes bulging with astonishment.

Virginio leaped off the bicycle, tossing it to the ground. Before he could draw another breath, he pulled his daughter into his arms. Her legs wound tightly around his hips. The tears rolled uncontrollably, mingling into a single stream.

"Oh, my Liliutti. Shhh, it's all right, Papa's here now." Virginio pulled the necklace out of his shirt. "You see that? Heaven was with me the whole time." Lilia continued to weep, as if releasing every worrisome thought and fear she had dwelled on since he departed. Giovanni, Riccardo, and Bruno clung to Virginio as if they would never let him go.

"Look how you've grown!" As he lovingly gazed at his children, their physical transformation took him aback—they were taller than he remembered and perhaps thinner, but healthy and smiling. He was thankful to be alive to see, hear, and feel them—and to be there to protect them once more.

Maria stood watching from the gate in pale-faced disbelief. She felt as if she were frozen in place. Could the one thing she'd been hoping for, for months on end, be true? The dormant, pent-up emotions—hopelessness, longing, joy, gratitude—erupted to the surface, melting her usually stern expression. As the children untangled themselves from his embrace, Virginio looked at her and smiled through his tears.

"Virginio!" Maria barreled towards him, shaking her hands in the air. "Oh God, oh my God!" She threw herself into his arms, and he held her tightly. The warmth of his body seemed to pierce through the cold ache that had been with her for so long—moving beyond the physical and touching her spirit.

"Virginio," Maria whispered as she kissed every part of his face fervently. "I didn't know—I didn't think—my God! You're home!"

Virginio felt her body tremble. The tears she wept were ones of elation, but they were also ones of great sorrow—for all they had lost, all they would never recover. Like their children, Maria had also aged. Her dark hair was threaded with silver, and the lines around her eyes were more pronounced. She looked beaten and worn and much older to him, but all the more beautiful. With each touch of his hand on her face, more tears fell.

"This feels like a dream—look at you!" Virginio gave her a kiss full of longing. "Maria, I—I almost didn't make it. Our moon, I followed our moon, and it brought me home, back to you."

Virginio, Maria, and the children walked back into the house, back to four walls that to anyone else were merely simple walls . . . but to Virginio, they contained everything that mattered.

"I was praying—" Virginio paused to collect his thoughts, hoping for good news. "Have our boys returned?" He looked around the room, "Where's Eliseo?"

"He's on a house-call with a client, and . . ." Maria released her hands from Virginio and drew them to her chest as an ugly acidity rose from her stomach. Her eyes filled with pain that seeped out into the words she knew, when spoken, would hurt them both.

"Maria! What is it?"

Maria breathed the memory of that day out slowly—the feelings still raw. "A military officer came here last winter with a telegram. He informed me—" she let out a soft whimper. "He said Erminio was missing in action."

A dull buzz sounded in his ears, and his vision blurred. Virginio's eyes darted left and right as a burning rage unleashed. He yanked the military beret contemptuously from his head and threw it into the roaring flames of the fireplace.

"Damn you, Hitler! Damn this war to hell!"

10 | THE GESTAPO

ও৯ত In the days following her father's return home, Lilia could hear the crackling air moving through his lungs. The wheezing sounded like a strange musical instrument. Lilia's concern deepened. She sat by his bedside where he lay resting.

"Papa, you don't sound good."

"Don't you worry, little one," Virginio patted her cheek gently. "Your Papa is strong!" He flexed his biceps, making Lilia laugh. Virginio smiled back at his daughter, although he had little faith in his own words.

Having served in both the Great War, and the war he recently survived, Virginio knew what it meant to live in the poorest of conditions. Lodged in mud and slush from the rains, finding a dry spot to sleep was challenging. And battle wounds were not the sole cause of death—trench warfare resulted in many illnesses among the soldiers, who fought not only for their country, but for their lives. After the Great War, every one of Virginio's war mates from Mussons had died from asthma. Even now, he wondered if his days were numbered. He dreaded the thought of his family being left alone to endure these difficult times without him.

When his last friend died, the church bells rang for a solid hour in his honor. "I'm next," were the words Virginio uttered to himself—and he believed them to be true. Maria's borage tea no longer soothed his breathing or calmed his erratic spasms. The local doctor paid Virginio a visit and prescribed him a costly medicine—the only hope for him to survive the attacks that came on without warning.

Virginio braved the days as best he could, attempting to smile through his coughs and keep the dread of death at bay. The Meneguzzi family surrendered to the quiet of night, which brought a veneer of peace in the midst of the larger chaos of war.

It was mid-November, well past midnight. Low black clouds had rolled in, endowing the village with an ominous atmosphere. As villagers lay sound asleep, a siren broke the silence, and turned into a continuous tone alerting them to take cover immediately.

Maria and Lilia hurried to wake the boys while Virginio and Eliseo gathered blankets. The boys were in a deep slumber, too tired to hear the bellowing sounds.

"Wake up!" Lilia attempted to get her brothers on their feet and help her mother dress them, but the boys were tired and fussy. As Lilia and Maria put one sleeve up their left arms, Giovanni and Riccardo pulled the sleeves off their right arms. Both boys whimpered and rubbed their sleep-heavy lids, insistent on crawling back into bed, while little Bruno launched into a nervous cry.

"Mamaaaa, I don't want to go. I want to sleep. Can't we stay here?" whined Giovanni.

"No, we have to go now!" Minutes were escaping, and Maria feared the worst. She grabbed both boys, still in their pajamas, and fled down the stairs. Lilia followed barefoot, shivering in her nightgown, with Bruno in her arms.

The damp air sank through their clothing, and breaths rose in puffs as they ran down the street in a panicked flurry. On this cold autumn night, the children's legs could not carry them fast enough, so Maria and Virginio sought cover for their family under the bridge behind the church. Wooden planks had been laid across the creek so villagers could huddle there in safety.

Amid the sirens, the permeating hum of the fighter planes grew louder and louder. The sky thundered like it was going to fall, rattling the children to their core. The boys buried themselves in Lilia's arms, and Eliseo covered them with blankets. Virginio gasped for air, trying to brave another impending asthma attack, but he doubled over and fell to his knees in agony. He didn't need to say a word. Maria saw the desperation in his eyes.

"Lilia! Run home and grab your father's medicine. Hurry!"

Lilia pounded the streets alone, her bare feet prickling with pain as they hit the hard gravel road. The sky filled with flashing lights, and the wailing sirens pierced her brain. She darted into the kitchen, clutched the medicine tightly in her hand, and tore back towards her father. The image of him collapsing was emblazoned in her mind.

Papa, I can't lose you.

A blast of cold wind at Lilia's back threatened to knock her over. She lost her balance, tripped, and fell to the ground, scraping both hands and knees. The awful howling of the planes rose and fell above her, sending shivers through her spine—but for Lilia, every second was precious, and she pushed herself back up. Her lungs screamed as she ran back to her family. The thought of losing her father was more terrifying than the raid itself. When she arrived at the bridge, Virginio looked like he was drowning—every struggle for a single breath seemed like it would be his last. Lilia watched in horror as the white stain of fear grew in her father's eyes and his fingers turned blue.

"Papa! I have the medicine!"

Maria grabbed the bottle and quickly administered the pills. Within minutes, Virginio's lungs opened and the attack dissipated—although weak, he was breathing normally again.

When the raid had passed and everyone was home safe, the children asleep in their beds, Virginio stood by Lilia's bedside, gazing upon her with adoration. His brave eight-year-old daughter had undoubtedly saved his life. In his hands, Virginio held the doll he'd pulled down from his and Maria's chest of drawers—it was still new and barely touched. Thoughts of the tattered doll on the train, the loss of his son, and the misery of war ran through Virginio's mind. Lilia carried the weight of the world on her young shoulders, and the fact that her efforts went unnoticed pained him.

Virginio gingerly lifted Lilia's limp arm and placed it around her Little Rose. "Enough. Enough now."

❧❀❧

The following day, the torment continued. An American plane was shot down in the nearby woods, and the Nazis were searching for both knowledge of the pilot's whereabouts and the partisans aiding his rescue. Armed Gestapo arrived immediately and patrolled the church, waiting for villagers to exit mass. As the bells of the clock-tower marked the end of the service, the large wooden doors opened to reveal soldiers with their rifles drawn. The blinding sunlight blurred out the Germans' faces for the villagers, who squinted their eyes from the glare as they were randomly pulled out one-by-one and forcefully pushed aside.

"Where are your papers? Papers! Papers!" one of the officers shouted as he directed several men and women with the tip of his rifle to form a straight line.

Tension blanketed the parishioners, and children were stunned into silence as they watched their parents tremble with fear before the soldiers. Lilia was among those children—she had attended mass alone that day. To her surprise, her teacher was in the line-up.

"Signore Maestro!" Lilia blurted out nervously.

"Lilia! Run to my home and get my papers from my wife!" He

198

cocked his head slightly towards her, pleading for help. Panic drenched his voice. Lilia saw large patches of sweat ringing his armpits, and his hands trembled as he tried to steady his legs with his knotted walking cane—the same cane he had so viciously and wrongfully used to punish her.

Lilia contemplated whether or not to help him. She despised him, but she had witnessed families taken away for questioning—some were released days later, while others never returned. Her teacher's imminent future was in her hands . . . tender hands that, not long ago, were swollen a livid blue.

His way of seeing the world was different from Lilia's, and perhaps his heart was also at odds with hers, but she prayed there was still a good man struggling to rise to the surface. Lilia eyed the armed soldiers and waited until they turned their backs and she was out of their line of sight. She slowly backed into the church escaping out the back door.

Every life matters rang in Lilia's ears as she hastened through the back streets to his home. Signore Maestro and his wife lived in the apartment above the dairy, catty-corner from her school. Lilia was left gasping for breath as she reached the top of the twentieth step. She knocked vigorously on the door until she heard a latch open.

"Signora, open, please!" Lilia was in a state of panic, and as her words blurred together, the woman could barely understand her.

"My child, slow down—what's wrong?"

Lilia's words tumbled out quickly. "The Germans are at the church. They are asking people for their papers. Signore Maestro doesn't have his papers! They have guns!"

Within seconds, the woman clattered down the stairs with documents in hand. She held them to her chest as she made a desperate dash for the church, with Lilia trailing at her heels.

As a result of Lilia's brave and timely action, her teacher was released. The three of them watched in agony, as the others were not so fortunate. At gunpoint, a procession of sobbing men and women were forced to stand facing the white cement wall of the building next to the school. In a short window, they were given a chance to present their papers, but many were unprepared for the invasion or didn't know where their documents were. The prisoners were loaded into a truck.

Signore Maestro's wife sank into his arms—her tears fell thick and fast. She then turned to Lilia with gratitude. "Thank you for helping us." She folded Lilia in a warm embrace. "You saved my husband's life!"

Lilia gave them both a tight-lipped smile. She was relieved that she'd been able to help Signore Maestro, but it pained her to see that so many others had met an unfavorable fate.

"You'd best get home to your mother now," said Signore Maestro awkwardly, with an air of aloofness, as he mopped his brow with a handkerchief. He looked at Lilia, and his eyes, which were filled with shame and regret, said more than his words ever could. They both knew her selfless actions had spared his life.

The soldiers departed, taking a handful of villagers to Morsano for questioning, some of whom were released the following day. Others were taken to Udine and then on the trains to Germany, never to return.

⚜

After the turmoil in the village had ceased and once the Gestapo left, Maria sent Lilia to collect winter wheat to feed the geese.

Lilia walked through the expansive field and marveled at how the sun-kissed wheat gleamed like gold and rustled in the breeze. Traumatized by the day's events, she was happy to be alone with her thoughts. Lilia rested her pail in the tall grass and lay back on her arms, craning her head up to the sky. She relaxed her eyes for a moment while staring wistfully up at the moving clouds, which formed into playful shapes: angels, kittens, horses. She imagined herself sinking into the softness of a fluffy cloud as the sound of the cool wind covered her ears, helping to silence the ugly sounds of the morning.

"When will this war be over? When will these scary Germans disappear?" Lilia sighed and closed her eyes. "And when will Arturo come home?"

As though he'd heard his little sister's words, Arturo appeared smiling behind her lids—and she smiled back. Lilia felt a tickle on her arm and opened her eyes to see a purple butterfly flitting about contentedly, with seemingly not a care in the world.

"In my next life, I'm coming back as a butterfly—a purple one. No one ever sees a purple butterfly. They are special . . . unique," she thought aloud. Lilia loved purple—the color of healing, faith, and courage. She lay watching the sky slowly cloud over, as though the heavens would soon deliver a storm. She pulled herself to her feet and quickly broke stalks of wheat to fill her basket before the sun disappeared altogether. An hour passed and the wind picked up, blowing the hair around her face and whipping it into her eyes. Her fingers were blistered from the ridged stalks and numb from the cold.

All at once, a blur of green flashed on her right as she turned her head. Lilia saw a soldier running low through the tall wheat field. A chill swept through her bones. She knew this must be the American pilot the Germans had attempted to hunt down.

Whispers of doom seemed to circulate on the wind, along with visions of shouting Gestapo bearing loaded guns. Lilia grabbed her basket and ran like the speed of light towards home. Careening around the church, she stumbled into a villager, nearly knocking him over.

"Careful there! You might hurt yourself! Where are you going in such a hurry?"

Lilia unconsciously blurted out words she would later wish she had kept to herself. "I saw a soldier running in the field to the dike. I—I have to go home!"

Remembering what Maria told her, to never speak to or trust anyone, Lilia tried to forget what happened. She didn't even tell her mother.

Later that evening, around dusk, there was a knock at the front door. Virginio had left with the other men in the village, carrying his blanket to a safe hiding place for the night, while Eliseo delivered orders that were weeks late. The stronger his love for drink had grown, the more his good service had dwindled, resulting in many lost clients.

Maria opened the door a crack and peered out. "Yes? What do you want?" She scanned the trio, aware that despite their civilian clothing, they were partisans—she had seen their faces long before the armistice on the streets of Mussons, when the village was still a safe haven.

"We need to speak to your daughter."

"My daughter? What do you want with my daughter?"

"We have a few questions."

Maria guarded the door, keeping it open no wider than her foot.

"Lilia! Come here!" As Lilia approached her mother, Maria's eyes narrowed into a reprimanding look. She was sure her daughter had done something wrong.

Lilia slid in front of her mother and leaned her head out. "Yes?"

"We don't want to cause anyone trouble, but we need to know what you saw today."

Maria opened the door wider, her stern face now at odds with the nervousness in her eyes.

"I—I don't know what you mean." Lilia's eyes darted from her mother to the men.

"We know you saw the American pilot today."

Lilia's mouth went dry, and her heart raced; so, did her mother's.

"We want to help him before the Germans get to him. Where did you see the pilot?"

Lilia looked up at her mother. Maria nodded.

"He was running to the dike by the river, next to the wheat field. That's all I know! I swear!"

The partisans thanked her and quickly left.

Maria rested her hands on the door, pausing for a moment as she closed it. Lilia crept back a few feet behind her mother, waiting anxiously. She was unsure if she would be punished.

"You tell me everything from now on, understood? You need to be more careful!" Maria chided. "You mustn't breathe a word of what you saw, not to anyone—there are eyes and ears everywhere!"

"Yes, Mama. I promise."

⋘❧ ❧⋙

The shock of the following days lingered as Germans stormed Mussons, questioning locals about the American. Families in the village took it upon themselves to move the pilot from trench to trench until he could be led to safety by the partisans.

News of the pilot's whereabouts had filtered through the streets like wildfire, inducing paranoia. Many people feared getting caught in the Gestapo's clutches, while others were more than willing to aid the American pilot in need.

Lilia's cousins, eighteen-year-old Ada and seventeen-year-old Speme, covertly took turns bringing the pilot covered baskets of food, warm blankets, and civilian clothing, braving the odds of being captured. They respected the Americans for their support during the war while despising the Nazis. The young women lived with their parents, Natale and Albina, and brothers, twenty-two-year-old Ferruccio and fifteen-year-old Gino. Any slip-ups would endanger their family. Keeping silent was vital to everyone's survival.

Early one morning, dark clouds dominated the sky, rain spattered, and thunder growled. Exhausted by her recent trials, Lilia succumbed to the comfort and warmth of her bed. She hoped to sleep longer than usual, but she was ripped from her stupor by the sounds of a soul being shredded from the inside. Lilia threw open her shutters, letting in a woman's blood-curdling cries, a flash of lightning, and rumbling from afar.

"Not my family! Oh, dear God, I will never see you again!"

Lilia darted outside to see what was happening. She found her parents at the gate, clutching one another and gasping in horror, while Eliseo stood trembling in disbelief. Lilia peeled her eyes to the street, where a scene of the purest pain played out before her. She saw Albina running after her husband and children, who had been seized by the Germans. Lilia's cousin Ada was among them—she was seven months pregnant. Lilia had believed this wartime terror could not get any worse, but now, she was face-to-face with its brutal reality.

When the Germans burst through their front door, Ferruccio panicked and, without thought to his family's safety, leaped out the upstairs window to save himself. He ran across rooftops to avoid capture and waited in hiding until the soldiers left—while his father, two sisters, and little brother were arrested and made to trudge on at gunpoint in single file. From the piazza, they boarded the army truck destined for the Udine prison. For most of his adult life, the villagers regarded him as selfish and uncaring when it came to others' needs.

A village spy had turned the family in for aiding the American soldier. Every thread of Albina's happy memories would be forever clouded by an emptiness more agonizing than death.

"Take me! Please, I beg you!" Albina locked her fingers together, her wide eyes desperately searching the German soldier's face. "Take me with you! I want to be with my family!"

"Look at you, you pathetic old woman," he scoffed, shoving her to the ground. "Go home."

Lilia watched him smile with contempt as Albina crouched in the rain, crying out of every pore, begging for mercy for her family. How much more grief could they all endure? Lilia felt utterly deflated. She felt like God and any sense of human goodness she'd ever believed in had fled this place long ago.

Is this all my fault? Lilia thought, as her throat burned from all the screams she was keeping at bay. *Is it because of me that they found and helped the pilot?*

Maria and Virginio ran to Albina, trying to pull her inside, but she was wildly hysterical. "I would rather die than be without them!" she continued to sob. "How can I live without my family?"

When the truck pulled away, Albina dissolved into despair and collapsed to her knees, moaning and groaning as she clawed the rain-soaked dirt. Virginio tried to peel her limp, wet body off the ground. Her unblinking eyes had gone seemingly blind, and saliva dripped from her loose mouth on to him as he lifted her into his arms. The people of Mussons were left stunned and frozen in place, behind their walls, behind doors, behind shutters . . . all the while knowing nowhere was safe.

◦◦◦ ◦◦◦

Hours passed, and when the heaviness cast upon the hearts of the villagers seemed unbearable, more incredulous news reared its ugly head.

Amilio was Lilia's second cousin. He lived in Torsa, a small village on the other side of the river. His uncle Antonio was Virginio's cousin living two doors up from the Meneguzzis. On occasion, Amilio stopped by Lilia's family. When visiting, being a known Garibaldi partisan, he hopped the fence from his uncle's garden into Virginio's to avoid conflict and to protect their families.

Amilio was Arturo's age, and like Arturo, he was undeniably handsome, causing passers-by to pause and turn for a second look. His eyes stopped one's pulse—they were intense like a deep blue ocean, honest and kind. Even young Lilia found herself mesmerized by them.

Amid the chaos of the armistice, Amilio fought to release himself from the clutches of his underground band. He no longer wanted to be associated with the dangers involved in battling the Nazis, for fear of risking his and his family's lives. The partisan leaders were suspicious and thought Amilio was a spy when he expressed his reluctance to partake in their insurgent activity against the Germans. Like the villagers, the partisans could trust no one, not even their fellow fighters—they threatened to punish him.

News of Amilio passing through Mussons alerted partisan leaders. He attempted to escape his band leader's clutches but was captured running for his life in the local cemetery. The partisans tortured Amilio for information, and in the end—castrated and with gouged-out eyes—left to die. It was a stab to the heart of his family and everyone who knew him. His tragic death made the papers, and the gruesome photo of his body circulated throughout Mussons until it landed before Lilia's eyes, the same day the Nazis captured Ada's family.

Seeing her aunt's world viciously torn apart, and now the horrific and merciless torture and killing of her cousin Amilio weighed her down with feelings of hopelessness. Never having seen anything like this, nor believing it was possible to treat another human this way, her face sank immediately into her hands, and her insides turned cold.

Death doesn't care, and whoever did this are monsters.

She felt the devil's hood would hang over her family forever. Haunted by war, she prayed, "God, let me grow up before I die."

මැ මැ

Not a week later, Ada was released from prison and reunited back into the arms of her mother and brother Ferruccio. The celebration was quiet. Too much pain had passed through their walls. Ada, Albina, and Ferruccio continued to pray that heaven would save their loved ones who had been shipped off to suffer in hell.

One Sunday afternoon, Ada visited the Meneguzzi family. Sitting around their kitchen table, Maria, Virginio, Eliseo, and Lilia listened to Ada. Her words alone bled their ears. Knowing they were true cut them to their core.

"When we got there, they put us all in different rooms. I didn't know what was happening, but I heard them cry through the walls—I was terrified for us all," her eyes glimmered with watery tears, "and . . . my baby."

"After two days, they put us in one room. We didn't know where they would take us, but at least we were together. When they released us from prison, trains were waiting outside. People were lining up. As we passed the checkpoint—" here, Ada broke down, "—they tore my family apart!"

Virginio grabbed her hands as waves of sadness rushed over him, too. "They sent Papa on one train, Speme on another, and Gino, my sweet little Gino, alone on a third train—I can still see his face." Ada looked up from the table. Anguish permeated every cell of the family's bodies—this was real.

"He was so scared, he couldn't cry. I kept my eyes on him for as long as I could, and then I was next—the last one. The German soldier was young, not much older than Gino. I overheard him ask a Polish woman why I was in hysterics. She looked at him pleading, pointing to him I was pregnant, and he pushed me aside. He looked at me with almost sad eyes—and then he let me go! The young soldier directed me to run to a point beyond the station, where I hid until he signaled me to escape. I could see him distracting the other soldiers as I watched the trains from around the corner of the building. Here I was walking away, with my life and the life inside of me—" Ada lovingly rubbed her belly, "—yet knowing my family was being sent to some dark unknown place. I wept for my freedom. I wept for their lives."

Virginio's face twitched when Ada spoke of the young soldier. His eyes glazed over with astonishment. Could it be that he, his niece, and her unborn child were spared by the same young German boy? Virginio knew in his heart it must be so. Tears fell down his face; to his family, this was a natural reaction to his niece's account of her close call. But they didn't realize his tears were for the soldier, for the overwhelming gratitude Virginio felt for him—one of the few who had apparently not been manipulated by Hitler.

"He may be a Nazi—" Ada paused, "but I'll never forget he spared me and my baby."

Ada sat back in her chair, spilling hot tears that carved new lines onto her fatigued face. "I turned and ran until I found a bus to Morsano—I ran until I was home. I will always hold contempt for those monsters, but I felt . . . if that young soldier could have, he would have saved us all."

11 | ARTURO

December 1943

ཀ On one of her many treks to gather firewood by the dike, Lilia spotted droves of unarmed men crossing the Tagliamento. By train or on foot, one by one, soldiers were running home to Mussons and neighboring towns—many dressed as civilians to avoid altercations with German forces.

Lilia's heart quickened as she scanned the stream of men in search of her brother, but Arturo wasn't among them.

Maybe he'll come tomorrow.

Over the next week, soldiers continued to funnel into the streets— battle-worn, haggard men met by loved ones and villagers who ran out to give them food and clean, dry clothing. Wives embraced their husbands, mothers their sons, and children searched for their brothers and fathers.

Day and night, Maria shuffled her tired feet across the kitchen floor to peer out the window. She patrolled the front gate, wishing for the hundredth time Arturo would appear, but Via della Chiesa grew quiet, and the sun rose and fell with no sign of her beloved son. Maria's gaze rested on his photo as she passed the buffet, but nothing could replace the sound of Arturo's laughter and his calming voice, or the gentleness in his eyes.

"I'd walk through the gates of hell to keep you safe." Maria brushed her fingers along the picture frame. "Come home."

Over the next week, she traveled from village to village with Lilia, approaching every farm and making her way through a continuous wave of soldiers.

"My son is Arturo Meneguzzi." His photo trembled in Maria's hand. "Do you know him? Have you seen him?"

"No Signora, I'm sorry."

"He's tall with blonde hair and blue eyes. He's from Mussons."

"No, I'm sorry, I don't know him."

Some men stopped to offer their apologies and courtesies, but many wanted to get home to their families.

After many days and failed attempts, Maria's head spun as she felt all the roads converge into a dead end on what felt like the end of hope.

"Mama?" The bottom of Lilia's stomach seemed to fall out as she saw her mother's despair deepen.

Maria's breath hovered in her throat. "He's gone. My boy is never coming back!"

Lilia struggled to hold up her mother, who all at once seemed weak and frail.

"Mama, he's coming back. Arturo promised me!"

Nothing Lilia said to comfort her mother seemed to get through. Maria felt like she was floating out of her body as she looked at her daughter, dazed. She was a forlorn wraith standing silently in the middle of the street as life continued and people moved around her.

Huddled together, they made the long walk back to a home filled with mourning.

Maria continued to watch other families reunite with their loved ones, and their joyous relief amplified her longing for her son to return. As she and Lilia entered the gate, they heard a young man's voice through the open window—it seemed familiar, but it wasn't the one Maria yearned to hear.

She pushed open the kitchen door and saw the back of a young man sitting in a wheelchair talking to Virginio and Eliseo. Virginio's eyes had glazed over.

"Maria?" He looked up at his wife, hoping for some positive news—any news. Maria slowly shook her head, and the young man wheeled around. For a moment, Maria froze as the shock rolled over her. The sight of him was all it took for weeks of tears to burst forth, despite her desperate effort to repress them.

It was Paolo, Erminio's closest friend in Mussons.

"My God, you're alive!" Maria wiped her face with the back of her hand and threw her arms around him, while Lilia's mouth fell open in astonishment. She couldn't help but fixate on the blanket that lay across Paolo's lap, barely concealing his amputated legs.

"Lilia, come, sit here." Eliseo motioned her over, tapping the seat next to him.

Virginio pulled a chair up for his wife. "Maria," he paused, knowing this news would be difficult for her to hear. "Paolo was with Erminio . . . in Russia."

Maria quickly turned pale and anxious. She sat back, pleating her apron with nervous fingers.

"Paolo, tell me. What do you know?"

Obviously reluctant to rehash the painful details, his swallow was hard and audible. "We were outside Stalingrad, and—" concerned for Maria, Paolo looked over at Virginio, who nodded, encouraging him to continue, "—and not prepared or trained to fight this battle. The army trucks were in short supply. We had to walk hundreds of kilometers with our light mountain gear in sub-zero temperatures. It was so cold, a cold you could never imagine. Soldiers were being trampled by Russian tanks and pushed into the deep snow. Many panicked, dropped their weapons, and turned back . . . but our commanding officer ordered us to advance . . . and so, we did."

"And . . . Erminio?" Maria braced herself, hoping she could handle whatever Paolo was about to say.

"He was the last person I saw . . . *after* I was hit—I couldn't move. I kept telling him to run—to save himself, but Erminio refused to leave me. We had little food left—my God, we ate frozen grass and snow." Paolo rubbed his limbs and let out a deflating sigh. His voice shook as he continued.

"I gave Erminio the last of my rations and told him to look out for himself, as the Red Cross would eventually come for me. I lay there nearly frozen—my face no longer moved. Had I not felt the blink of my eyes and heard Erminio cry over me, I would have thought I was dead. He held my hands, which had fallen into a numb sleep. We said our goodbyes, and then he was gone. I watched Erminio disappear into the white-out—that was the last I saw of him. I don't know how much time passed, but I was losing consciousness until the medics finally carried me out. I spent many months in the hospital. I remember passing by garbage bins filled with gangrenous limbs, and soldiers moaning in agony. War is hell."

His next words were slow, as though his brain were struggling to process them. "I came home half a man, without my legs . . . without my best friend." His voice trailed off as he dropped his gaze to his lap.

Maria reached over and caressed his face lovingly like she would her sons. Her voice was soft when she spoke, "Thank you."

That night, Maria prayed until sleep enfolded her. With each touch of the rosary beads, she wished for Erminio's soul to rest in peace. He appeared to her, beaming his boyish smile and his eyes twinkled with laughter. He seemed happy. "You were my cherished son, the flesh of my flesh, the closest to my heart. Until my dying breath, I will thank God for giving you to me." Maria couldn't focus on her memories of him anymore, as they cut too deep. In her final prayer, Maria's insides turned tightly. She asked for one miracle.

ৡৢ ঀৣ

Early the next morning, Maria awoke to a choir of voices pouring in through the open window. Her eyes rolled open and glazed over; the rosary was still wrapped around her hand. The clamoring grew louder as a villager hollered at the gate.

"Maria! Maria! Look who's coming! It's your son!"

A rush of adrenaline coursed through her body. "*Erminio!*" In a moment of befuddlement, his name sounded on her lips, but Maria caught herself—it had to be Arturo.

My God, could it be?

She threw the covers off, hurriedly pulled on her clothes, and stumbled out into the hall, banging against the walls as she dashed downstairs. Her euphoric cries echoed through the house.

"Lilia! Boys! Wake up—Arturo is coming!"

Maria's excitement stirred everyone around her. She blew open the front door.

"Virginio! He's coming!"

Virginio had already dropped his tools and tore out of the barn and into the street. Breathless, Maria ran behind him. Her arms flailed and tears of joy and disbelief poured from her eyes as they strained into the distance. After weeks of prayers and the chaotic retreat of thousands of soldiers, Arturo was making his way down Via della Chiesa, leading the last of the troops. He was thinner and ragged, dressed in civilian clothing and covered in dirt and mud. His eyes appeared smaller and looked tired. He had been transformed. Maria

214

saw lines in his face she had never seen before, but to her, Arturo was as beautiful a vision as ever.

"Oh my God, my son! My *son*!"

The dark visions of war were instantly yanked out of Arturo the moment he saw Maria. It was like walking through one of his many dreams, but this time it was real.

Arturo embraced his mother, who unraveled in his arms like a spool of delicate lace. "It's all right, Mama. Don't cry." Her warmth and love radiated through his entire body.

"Papa!" Arturo looked up to see his father's tear-streaked face break into a grin.

"My boy!" Virginio pulled him into a tight embrace.

"It's good to be alive, Papa," Arturo whispered, tears stinging his eyes for all the time they'd missed. "It's good to be home."

Lilia felt her entire world burst into sunshine as she ran into her big brother's arms, the young boys flanking her sides. Everything felt brighter, crisper. The greyness of the landscape gave way to color.

"Arturo! I knew you would come back!"

"I always keep my promises." A smile he had not felt in over a year cracked on Arturo's face as he caressed Lilia's hair. "How's my favorite girl? And look at you, boys! How big you've grown!" Arturo pinched Bruno's cheeks, and with the last of his strength, threw Giovanni and Riccardo over his shoulders, generating a chain reaction of laughter.

This long-awaited family reunion was a sight to behold for villagers, who watched in adoration. Amid the celebration, Maria dropped to her knees to kiss the ground. "Thank you, Lord, for answering my prayer . . . for bringing him home."

Back at the house, Maria fluttered contentedly in the kitchen, as if the room were alive with music.

"Arturo, my love, sit. You must be starving and exhausted. Lilia, go to the pump and fill the bucket with water so your brother can take a bath. Virginio, light the fireplace and while you're in the great room, get our boy some food from the cantina," She caressed her son's head repeatedly and squeezed his shoulders. "You're here!"

Arturo reached for her hand. "Mama, relax, I'm *fine*. All I need is a long night of sleep, and tomorrow will be a new day. I promise it will be like I never left. Nothing that feels this good right now could go wrong again—being with my family is the only place I want to be." He kissed her hand as Virginio, and Eliseo strolled in with fresh cheese and a stick of salami—they were grinning, ear to ear. The boys followed with a basket of bread, giddy from all the excitement.

Arturo looked expectantly around. Any moment now, he knew he would see his brother Erminio strolling in with a mischievous smile, slicked-back hair, and lipstick kisses smeared on his collar and cheeks.

"So, where's Valentino?" Arturo let out a chuckle. "Where's that good-looking brother of mine?"

Lilia had arrived into the kitchen with the bucket of water. She tentatively placed the pail on the floor. Her face flushed red with sadness. Maria turned to the window to shield her pain, and Eliseo quickly gathered the boys and took them upstairs. Virginio pulled out a chair and sat down next to Arturo. He knew this moment had to come, but he still didn't feel prepared to share the news with his son.

Arturo felt the palpable change in his family's mood; their previous carefree joy had been sucked out of the room.

"Somebody please tell me what is going on?" Arturo beseeched his father. Virginio's face drained to a pale shade of dread.

"He's gone!" Maria blurted out. "Your brother is dead." The force of her words shocked everyone, including herself. Maria clamped her hands over her mouth and whimpered. A chill permeated the room, and the news fell like darkness snaking around Arturo's mind and body. Darkness that Arturo had come to know as his reality over the last several years.

He quivered in outrage. "No, no, no!" Arturo stood up, but his tired legs buckled. His father leaped up to support him. "Papa? What happened?!"

"The army stationed him in Russia—they never found his body." Virginio's throat clenched as he tried to breathe through the resurgent grief. "They declared him missing in action."

Tears prickled Arturo's eyelids, blinding him. "If I had been there, I could have protected him! Saved him! I should have been there!"

Virginio could feel the pain and guilt that choked his son's words. "It was out of your hands, son, out of all our hands. Erminio is with God now."

"He should never have left!" Arturo cried into his father's shoulder. "It should have been me who died."

The remainder of the day felt heavy and numb. Arturo knew how frightened Erminio had been of war, and images of the traumatic ending he must have endured flooded Arturo's mind, even as memories of his beloved brother continued to ambush him.

He didn't know how to accept the unacceptable.

He lay awake most of the night, staring at the empty bed next to him. Nothing remained of Erminio but an armoire of his dapper suits and shiny, well-polished shoes. Like a gust of wind, Erminio had left Arturo's life.

"I'm sorry, brother. I'm sorry I wasn't there. You didn't even make it to your twenty-first birthday." He breathed a deep and heavy sigh. "What is this all for . . ." Arturo was inundated by grief, but as always, a whisper of hope managed to trickle in. He had managed to save some of the letters Angelina had written him while still stationed in Udine before the army sent him away, and she nor his family knew where he was. They were worn and creased from so many readings. Each letter ended with, "I miss you."

Arturo pulled one of the letters out of a large, stained and wrinkled, manila envelope. He held the paper close to his face—it smelled of her, of Angelina's sweet vanilla scent. He had envisioned her writing to him; he could almost hear her gentle voice with each word that graced his eyes, words that gave him warmth on many cold nights, promises that led him home. She was the one who could chase the heaviness from his soul and revive him to life.

⁂

The morning light swelled through the window. It felt stark and cruel against Arturo's puffy eyelids. His limbs were heavy, yet he pulled himself up to face the overwhelming echo of death in the room and the loss that surrounded him.

Erminio should be here with me. We should have woken up together, and I should be listening to him ramble on about girls.

"Arturo?" A sweet, soft voice broke the eerie silence. Lilia stood at the bedroom door in her nightie. She, too, was staring at the empty bed, which she had been avoiding ever since they'd learned about Erminio's fate.

"Come. Hop in." Arturo sensed Lilia's need for his attention. He felt sorrow over his bittersweet homecoming; it didn't seem fair that his family should celebrate his return as they mourned Erminio's demise.

"Are you staying this time?" Lilia folded her legs beneath her nightie and tucked herself into her brother's side. Arturo stroked her back in circles and kissed her hair.

"I'm done fighting, piccina. I'm not going anywhere."

"Are you going to see *that* girl again?"

"Well, I have been gone for a long time. I miss *that* girl, too, like I missed you."

"I don't *like* Angelina." Lilia pouted while continuing to fiddle with the buttons on her brother's shirt.

Arturo laughed. "Have you and Mama been plotting to break us up?"

"No, but I *feel* things. And whenever I see her, she ignores me. She's not like us."

"Fair enough, but give her a chance. Look, once you get to know Angelina, you'll change your mind, but until then—" Arturo tickled Lilia's sides, throwing her into a fit of giggles.

"Stop . . . *stop it*!" Lilia squealed as she wiggled away.

"All right, last one downstairs is a dirty, rotten egg!"

Lilia leaped forwards, running ahead of her brother. The hollow pit in his stomach felt less painful. The pain had been alleviated, at least for a moment. For Arturo, his sister's lightheartedness brought him back to all that was good and kind in the world, even in this time of utter chaos and a loss that seemed unending.

⁘

It was midday, and the villagers had turned in for their riposo. Arturo thought it was the perfect opportunity to surprise Angelina. Despite time and distance, Arturo felt more devoted to her than ever. He had already married her in his heart.

He commenced with his old ritual of throwing pebbles at her bedroom window to alert her of his arrival. She would sneak out and climb down the adjacent apple tree to meet him, and together they would float off to their secret hiding place in the woods—a place unknown to anyone but them.

Standing under her window, he proceeded to ping the shutters. Minutes passed, and she didn't show up. Arturo climbed the tree and peered into her room; the bed was made. She was gone. Perplexed, he wondered where she could be. Still, knowing they would soon be together forever was all Arturo needed.

Anything is possible in this world with Angelina in it.

Arturo decided to go to their secret spot, hoping maybe she was there missing him, too.

She must have heard I was home.

Over those long months, thoughts of Angelina had pulled him out of the darkness of war. He had waited so long to hold her, kiss her, spend an eternity with her. Arturo felt like the luckiest man alive.

The weather was fresh and crisp. As Arturo walked through the woods under a canopy of bare branches and evergreens, the sunlight playfully danced through the trees, mirroring his dreamy state. The sparks of being in love tickled his insides as he neared the oak tree where he and Angelina had spent many afternoons. He shivered not from the cold, but from the sheer excitement and hope of her being there. Through the rustle of the breeze and the leaves crunching under his feet, the silence of the forest broke with a familiar sweet sound—it was Angelina.

Arturo halted, holding his breath to listen until another voice surfaced—that of a man. Although frantic, he crept noiselessly through rows of bushes to reveal a Nazi soldier laying his head on Angelina's lap. She ran her fingers through his blonde hair and caressed his chiseled face. She flirted with words that, to Arturo, felt like shrapnel in his chest.

"You're so strong and powerful—a real man." Angelina playfully dangled her hair over the German. "And I love this jeweled hair comb you bought me. I feel so regal!"

"You like sparkly, shiny things, don't you?" He leaned closer brushing his lips against hers while winding one of Angelina's long tresses around his hand. "A woman like you must have many boyfriends buying you special gifts." Their intimate exchange pierced Arturo's heart like a dagger.

Angelina laughed, and the sweet silver sound pierced the air. "No, but there was one man, and he was penniless. Besides, he left for war, and he'll probably *never* return. He wasn't that special."

"Well then, next time I'll put something *pretty* . . . here." He leaned in to kiss her neck.

Arturo felt the blood drain from his face as he slowly pulled back; he could taste the betrayal. Angelina had deceived him with the enemy.

He quickly turned to run away and stumbled over piles of fallen twigs. His knees faltered, and he toppled on to a bed of decaying leaves.

"Who's there?" The German stood, prepared to fire when a brown squirrel scampered up the adjacent tree with an acorn.

Angelina laughed. "It's a poor squirrel—ignore it. Now, come back to me."

A sense of foreboding hung in the air. Arturo weaved through the forest in a wild daze, disoriented by the light flickering through the trees. A once-peaceful escape was now a hell where he had left his happiness for good.

She didn't wait for me! She lied!

There were two wolves in the forest that day—the worse of them was his betrothed. Arturo walked for hours by the river, trying to clear his head. All he'd ever felt for Angelina was blown away in that gut-wrenching moment, like ashes in the wind, with nothing left but an aching hole where love used to be.

⁂

Dinner came and went, and there was no sign of Arturo. Maria grew worried.

"Did he tell you where he was going?"

Virginio raised his shoulders. "He didn't say, but I imagine he went to see his friends and lost track of time. He's a big boy."

"He went to see *Angelina*." Lilia demonstrated her disapproval with an eye roll.

"Oh, I see." Maria put away the dishes and tried to embrace her gratitude—at least Arturo was safely back home.

Hours passed. It was near midnight. Maria and Virginio sprung awake to a loud ruckus that filtered throughout the house. Voices rose to a raging crescendo and banging rattled the walls. Alarmed, they rushed downstairs to find Arturo shoving furniture and yelling profanities. Maria had never seen nor heard her son behave in this manner; she instantly broke into a fit of tears. Arturo's friends were also there, trying to hold him back, but he was clearly intoxicated. In a drunken fit, he resisted them.

"Arturo, don't do this, please!" Maria begged him to stop as she circled him, desperate to calm her son. "Virginio, do something!"

Arturo drove his fist through the kitchen door, nearly taking it off its hinges, despite his father's attempt to restrain him. "Get off me!" His knuckles bled crimson. "I'll kill him!" He kicked and screamed, trying to wrestle out of Virginio's grip.

It took all five men to pin him to the floor. Lilia and Giovanni came running and hovered on the landing as they watched in horror.

"Get back to bed. Now!"

They obeyed their mother immediately but stayed in the darkness of the landing, crouched in fear and confusion as they listened to the drama unfold.

"She left me . . . to be with that Nazi scum—and not just one of them!" Arturo let out a blood-curdling scream. "Everybody knew!" His rage slowly subsided into heart-breaking sobs in his father's arms. "How could she do this to me? I would have given her the *world*."

As Maria watched her son, she knew she would never forget the inferno in his eyes and the whore who'd lit the match.

જાછ ૭ે

It was late morning. Arturo awoke with a gray aura around him. His head pounded, and his throbbing hand was still bruised and swollen—he faintly remembered how it got that way. Arturo sat hunched over in his bed with a powerful sense of loss, one from which he feared he would never recover. Regretful of the previous night's eruption, Arturo sought out his parents to ask for forgiveness.

Maria and Lilia had taken over the dining-room table and were kneading and rolling out balls of dough into thick, long ropes. Excited to see her big brother had surfaced from his stupor, Lilia beamed up at him, her eyes aglow. She was speckled in flour. "I'm making gnocchi!" Lilia's smile warmed Arturo's heart in a way the sun never could—especially now.

"*Piccina*, shouldn't there be more flour on the dough than on your face?"

Lilia giggled and shrugged.

"Less laughing, more working, young lady!" Maria cut the rope into small pieces and shaped the gnocchi. "Lilia, watch what I do with the fork." She rolled the gnocchi along the tines to flatten them and to create the traditional decorative ridge. "Now, you do the rest, and when you finish, cover them with the dishtowel—we'll boil them right before dinner time."

"Mama?" Arturo pulled his mother aside, while Lilia flattened one too many gnocchi into mini pancakes. "I wanted to apologize to you and Papa for my behavior last night. Saying sorry feels meaningless after what I did. It won't take away the heartache I put you both through, but . . ." Arturo looked around to evaluate the extent of the damage he'd caused to the house and was overwhelmed with shame. "Mama, I'm so sorry."

Maria glanced at the hole in the kitchen door, her son's saddened face, and the black and blue bruises on his hands. "I don't know what to say. It's not a side of you I've seen, and I hope I never see it again."

Arturo sighed with remorse. He'd never imagined anything would drive him to drink, let alone that much, or to lose his temper in such an extreme way. His face crinkled with the full realization of what he'd done . . . and now that Arturo was sober, the painful truth of Angelina seeped in.

Maria softened at that moment. She could tell he was fighting a battle he would ultimately lose—and he needed to feel the awful truth to let it go.

"She didn't deserve your tears, or this—" Maria cradled his

swollen hand. "She didn't deserve *you*. Spend some time in the garden and pull up a few bushels of radicchio for later. The fresh air will do you good, son."

Lilia had finished preparing her culinary masterpiece and noticed Arturo had been gone an unusually long time. She traipsed through the garden to find him. Nearing the pathway, she saw wisps of smoke at the end of the row; they were twisting up towards the sky. Her brother was crouched on his knees, his back towards Lilia.

"Arturo, what are you doing?"

Abruptly, he rose to face his little sister. There was no trace of tears, but his face had reddened. His eyes flashed with indignation and pain.

"Starting a new chapter, piccina, starting a new chapter." He brushed the flour out of her hair with his fingers and shook his head, chuckling. "I'll wash the radicchio and bring it inside." He gave her a knowing wink and whispered, "Maybe you should clean up your hands and face before dinner—you know Mama!"

As Arturo left, Lilia's eyes drifted over to where he was in the garden. The smoke had cleared, and all that remained was a small bed of ashes and a ripped piece of singed paper. She picked it up, dusting off the soot and dirt. Lilia could still make out the words, "I miss you." She quickly shredded the paper and buried those betraying words deep in the dust.

∾⊛ ⊛∾

The dinner was set, and eight pairs of hands folded around the table.

"Do you want to say grace?" Virginio asked, squeezing Arturo's hand.

All heads bowed in prayer as Arturo pondered for a moment.

"Dear Lord, thank you for putting us together again—for the gift of family. We come into your love with grateful hearts—" Giovanni and Riccardo fidgeted. Lilia kicked them gently under the table, while Maria gave them a stern look. "Bless my sisters, Ermides and Dina, who cannot be here—keep them safe from harm," Arturo raised his eyes to Eliseo, "and bless Mariutta, whose sweet soul is greatly missed. And—" Arturo paused as an involuntary whimper escaped him. Virginio grabbed his shoulder in compassion, "—help us cope with the empty seat at our table. Our family chain is broken since you called Erminio away. He will always be beside us to comfort us, behind us to protect us, below us to support us, and above us to bless us. We pray you watch over him until one day, one by one, our chain will link again. May this food nourish our bodies and provide us with the strength we need to endure the days ahead. Amen." A wave of stillness washed over the table.

"That was beautiful, son, thank you," Virginio said softly. Deeply touched, Eliseo was at a loss for words. He gave Arturo a gentle nod.

Maria felt water creep out of her eyes, too. She quickly squared her shoulders and released a deep breath. "All right, children, sit up straight! Chew with your mouths closed, and don't talk with your mouths full!"

Disenchanted with his meal, Giovanni flipped the dumplings around on his plate. "Mama? What happened to the gnocchi? Almost all of mine are flat!"

"Mine, too." Riccardo speared three on his fork, while Bruno was content to be handling his utensil well.

Maria's eyes narrowed as she gave Lilia a sideways look. "Ask your sister."

Lilia dropped her shoulders and slumped in her chair.

"You know what, boys?" Arturo shot Lilia a wink of encouragement. "Just because something doesn't look perfect doesn't mean it isn't good."

"And because something looks perfect doesn't mean it will make you happy," Lilia intoned as she looked her brother lovingly in the eye. She adored the bond they shared and the way they understood each other without having to do or say much at all—she would do anything to protect him. Her being with him was the purest form of comfort she had ever felt.

Arturo smiled at her in amazement. "Liliutti, you are so wise for your age. One day you are going to change the world."

⁂

The occupying Nazi troops were notorious for seeking out women for pleasure. As food was scarce, some women had sex with the Germans for the sake of survival, and to protect their families. Others, having lost their husbands to war, imprisonment, or death, eased their grief and loneliness with these fleeting dalliances. Angelina and Frida, the one friend she had left in Mussons, accepted liaisons with the Germans for the allure of money and decadent parties, as well as a glamorous lifestyle they had always craved.

Women caught fraternizing with German soldiers were labeled prostitutes. Many were chased by mocking crowds, who stripped them naked and forcibly shaved their heads. They were beaten and humiliated in public as punishment for their adultery.

The community suspected Angelina and Frida of consorting with the Nazis weeks before Arturo's return. The two were shunned when roaming gossip confirmed both women had contracted gonorrhea. Angelina had disgraced her family and the village she'd once called home, which to Maria was fitting retribution for sleeping with the enemy and betraying her beloved son.

⚬◍◐ ◑◍⚬

Time passed. Over the next few months, Arturo cast his heartache aside and refocused his time and energy on his newly appointed position. In the field, he was an explosives expert and a high-ranking officer; the military revered him as a hero for saving a general's life. Arturo was awarded a gold medal of valor for outstanding gallantry in war and assigned the highly sought-after role of Head of the Night-Duty Watchmen by the mayor of the province. He and his men enforced a curfew and patrolled the streets. Around the clock, they protected the people of Mussons and neighboring villages and towns from bombings and gunfire.

Since Arturo's new appointment in April, his childhood acquaintance, Marcello, made unusually frequent visits to his house in an attempt to recruit him to the resistance, which was now at its peak. They had grown up together and lived a few streets apart. As the only child of a war widow, Marcello was exempt from going to war.

While the villagers admired Arturo for his bravery, valuing him as an essential member of the community, they treated Marcello in a less favorable light.

Because he'd never earned the same level of respect, not even from his own family, Marcello was blinded with envy and resentment. Even when they were young boys, he'd secretly despised Arturo. Marcello vied for Arturo's new position, not for the desire to feel indispensable like his friend but for the power of control it held; after all, heading the night-duty watchmen was the perfect way for the underground to retrieve information.

One afternoon, Marcello confronted Arturo outside the gate of the Meneguzzi home.

"Arturo, come join us." Marcello scanned the street, conscious of watchful eyes and attentive ears.

Arturo ignored him and blew through the gate, stalking towards the barn, which was now his designated office space.

Marcello followed him in earnest pursuit. "With recruits swarming in, we need arms and supplies—you can help. The movement is stronger than ever. The underground needs a man like you! Come on, why are you wasting your time policing these streets?"

"No, Marcello. I've told you time and time again, no! I don't want any part of it."

"What, are you too good for us now with your medal of valor, *night-duty watchman?*" Marcello mocked.

Arturo grabbed Marcello's arm and forcefully yanked him inside the barn, away from view, "We are done having this conversation." Irritated, Arturo rustled through papers on the workbench. "The last thing I want is to endanger myself and my family." Arturo turned to Marcello with incredulous outrage. "You *know* how this will end. One for ten—you take one of them down, they kill ten civilians! The Germans will break our legs, burn our houses, rape our mothers and our sisters, put bullets in our heads—worse, take us all to the camps!" Arturo braced himself against the workbench and dropped his head as he took a deep breath. "I *hate* them more than you know, but I love my family *more*. And I care about what happens to people here—they need me!" Arturo's head came up, and he looked Marcello square in the eyes. "I'm the one who fought in the war, not you! No one can do this job better than I can—especially not someone who is always out for himself. You always were . . . and nothing has changed. Go back to your dark corner of the world. You're on your own—get off my property and don't come back."

Marcello's chest rose and fell in angry breaths. He gave Arturo a caustic grin. "You think you're better than me? I'd watch your back if I were you—evil lurks in the most unsuspecting places and people." After a long and seething pause, he stormed off.

Maria quickly released her hand from the curtain and hid from the kitchen window. She knew she had witnessed an intense altercation. Maria was consumed with worry. Trouble always followed Marcello. He'd always been a defiant, selfish child and master manipulator—it seemed he'd left his mother's womb destined to be a wicked man.

Flinching at the slam of the gate, Maria ran out to her son. "What happened? What did he want?"

Arturo was noticeably agitated. "Nothing, Mama. We won't be seeing him anymore."

঩ඏ ඏঌ

June 1944

At the crack of dawn, a dull humming sound was heard coming from the piazza. It had been weeks since Mussons had felt the rumble of German vehicles. Maria lay still, straining her ears. As soon as she and Virginio instinctively grabbed the children, they heard the gate rattle—the Gestapo were at their home.

"Open the door!"

"Mother of God! Virginio, what do they want?"

At the same time, Arturo and Eliseo came running down the hall.

"Papa, stay here with Mama and the kids! I'll go!"

"No! You're not going. Let your father go!"

Virginio hurried downstairs with Eliseo. The moment they lifted the latch, the Germans exploded through the door, pushing them aside.

Two Gestapo proceeded to search the grounds and house, while three others escorted Arturo, Maria, and the children down into the great room.

"What do you want?" Virginio stood up to the Nazis and shot Maria a quick, anxious look.

"You!" The officer waved his rifle over to Arturo. "Are you Arturo Meneguzzi?"

"Yes, I am."

"You need to come with us."

"What is this about?" Arturo kept his composure, thinking of his family's safety.

"We have orders to take you for questioning into Udine headquarters."

Lilia let a frightened gasp escape her lips. Virginio fixed his gaze on his daughter, giving her a subtle nod so she would not make another sound.

Silent terror filled Lilia's eyes as Arturo grew increasingly nervous. "Headquarters? For what? Why?"

"We have been notified that you are in possession of your service weapon."

"That's not possible. I turned it in!" Arturo was incredulous. "Where did this notification come from?"

"There are no guns in this house, I can assure you." Virginio made himself sound as confident and resolute as he could manage, despite the cold sweat that trickled down his back.

The soldiers searched the property and tore up the house, leaving no piece of furniture unturned. They found nothing. Watching the

Gestapo invade and destroy his family's home brought Arturo right back to that heart-wrenching night when he lost his way over the woman who betrayed him and wounded his soul.

"Until we have verification, you must come with us. We have also been alerted on secret authority from our informants that you're covertly aiding the rebels."

"My son, a *partisan*? Never!" At that moment, Maria was haunted by a memory she would not soon forget. She realized who she was talking to: the evil-eyed Nazi who'd raided the house and threatened her had returned to take something valuable—Maria's son. She lunged wildly towards him as Virginio held her back.

Arturo turned to his parents, disbelief wracking his body. *How could this be happening? Who is responsible for these lies?*

"He has a medal of *valor*! He's a good man! Why are you doing this?" Maria implored.

"There must be some misunderstanding. Arturo is a respected military officer. He is not working with the underground." Virginio hoped that by remaining calm and diplomatic, he could reason with these men.

Lilia was pinned into place in the corner of the room while her little brothers clung to her. Her tiny body shook uncontrollably with hatred.

I can't lose my big brother now!

A tremor overtook Lilia. She broke free from her thick wall of fear and lanced through the room. She pushed past the Germans and pulled on Arturo's arm, her voice trembling as she pleaded through her tears.

"You can't go! You *promised*! You promised!"

Arturo detached her hands and shoved her gently away. "*Piccina*, I have to go." He stared at his parents with a strained, beseeching look. There was so much he wanted to say, but in this life-or-death moment, he knew he couldn't.

Lilia slowly withdrew and moved back towards her little brothers to comfort them. She sensed her world closing in around her again. Her heart sank as she watched the light dim in Arturo's eyes.

"Arturo, don't go with them! If you do, I'll never see you again!" Maria fell to her knees in a disheveled heap, tears coursing down her face. Even as she begged at his feet, she knew it was hopeless. She knew what darkness was to come.

"Mama, if I don't go now, they will kill us all."

12 | STAY WITH ME MARIA

🌀 Dina had just poured herself a cup of tea. She sipped from the cup in her hand while reading a letter sent to her by her father. Dina jerked upright in sheer panic as her father's words rolled through her veins with dread—words that pierced her heart like sharp needles. Dina dropped the teacup, shattering it on the tile floor. She collapsed to her knees. Dina's chest tightened, and her stomach surged at the thought of her brother's fate now in the Nazis' grip. One week had passed since Arturo's arrest. Every minute for him would be hell, as most Nazi arrests were a death sentence.

> *. . . and after what Angelina did, he was destroyed for months—we'd never seen him like that. When the Gestapo showed up at our door and arrested him, we tried to stop them. They accused Arturo of not turning in his military weapon and of working with the partisans. A partisan? That's inconceivable! He's innocent! Someone framed your brother. Mama believes it was Marcello.*

> *Your mother is distraught that we'll never see Arturo again. We all are. You're there in Udine. Find out what you can. We love you.*

> *Papa*

Dina felt every second of Arturo's life was dependent on her—and time was running out. She was the only one who could see him, and in her mind, she was her family's last chance to bring what was hidden to light. She was determined to uncover the truth behind his unjust arrest and wrongful imprisonment. She would prove her brother's innocence and set him free.

Sleepless hours tormented Dina as the night wore on. She tossed and turned, fighting the morbid thoughts that tumbled through her mind. Could she truly prove Arturo's innocence and save him? She wrestled in tangled sheets until morning. With the darkness now looming over her brother's life, Dina believed she was the only hope he had left.

Dawn had broken, and the stark daylight splashed into Dina's tired eyes as she boarded the bus to see her brother in prison. *What will I find there? Is he being mistreated? Will they let me see Arturo? Will he be released?* Questions with no answers burned her brain, but Dina was determined to clear his name of any accusations and convince the Germans to let her bring Arturo home. Before arriving at Nazi headquarters, Dina witnessed an open field of prisoners from her window seat. She felt sick to her stomach as the bus inched by. People were bundled in groups and loaded into separate boxcars. Under the watchful eye of the Gestapo, families were separated. The innocent were stripped of their freedom.

Are they all headed for Germany? Dear God, please don't let Arturo be among them. I pray I'm not too late!

A sickening sensation came over her as she moved closer to the place where her brother was being held captive. Towering Nazi flags draped either side of the stone wall. The swastikas rose as high as her eyes could see, sending a chill of intimidation through Dina's body. She saw Gestapo and SS officers exit and enter the building. Their ominous presence blanketed the grounds with darkness, seemingly sucking all the light up into the sky.

Dina stepped off the bus in a sweat. She felt herself turn pale as she neared the two, stoic, armed guards operating the front gate.

Dina caught a glimpse of other civilians leaving the prison. As they moved to her right, they made brief eye contact, terrified of showing their emotions in front of security—stunned into silence. Perhaps they, too, had a loved one imprisoned here.

Dina's heart beat loudly; she was certain the guards could hear it.

"My brother was arrested one week ago. I have come to see him."

"Let me see your papers."

Dina extended her identification with quivering hands. Hitler's rants echoed and re-echoed in her mind as she sized up the fierceness of the guard's face. Her insides seized at the thought of her brother being held prisoner by these monsters. The guard returned her documents with not so much as a word. Dina assumed this was her cue to advance towards the door.

The visitation line had dwindled, and she was next to approach the sign-in desk. She introduced herself to the warden, who was logging everyone who came and went.

"I'm here to see my brother, Arturo Meneguzzi." Dina's jaw clenched, and despite all efforts to conceal her deep loathing, her eyes could not hide their contempt. "He was arrested in Mussons and brought in for questioning a few weeks ago."

The warden ignored Dina's request, keeping his attention on his paperwork. "Wait over there." He motioned her over to the far wall. It was cracked, covered with peeling, army-green paint, and streaked with water stains. A row of hard, upright metal chairs lined the narrow hallway. The prison smelled of stale air, cigarette smoke, and the stench of the Nazis and all they represented.

Dina clutched her purse tightly against her chest and eased herself into the seat—it felt cold against her bare legs. Her knees bounced, and her fingers twitched. An uncontrollable dread flooded every part of her body. Her senses were acute. She could hear weeping from behind the detention rooms and German voices rising in anger. Dina watched as a stream of Gestapo and SS officers marched the corridor—their shoulders squared, jaws rigid, and gait stiff, as though they could barrel through anything or anyone. Like dark clouds, they blocked the afternoon light that beamed through the high windows. The sun may have been warm, but Dina was chilled to the bone as she observed the Germans' faces. Each of them shared the same cast-iron, immovable expression.

Straight ahead of Dina hung a photo of Hitler—who looked more steely and determined than maniacal. Bile instantly rose in her throat. She shifted her eyes away from its invasive view, when the warden called out to her.

"You! Come here."

Dina approached his desk.

"You are here to see Arturo Meneguzzi?"

"Yes, I am. Arturo is my brother."

"His visiting privileges have expired, and according to my chart—" he gave her a cutting, accusatory look, "—his *sister* visited him this morning."

"What sister? *I'm* his sister! Dina Meneguzzi!"

"It's marked here: A woman from Mussons signed in as Dina Meneguzzi four hours ago."

"That's impossible! What woman? What did she look like?"

The warden peered over his clipboard and turned to a group of officers. They exchanged a few words in German while Dina waited impatiently. Her anger intensified as she clamped her fists and ground her nails into crescent moons in the palms of her hands. Laughter rose among the men. The warden looked back at Dina and raised his brow. "It appears she was a beautiful blonde." He smiled smugly, sizing up the brunette Dina with a leer.

Dina's face flushed, and her eyes gleamed with rage and disbelief. She rustled in her purse and pulled out her papers.

"Look!" She shook them in a temper. "*I* am Dina Meneguzzi! Arturo is my brother!"

The warden acknowledged her documents, shook his head, and let out a sarcastic cackle. He shrugged in mock sympathy. "Women. What whores they are."

"I want to see my brother!"

"He's a prisoner of war and leaving on the next train. There will *be* no more visits."

"Train! Train to where?"

He gave Dina a scathing look as his words razored through her heart. "Germany. But I'm sure once your brother has quarried enough stone, and if he's on his best behavior, they'll send him home in a year."

Right then, the doors swung open, and the light blazed through with intensity, sharp and blinding like the warden's words. Dina was numb. Lost. Unable to complete her thoughts. A sudden pain squeezed the front of her head as the guards escorted her through the gate.

The city bus pulled away, and a river of emotion ripped as gut-wrenching sobs tore through her chest. Like blood before her eyes, all she could see through her blurry vision was the prison, cloaked in Nazi flags, drifting out of sight. Dina knew she had lost her chance of ever seeing her brother again.

What happened? Who used my identity? And why?

As she thought about Mussons, Arturo, and her father's letter, the evil truth struck her cold.

Oh, dear, God! It was Angelina! Hasn't she done enough? What did she want! How could she do this?

Dina had never approved of Angelina, but she'd never dreamed that Arturo's lover could be so conniving. She had ruined Dina's chance to testify her brother's innocence against all these false accusations.

The woman who had betrayed her brother had determined his fate. Bitter regret swirled inside Dina.

If only I knew what Angelina said to Arturo. Why she lied. Why she ruined my brother's last chance at freedom. Faced with writing the most challenging letter in her life, she felt plunging pain in her core, knowing the devastation this news would have on her parents. Her family would never know peace in their hearts again.

Weeks had passed since the news that Arturo had been branded a prisoner of war. Not knowing which German camp he'd been sent to or if he would return, the Meneguzzis remained hopeful. They prayed for the end of this ordeal, for Arturo to find his way home as he had months ago.

Amid the torture of waiting, Maria was feeling unusually tired. She knew this feeling all too well. She suspected her family would be growing once again.

⁓⊙⊙⊙⁓

It was an August morning. The light of the sun was oddly bright, or so it appeared to Maria as she released the shutters from their iron hooks to push them open. An abrupt dizziness seized her, and she fell against the windowsill. Overwhelmed by shooting pain, Maria pressed both hands to her stomach. Her head felt like it was on fire. Despite her disorientation, she could sense something wasn't right. Her acute pangs increased. She reached for the bed and instantly doubled over as dark clots of blood streamed down her legs.

"Lilia! Come quickly!"

Lilia heard the breathlessness in her mother's voice and instantly ran into her parents' bedroom to find Maria pale-faced and in distress.

"Mama!"

"Go call your Aunt Theresa. Tell her to come immediately!"

Several minutes later, Lilia returned with Theresa and a few other women from the village. They scurried to Maria's bedside.

"Lilia, where's your father? Where's Eliseo?" Theresa quickly pulled the sheets off the bed.

"Papa's finishing some carpentry work at a neighbor's house. Eliseo left to see his son in Turin."

"Take the boys to Cornelia's now! And then wait downstairs!"

Lilia obeyed her aunt and whisked her brothers next door. Confusion dominated her every thought. Her mother's screams of agony made her cringe.

What is wrong with Mama?!

When Lilia returned, one of the women hurried down the stairs and out the front door, carrying a heap of blood-soaked sheets in her arms. She soaked them in the courtyard washbasin.

"Go find your father!"

Lilia didn't understand what was happening. As she tore out to alert Virginio, he was entering the gate, walking beside his bicycle, his tool pouch draped over the seat. Lilia's pallid face frightened him. Her eyes were wet with tears. She was visibly shaken.

"Liliutti, what's wrong!"

"Mama—something is wrong with Mama! There is blood everywhere!"

Virginio dropped the bicycle. "Wait here, Lilia!" he ordered as he ran to his wife. The house was filled with the echoes of Maria's agonized cries, which caused Virginio to imagine the worst. He pushed the dreaded thoughts away and forced himself to be present.

After minutes of waiting and listening to the murmurs and soft cries that came from her parents' room, Lilia ran upstairs. She found her father sitting on the edge of the bed, crying, with Maria in his arms. Her head was buried in his chest. Her eyes barely flickered.

The women were soaking up the blood from the floor and mattress and wringing the rags out in a bucket of reddish-brown water. Theresa had peeled off Maria's undergarments and wrapped her in linens to keep her warm; a cold cloth lay across her forehead.

"Papa!" Lilia felt a flurry of panic and gasped as the sight of her mother. She instinctively stepped back, even as she wanted to draw closer. "Is Mama dying?!"

"Stay with Aunt Theresa while I find someone to take Mama and me to the hospital."

"I'll watch the children, Virginio! Don't worry!" Theresa's hands were once again covered in Maria's blood, which continued to drench the blankets. "Hurry!"

The hospital was fifteen kilometers away, in San Vito, the same hospital where Bruno was born. All Maria's other children had been birthed at home with the assistance of a midwife. Because the journey to San Vito was far and fatiguing, it was only during emergencies that Maria and Virginio endured it.

Virginio was distraught as he cycled through the village, knocking on doors to beg for help. Few people owned a car in Mussons. Those villagers were apologetic as they refused him; naturally, they feared the checkpoints, as well as the danger of being arrested by Germans. With nowhere left to turn, Virginio frantically turned to the owner of the bar.

"Signora Bertoni, please, I need one of your sons to take Maria and me to the hospital. She's hemorrhaging!"

"Oh, dear God, Virginio! What happened to Maria?"

"I don't know. There is no time! Please, can you drive us?"

The woman searched his troubled face. She wanted to help, but the thought of her family's safety gave her pause.

"Forgive me, Virginio. The Gestapo are everywhere, and I don't want to endanger my family." The expression of helpless despair on his face was too much for her to bear. "Signore Moretti has a carriage parked behind the church—I'm sure he will take you. My prayers are with you!"

Virginio sprinted up the street on his bicycle and careened past the church to implore the man for help. Without much need for words or explanation, Signore Moretti felt the urgency of Virginio's request and offered to take him and Maria in his white horse-drawn carriage wherever they needed to go. With not a second to waste, he pulled up to the house, saddled and ready. Neighbors spilled from their homes, converging to assist, and several made the sign of the cross and kissed their rosaries. Whispers of concern and prayer floated in the breeze.

Stunned and horrified, Lilia watched her father carry her mother out of the gate. Maria's body lay limp and motionless in Virginio's arms, her blood dripping a trail on the walkway.

Virginio cradled Maria in the back seat of the carriage, holding her as still as possible. "Don't you leave me! You're the strongest woman I know. Stay with me, Maria. We're going to fight this together!" He felt a warm sensation on his pant legs as they soaked red, and the breath of life escaped his precious wife.

ೋღ ღೋ

On arrival, the emergency room was in complete chaos. Gurneys rolled down the narrow corridor, barely able to pass each other. Orderlies and nurses in white uniform paced in earnest from room to room, and trolley wheels rumbled on the uneven floor. The walls flaked layers of pale blue paint, revealing the dull gray concrete underneath. The light was much too abrasive for Virginio, as it magnified the audible cries of human distress. His savior was the wooden effigy of Christ on the cross that hung in protection, suspended above all the turmoil that passed through these walls. Virginio sent a silent prayer begging for His helping hand before yelling out, "Please, someone help us! My wife is losing blood!"

Nurses came running and lifted Maria on to a bed, wheeled her into a room, and pulled the curtain closed. Overloaded with a barrage of patients, the chief trauma surgeon arrived wearing a butcher's apron. He immediately pushed Virginio aside.

"Sh-she won't stop bleeding!" Virginio's voice trembled with helplessness.

After taking Maria's vitals and a brief assessment, the doctor turned to the nurse who'd brought Maria in, his face impassive. He shot her an irritated look. "Why are you bringing me a dead woman? We need this bed." The doctor swung open the curtain and stormed down the hall. His words left his lips with the same cruel carelessness that drove a dagger into Virginio's heart.

"W-what are you saying? No, no, no, no! My God, no!"

The orderly turned to Virginio, his face somber. "I'm so sorry, Signore Meneguzzi, your wife had a fatal miscarriage."

Fear gripped Virginio. He shook his head incredulously. It couldn't be!

The nurse and orderly tried to calm and console him, but all Virginio could hear was monotone and muffled noise.

"Oh, Maria, this is all my fault! Maria! I'm sorry, I'm sorry, don't leave me!" Virginio draped his body over hers, as if to keep the last spark of life from trickling out of her. "My God, why have you taken my wife, too? She lived through so many hardships—was that not enough torture? Is this what you want for her? For us? Have mercy!" After a few long moments, the orderly gently eased Virginio out of the room and into the hallway. His eyes were glazed over as he stared into space. He felt hollow. Dead. "It's my fault." The words dribbled off his lips again and again. Virginio had seen death many times, but this was different. He felt entirely purposeless without Maria. He sank against a hard-backed chair, his blood-stained fingers spread out before him.

Is this how it ends? She was the love of my life.

Pity rose within the orderly, alongside contempt for the cruel doctor and his cutting words. The adoration he'd seen in Virginio for his wife had deeply moved him. He witnessed death daily, but this display of a husband's devotion made Maria's loss an especially painful tragedy. He placed his hand on Virginio's shoulder. "Signore Meneguzzi, take some time, and when you're ready, we have release forms for you to sign. I need to move your wife to another floor—you can spend as much time as you need with her there."

Virginio remained still, staring into nothingness. "I have four small children at home. I lost one son to war—another was taken to a German camp. What am I to do without my wife? What have we done to deserve so much suffering?" He lifted his head to the cross and then to the orderly. "Why?"

The orderly breathed a deep sigh. "I don't know, Signore Meneguzzi. I will never understand the whys of the world." Words seemed ineffectual. He bowed in sadness and retreated to Maria's bedside to pay his respects and prepare for the transfer.

Beams of light streamed through the window, casting an eerie glow over Maria's body. The sun's warmth drew some peace into the wretched moment, as if heaven had momentarily descended onto this hell. The orderly caressed Maria's weathered but still beautiful face.

"You were so loved, dear lady."

No sooner had his words floated about the silent room than he thought he saw one of Maria's pale fingers twitch. He blinked, knowing it was impossible. Had his eyes played tricks on him? He looked more closely. The finger moved again.

"Maria? If you can hear me, move your little finger on your right hand for me!"

Maria raised and lowered it ever so slightly.

This woman is still alive!

The orderly was flooded with amazement. She must have heard the doctor dismissing her. *She must have thought of her children and her devoted husband. This woman is a fighter! Maria, you're not ready to die!*

The orderly fumbled back into the corridor and knocked over a trolley. His arms flailed wildly in the air as he ran after the doctor, shouting, "She's alive! Signora Meneguzzi is alive!"

Virginio sprang from his chair, half-dazed, to the most magnificent words ever spoken. He watched the doctor and nurses barrel past him to Maria's bed. A mix of confusion and euphoria made him shiver from head to toe. His body couldn't seem to catch up to the reality of what was happening. Virginio attempted to move towards the bed, but the doctor restrained him from getting too close and forced him to the back of the room. Virginio peered through a trail of medical staff and equipment and fixed his eyes solely on Maria, when he felt a familiar hand upon his shoulder.

"Your prayers may be answered yet, Signore Meneguzzi. Your

wife is not out of danger, but hope prevails! Perhaps God heard you," the orderly said softly.

It seemed that Maria had lost too much blood and urgently needed a blood transfusion. She was rushed into surgery.

The surgeon who had dismissed Maria so callously turned to Virginio. "Signore Meneguzzi, your wife has a rare blood type. We need a family donor. Is there anyone you can call? There is a phone you can use here in the hospital—the nurse will direct you and give you the pertinent information." And with that, he hurried down the hall.

Virginio hovered over the nurses' station, their phone in his hand. Minutes felt like hours as he frantically summoned to mind the numbers he could remember . . . Maria's sisters, brothers, Ermides—but no one was a match. Dina was the last one left to call.

"Dina! It's Papa. I don't have time to talk. Mama is in the hospital in San Vito. She's in critical condition. Do you know your blood type?"

"AB negative. Why? Papa! What happened?"

"There's no time. Come quickly! You may be the one who can save her."

"I'll be on the next bus and there in a couple of hours!"

When they thought Maria couldn't hold on any longer, Dina arrived at the hospital and was immediately taken to have her blood drawn. What could have been a tragic ending became an earnest, and successful, fight for survival. The recovery would be arduous, but Maria was alive.

The following morning, Maria roused to partial consciousness and was able to recognize Virginio and Dina smiling over her. Once she was fully coherent, the doctor explained to her what had transpired from the time she'd arrived. Maria struggled to focus on the grim news.

A solemn tear slid down Maria's cheek as she slowly stroked her stomach with a brush of her hand. She closed her eyes to gather whatever strength she could muster. What was to be a joyous moment was dampened when Maria uttered her next words.

"I lost our baby." Maria's face was blank.

"Shh, don't talk," Virginio caressed Maria's brow. "Please, try to rest. You're alive, and that's all that matters."

Maria's voice trembled. "I've lost so many babies, and my boys . . . gone . . . forever." She raised her weary eyes to Virginio. "Why am I here? Alive? And for what? Why is God sparing my life, and taking my children?" Maria strained to turn her head towards Dina.

"And you! Why did you come?" Barely able to speak, Maria slurred her words. "You should have let me die."

"Mama, don't say such things." Dina felt a blow to her heart, and for a moment, she felt guilty for expecting gratitude for her selfless action. "Lilia and the boys are waiting for you. Your family needs you."

Maria turned her gaze towards the window, unable to feel grateful for anything. She was tired of it all.

"Your mother's tired, Dina." Virginio gently nudged his daughter out of the room. "She needs her rest . . . most of all, she needs time."

Maria remained in the hospital for nearly three months. In her absence, nine-year-old Lilia was taken out of school to care for her little brothers. At the same time, Dina stayed in Mussons and visited her mother intermittently throughout the weeks, until Maria was well enough to return home.

During those months, German invasions were on the rise as partisans grew to over 200,000 strong, becoming the strongest anti-fascist army yet and immobilizing a quarter of the German divisions in

Northern Italy. Soldiers still in possession of their military weapons and released prisoners of war were recruited. They fought against the German occupation, Italian fascists, and the ruling elite by destroying transportation centers and communication lines throughout the region. Although the various resistance groups were at odds with one another, partisans stood united.

In the meantime, the Nazis were on a rampage to eliminate every Italian rebel or civilian who joined or aided the underground activities. News quickly spread that partisans had been captured by the Gestapo and hanged in the center square of Villanova, a twenty-minute walk from Mussons. This act of cruelty demonstrated Hitler's absolute power and instilled fear within the villagers with the repeated warning: *one for ten—you take one German down, we'll kill ten civilians.* It was reminiscent of the tragic incident in Rome months prior, when partisans bombed an SS unit, killing thirty-three soldiers; this was followed by the Nazis executing 335 innocent Italian civilians in retaliation.

Dina had always been a curious and adventurous young woman and, in light of her brother's recent imprisonment, she made it a point to keep abreast of all that was happening. Upon hearing about the public hanging, Dina went to witness a clan of partisan rebels strung by their feet in the town square of Villanova—they had been beaten and shot to death.

The horror was more than Dina had anticipated. She stumbled to the ground and vomited repeatedly.

It was all too much—even for the strongest of souls. The collective impact of being denied her one chance to see her brother, nearly losing her mother, and witnessing the gruesome public hanging left Dina in shock and traumatized.

After her experience in Villanova, she left Mussons early the next day at the crack of dawn. With her knitting bag in hand, she hid in the trenches by the river for hours. Dina was terrified of the possibility of a home invasion as they only produced suffering for the villagers and her family. She had an uncanny ability to sense things before they happened, and she wondered if her dread was in fact a premonition. Dina wasn't mentally prepared to take the risk. For several days in a row, this became her ritual: leaving home early in the morning and waiting in the trenches until the gnawing feeling in the pit of her stomach lifted. As irrational as it may have seemed to anyone else, Dina felt compelled by something she could not explain.

With her mother still in the hospital and four siblings at home, a momentary lapse of sanity was unacceptable. Virginio was preoccupied with his wife, trips back and forth to the hospital, and now also his daughter's state of mind. Lilia was worried too that something tragic would happen to her sister by the river—as she'd feared with her big brothers, the possibility of losing Dina felt all too real.

After a week of Dina hiding out in the trenches, Virginio's concern turned to impatience. Arriving home from the hospital, he instructed Lilia to check up on her big sister and coax her home. "Your sister should never have gone to Villanova. She may be nineteen years old, but what she saw is not for the eyes of a young woman—not for anyone. I'll watch the boys. Your sister is no safer by the Tagliamento than she is here in the village with us—we're a family, which means we stay together."

Lilia heeded her father's words, made and packed some food for herself and Dina, and departed for the trenches. The thought of an invasion gave Lilia plenty of reason to worry, but her strength was stronger than her fear. She may have been young at nine years of age, but Lilia had lived through more horrific and frightening experiences than either of her sisters. She wanted to protect Dina, and she knew she could give her solace.

En route to see her sister, Lilia spotted two partisans up ahead walking towards the church. Behind them were two, armed, German soldiers. She knew these men were marching to their deaths. Lilia kept a slow pace, observing from afar until she felt safe to continue to the trench hidden in the river dike. The village of Mussons had lost any hope of safety. The stench of the Nazis' endless brutality and bloodshed was ever-present.

Once Lilia arrived at the dike, she found her sister huddled just inside the open door of the twelve-foot trench. The strong sunlight streamed in, making a spotlight on Dina's face. She was sitting against the concrete wall knitting furiously.

"Hey!" Lilia cried out.

Utterly surprised, Dina threw her knitting, bouncing it against the far wall. Caught off guard, she struggled to catch her breath. Her startled response quickly gave way to annoyance when she saw her sister standing before her. "Don't do that again! You scared me!"

"Are you going to stay here all day?"

"I don't know. Why?" Dina shot back.

Lilia was unmoved by her sister's hostility; she stepped inside the trench and sat down beside Dina. "Papa is worried about you. I am, too." Lilia pulled the food out of her bag, handing Dina a sandwich. She took a bite of her own. Dina smirked but gave her little sister a nod of gratitude.

"Thank you." Dina collected her knitting needles, now embarrassed by her cowardice in the presence of a nine-year-old. "I should be the one rescuing you." Dina gave her little sister a sideways look. "It turns out you're the glue that keeps this family together."

"Papa thinks we'll all be safer if we stay together, at least until Mama comes home, and then you can return to Udine. He's right."

"I'm not going back to Udine. I found a better job in Milan."

Lilia sighed at her sister's news. "You're always leaving. Everybody dies or leaves. Mama almost died. I sometimes worry she won't come home. I miss her."

Dina pulled her little sister into her arms and patted her gently. "I remember, years ago, before you were born, Mama had another miscarriage. It was awful. She was maybe six months pregnant, and the baby girl died. Mama didn't know for a few weeks, and then realized the baby wasn't kicking any more. I remember the doctor laying her on the kitchen table with stacks of towels and a pail of hot water. He then pulled out these metal forceps—they looked like long-hinged scissors—and he used them to remove the baby. I didn't see what he did, as I was nearly your age and not allowed in the room, but I heard Mama screaming with her entire body—it tore through me like glass. My heart thudded as she kept screaming. I was sure the entire village could hear."

Lilia cringed as she listened, her eyes wide with horror.

Dina stood up and leaned her head out the door, gazing up at the sky, mustering a sense of lost courage as she thought of all their mother had been through over the years. "If Mama could survive that, she will survive anything! She's tough, like you. She'll be *fine*."

Lilia looked up at her sister with pleading eyes. "And so will you! Now, can we get out of this trench already?"

Dina wrapped up her knitting bag, and the two sisters walked out of the trench from under the dike and on the pathway home, both relieved to be surrounded by full daylight.

Dina refocused her eyes and pulled herself together, back to her senses.

"I'm sorry for not having been there for you all these years." Dina swept Lilia's bangs from her forehead and smoothed her braids, taming some of the hairs that had escaped and then kissing her sister's cheek. "You've battled and grown through some incredibly difficult and scary times. You are strong, Lilia, like Mama, and so much braver than I will ever be. Let's go home."

⁓⊙ℰ ℰ⊙⁓

With the stress of nearly losing his wife, Virginio's asthma took a turn for the worse and he fought a bout of severe episodes that left him bedridden for days. Lilia was left to watch over her father while Dina went back and forth between Mussons and the hospital before leaving for Milan. To lighten Lilia's load, neighbors offered to take the boys in until Virginio regained his strength.

It was twilight, and Dina had left for San Vito on her father's bicycle. An hour later, Lilia could hear Germans shouting outside her window, and dogs barking in the distance. She carefully pushed open the shutters a crack, and although the sky was dark, a delicate play of pink light reflected off their uniforms as the Gestapo approached her house. Lilia gasped for air as panic rushed up to her throat. The memory of the soldiers taking Arturo and the sound of her mother's anguished cries brought her right back to that frightful and traumatic day. She drilled her fingers into her pulsing temples, wishing the soldiers would go away. A sudden hammering was heard at the door.

"Open!" The pounding and shouting escalated. Lilia was alone with her father. Eliseo was at the bar, whose doors had barely opened for business.

Virginio's body was utterly weak. It didn't matter what the

Germans were after—their loud voices made him give in to his impulse, which was to run and hide.

"We said, open!" The sound of barking dogs ensued.

Horror-struck. Lilia watched as her father, wheezing and trembling, scampered under the bed, then hid in the closet before attempting to climb out on to the terrace. But there was no way out—he realized he was too frail. The German's shouting escalated with insistent pounding on the door. Virginio crawled back under the covers and prayed to the Almighty that he would be spared from the soldiers' clutches.

Lilia crept down the stairs, her heart leaping violently with every bang on the door.

If I don't answer, they'll burst in, anyway. And maybe if I do . . . if I show them we'll cooperate, they won't hurt us . . .

Lilia bravely released the latch, letting in the hounds of hell.

Four, armed soldiers stormed in at gunpoint and tore up the stairs, causing Lilia to flatten herself against the wall. Adrenaline jolted through her body. Without hesitating, she rushed after them and to her father's side.

The Germans found Virginio quivering in his bed, gulping for breath.

"Get up!" the officer in charge barked as he prodded him with his rifle. "We are taking you to headquarters for questioning!"

Virginio had no choice but to follow orders. With four guns pointed straight at him, he pulled himself up from his bed as he gasped for air. Lilia had pinned herself to the darkest corner of her parents' room. Every ounce of her being shook with loathing, rage, and terror . . . but she could do nothing except watch and wait. Her eyes slowly shifted towards her father. She watched him struggle to stand. His legs wobbled. Urine trickled down to his bare feet, soaking his pajamas and pooling into a puddle on the floor.

At that moment, Eliseo, who had heard the dogs howling, bolted into the house and burst upstairs. He raised his hands to demonstrate that he was unarmed and immediately spoke his best German. "Please, officers . . . please let this man be. He is weak and ill. His wife is near death! He has lost both his sons to war, and all he has left is four small children. Surely, you can see that he is of no use to you."

"We found the partisans!" At that moment, another soldier bellowed from the courtyard, alerting the men in the room to retreat at once. Before departing, the commanding officer turned to Virginio, sending him a seething look. "It's your lucky day, old man." He looked at the puddle with disgust. "Useless peasant." He spat upon the floor before retreating downstairs.

As the soldiers left, Virginio shot Eliseo a wordless look of gratitude. For all his perceived weaknesses, Eliseo was a true friend, always there for Virginio and his family. In one unutterable moment, the two shared the realization that, had it not been for Eliseo's intervention and the soldier in the courtyard calling the other men . . . Virginio's life might have ended. Eliseo smiled through misty eyes, nodded in relief, and quickly bowed out of the room.

Depleted of all energy, Virginio collapsed to his knees, sobbing in despair and shame. Lilia ran over to her father and knelt beside him. She rubbed his back and leaned her head against his quivering shoulder.

"What kind of man am I? Look what I've done."

Lilia's heart filled with compassion. Her father, who had always been her anchor, now seemed small and fragile in her arms. "Papa, I'll clean it up. Don't worry. They are gone. We are safe now."

13 | ARBEIT MACHT FREI

February 1945

༄ At the crack of dawn, Bruno's intense screams demanded urgency.

"Sh-sh-sh. What's wrong? Please stop crying!" Lilia rocked her baby brother slowly as his tears soaked her nightie, but she was unsuccessful in her efforts to calm him or stop him from scratching his head violently.

"My head!" Bruno proceeded to then rub the inside of his ears.

"What's wrong with your head? Stop scratching. Get your fingers out of our ears!"

"I can't! Something's moving all over my head!"

Lilia grabbed Bruno and ran downstairs. Riccardo and Giovanni followed; both boys were agitated and also madly scratching their heads. Lilia was irritable too, fussing with discomfort as she rubbed her ears and the scruff of her neck, her braided locks swooshing side-to-side.

"Mama, he won't stop crying! I don't know what to do!"

Maria took Bruno in her arms. His lashes blinked, heavy with tears. She took one look at her other children, rolled her eyes, and slapped her forehead. "And here we go again! Virginio!" Maria hollered at her husband, waving him in from the barn. "I need help! Bring your clippers!"

Lilia grew paranoid as she continued to twitch her head. "Mama, what do you need *clippers* for?"

Virginio dashed into the house. "What's wrong? What happened? Who's hurt?"

By the exasperated look on his wife's face, one screaming child, and three more with tousled hair doing an antsy dance around the great room, Virginio quickly clued into the situation at hand.

"I'll go to the pharmacy," he chuckled to himself and handed Maria the clippers. "You can shave their heads."

"*Shave?*" Lilia panicked. Her eyes pooled with anxiety. "You're going to shave my head?" She stumbled backward as she smoothed her fingers over her long precious braids.

"Lice. You all have lice!" Maria threw up her hands theatrically as her children hurled themselves into a tizzy.

"Lice?"

"Bugs?"

"Something's moving on my head!"

"It's going in my ear!"

"What?"

"Yes, you have bugs in your hair. We need to get them out before they lay eggs."

"*Eggs!*"

Lilia, Giovanni, and Riccardo stared at each other in horror, now screaming in unison and frantically scratching their eyebrows, hairline, and behind their ears, while Bruno continued fussing endlessly—his red face wet with tears.

"Lilia, this is the one time that it's a blessing to be a girl—your father is getting you an expensive medical treatment to kill those pesky crawlers, otherwise you'd lose that long precious hair and be shaved bald like your brothers are about to be."

"Why did we get these? Is it because we're poor?"

Maria laughed at her daughter's absurd question. "Of course not!

Rich, poor, it's doesn't matter. The Bible says even the Egyptians were plagued with lice." Maria shot a look through the front door and across the street. "I'm sure you got them from that damn whore, Giovanna, and her dirty children . . . those poor children." Maria shook her head in pity. "Your older siblings had lice, too, when they were young." Maria's eyes glazed over and she quickly caught herself before she could reminisce over a scene that seemed a lifetime away—time she would give anything to have back.

Reminded of the cavernous hole in her heart and now irritated by the task at hand, Maria lamented to herself. *Was it not enough those German scum took my sons and brought the rest of my family scabies and fleas, and now I need to deal with lice, thanks to my filthy neighbor?*

"Well, at least I don't have to bathe you all in urine as we did when you got scabies—that nightmare lasted for weeks." Maria pulled up a chair from the dining table. "Boys, take your clothes off and put them in a pile outside. Lilia, run upstairs and remove the linens from the beds, and give me your clothes, too. Once your father returns, I need you to take everything to the river and wash it well. We'll then tie the clean laundry into a bedsheet and leave it in a bucket of hot water covered in wood ashes to soak overnight."

One by one, the naked boys plopped themselves on the chair while Maria shaved their heads. Their jaws chattered and their bodies trembled in the winter air as it wafted in through the front door. They could hear their mother squeeze the lice between her fingers, making a dry cracking sound. Giovanni, Riccardo, and Bruno winced in disgust, while Lilia boiled hot water to bathe them.

"When we're done here, you're all jumping in the bath."

Upon Virginio's return, Maria doused her daughter's long hair in a medical, paste-like cream that smelled of sulfur before wrapping it in a towel. Lilia cringed at the pungent odor, screwing up her face.

"It smells awful, but it works," said Virginio. He was grateful they could at least keep her beautiful hair intact.

"You need to keep it in until morning," ordered Maria, "and then we'll wash it out and give you a good combing."

Even though Lilia felt irritated and her scalp tingled uncomfortably, she still emerged from the day's events reasonably unscathed—at least she still had her precious hair.

After a traumatic day, Maria and Virginio tucked their children into bed. Exhausted themselves, they lay back against their pillows, reflecting on the jagged shards of painful memories and all the tribulations placed upon them and their family in recent months.

"Maria, I watched our boys tonight, in their matching pajamas, heads shaved, huddled together in bed, and the grimace on Lilia's face—she must be feeling punished by that horrible smell. I thought to myself—we saved them from a little hell today, and yet we were helpless in keeping Arturo from the worst evil of all."

"I know . . . I'll never let go of the night they took him. I've heard things in the village about the camps and what the Nazis are doing to people. Our son is there, somewhere. Dachau? Auschwitz? How will we ever know? What if he never returns? What if they hurt our son?" Thoughts of Arturo being tortured raked her insides.

Virginio lay in silence for several long moments. Even after all they'd been through, and in the midst of so much death and destruction, he felt the slightest quiver of hope stir his heart. "We almost lost him once, Maria. God willing, he will be spared and sent back into our loving arms."

Arturo was arrested on 24 June 1944, and detained for questioning at Nazi headquarters in Udine, Italy. Since the armistice, the Italian city was under German administration. Unknown to his family, the SS labeled Arturo a political prisoner under protective custody and sent him to Buchenwald on 14 July 1944, where he joined more than 60,000 other inmates. The goal of the camp system was to dehumanize prisoners with beatings, torture, starvation, and by working them to death. Fortunately, Arturo had learned the butcher's trade from his father, which singled him out from the other prisoners. The SS moved him into the kitchen.

After four months of imprisonment in Buchenwald, Arturo was loaded into a crowded freight car of 250 prisoners headed for Porschdorf, one of the last eighty-one slave labor subcamps of Flossenbürg, in the Bavarian forest, near the Czech border—also known as the Bavarian Siberia. When Auschwitz was later liberated by the Russians on 27 January 1945, the army advanced towards Porschdorf, meaning the subcamp was short-lived; hence, the death toll was relatively low. However, the main camp at Flossenbürg was a different story.

Upon arrival to Porschdorf, camp authorities assigned Arturo a second matriculation number. In Buchenwald, 29791 was tattooed on the inside of his left arm. The new Flossenbürg camp number, 38887, was patched on to his blue-striped prison uniform next to a red triangle with the letter I, signifying he was an Italian political prisoner.

Twenty-six SS guards, their dogs, and Kapos awaited the train of workers with wooden clubs and a grueling regimen. The Kapos, mostly German criminals, were assigned to supervise forced labor. The prisoners moved by foot and were forced to dig tunnels and load rails on to barges in the Elba River. Like slaves, they were driven to break rocks and build an underground facility processing coal tar, which was converted into petroleum for airplanes.

The Flossenbürg SS guards, known to be the most vicious unit of all the concentration camps, ordered the Kapos to mercilessly beat prisoners. In some cases, they released their rage by murdering them. Those men deemed unfit to continue with the rigorous work at Porschdorf were sent to Flossenbürg to die.

On 27 February 1945, Arturo, along with other emaciated inmates, were sent by cattle train to the main camp at Flossenbürg. The journey was horrendously cold, as the freight car had no roof nor straw for warmth, and the bombardment by the Russians and Americans overhead cast a constant threat. Prisoners were packed like sardines with barely enough standing room. The only protection they had against the elements was the clothing on their backs as they battled hours of heavy snow, sleet, and rain. Without food or water, their only source of nourishment was pieces of ice, if the prisoners were lucky enough to find them or the flakes of snow that landed in their hands.

The train stopped as the railway came to an end. Prisoners were herded on foot for miles in deep snow under -30° Celsius temperatures to the remote Bavarian camp. After having endured months of despair and survival, many prisoners were shot for collapsing from exhaustion or falling back in the march. They were left to die on the side of the road.

⁕⁕⁕

Upon reaching their destination, the men were corralled among droves of new prisoners huddled together, panic-stricken, sinking further into fear and dread—haunted by uncertainty. A high, double barbed-wire fence enclosed the grounds, which were monitored by three watchtowers.

When prisoners arrived at the camp, guards spoke in German. Despite months and years of prisoners being transported between camps, crowds of people from vastly different cultures were still unable to understand each other, much less the rules of the SS. It was clear from the terror, agony, and befuddlement on their faces that they had stumbled upon questions to which there were no answers: *Why are they still shooting people? Beating us? What have we done to deserve this?*

Horror blanketed the minds of intellectuals, teachers, peasant workers, priests—individuals with faces, names, hearts, and souls . . . human beings reduced to mere numbers.

Two stone pillars flanked the wrought-iron gate of the entrance; the left column displayed a sign with the slogan, *Arbeit Macht Frei,* which translated to 'Work Will Set You Free.' For many prisoners, those were familiar words—the lies the Nazis fed them from other camps. Prisoners were forced to memorize the Nazi slogan. *There is a path to freedom, and its milestones are called obedience, sobriety, truthfulness, a spirit of self-sacrifice, and love of the Fatherland.* The proverb was written on visible rocks in the camp. It was Hitler's way of masking the brutality as institutional rehabilitation.

"Hard work will set you free. If you don't work hard, that is where you will end up!" the SS officers shouted to prisoners while pointing towards the crematorium chimney, smoke billowing out of its pipe. "And if you cross the white lines of the perimeter," demonstrating the five-meter line from the wire, "we *will* shoot you."

As Arturo approached the camp, stories of the inhumane acts it housed flashed before him. A more experienced prisoner, like Arturo, focused on fighting exhaustion and battling the severe cold and mind-numbing hunger. Arturo knew the stronger and more useful he was, the longer he would survive.

Still, he was assaulted by an onslaught of questions. How much more could he endure? Would life be worse or better here? Would he ever see his home and family again?

As the son of a butcher and from his months spent in Buchenwald, Arturo was exempt from the Flossenbürg quarry and granted a position in the kitchen. For him, this was a blessing compared to his grueling months digging tunnels in the Porschdorf subcamp, and the risk of being one of the many dead bodies carried back to the camp from the quarry.

Arturo knew the importance of complying with the rules in order to stay alive. But from the moment he arrived in Flossenbürg, he fought to lift the flagging morale of others . . . and his own. Despite the horrific conditions of the camp and the mortal fear he had of losing his life, Arturo never stopped caring for people or standing up for the less fortunate. Through the stifling layers of his depression, he had to believe hope would prevail.

The Germans assigned Arturo the role of helper in the kitchen. The batch cooking was the same soup and stale bread day in and day out. Not a week later, a Jewish prisoner from Poland joined Arturo in the kitchen. His name was Pepick. Arturo prepared the food to bring to the other men in the barracks, and Pepick washed the large pots. They were supervised by a German political prisoner named Hans. The SS officers entrusted and armed him with a pistol, as the Americans and Russians would soon be encroaching on their territory.

Hours after the last meals were distributed, Arturo and Pepick found themselves alone in the kitchen building. It was finally safe for them to speak.

"Sprichst du Deutsch? Cesky? Do you speak German? Czech?"

Arturo asked as he stored the leftover food supply in large metal containers. He noticed the other helper who was washing the pots wore a star on his uniform.

"After three long years of the German occupation, being in the ghetto, and working in the camps, I speak almost everything," the young man replied in Czech. "My name is Pepick."

"I am Arturo—Italian." Arturo stretched out his uniform from its baggy state—the uniform that months ago his body had been able to fill—to reveal his own patch. "You can call me Artu . . . my friends call me Artu. With all this hell around us, we are lucky to be in this kitchen. The SS shoot prisoners dead if the stones they carry are too small, if they put up a fight, or stand up for someone. Kapos hang innocent men every day and brag about the numbers they've killed. When I see the young boys, they look so frail and weak . . . innocence lost." Arturo ground his teeth in anger but refused to let the wrongdoings of ignorant men turn his heart black. "We will keep stronger here, better fed—we can scrape the bottom of the food barrels and trade bread for better shoes. All the same, I miss home . . . I miss what life used to be. This memory is what has kept me alive." Arturo felt a twinge of guilt, knowing he was fortunate compared to other prisoners—he was still alive . . . yet he desperately yearned for what he'd once had. "I see you are Jewish. Why did the Germans bring you to work here and not in the quarry?"

Pepick continued to wash the dirty pots as he lamented, "I was in the ghetto when the Gestapo took me from my family. My mother feared for my life and safety. She gave me her wedding ring and told me to safeguard it that I might need it one day. I have kept that ring hidden for over two years! You asked how I was given this job in the kitchen? I have my mother to thank for saving my life—I traded her beloved ring, with all the love it held, for my security. Hans has it now. And this, my friend, is how I am here." Pepick paused, looking at Arturo with admiration. Although Arturo's face was gaunt and pale, his eyes were kind. "Artu, the Germans need us, at least for now. This kitchen, these four walls and the scraps they contain, is our last hope. There is too much pain and suffering out there."

Arturo nodded in agreement and then turned a curious look upon his new friend. "Where did you hide the ring all that time?"

"Where no one ever checked." Pepick opened his mouth and pointed inside. "I'm amazed I never swallowed it!" For a brief moment, they shared a laugh, and then the reality of what had become of their minds, bodies, and souls washed over them.

"You know, before Hans brought me here, I watched you stealing extra soup and bread and bringing it to the other prisoners, to sickbay, where hundreds are dying every day. Your heart is pure, Artu. And I sometimes hear you sing a beautiful Italian song from my block. Your soothing voice rises amid the ugly noise in our heads. You uplift the men, and you uplift me." Pepick let out a deep sigh. "I am twenty-one years old. What could I have possibly done to deserve this never-ending nightmare?"

"I celebrated my twenty-fourth birthday in November breaking rocks and building tunnels in Porschdorf," sighed Arturo. "I hated all that Mussolini stood for, and his fascist regime. I was captured and labeled a rebel, but I wasn't a partisan. I was in Buchenwald four months and saw things my eyes couldn't believe. The SS did medical experiments on people, skinned the tattoos from the bodies of dead men, and used their skin for things like lampshades and books! How can one man possess such evil and control an army of soldiers and officers, twisting their minds into believing what they are doing is humane? To answer your question, Pepick, we have done *nothing* to deserve being treated worse than animals. If there is hell on earth, this is it."

Arturo paused to watch a prisoner pass by the kitchen window. He was bracing his body against the bitter cold and walking with two other men, his head lowered in despair. Arturo pointed him out to Pepick.

"You see that man, the one in the middle? He's an Italian major-general used by the SS as a scribe to log the daily body count. They chose him for his skills as a calligrapher. I'm sure this mandate has saved his life all these months, but what darkness and horror he must bear. They lock him in a barrack with hundreds of dead prisoners. One by one, he has to catalogue each matriculation, matching it to the deceased person's registration on arrival to this evil place. The Germans let him sleep during the day, so at night they can break his soul. Look what Hitler has done to millions of people. I pray for God to help us, Pepick, but He does nothing." Arturo turned to his friend, a fire still burning in his eyes, "Retribution will be served. If not in this lifetime, the next, and the next, until all hatred comes to an end."

Pepick released another deep sigh and nodded. Not knowing when Hans would return, Pepick pressed on. He wished to learn more about this good Samaritan, who under the worst circumstances had brought him and others so much hope and comfort through song, strength, and a clear love for humanity. Who was he? What had his hopes and dreams been before coming here?

"A man like you must have left a beautiful woman at home . . . someone special waiting for you."

Arturo peered out the snow-framed window into the darkness and saw his gaunt face reflected in the glass—his eyes still filled with the pain and confusion that had overcome him months before becoming a prisoner.

"That 'someone' is dead to me now." Arturo's thoughts quickly turned to Lilia's smile, a smile that lit up his insides. "A wise little girl once told me, 'Because something looks perfect doesn't mean it will make you happy.' The meaning of happiness is far simpler now."

Arturo cast his silent prayers out into the heavens: *Mama, if I could hold you in my arms again and calm your troubled heart. Papa, to have that drink and laugh with you once more. To see my sisters at peace and thriving—their lives filled with joy. To watch my baby brothers, grow into strong men with integrity, adventurous to see the world. And my precious Lilia, how I wish to share in these years of you blossoming into the incredible woman I know you will become. To know you'll marry a man worthy of your love, who gives you the life you so rightly deserve. Dear God, why You put me here, punished me, I will never understand, but if You're listening at all, if You haven't forgotten me, let this unjust fate pass so that I may return home . . . where my heart lives.*

A light shone in his eyes when he looked at Pepick. "Family—my family is waiting for me."

Pepick's face momentarily brightened as he hummed a familiar tune. "Artu, sing the song again. I memorized the words—words I will never forget."

In a quiet breath, Arturo sang, swaying his worn body slightly as his voice graced the silence. His eyes fixed on the winter sky—the stars clouded by the ashes of burnt flesh . . . bodies that burned into the night.

**"When we are free, we will forget our suffering.
We will tell the world about all the friends we lost
Here, in this place of horror . . ."**

His voice trailed off as a lump rose in his throat. "Pepick, you only die once. Today is not the day. Not in this place."

Arturo gently grabbed Pepick's shoulders. "One day, my friend, you'll be telling our story to your children and the world. One day, we will meet again."

ఇం ఆ

Mussons, March 1945

Lilia struggled to wake herself up from a nightmare. Her internal screams paralyzed her fight to break free and drowned in tears on her pillow.

In her dream, she was in a stark room. The light was dimming. It was cold—she was left alone to die. No one came. No one heard her cries. No one remembered her name.

Lilia jolted awake to the sound of Arturo's voice, calling out to her . . . Piccina . . . He was smiling behind her lids. Maybe it was a sign he was coming home!

Lilia sprang out of bed. She inched to her big brother's room and leafed through his closet. Lilia grabbed Arturo's pajama top—the one he'd worn the last time he was home. She crawled back under the covers and wrapped herself in his nightshirt. She felt safe and protected, sensing Arturo's soothing energy everywhere. His love felt abundant.

"You're not alone," she whispered, pulling his shirt tight.

14 | BRING MY BOY HOME

It was April 1945. Chaos was rampant, and panic stirred among the Germans as the Americans advanced. SS officers left the Flossenbürg camp in droves, leaving few guards to watch over the prisoners. In their own agitation, the guards became more aggressive, shooting anyone who posed the slightest threat or problem. Some prisoners tried to escape, while others hid in unsuspecting places. Some were victorious in their attempts, while others met their demise.

With the Allies fast approaching, 40,000 prisoners were evacuated by the SS on a grueling death march that lasted days. Those who survived the journey were loaded into open freight cars; those who fell back in the line were shot dead. In the main camp, many prisoners were left behind to die, while hundreds were thrown on to piles and burned. This was how the SS removed any evidence of executions.

Flossenbürg was liberated on 23 April 1945, by the 90th US Infantry Division. The inmates awaited the US soldiers with a hand-painted sign that read: *"Prisoners happy end! Welcome!"*

The Americans were horrified by what they encountered: mountains of corpses, and nearly 1,500 emaciated prisoners on the verge of death. Those who did not survive the liberation were respectfully buried in the town center of Flossenbürg. It was the one dignity bestowed upon them after months and years of inhumane suffering.

Like lambs to the slaughter, dark fate led innocent souls into the hands of evil—the nightmares of the Holocaust. And like Arturo Meneguzzi, many waited for God to intervene.

On May 8th, after partisan rebels executed Benito Mussolini and one week after Adolf Hitler had committed suicide, Italy, like all Allied countries, celebrated the surrender of Nazi Germany, ending World War II in Europe. Twenty-three years of a fascist dictatorship and five years of a grueling war had come to a close.

The news spread like wildfire through Northern Italy: the war was over.

British and American troops drove through villages in jeeps and trucks, embracing the roaring crowds. As they paraded through Mussons, women ran out after them, touching them, kissing them, throwing roses at them, and praising these great heroes with tears of gratitude.

"God bless you! Thank you! We love you!"

Men raised their fedoras in salute and shook hands with the soldiers, while children waved from their mothers' arms. Flapping white handkerchiefs lined the streets and brightened every open door and window. The village was bathed in long-awaited joy. After years of pain and suffering, soul-harrowing fear, death, and destruction, people were left to pick up the pieces—and peace had finally come home.

"Mama! Papa!" Lilia threw open the front door and ran outside with her brothers. All of them waved their hankies. "The soldiers are coming! Look!"

Maria and Virginio ran out to the street, their eyes lit up with hope. Finally! Arturo would soon return!

⊷⊙ ⊙⊶

July 1945

"Maria, I heard they're coming back from Germany! Prisoners were rescued and have returned home to Morsano, San Paulo, and Villanova."

Like all families in Mussons awaiting news of their loved ones, Virginio continued to ride on the hope and faith he would see his son soon. Although it had been two months since the war ended, Virginio knew the aftermath of this grueling nightmare would prolong the return of many. Knowing Arturo was one of the last soldiers to come home following the Armistice of September 1943, his father was aware of the sobering reality that his journey back from this hell could take far longer.

"Go talk to them! Maybe someone saw Arturo! Maybe they know where he is! When he's coming home!" In that split second, every nerve in Maria's body fired with anticipation, all the way to her toes. The thought of holding her son again, or at least knowing he was somewhere alive and safe, sent her spirit soaring.

While waiting for Virginio's return, Maria couldn't sit still while her mind danced in a million directions. She pulled weeds in the courtyard, pruned her garden, cook and cleaned.

Where did they take him? Is he alive? Hurt? On a train? What did those animals do to my son? I want him home!

Virginio rode his bicycle from morning until night-time through the villages, connecting with survivors from Auschwitz, Bergen-Belsen, Buchenwald, Ravensbrück, and Dachau—people who were stripped of humanity and forever changed, mentally, physically, and spiritually, by the horrors they had endured. He held a photo of Arturo in his hand, searching for answers about his son's whereabouts. One of the survivors recognized Arturo's photo. He, too, was a prisoner in Buchenwald. The man invited Virginio into his home.

"Please, come in."

"Thank you. I won't stay long." Virginio's heart sank with pity at the sight of him as he watched the man shuffle his feet into the house. He was weak and worn. From the family photos on the walls of this humble abode, it was clear this man was a skeleton of his former self. His eyes were vacant but instantly pooled with tears as he looked at Virginio and again at the photo.

"Yes, I remember him. We were prisoners together in Buchenwald. He worked in the kitchen butchering meat for the Germans." The man tapped the photo with certainty. "Wait for the trains—I'm sure he'll be on the next one."

The man unsteadily teetered from side to side. His face emitted years of torture and suffering. "I've been having trouble sleeping, so the days are long. I need my rest." His hand trembled as he grabbed Virginio's arm.

"Don't lose hope, my friend. May God be with you." Virginio embraced the man and wished him well on his way back to recovery, back to the way things used to be . . . if they could ever be that way again.

As Virginio made his way back to Mussons, his brain exploded with dark visions of his son and the state he must be in—the mental anguish he must have endured in those ten months since his arrest. Virginio had heard rumors in the villages of the torture thrust upon prisoners in the camps, but he could not allow himself to dwell on such heart-wrenching thoughts—he had to believe Arturo had been spared the unthinkable. Virginio could still feel his son's embrace the day he came home. He remembered the smile on his face, the peace in his heart. To Virginio, that beautiful moment was all he could hold on to in order to withstand his anticipation, which vacillated between dread and hope.

I fear what awaits us, but all I want is for my son to be alive. Bring my boy home.

⚬◉⚬ ◉⚬⚬

Maria, Virginio, Lilia, and the boys waited months for Arturo's return, but there was no sign of him or any of the other men, women, and children who were taken from Mussons.

It was November 2. The villagers were celebrating All Souls' Day at Saint Osvaldo Church. A requiem mass was held at dawn to commemorate those loved ones who had departed—some of whom had been proclaimed dead and others who simply never returned. After the ceremony, families visited the cemetery, leaving the traditional chrysanthemums on their beloveds' gravesites. For those men and women whose bodies were never found or returned, a large white cross was planted in the ground to honor their souls.

Maria and ten-year-old Lilia knelt in prayer as the priest prepared the chalice for communion. His voice echoed through the vaulted aisles, blanketing the murmurs and whispers of the congregation.

"Lord, I am not worthy to receive you, but only say the word and my soul shall be healed." As parishioners rose to join the line to receive the holy sacrament, Maria heard sniffles and soft sobs. She noticed her relatives, neighbors, and other villagers beholding her with pity, as if they knew something she didn't.

Why are they looking at me? What is going on?

Grim expressions scattered the church. Maria grew worried as villagers shielded their tears from her sight, not discreetly enough to evade her notice.

After mass, Maria and Lilia started back to the house. Passers-by continued to bow their heads to avoid eye contact. Maria now sensed a change in the air—Lilia did, too. Something was wrong.

"Mama? Why is everyone staring?" Lilia furtively glanced around her. Her shoulders were covered, and there were no rips or stains on her blue dress. *It's not me . . . is it?*

"I don't know, but I'm going to find out!" Maria was irritated that everyone she knew and trusted in the village seemed to be ignoring her. Maria's eyes squared towards the bar, where she saw Arturo's friends lingering outside, smoking cigarettes; as they caught her expression, theirs changed.

"Lilia, get your books and go to school. I'm going to go speak to those boys for a minute."

Maria stormed towards La Bottega, her fists clenched at her sides and her face contorted with anger. "Nando! Marco!" Her eyes were blazing. "Is there something I need to know? Have you heard news about Arturo?"

Arturo's friends immediately panicked, dropped their cigarettes, and turned pale.

"N-no, we don't know anything." Maria caught Marco's sideways glance at Nando, who appeared nervous. He nodded in agreement, but both boys' eyes told Maria a different story.

She shot them both a look charged with distrust before stomping back to the gate, grumbling aloud. "What the hell is going on! No one is telling me anything!"

When Lilia arrived at school and took her seat, a surprise math test awaited her. She flipped through the pages, and her mind drew a blank. Erasing her answers and rewriting them, Lilia struggled with the questions and the odd stirring feeling that had unsettled her stomach since mass. *What do the villagers know that she and her mother don't?* A sudden knock on the classroom door startled Lilia, releasing her from the frustrating world of numbers and equations. She blinked, focusing her gaze outside the window and up the street to see a line-up of people leading to her house.

An internal alarm bell set her heart racing. It was her cousin Anita who'd interrupted the class. She whispered to Signore Maestro, whose face twisted into a frown as he looked over at Lilia.

The teacher's silence sent a flurry of chills through Lilia's body. She abruptly stood up. She knew something was wrong.

Signore Maestro approached her desk and lay his hand on her shoulder, which she tried to unobtrusively shrug off. "Your mother needs you. Go quickly. You can finish the test another day."

Without a moment's thought, Lilia tore out of the classroom and ran home. As she neared the gate, the tear-filled eyes of relatives and neighbors were fixed on her. Like Moses parting the red sea, they gave way, letting Lilia through to the front door. Villagers reached out to stroke her hair and caress her arms. Weeps became sobs. They spoke words of comfort and sadness, but Lilia could not hear them. Her cheeks flushed red and her body trembled—she was in her own world. She could hear her mother's guttural wails spill out the windows.

Lilia stopped in the doorway, confused and terrified. She watched her mother slumped on the ground, crawling on all fours, screaming her brothers' names. "Arturo! Erminio!" And then again, in a mournful wail, "Arturo!"

An officer stood by Maria, his face drawn into an expression of agony as he watched the raw suffering before him. "My deepest sympathy, Signora Meneguzzi. The death of your son is beyond tragic. His ashes were scattered with thousands of others' in the camp—I'm so sorry, Signora. In the end, evil will not prevail. These Nazis will pay for their crimes."

For Lilia, everyone's lamentations and her mother's agonizing cries drowned into a dull hum. All she could hear were the words death and ashes, as they bore into her soul.

Lilia's beautiful brother, a man of peace and a protector in a time of war, had been tortured and burned.

Her throat grew tight. She was barely able to breathe through her despair and anger. *Whose sins are we paying for?*

Lilia watched the priest and friar praying over her mother, but their words of benediction and hope meant nothing. *What good is that now? Where was God when we needed Him?*

Padre Munnini reached out to touch Maria's shoulder.

"Maria, you need to have courage and give your son back to God."

Maria swatted his hand away. Her eyes seethed with contempt.

"They burned my son! *BURNED HIM!*" Primal sounds erupted from her. "Get out of my house!" Maria's arms rose and fell as she rocked back and forth on the floor. Lilia wanted to go to her, but a mixture of fear, disbelief, and shock repelled her.

"What do you know about children? He was *my* child!" Maria beat her chest repeatedly, and spittle fell from her mouth as she violently disgorged her words. "*My* son! Get out of my house! *GET OUT OF MY HOUSE* and take your *GOD* with you!"

This day was the darkest of Lilia's life. She saw the pain in her mother's eyes. She felt her heart cry words she could never speak. Lilia watched Maria release her rage and agony, which seemed to spill like a puddle of memories around her. Memories of Arturo . . . Maria's firstborn and Lilia's favorite brother.

And yet again, another son, another brother, who would be buried without a body. Without a resting place from which to pray.

At that moment, Lilia knew Arturo had been saying goodbye in her frightening dream so many months ago. The idea that life would now go on without him threatened to engulf her. Lilia pulled away. She felt strangled by the darkness as it unfolded and rolled over her like an ominous cloud. Tears rained down her cheeks as her little body shook.

Her big brother was dead.

A silent scream rumbled inside. She hated the Nazis. She hated this life. How could God let this happen? With so much death, Lilia's eyes could no longer see past the grief. What future would she possibly have without Arturo? How could she ever feel happiness again?

Lilia's thoughts quickly turned to her father.

Papa!

She ran upstairs to find Virginio sitting on the edge of his bed, his face whiter than a sheet. He was barely able to look at Lilia through his puffy lids. Virginio held Arturo's photo in his quivering hands. He looked empty, as though he had lost sight of all that could have been. War had taken away his sons and destroyed his family.

⚬◎◐ ◑◎⚬

Arturo's tragic death was the first of many. One by one, others in Mussons suffered the same painful news—lives lost, families destroyed.

For Maria, her world had ended. In the days that followed, intense pain took her mind prisoner. Everything lost meaning. Smell, sight, taste, and sound vanished—and her battered heart grew cold. She no longer wanted to fight the pressure that rested on her shoulders, but to succumb to it, at last. She was tired of being strong.

Maria fell into a deep depression, followed by a nervous break-down. She confined herself to her room and refused to eat or speak to anyone. She didn't want to get up; she didn't want to move; she found no reason to. Her heart moaned, but she didn't speak a word as she suffered in silence. With Eliseo having left to visit his son in Turin, neighbors stepped in to help care for Giovanni, Riccardo, and Bruno, leaving Lilia and her father to tend to Maria.

"My love, you have to eat. *Please.*" Virginio sat by her bedside with a tray of food one afternoon. But again, it was to no avail.

"I don't want it." Maria pushed the tray away and refused to make eye contact with her husband. "Take it away and leave me alone." She turned her back on Virginio and pulled the covers up high over her head until she was out of sight.

For the next few days, Virginio tried to get through to his wife, but she continued to turn away meals, and to speak only when she was refusing them.

"Maria, I've been hearing about this man, Major Ubaldo Pesap-ane—a survivor from Flossenbürg. He was interned at the same time as Arturo. While there, he somehow managed to access the German records of all the Italians who died in the camp. The Major has been sending letters to families to let them know where their loved ones were imprisoned—where they died. I wrote to him, hoping to find out more information. Perhaps it will give us some closure."

"Closure for what?" Maria snapped. "Our son is dead."

"Maria! Enough of this! You're not the only one who is suffer-ing!" Virginio ran his hands through his hair in frustration. For the first time, his patience had worn thin as he struggled to deal with his own depression. Virginio didn't want to argue with Maria, so he pulled her against him instead. "Arturo was *my* son, too!"

After years of comforting Maria through dark times, through the loss of their other children, and through her nearly losing her life, Virginio lost his strength to absorb Maria's pain, as he was consumed by his own. He buried his pain in work, and although it didn't take away his sorrow, as a soldier, he had learned to accept the inevitable consequences of war. Still, knowing the horrors his son suffered was more than Virginio could bear. He'd had no control over Arturo's fate, and yet as a father and a protector, Virginio regretted not having been able to do more for his son.

Maria pulled away and turned her back once again.

Alone in his grief and emptiness, Virginio stomped downstairs, threw the tray into the sink, and wept until he was exhausted, body and soul.

Lilia watched her father unravel before her eyes. She, too, felt lost and needed comfort, but the days of being tucked into bed and counting on Virginio's strength alone were long gone. Like her father, she threw herself into her chores, cooking meals and watching over Maria as best she could, leaving little time to feel the loss of Arturo but also of her mother, who was rapidly fading. Both of Lilia's older brothers had been ripped from her life but letting go of Arturo was the most painful. He had come back promising he'd stay, and now he was gone forever. Once the news traveled to Ermides and Dina, they too suffered in silence. Separated by miles and responsibilities, there was not much they could do, but pray for their family and continue to send money home.

Growing up through the intensity of this savage war was a painful rite of passage for Lilia. She seemed to have leapt into adulthood overnight. She could no longer be the little girl who needed protection from the torment of war. War was now practically all she knew. It was up to Lilia to offer solace to her grief-stricken parents, to pick up the pieces and be the glue that kept them together. It was simply her cross to bear.

"Papa, go to work." Lilia rubbed her father's arm to soothe him. "Let me clean this up, and later today, I will bring Mama some soup and try again."

Virginio caressed her face tenderly. "I'm sorry, Liliutti." His voice was apologetic, his face soft. "And who is here to help heal your heart? How are we ever going to get through this? I don't know what more I can do." He squeezed her shoulder. "As broken as I feel, I'm still your father, and I will do my best to be here for you."

For the first time, Lilia had little to say. She, too, was silent with her words and feelings. With her little brothers being cared for by the neighbors and her father at work until dusk, Lilia grew lonely in Maria's absence. Despite their years of emotional strain and distance, she feared her mother would never return to how she once was.

Hours passed. Lilia prepared the tray once again with a light soup made of chicken broth and tiny star-shaped pasta both Lilia and her mother loved.

"Mamina?" No reply. "Mama?" It was mid-afternoon, and the shutters were pulled tight—Maria took comfort in the coldness of the darkly lit room, which mirrored the vast emptiness in her heart.

Lilia placed the tray on the dresser and opened the window to let in the sun's warmth and fresh air. The sight of her mother was horrific as the sunlight fell upon her face. Maria's eyes were glazed over and seemingly dead. Lilia watched her mother stare through her as though she were invisible. Anything Lilia said seemed to pass through Maria. Her body was lifeless, like scattered dead leaves. It was as if Maria's soul had departed.

Lilia gazed out into the courtyard. Even the leaves twirled in the occasional wind.

Maria made no effort to acknowledge her daughter's presence.

How can my mother, a powerful woman, so fiercely alive and in control, now disappear from life, give up on our family?

"Mama, the soup is hot. Please try to eat something." Lilia waited for some sign or movement. "Mama, Papa and the boys need you . . . I need you."

The weight of Maria's silence felt like a vice on Lilia's heart. She bowed her head as she shuffled to the door, but when she turned to look at her mother, pity and courage inflated her little body. "I miss him too, you know. My stomach tangles in knots every night before I go to bed. I miss telling him things. Arturo was the only one in my life who saw me for who I was. I hope I can still be that girl for him, but right now, I'm afraid I might shrivel up and die . . . like you." Lilia looked up, still hopeful for a word—anything. Her mother faced the window and didn't flinch. Lilia pulled the door closed as a single tear trickled down Maria's cheek.

Lilia had no choice but to take time off school to tend to her brothers. Giovanni, Riccardo, and Bruno returned home after having been gone for days. Too young to understand the barbaric cruelty of Nazi camps, they were spared the painful truth and told their war hero brother had died in battle, joining Erminio in heaven. Their sadness was more a reaction to their parent's and sister's suffering, the dark mood lingering in the air, and the cries that echoed off the walls.

Still in shock over Arturo's death, Lilia struggled through her feelings by going through the motions and doing what was expected of her, as she always had.

Will this be my life forever? she wondered.

As much as she dreaded the math equations which she'd slogged through in class days ago, Lilia wished she were back at school, behind her desk. At least she'd be away from home, removed from the overwhelming sadness and inescapable duties, from which there was seemingly no way out.

All I want is my brother. Without him, nothing else matters.

༄༅ ༄༅

Two weeks later, on a Sunday morning, Virginio, Eliseo, Lilia, and the boys were sitting at the kitchen table when they heard footsteps slowly coming down the stairs. They shared a look of surprise and relief.

Maria caught her reflection in the mirror of the buffet and didn't know who was staring back. *Look what's become of me.* She let out a heavy sigh and shuffled into the kitchen. The room fell silent.

Maria looked haggard. Exhaustion covered her face like a veil. Her skin was gray and flaky, as if all her blood had drained away. Maria's white-streaked hair was greasy and matted; her eyes were sunken, rimmed in charcoal circles, and drained of life. Her voice cracked with regret as she expelled her first words in weeks: "My grandmother came to me in a dream last night."

"Mama! Mama!" Overjoyed, the boys ran to Maria and threw their arms around her, not particularly interested in her dream. She proceeded to finish preparing the breakfast Lilia had started, as if it were a typical day.

"Boys, come, sit down. Let your mother breathe!" Eliseo corralled the boys, sensing Maria needed time.

"So? What did Nonna Rosa say?" Lilia missed her mother too, but she wanted to give Maria the space to express herself, to feel heard and held.

"She was angry with me. She told me: 'Maria, what are you doing? You have a husband who loves you, and four children who need you. Be with them. Go be their wife and mother.'"

Virginio watched his wife. Even though she'd mustered the strength to come back to him and their family, he could see the pain had not ceased. It had simply gone underground. He struggled to understand how they could hold both the fond and distressing memories and navigate their lives to regain hope for the future. How could they embrace the sun again, laugh again, find the courage to accept peace amid so much suffering and hate? How could they forget all that had torn their family and lives apart?

"Maria, I know it feels like you're drowning, but only you and time can heal your heart. I'm with you through it all, my love." Virginio looked over at Eliseo, the boys, and then at Lilia, squeezing her hand. "We all are—you are not alone. We are still a family." Virginio rose from the table and gave his wife a gentle peck on the cheek before whispering in her ear, "The light will find us again. It doesn't rain forever."

♖♖

Just over a year after Arturo's death, Mussons was gearing up for its annual Catholic procession, the Assumption of the Virgin Mary, in celebration of her body's ascent into heaven, and for her piety and love for the poor. This was a day to embrace hope, peace, and brotherhood, which were all so needed in a place that had undergone so much pain and suffering.

The Assumption commenced early in the morning after the villagers adorned the statue of the Madonna. They decorated her with garlands of chrysanthemums and lilies from their gardens. The virgin flowers symbolized Mother Mary's purity and connection to the divine. With the shadow of war still looming in their hearts, this day brought villagers a necessary sense of community, shining a bright light upon memories shrouded in darkness. The parishioners escorted the effigy from St Osvaldo, down Via della Chiesa past the village square and back to the church in time for the Holy Mass in Mother Mary's honor.

Every year, female members of the church group walked the procession. Each carried a lit candle that symbolized the light of Christ beaming on to the world. Deemed old enough to join, Lilia was granted the opportunity to join the procession, filling her with feelings of pride and acceptance.

"Lilia, hurry up, or the priest will leave without you!" Maria hollered.

"Yes, Mama!"

Lilia arrived at the church out of breath, just as the priest emerged on to the street.

"Good morning, Lilia." He nodded as he lit her candle. "Get in line. Quickly now."

"Sorry I'm late, Padre." Lilia's heart throbbed with excitement to be invited into the celebration. As the youngest girl bestowed with this honor, she felt special. Lilia balanced the tall pillar in both hands and watched the statue of Mary with adoration as it was hoisted high above her head on a wooden platform, carried on the shoulders of four men.

Maria watched the procession from her kitchen window. She waited to be sure her daughter had arrived at the church on time and was holding the candle. As the pilgrimage approached Maria's house, she strained her eyes and looked more closely, unsure of what she was seeing. Through the dense crowd, Maria spotted Lilia walking behind the priest . . . and behind her was Angelina. She had been gone from Mussons for over two years. Her cheeks were gaunt, and like gray stones, her eyes had lost their luster. She was thinner, dressed in a plain, modest dress, her posture no longer upright and dignified. Angelina's long blonde hair was cut shorter; it was unkempt and had turned dull. She was no longer the beautiful woman she once had been. Guilt had consumed her. Frida was standing by her side, similarly transformed, destroyed from the inside.

Their lost beauty offered no condolences to Maria, whose blood instantly reached a boiling point. She stuck her head out the window screaming vulgarities. "Angelina! You whore! You killed my son!"

Padre Munnini halted the procession. The crowd gasped in horror and surprise at Angelina's presence—an insult to the community of Mussons. The villagers moved away from her and turned their eyes towards the gate. Maria burst into the street as a raging fury overtook her body. She had come to accept her son's death as best as she could, but she would never forget it was Angelina who'd burned her son to ashes.

He loved Angelina, and she betrayed his heart. She lied. She had the power to save him and did nothing!

Blinded by determination, Maria pushed people aside and ran up to her son's former beloved. She slapped Angelina's face so hard that it knocked her to the ground. She lunged into the young woman as several villagers tried to pry her off. Maria's knuckles were white as her fingers coiled into fists.

"You killed my son! It's *your* fault! You slept with the Germans! You could have said something, done something! You saw Arturo in prison and did nothing to save him! You let him *die*!" Maria shook her head with such hatred that her hair exploded out of its bun.

All the while, Padre Munnini remained silent and Lilia looked on in shock at her mother's public display. She could almost see the flames roaring in Maria's eyes. Although heart-breaking to watch,

Lilia felt every word being spewed—words that were true, as she harbored them, too.

A villager leaped out from the crowd and spat on Angelina. "How *dare* you show your face here again after what you did! You're nothing but a filthy Nazi tramp!"

"*You*!" Julia, Pietro's mother, ran out from her house with a stick in her hand. Her face was beet red. "Traitors! Both of you! The Germans dragged my son out by his feet, screaming! You could have stopped them from taking him away!" Angelina and Frida crouched on the ground, shielding themselves, never breathing a word as Julia beat them. "You killed our sons. You slept with the Nazis! And you did nothing to save our boys! It should have been you they burned!"

Before more trouble could ensue, Julia was pulled away, and Angelina and Frida beat a hasty retreat. Arm in arm, they limped and whimpered in shame down the street. Julia continued to taunt them. She stood in the center of the crowd, all five feet of her, waving her stick, and vomiting every thread of pain tangled inside her body. "There is no dignity in whores like you! You spread your legs for that scum. Commanders! Colonels! Generals! It will take a kilo of lemons to shrink those infested vaginas. Run like cowards! Run! Never show your faces here again!"

⁊⊘ ⊘℩

With Angelina and Frida out of sight, the crowd's anger subsided, and the whispers of hatred evolved into peaceful prayers. The procession continued. After mass, Lilia arrived home to find Virginio consoling Maria in his arms. At that moment, and after the pain of seeing Angelina again, Lilia found herself submerged in grief—grief she had been suppressing for far too long because she felt she'd needed to, for the sake of her family.

Lilia ran to the fig tree, the same tree where she and Arturo had shared a moment of reflection and closeness before he and Erminio left for war. Like her big brother, she sat on the patch of grass and clasped her arms around her knees.

His words still lingered in the air: "Come on, put your head back like me, close your eyes, listen to the sounds, and feel the breeze on your skin. If you lay real still, you can almost hear butterflies flutter."

Lilia remembered how much Arturo loved the sun on his face, the infinite blue sky, and the scent of their mother's roses.

Tears spilled down her face as she spoke aloud. "I miss you, Arturo. You loved and protected everything and everyone. How could someone so good die so young? I thought when we die, our light dies with us, but maybe your light lives on in me. I'm sitting here in *our* place . . . wishing you were here."

Lilia leaned back, gazing up at the white clouds as they sailed across the sky. She wished to be on them, soaring free to faraway places and away from the stark reality—her brother was gone. As Lilia closed her eyes to the world and the troubles around her, a smile played across her lips. She could sense Arturo in the breeze. She could almost feel his arm around her and hear him calling out her name: "Liliutti, how's my favorite girl? Be happy, *piccina*. I'm fine, and I'll be here for you every step of the way."

Lilia felt a sudden tickling on her nose. She opened her eyes to see a purple butterfly hovering above her. She loved purple now more than ever. She reached her hand up and watched these delicate wings dance across her fingers.

Lilia reached over to the bush and plucked a red rose. She laid it gently under the tree.

The deep pain I'm feeling in my heart is the price I have to pay for loving you so much. But I will never stop loving you, Arturo, and I will never forget.

15 | GONE WITH THE WIND

Spring 1947

"The Grand Hôtel?"

What is she doing reading this garbage! *And why is she hiding them under her mattress?* Maria thought. Stunned, she angrily flipped through the weekly magazines. She was appalled by the fotonovelas—romance comic strips of movie stars with adult dialogue. Despite Maria's no longer being a major proponent of the Catholic church, she knew such material was heavily opposed in the village. Maria thrust her head out the bedroom window.

"Lilia! I found this under your mattress! Who gave it to you?" she shouted as she waved the rolled-up magazine in her hand. Her cheeks flamed red, and disgust tinged her words.

Startled, Lilia gasped, dropping her broom in the pile of dirt she had groomed on the walkway. She looked up and cringed. Her mother's tone assailed her like a hail of bullets. *Thank God Papa and the boys are not home for this embarrassing display. I should have gone to the farm with them.* Exasperated, she bowed her head, readying for the impending onslaught, "Solidea gave it to me. She bought it in Morsano after school."

Maria launched the magazine into the courtyard, nearly clipping her daughter's head. Lilia braced herself with her arms. "Throw it away, or I'll get rid of this nonsense myself by burning it in the fireplace! What if Padre Munnini caught you reading this? You'd be feeling the back of his hand far before mine!"

"But Mama, all the other girls are reading it!" Lilia offered her weak defense.

"And this makes it right? Solidea's parents should be ashamed of themselves! She should be home helping her family, not wasting time going to school, and not reading this filth!"

Lilia sighed as she thought of Solidea's life, which seemed like such a luxury compared to her own. Day in and day out, Lilia waved Solidea and her other friends goodbye as they cycled to and from the middle school in nearby Morsano.

It had been two years since Lilia completed her fifth and final year of classes in Mussons, and as misfortune would have it, she failed her final exam. The denial of her diploma left her with yet another disappointment. Lilia knew she deserved recognition and the feeling of accomplishment, but there was never enough time to study between chores and helping to raise her brothers. Lilia could have rewritten the exam, but her mother didn't see the value in it—she didn't see the value in her.

"You're a *girl*!" Maria had flared, emphasizing the word *girl* with scorn. "Girls don't need an education!" Beyond the fact that Maria didn't see the utility in sending a girl to school, advancing Lilia's education was too expensive. Maria and Virginio planned to set enough funds aside to bestow this privilege upon Bruno, who, at age seven, offered sufficient time for them to build up their savings.

Although the Meneguzzis had always been poor, post-war life had made the strain on their finances more palpable. After the war, the escalated cost of living and the rise in unemployment rates collapsed the Italian currency. Villages, towns, cities, and their people had to be rebuilt physically and socially. The recovery would be slow, and Lilia knew she would soon be following in her sisters' footsteps, working as a maid to help supplement the family income. Although cleaning other people's homes wasn't Lilia's dream life, and although she yearned for her diploma and the chance to graduate high school and have more choices, she resigned herself to the fate she had.

Lilia grabbed the magazine from the ground, rolled it up, marched over to the outhouse, and released it into the deep and dark pit along with her dreams. She had grown exhausted from her mother's disapproval of everything she'd ever done or wanted to do—anything she hoped for in her life. There was no sense indulging in her childish pleasures any longer. One day she would stand on her own, but as long as Lilia was under the weight of her mother's oppressive thumb, she didn't exist.

⁂

As a natural jack-of-all-trades, Virginio was also a barber and offered the villagers the use of his grooming tools. At twelve years of age, Lilia had grown curious about the young women who frequented the house to use her father's razors to shape their brows. He kept his tools neatly stored in the drawer of the living-room buffet.

Maria mocked these women under her breath, feeling all this pampering was a waste of time. Although severe in her beliefs, under her tired, ragged face, Maria was a beautiful woman; but Lilia had never seen her mother pay much heed to her appearance or use any enhancing instruments and tricks which would turn back time. In fact, Lilia lacked experience in the feminine arts, especially since Ermides and Dina had left home so long ago. Still, Lilia had a natural yearning for beauty, and she was intrigued by the confidence and easeful sensuality with which some of the young women of Mussons carried themselves.

Norma, Tosca, and Victoria were sisters in their twenties and, in Lilia's eyes, the most elegant women in Mussons. Compared to the other locals, they were known as socialites with a glamorous lifestyle, venturing out to places like Milan, Turin, and Rome—cities Lilia dreamed about and hoped to one day explore herself. As remote of an idea as it seemed, she fantasized about being these young beauties, or at least growing up to look like them—heads held high and the sound of their stilettos clicking on the floor as they waltzed into a room with flair and style.

Lilia marveled at the effort and time they put into their appearance and stealing into the house to watch them groom themselves felt like she was partaking in a secret ritual.

One afternoon, Norma, Tosca, and Victoria approached the front gate. "Signora? May we use Signore Meneguzzi's razors to trim our brows?" The girls giggled with excitement as they pranced into the courtyard in their back-seamed stockings and high heels. "We're off to the big city for the summer!"

Maria scanned the girls up and down and quietly scoffed, appalled by their appearance. *Look at those scarlet lips—and their legs showing for all the world to see! Their skirts are too short and too tight! What are they trying to prove except that they are stupid girls, on their way to breaking their necks in those ridiculous shoes!*

Maria nodded dismissively. "Yes, yes, go inside. You know where he keeps them." Maria slapped the dirty clothes hard against the washboard basin. As the girls sauntered away, she muttered to herself, "Hussies!"

Lilia hid quietly behind the kitchen door, spying on the sisters and observing them with admiration and a tinge of envy. She watched as they brushed their long golden locks, rolled up tubes of red lipstick to paint their lips, and demonstrated the fine art of sculpting brows as pencil-thin as Marlene Dietrich's. The villagers, like much of Europe, adored the well-respected German actress, who was known for her humanitarian efforts during the war. From housing exiles to helping Jews escape from Germany, she funded refugees with her own money and performed on the front lines to boost morale and sell war bonds.

Fixated on their transformation, Lilia stroked her brows. She felt the thickness of the unruly hairs under her fingers, which made her sigh. *Could I look like them if my eyebrows were thinner and arched higher?*

As the sisters leaned into the buffet mirror, shaping and shaving with the greatest of ease, Lilia crept into the great room, grabbed one of her father's razors and a hand-held mirror, and slipped back into the kitchen. With blade in hand, Lilia proceeded to shave a little off the top and a little off the bottom, careful not to cut herself. While tilting her head to sneak one last peek at the girls, Lilia lost her balance. With a careless move and slip of the wrist, she accidentally shaved off one of her beloved brows. Lilia gazed at her reflection in the mirror mournfully, her eyes wide with shock as she took in the strange-looking girl before her—she was thoroughly rattled.

Oh my God! What have I done? Mama is going to kill me!

Lilia instantly broke into a sweat as she imagined the merciless scolding she'd get from her mother. She raced upstairs, grabbed a scarf, tied it around her head, and pulled both corners down far enough to cover her bare brow bone.

"Lilia! Where are you?"

Through her bedroom window, Lilia could see her mother hanging linens to dry on the clothesline, and heard Norma, Tosca, and Victoria's giggles as they disappeared out the gate.

"Mama, I'm upstairs!"

"Come outside and help me with the laundry."

Lilia knew avoiding her mother was out of the question. She

braced herself and descended the flight of stairs. Each step triggered a different vision of what might transpire. *Will Mama be angry? Will she punish me? Will she tell Papa I touched his tools?* Lilia stepped outside with her head down and refrained from making eye contact with her mother. She busily threw herself into the handwashing while keeping out of Maria's sightline.

Through the billowing white sheets, Maria noticed a scarf strangely positioned over her daughter's head but made nothing of it and continued pinning wet clothes on the line.

I've never seen Lilia wearing a *headscarf*, she pondered. Maria continued to observe her daughter with a watchful eye and growing suspicion.

"Lilia, come here."

Lilia's breath quickened. She felt the rush of both panic and nausea. Lilia knew she'd made a terrible mistake. She had no business touching her father's tools, but facing her mother was much worse than losing her eyebrow. Lilia shuffled over to Maria like she was headed to the gallows.

"Why are you wearing a scarf on your head? It's covering your eyes! You can barely see what you're doing!"

"It's too hot outside, and my head hurts. I wanted to shade it from the sun."

"You expect me to believe this? What are you hiding? Take it off!" Maria didn't wait for Lilia to respond. She yanked the scarf off her daughter's head. Lilia instantly shot both hands up to hide her brow.

"Let me see!"

Lilia trembled as her hands slowly slid away from her face.

"Oh my God, you stupid girl, what did you do?"

Lilia could feel her face flush and her stomach turn. She braced herself against an imminent slap, shrinking into herself as she awaited her mother's punishment . . . but instead, Maria erupted into laughter.

"Eliseo! Come see what this silly girl did!"

Eliseo, who had been suffering from a chronic chest cold, had not been well for weeks, but he was in good spirits, as ever. He crept out the front door with his tightly wrapped sweater, and the sight of Lilia threw him into a fit of coughing and laughing, seizing him so hard that it made him bend over.

Although she was embarrassed, Lilia was relieved not to have suffered her mother's wrath and laughed along with them. *I am a stupid girl. The one who will suffer now is me, waiting for my eyebrow to grow back—if it ever will!*

Maria's laugh quickly dissipated as her suspicion rose once again. "Young lady, why are your cheeks red? Did you put makeup on?"

"Mama, no! I promise!"

With Eliseo watching, her cheeks flushed even brighter from embarrassment. Maria yanked a handkerchief from her pocket, spat on it, and proceeded to rub Lilia's skin repeatedly. She withdrew the cloth and frowned. She was almost disappointed it came away clean and unmarked. She'd been wrong, after all. "Well, thank goodness. You don't want to be like those trampy girls. Now go clean up their mess before your father gets home."

"Yes, Mama."

Although things had turned out badly for Lilia and it would take several weeks for her brow to grow back in, she felt a little spring in her step. At long last, she'd learned a little about what it felt like to be a woman . . . to be beautiful, elegant, and sure of herself. Still, she yearned for someone, anyone, to teach her how to carry herself with the confidence of a princess. How else would her true knight appear? How else would she be saved and whisked away from this endless drudgery?

୬ଡ଼ ୨ୡ

October 1947

"Lilia!" Maria yelled out from the kitchen window, calling her daughter inside. "Go check the candles upstairs. Make sure they're still lit, haven't fallen over, and didn't drip on the bed. I'm busy making food for everyone."

It was a cold late afternoon, and the sun was gradually melting behind the soft, gray clouds. Lilia looked up at the warm light escaping the bedroom window and felt sick to her stomach at her mother's orders. Lilia ran across the street to her friend Ana's house to enlist her support.

"Ana, come with me! To the upstairs bedroom. Please!"

"You want *me* to see the dead body?"

"I don't even want to, and it's in *my* house, but yes!" Ana could see Lilia's trepidation.

"Yes, I'll go with you. You shouldn't have to do this alone!" Ana's eyes began to fill with curiosity, "You know, I've never seen a dead body before!"

"I hate that my mother is making me do this. I've been avoiding the room since yesterday, when Padre gave his blessing."

Without wasting another moment where she might change her mind, Ana led the way across the street and through the gate. Like two young explorers off to challenge the unknown, they entered the house of death and burning candles.

The girls climbed the staircase to the landing and stood there for a moment, gathering their courage. The walls and ceiling came alive with moving shadows as the distant candles flickered in the room at the end of the hall. Lilia and Ana held hands. Their fingers intertwined tightly as they inched towards the bedroom, fixated on the foot of the bed where the dimly lit figure became increasingly visible. The sound of the creaking floorboards and their rapid breathing permeated the air.

"Your hand is wet." Lilia unclasped her grip to wipe the moisture of nervous sweat on her dress.

"Well, yours is cold!" Ana grabbed Lilia's arm, pulling it snugly against her body.

The girls arrived at the doorway and froze, immobilized by the scene before them.

Lilia squeezed her eyes shut. "I can't do this!"

"You have to! We'll do it together. Come on."

At a snail's pace, the girls neared the bed, which was framed by four pillar candles. Their pulses raced and their eyes grew wide as the lit, wax tapers cast an eerie glow on Eliseo's calm face. It spoke of a world beyond, a dimension after death, a place unfamiliar to Lilia or Ana's imagination. Lilia always knew him as jolly and playful, but the joy had left his body like the sun on a gloomy winter day. His soul had departed.

Who is this man? thought Lilia. *He is a stranger to me.*

Eliseo was dressed immaculately in his best three-piece, navy-striped suit and starched, white shirt. Maria had bathed and clothed him in preparation for the all-night vigil, and she'd set a palm frond in holy water for people to bless his body.

"It's freezing in here." Ana wrapped her arms around herself, unable to stop shivering. "Why is the window open? I can almost see my breath!"

"Padre said, 'It's to light Eliseo's spirit on its way to heaven'; but Mama said, 'It's to keep his body from smelling.'"

Ana observed the corpse. Her mouth was dry, and her limbs

trembled. "What if his lips twitch, and his eyes move in their sockets? What if they open?"

"Ana, stop! You're scaring me!"

"My mama said pneumonia took his life."

"Yes, it happened quickly. Eliseo got sick, and in a few months, he was gone. I was here when he died yesterday. I watched him take his last breath. It felt like something out of a nightmare, so I looked away. And then everyone started crying and praying. I ran out of the room. I don't like death, Ana. Death doesn't care about anyone or anything. It takes all the people I love."

Ana stared silently at the dead man she had known as the village tailor while Lilia checked for drips of wax on the bed and his clothes.

"He looks peaceful with his arms folded, and his hands wrapped in the rosary. It makes him look like he's praying." Ana's trepidation had been replaced by intrigue and curiosity as she crept closer to the body. "He looks elegant in his suit, don't you think?"

"Ana, let's go. I don't want to be here anymore." To Lilia, he didn't look like her long-time, family friend, but a soulless, stone statue.

"Lilia, he twitched!" Ana blinked rapidly and drew closer. "I think his face moved!"

Lilia averted her eyes and shook her head. "No, it didn't!" Her stomach lurched, and her heart hammered against her chest. Immediately, she ran for the door.

"Wait for me!" Ana squealed. Both girls barreled down the hallway and stairs, headed for an escape out the front door, but skidded to a halt when they saw Maria.

Maria shuffled out of the kitchen in her black slippers and a stained white apron, stirring a large bowl of pasta with a sauce-coated wooden spoon. She looked tired. Her face was drawn, and strands of wiry gray hair poked out from the black scarf on her head. It was clear she hadn't slept in days.

"What's wrong with you girls, pale as a sheet and out of breath? You look as though you've seen a ghost." Maria failed to realize the cruelty of the task she had given her twelve-year-old daughter. "How are the candles?"

"They're *fine*, Mama." Lilia looked at her mother in consternation and confusion. Why in the world had Maria put her through such an ordeal?

"Say goodbye to your friend and come help me set the table. Eliseo's vigil will go on until the funeral in the morning—your father and I will be feeding people all night."

Lilia and the boys were unable to sleep that evening as they listened to the creaking footsteps of friends and family members who were there to pay their respects to Eliseo.

"I'm going to miss him." Giovanni let out a mournful sigh as memories of Eliseo ebbed from his mind. "I'm going to miss his jokes and the times he hung out with us because he wanted to."

Riccardo's face fell as he met Giovanni's gaze. "He made me laugh, too—he was like an uncle to us."

Bruno lay quietly between his older brothers on the double bed. He didn't understand why everyone was so somber. Death, for him, was still an abstract matter. He couldn't fathom not seeing Eliseo, whose illness had come on so quickly, ever again. Bruno wondered if Eliseo would still be able to take him to the bar—or hold his hand like they were the best of friends.

"We were lucky he came into our lives." Lilia glanced over at her brothers huddled together under the covers. "He saved Papa's life once, and maybe all of ours in one way or another. I guess, like Arturo and Erminio, he's up there among the bright stars." Lilia looked out the window to the darkened sky. "He loved us like family, and we loved him the same. His light will never die, like our memories of him."

Lilia rolled on to her back, reflecting on the years gone by. She lay awake for hours as the endless stream of visitors, whispers, whimpers, and prayers lingered in the silence. The light from burning candles continued to flicker beneath the far door and trickled under hers—a constant reminder of Eliseo's dead body lying a few yards away. Spine-chilling sensations descended upon Lilia, and gruesome unwanted thoughts tumbled through her mind. Although she loved Eliseo, she was grateful she no longer had to check for dripping wax. However, in the back of her thoughts, Lilia knew his bedroom would one day be hers. One day, she would be sleeping in his bed.

◈◈◈

Summer 1948

"What does it say? Is everything fine with Ermides?" Maria sat at the dining-room table, folding clean laundry from the wicker basket, while Virginio eagerly read his daughter's letter. He looked up from the pages in his hands, removed his spectacles, and turned to his wife, his eyes brimming over with sadness.

"She's been seeing a divorced man named Eolo."

Maria scoffed aloud. "Well, it won't last long now, will it? The church will never allow her to marry a divorcé, and she would never disgrace our family by living in sin. Why the long face? What else did she say?"

"The family in Rome is short of help. Ermides wants us to send Lilia there for at least a year." Virginio's voice petered out as he watched Lilia in the courtyard busily wringing bedsheets at the washbasin and hanging them out to dry. Maria sensed his fatherly concern, having to send another daughter away and miss seeing her grow up.

"You knew this day would come. As much I need her here, we need the money more. And she's thirteen now, older than the other two when they left. It's time."

"How are we going to get her there?" Virginio tried to focus on the logistics of making it all happen, but his thoughts were elsewhere. He couldn't help but feel guilty about the decision they were about to make. He wanted Lilia to experience a world he and his wife could never give her. He knew his daughter's destiny would surpass any future she could ever have in Mussons. She worked so hard here, and so many burdens—including Maria's harshness and disapproval—seemed to hold his sensitive young daughter back. Perhaps if she had a taste of what life could be like elsewhere, she might experience the youth that eluded her here.

"I heard the Favaros' youngest boy, Bepi, finished his eighteen-month service and needs to report to his military base in Bologna, and then he's off to work in Rome. I'll ask his mother if he can take her."

Virginio pulled out a blank sheet of paper from the hutch drawer and wrote to Ermides. Her request would be fulfilled.

One week later, Lilia's small suitcase was packed, and she was ready at the gate with her father, waiting for Bepi to collect her. She'd lain awake most of the previous night, flitting in and out of vivid dreams, and spent the early morning running back and forth to the outhouse with bouts of diarrhea. Lilia was wrought with nervous tension. Her jaw tightened and her stomach cramped with apprehension. She felt conflicted over her feelings about home. Everywhere

Lilia turned, stories from her life flooded her heart and mind: Bruno's first steps, Giovanni and Riccardo's antics, precious moments between her and Arturo under the fig tree, Erminio trailing Lilia on the bicycle, blissful days parading down Via della Chiesa on stilts and playing buttons with her friends.

But each memory she caught seemed to evaporate into the air like wisps of a dandelion. Lilia's beloved big brothers and Eliseo were gone—her childhood was over. Lilia had always dreamed of leaving this place, which seemed to hold equal parts joy and sorrow, but she wondered who she would be and what awaited her now. What would become of her dreams—of finally finding love and lasting happiness? Was everything she had ever yearned for attached to this house? And if she left, would she change? Would the positive memories, which she had attempted to weave together into something precious and endurable, abandon her altogether?

I'm moving to go live with a sister I barely know, to a city larger than my imagination can bear. I'm terrified.

"Papa, I'm scared," she turned to her father with pleading eyes. "Don't make me go!" This was her first time leaving the cocoon of home—which, although never comfortable, had always been familiar. She prayed she could take with her the memories of home wound tightly in her chest. "What if I don't like it there?"

"Liliutti, you will *love* it. It's Rome!" Never having been, Lilia's father reassured her with his broadest smile, although deep down, he hated seeing her go. *Another of my daughters forced to leave the nest far too soon. What's left of me as a man if I can't support my family?* Still, despite his reservations and frustrations, Virginio hoped the experience would be enriching. Sending Lilia off was the right thing to do.

"But what if this rich family doesn't like me? Am I good enough to be a maid?"

"You are more than good enough. Your big sister will be with you. You won't be alone, and this will give you two a chance to spend more time together. Think of all the incredible places you will see! Look at this as an adventure! As the first day of the rest of your life!"

Lilia nodded, but she felt sick to her stomach. As the jeep pulled up, the sound of the honking horn intensified her anxiety.

"Boys! Come down, Lilia is leaving!" Maria ran out to the gate with a cloth handbag and placed it over Lilia's shoulder. "Here is some food for the trip. Be a good girl, and do what Ermides tells you." Maria hugged her daughter and grabbed her gently by the arms. "You're a strong girl, Lilia. Make us proud and remember to keep those shoulders back—nobody likes a sloucher!" Within seconds, six feet scurried down the stairs. Giovanni, Riccardo, and Bruno dashed outside with sleep still in their eyes and in their pajamas. They managed to give their sister a lazy wave. Having said their goodbyes the night before, she hugged her brothers and released them back to bed.

"We're always here if you need to come home." Virginio embraced his daughter, kissing her cheek repeatedly and whispering in her ear, "Papa's already proud of you."

Lilia had grown tired of goodbyes; she had said too many over the years and knew they seldom came with a happy ending. She trembled like a leaf but couldn't bring herself to cry, and now she was in the hands of a man she hardly knew, facing a whole new world. Leaving behind her parents, siblings, friends, and the one home she'd ever known felt far more daunting than the journey ahead of her.

Bepi lifted Lilia and her suitcase into the jeep. Virginio shook the young man's hand and looked him squarely in the eyes. "Take care of my little girl."

"Signore Meneguzzi, you need not worry. I assure you, she's in good hands."

Lilia waved to her little brothers as their gazes dropped to the ground and sad sniffles ensued. As the jeep drove away, Lilia could almost hear Little Rose, Eliseo, and her big brothers saying goodbye, along with the ghost of her childhood. She took a deep, quivering breath and filled her lungs, her eyes never once leaving her father's kind face and his encouraging smile as they became smaller and smaller on the horizon.

ఴౚ ౚఴ

When they arrived at the station in Latisana, the train was wall to wall with soldiers on their way to report to their compulsory military training, while others, like Bepi, reported for discharge. Dismounting the jeep, Lilia's eyes moved quickly left and right—there were no other girls on the grounds but her. Although the morning breeze was warm, she felt shaky and out of place. She had never been on a train before.

"Bepi?" Lilia's voice cracked as she watched young soldiers leaning out the train windows, smoking cigarettes, laughing, and shouting at each other. She took a shuddering breath. "Are you sure I'm allowed on there?"

"Stop worrying! You're safe. I promise." Bepi quickly scanned the train, which was about to depart. "Wait right here!" Lilia nodded, gripped her suitcase handle tightly under her cupped fingers, and watched Bepi through the crowded platform as he engaged with an officer. Once the officer walked away and was out of sight, Bepi shot a glance back at Lilia, smiled, and then quickly boarded the train. He made his way through a long line of men until he reached open seating. He waved Lilia over.

"Give me your suitcase!" She raised herself on her tip-toes and lifted her square brown bag to the window. Bepi then pulled both Lilia and her handbag into the car.

Lilia took her seat and shrank herself as small as possible. Her senses felt drowned by the smoke and the noise of the rowdy soldiers. She knew she wasn't supposed to be there. The men were kind to Lilia. They asked her polite questions, trying to ease her obvious discomfort amongst a train of boisterous male travelers, but an unfamiliar shyness overcame her, making her long for home even more.

"Hello there, young lady." One of the soldiers in the aisle smiled and winked at Lilia. "Is this your first train ride?"

Overwhelmed by the barrage of men, Lilia felt a flush of pink on her cheeks and a sudden lump in her throat. Her uneasiness felt thicker than the crowded atmosphere. She wanted to respond but didn't know what to say or how to say it. She made her best effort to give him a genuine smile before quickly using her luggage as a shield against further questions.

Please, don't let anyone else talk to me!

Lilia bit her quivering lip and kept her eyes on her feet for much of the five-hour ride to their destination, Bologna.

Once they disembarked in Bologna, Bepi sat Lilia on a park bench across the street from the station. "Wait for me here. I can't take you to the base, but I'll come back soon, and we'll board the train to Rome. You'll be safe as long as you stay put." Bepi gave Lilia a sympathetic smile. He felt sorry for leaving her, but there wasn't much more he could do. "Are you going to be all right?" Lilia gave him a polite nod while fighting the urge to cry. What choice did she have?

Someone could hurt me, and Bepi won't be here! What if he has to stay overnight at the base?

She sat hunched on the bench for what seemed an eternity,

watching the stream of passengers and passers-by, pigeons circling overhead, and squirrels scurrying into flowered bushes and up trees. She gazed at the cirrus clouds high in the sky and stared into space. Her mind drifted back to the many times she and Arturo had sat outside enjoying the sun and breathing in the delicate fragrance of nature, but it didn't soothe her this time. She felt abandoned, not only in the park, as the light dimmed, but in her plummeting heart. Lilia laid her suitcase on her lap and wrapped her arms around it, shutting out the world. Tears clouded her brown eyes as she held on tight to all the memories left from the one home she knew, the one she'd been forced to leave behind.

After a torturous waiting period, Bepi returned to find Lilia's face fraught with panic.

"I'm sorry I took so long! What did you do while I was gone?"

Lilia didn't feel like being cheerful. She sat up and regarded Bepi stiffly. "Can we go?"

As the two traveled three hours south to Rome, their train passed through a succession of long, dark tunnels. Lilia could no longer see daylight behind her and feared the light would never reappear. As the darkness closed in, Lilia's heart pounded so loudly she could hear it in her ears. Finally, they reached Termini Station, on Piazza dei Cinquecento. Lilia was relieved to get off the train and step into yet another new experience—riding her first streetcar.

"Lilia! Welcome to Rome, the city of my dreams!" Bepi immediately lit up as he opened his arms to the hustle and bustle of the busy street. To him, Rome was a tiny piece of heaven, and in less than an hour, he would safely deliver Lilia to her sister and make good on his promise. From her seat in the streetcar, Lilia roamed the majestic scenery—a feast for her eyes. She watched as every class of people paraded the streets, which were lined with enchanting four-story buildings and stone arches. Fountains, ornate churches, narrow side alleys, lively neighborhoods, and the glistening Tiber River momentarily caught Lilia's breath, silencing her words.

"Isn't it incredible?" Bepi rattled Lilia's shoulders in excitement, but for her, the journey had been too overwhelming to leave room for joy.

"When will we get to Ermides's house?" Lilia felt drained by the emotions she'd been holding back since leaving her family, and by the journey itself.

The streetcar stopped on Via Antonio Bertoloni. Bepi and Lilia stepped down. The tram pulled away.

"Lilia, we're here! Look! There's the address across the street!"

Lilia looked up awestruck. Her eyes bulged in disbelief at the sight of this palatial building rising five stories tall. The exterior walls were painted a pale shade of peach with sculpture detailing of carved flowers and cherubic figures, and white stone pillars framed the windows with dark green shutters. Under a triumphal arch and stained-glass pendant and atop six marble steps, the richly carved, oak front door rose ten feet high. She felt transported into another world, as though she had fallen into one of her fairy tales.

With each step up, Lilia's nervousness grew. Startled, never having seen or heard a doorbell, she jumped back when Bepi rang the button for the fifth floor.

"Lilia! I'll be right down!" Lilia ran back down to the sidewalk to see Ermides waving her arms and shouting from the top-floor balcony, with its ornate, cast-iron railing. Lilia grew quiet as her eyes watered and her lips trembled. After all, it had been years since she had seen her big sister. Within minutes, the door pushed open and Ermides appeared amidst all the grandeur. Lilia dropped her suitcase and ran into Ermides's arms, weeping inconsolably. Finally, she could give in to the tears which had nearly consumed her since leaving the comfort of home. They were tears of bittersweetness—they were tears of relief. It had not escaped Lilia's attention that she would no longer be tasked with caring for her brothers; nor would she have to suffer chastisement from her mother for not being good enough. She had no idea what life held for her from this day forth, but she could finally be herself—a thirteen-year-old girl.

"What's wrong?" Ermides chuckled. "Are you not happy to be here?"

Lilia, now curious, stepped back to consider her sister. So much time had passed, and with twelve years between them, Lilia felt shy and uncomfortable in the midst of this beautiful reunion. Lilia's fondest memory of Ermides was when she gifted her with Little Rose. The mere thought of the beautiful doll, who had provided her with such a sense of solace during some of her darkest moments, filled her heart with love. On some level, although Ermides hadn't been there for most of Lilia's life, she knew her. Lilia beamed up at her sister in gratitude through a mist of tears.

I must try to embrace this new place . . . this new life.

Bepi interrupted the moment. "Ermides, remember me? Bepi, Nando's younger brother." He extended a hand. "It's been a long day for Lilia. I'm sure she's tired. You have a brave little sister there."

"Yes, I remember you. You were a young boy when I left Mussons some thirteen years ago, before Lilia was even born! Thank you for taking care of her today. Would you like to come in for a drink or something to eat?"

"No thank you. I need to be going."

"All right then. Next time you see your big brother, please give him my regards."

"Will do!" Bepi snuck Lilia a wink. "I told you I would get you here safely! You will fall in love with Rome, and it will love you back. You'll see!" Bepi waved as he ran down the street to hop on the next streetcar. Lilia waved back while still clinging to Ermides.

"Hey, city girl! Let's go inside. Welcome to your new home."

⋅୧ଅ ଅ୨⋅

Lilia followed her sister up another set of marble stairs to the mezzanine while taking in the intricately tiled floors, rich wood-paneling, and high ceilings. She slowed her pace, admiring every detail before her. Lilia watched Ermides pull open a metal-framed glass door and step into what appeared to be a dark and cold-looking box built into the wall.

"Well? Are you coming?"

Lilia looked over at the stately staircase to her left and back at her sister. She felt confused and utterly disoriented. "What *is* that?"

Ermides smiled, thinking back to her own firsts so many years ago. "It's called an elevator. It's a genius invention, and besides, the stairs take too long. However, on the days we have bags of groceries, we'll take the walk-up, as there isn't enough room in here—we must be considerate of the other tenants and visitors." Ermides motioned her in. "Come. It's safe!"

Lilia timidly stepped inside. Her throat tightened as the door clanged shut. Ermides pushed a button with the number five on it, and the elevator moved. Startled, Lilia lost her footing and stumbled against the back wall as the floor ascended, higher and higher. Lilia's heart raced as she braced herself, her eyes riding up while each passing floor rode down.

The elevator came to an abrupt halt. "Ta-da! We're here! See,

Lilia? It's like magic!" Ermides pushed the door open and Lilia quickly leaped out, throwing her sister into a fit of laughter.

"You'll get used to it. I find it fascinating how random people share this tiny space. Some are friendly, while others don't say a word, especially to the staff."

Ermides unlocked the front door as Lilia ran her hand over the brass, lion-head knocker. She tingled with excitement upon entering the large foyer of this magnificent home. It was grander than any journey Lilia had experienced while reading her fairy-tale books. Dropping her suitcase, she stood dazed and bewildered. Lilia turned in circles, letting her eyes roam over the vast, opulent space. Dazzling art hung on every wall. Lovely, arched windows were framed with thick, baroque drapery, and Persian carpets covered the polished, wooden floors pouring into each room. A chandelier with an array of branches, encrusted in teardrop-shaped crystals, illuminated the dining room and an exquisite table which seated a small army. It was covered in a hand-woven linen cloth and adorned with porcelain and silver. The living room was richly decorated with antiques, silk lamps, pillows, and furniture enveloped in luxurious upholstery.

Ermides observed the moment with gratitude as Lilia stood speechless, her bewildered gaze traveling over every detail in the house. Ermides was ecstatic she now had her little sister's helping hands, but she was also thrilled at the thought she'd saved Lilia from a life of continual hardship in Mussons and the watchful eye of their strict and unforgiving mother.

"It's a sofa, Lilia. Go on, sit on it."

Lilia fell back into the soft seat and gently stroked the velvet armrest. She gazed up at the frescoed ceiling with dreamy eyes.

"You live *here*!"

"And now, so do you," Ermides smiled. "We work hard too, so

be ready. The chef left, so I'm now in charge of cooking. You'll be dusting, doing laundry, making beds, vacuuming—"

"Vacuuming? What's that?"

"We use a vacuum to clean the carpets, floors, and drapes. The first time I used one, it ran away from me."

Lilia gave her sister a puzzled look. How could an object run away from a person?

Ermides laughed again. "In due time, you'll see and learn many new things. You will serve meals to the owners, Signore and Signora Zamparelli, and their two children, Julia and Leonardo, and at dinner parties. The girl is your age; the boy is 19. Julia is at summer camp now, and Leo is off cruising the coast with his friends—lifestyles of the wealthy, my dear! You will be taught proper table setting and etiquette. Oh, and we dress in uniform during work hours, which are Monday through Saturday."

Lilia's face grew pale and bleak upon hearing the long list of responsibilities. When would she ever have time to enjoy her luxurious surroundings . . . or to simply be a young girl?

"Don't worry, Lilia. It's mostly nothing you haven't already done. You'll catch on soon enough. Signore Zamparelli and his brother own an olive farm in Matera—he and the Signora are there for the weekend. Dina works for the brother and his family. Signora Zamparelli is an elegant socialite, always planning extravagant soirées. Sunday is our day to do whatever we want! Come, I'll show you the kitchen, our bathroom, and the bedroom we'll share. We're in the maid's quarters at the end of the hall."

Lilia followed her sister through the house, nearly falling over her own feet. It was a constant challenge not to let her jaw drop, bump into the expensive furniture, or knock over the fragile but expensive furnishings.

"Here's our bathroom." Ermides pointed to the features. "Your first toilet, and a real bathtub! What do you think?"

Lilia marveled at the fancy tiles on the floor and walls, the ornate fixtures, and plush, rose-colored towels. "A toilet?" Curious, she lowered and raised the lid. "And what's this?" Lilia yanked the chain hanging from the ceiling, causing the toilet to flush and jarring her out of the moment. Lilia was fascinated as she watched the water spin and disappear into the hole. She yanked the chain again while Ermides giggled.

"Sorry!" Lilia drew back her hand and refrained from touching anything else.

"Don't apologize. How else are you going to learn? Go ahead! Touch. Pull. Turn. Do whatever you want, but for the love of God, don't break anything!"

Lilia noticed the roll of delicate white paper held up by a brass handle hinged to the wall. She pulled on the neatly folded corner of the first sheet. "And this? What do you do with this?"

Ermides shook her head with disgust, reflecting on her harsh, peasant upbringing. "I sometimes forget where we come from." She rested her hands on Lilia's shoulders. "There will be no more wiping with those dreaded leaves from Mama's garden, and no more bedpans at night."

Lilia nodded excitedly. "And this?" She pointed to what looked like a second toilet.

"It's called a *bidet*, and it's used to wash your lower half after you use the toilet—it's cleaner than using the paper. It's the same as when Mama had you wash with a bowl of water and a cloth."

"How does it work?"

Ermides demonstrated the process. "You crouch on it like this and run the water by turning these taps. One is for hot water, and the other for cold. It might feel strange at first, but you will soon appreciate it."

Lilia hid her face in embarrassment.

"Hey, what's with the face?"

"I feel stupid. I don't know anything."

"There will be none of that talk. Look at me."

Lilia raised her head slowly as tears pooled in her eyes.

"You've had a long journey. You're tired. This is your first time in a big city, and this house is a big change for you. It will take you a few weeks to acclimatize, but everything will soon make sense and you'll feel right at home. Let's unpack your suitcase and get some food in you." Ermides put her arm around Lilia, giving her a squeeze. "Look around—this, my dear, is how the civilized world lives—*la dolce vita*!" She kissed her little sister on the cheek. "Tomorrow, your new life begins!"

Waves of relaxation washed over Lilia's entire being, shedding years of sadness and dark memories. Her heart was full, and her pulse raced with newness and anticipation. Hours ago, she had left her tiny village, feeling frightened, hopeless, and insignificant. Now, upon stumbling into this magical world, she almost wanted to pinch herself to see if she was dreaming. Despite her exhaustion from the events of the day, in Lilia's mind, she had died and gone to heaven.

This time, the dream was real.

◦◦◦◦

Lilia's days were filled with many firsts, and although terrified of failing, she learned quickly, and her tasks soon became second nature. In the weeks following, Lilia was in charge of setting her first table for an elegant dinner party while Ermides, now the head chef, orchestrated a five-course meal.

Signora Zamparelli observed as Lilia carefully placed the table settings on the linen cloth. Signora's watchful eye made Lilia anxious as she continued to wipe the sweat from her hands on her apron. Lilia mentally visualized the setting placements as instructed by her sister. *The dinner plate, half a thumb from the table's edge, the starter and dinner fork on the left, the two knives and soup spoon on the right—*

"Ah, ah! The blades turn inward, dear. We don't want any bloodshed!" the Signora spoke softly. Unlike her mother's customary remonstrations, Signora's voice was patient and kind.

"Oh, yes, of course! I'm sorry, Signora!" Lilia stuttered. *Small fork and dessert spoon above the dinner plate, bread plate to the left, butter knife.* Lilia caught Signora's smile of approval, which filled her with encouragement. *White wine glass to the right, water glass left, red wine glass far right, champagne flute, small liqueur glass.* Lastly, Lilia folded the napkin like a rosebud and placed it on the dinner plate. She let out a sigh of relief.

"Bravo, Lilia! Yes! You want to dazzle the senses! Always make sure the crystal sparkles, the silver shines, and the porcelain glistens—and most importantly, serve the food on time! Well done!"

Lilia couldn't help but smile from ear to ear. Finally, she was in a place where she felt she mattered, and she was appreciated. Pride bubbled within her, causing her to stand a little taller. She was a full-fledged lady's maid!

On Lilia's first Sunday in Rome, she and Ermides hung up their black-and-white uniforms and explored the eternal city. From St Peter's Basilica to the Spanish Steps, the Colosseum, and the Sistine Chapel, Lilia was swept up in sheer amazement. She experienced her first marionette puppet show in Villa Borghese, surrounded by beautiful gardens; then, she strolled through the market in Campo de' Fiori and threw her first penny into the Trevi Fountain.

"What did you wish for?" Ermides asked.

"If I tell you, it won't come true!" Lilia responded gleefully, soaking up her newfound good fortune. She shrieked with laughter when Ermides drew some water from the fountain and splashed her. Lilia quickly ran for cover. She had never felt such a sense of exhilaration and freedom. She had almost forgotten the war and how life used to be.

"Ermides, I *never* want this to end! I love Rome!"

"Tonight, you'll meet my boyfriend, Eolo. He owns a grocery store. He's adorable and sweet. We'll take you for gelato in Piazza Navona."

Lilia had overheard her parents discussing how Eolo was divorced and how the church would never permit the celebration of a second marriage. Although Maria and Virginio disapproved of Ermides' choices, Lilia could tell from the softness in her eyes whenever she spoke of Eolo, Ermides was truly in love.

"Oh, yes! I would love gelato!"

"One of these Sundays we'll take the train to Ostia, shuffle our feet in the warm white sand, and bathe in the sea! And I'll take you to the movie theatre. Do you remember when I told you about the movies?"

"Yes, I never forgot! The room which looks like a church with a big sheet on the wall!"

Ermides beamed at her sister, who lit up like a lamp at the memory.

It was her greatest pleasure to have pulled Lilia out of Mussons, away from such dark memories. Her little sister deserved a chance at happiness.

Neighborhood after neighborhood, Ermides exposed Lilia to a vibrant maze of restaurants, shops, and the many piazzas filled with live music and people from every corner of the world. Of all their Sunday excursions, the chance to admire the fashion mannequins captured Lilia the most. She longed for the magnificent clothing on display by designers she had never heard of, such as Guccio Gucci, Mario Prada, and Edoardo and Adele Fendi. Lilia knew she could never afford even the most modest of dresses, as her salary was sent directly home to her parents. Still, catching sight of her reflection in the glass storefront windows, she couldn't help but fantasize about trying on the delicate gloves, sheer pantyhose, and chic expensive dresses gracing the lovely mannequins.

At some point, Signora Zamparelli took notice of Lilia's peasant smocks and sensed her sadness. It was clear this poor invisible village girl desperately wanted to fit in. The Signora immediately collected a small selection of clothing from Julia's closet, and one day, she presented Lilia with her own small wardrobe.

The hand-me-downs became Lilia's treasures, for they made her feel beautiful for the first time in her life. Her world felt permeated by the magical atmosphere of the city and small luxuries she never thought she'd get a chance to experience.

Finally, Lilia was experiencing what it meant to be a girl—carefree, and with everything to look forward to.

On 12 March 1949, the American film *Gone with the Wind* opened in Rome at the Cinema Metropolitan. While waiting in line with Ermides, Lilia stood mesmerized by the marquee that framed the stately Art Deco building greeting the patrons.

"Now, when we go inside, Lilia, don't be scared. The auditorium is dimly lit, so grab on to me, and you'll be fine."

Lilia gripped her sister's hand tightly, more from anticipation than fear. She could not fathom what she was about to experience: American actors larger than life on a huge screen. It felt like a kind of sorcery. Upon entering the theatre, Lilia's eyes were greeted by over 200 seats spanned across the room. The walls were designed with Spanish-Moroccan plasterwork in gold and blue.

Ermides leaned in and whispered, "This is your first date with the movies!"

Lilia wanted to scream her excitement but instead gave a polite whisper. "This is beyond my imagination! I can't believe a mere theatre could be this grand!"

Throughout the film, Lilia visualized herself walking on to the stage, like Scarlett O'Hara, in velvet robes and an ivory satin wedding gown and long pin-curled hair. She had been transported into her fairy-tale dreams. As the credits rolled, Lilia's face flushed. She immediately erupted into questions. "I can't believe he left her! But she was so strong, and nothing could break her."

"Are you crying?"

"This is the *best* movie I have *ever* seen!"

"Lilia!" Ermides broke out in laughter, "It's the only movie you have ever seen!"

"Doesn't he love her?"

"Yes, I'm sure he does."

"Do you think Rhett will come back?"

"Well, the movie is over, so I guess you will have to create your own ending." Ermides paused in reflection. "You know, sometimes, saying goodbye is a painful way of saying 'I love you.'"

Lilia noticed a sudden change in her sister's mood. "Is something wrong?"

"Eolo wants to marry me, but he's divorced, and in the eyes of the Catholic Church, I can't marry him. Living with him would disgrace our family, and Mama would never forgive me. I broke up with him a few days ago." Ermides grabbed Lilia's hand and shook it, as if she needed to convince herself into believing the words she was about to say. "Oftentimes, we have to do whatever is necessary to care for the ones we love, even at the risk of giving up our happiness."

"No! If you love him, you should be together!" The unfairness of it all made Lilia's blood boil. "Why does the church control everything we do? Love is sacred. Papa believes in love; I know he would support your choices! Mama's never been happy, so you shouldn't listen to her!"

Ermides gave Lilia a gentle smile, moved by her sister's passion and naiveté. "It's not as simple as you think, sweet one. We can't always have what we want. Sometimes . . . love is not enough."

Like Rhett walking away in the morning fog, leaving Scarlett in tears, Lilia could tell her sister had been left broken-hearted by forces beyond her control.

Lilia's unspoken wish at the Trevi Fountain was to one day find a wondrous love to ignite hope for her future and change her destiny forever.

I will survive in the face of adversity. My dreams will rise above my scars. When I become a woman, my chosen path will lead me towards an unforgettable and inspiring journey. No one will ever take that away from me.

Right then and there, Lilia vowed to save her heart for love everlasting—the kind of love which rightfully belonged on the big screen.

16 | YOU WILL NOT BE FORGOTTEN

Rome, Summer 1949

🙼 Grateful shades of night fell upon them. Ermides and Lilia were exhausted after another laborious day. From washing the brass pots, and china plates to polishing the crystal and silverware and kneading bread for the morning took the last of their energy—they collapsed on their beds. Lilia pulled back the Egyptian cotton sheets and lay snuggly in her double-size, mahogany bed, feeling content with all her blessings, while Ermides sat on the bed next to her, leafing through the mail.

"There's a letter from Papa!" Ermides scanned the few lines of her father's scratchy penmanship, paused for a moment, and then slowly folded the letter. She took a deep breath before shifting her gaze to Lilia. Ermides could not conceal the disappointment on her face.

Lilia grew concerned as she saw her sister's eyes glaze over. "What's wrong? What did Papa say?" Ermides fumbled as she tried to cram the paper back into the envelope. But Lilia yanked it out of her hands and mumbled the words aloud until her face grew pale.

"Your mother has taken ill with influenza. The doctor has it under control, but she needs bed rest for a few weeks. I'm sorry to have to be the bearer of news which neither of you will want to hear, but you must put Lilia on a train at once so she can resume her duties at home."

Lilia's heart sank. The morning had been filled with the warm flush of excited anticipation of new adventures in Rome. Now it felt cold and bitter, like day-old coffee waiting to be thrown in the garbage.

"Hardship always finds me! Why am I not allowed to be happy?" she beseeched her sister.

Ermides's heart also plummeted at the despair etched in her sister's face. She wrapped her arms around Lilia's sagging shoulders. "I know this is hard, but our family comes first, and Mama needs you. Perhaps in time, you will return to Rome. Unfortunately, while I know the Zamparellis adore you, they will surely replace your position—and soon. I'm sorry, Lilia."

"No!" A tear fell on to the letter, and then another, until Lilia lowered her head sobbing, the paper crumpled in her hands. "I don't want to go back!"

Ermides tried to wipe her sister's tears away, but Lilia refused her consolation. "No, it's not fair!"

"Lilia, most things in life are not fair."

Lilia tried to sleep through the night, but each time she closed her tired, swollen eyes, she heard her mother yelling out orders. "Take the clothes to the river and wash them; feed your brothers; the floors need scrubbing; go chop and fetch the wood; empty the bedpans!" Gone were the luxury bath, toilet, and bidet. There would be no more dinner parties to serve, no more Sunday excursions, no more magical evenings at the movie theatre. Once again, her life would not be her own. Once again, Lilia would feel invisible and trapped in the strict confines of her village, beneath her mother's oppressive thumb.

Letting go of all the wondrous things she had to leave behind and the experiences yet to be lived and tasted, to return to a place that felt so dull and distasteful in comparison, had finally broken Lilia's spirit.

The following morning, she bade her farewell to the Zamparellis and the house which had become her home. She took in the opulent foyer one last time, quietly kissing it goodbye. "Thank you for everything! I will never forget you and all the love and kindness you have shown me!" Her heart was beating so fast and hard, she could hear it. Lilia tried to contain the waves of emotion as they rumbled in her being, but her lips trembled, and her eyes overflowed with sadness.

"Oh, there, there, dear. It's four walls, Lilia, on one of many streets in Rome. Whatever new maid takes your place, she won't have your grace and your brilliant smile—a smile which lights up all our lives."

Lilia threw her arms around the Signora, unable to hold the tide of tears back. "A piece of my heart will always be here."

"Well, this is the beauty of a big heart now, isn't it? There is enough of it to go around." The Signora lovingly caressed Lilia's cheek and moved her hair behind her ears. "A part of your soul is imprinted on these walls now, my sweet girl—this is the gift you leave with us. You will not be forgotten."

Lilia ran her hand over the lion-head knocker one last time as Ermides pulled the door shut behind them.

⁂

It was evening at Termini Station. Between the melancholy of leaving and the anxiety of traveling alone, Lilia's stomach was in knots. "You'll be fine," Ermides assured her with a confident smile. "Sleep on the train, and Papa will be waiting for you in Latisana in the morning."

Lilia nodded despite her misgivings and doubt. "Ermides?"

"Yes, Lilia?"

"Thank you for everything—for letting me be a part of your life here. You've given me hope there is a place for me in the world . . . someday . . . somewhere." Lilia stared off into the distant night sky.

Ermides grabbed Lilia's hands and gently rubbed them. "Hold on to these dreams. Your fire burns bright, and I know, one day, your perseverance will see you through. God has a plan for us all—He won't forget you."

Lilia boarded the cramped train after it approached, and she waved goodbye to Ermides—the sister she had known so little before her arrival in Rome . . . the sister who had become her friend and confidant, and the key to Lilia's freedom, in this last year.

Lilia fought against the crowd of people, who pushed and shoved as they attempted to board the train, and she managed her way through the narrow aisles packed with grumpy passengers. She located her compartment; of the six seats, she settled into the open one by the window. She sat next to a robust woman who seemed to be in her forties. Their eyes met, and her kind smile made Lilia feel slightly less alone.

As the train moved, every beautiful moment she'd experienced in Rome came and went like a flame going out. Lilia felt utterly bereft of joy as her journey back to Mussons was one of the most unpleasant experiences of her life. The compartments, halls, and bathrooms were chaotic, crammed with people and piles of luggage. The air was heavy with cigarette smoke, forcing Lilia to cover her nose and mouth. With the passing hours, the lingering chatter of her fellow occupants ceased, apart from the inescapable snoring lingering through the night.

Time elapsed. Lilia had been battling the constant urge to relieve herself. She wanted to avoid the crowds, but she could not control her bladder any longer. She stumbled towards the bathroom, stepping over bags and sleeping bodies. On her way, she saw a man urinating out the window. She swallowed hard. *My God, I pray I don't have to do that.*

When Lilia arrived, she poked her head inside the door, calling out to anyone who would listen or care. "Excuse me?" her voice barely sounded. "I need to use the toilet." The train was horribly overcrowded with passengers splayed out wherever they could find space, including the bathroom floor. No one paid Lilia any attention. "Please, I need to use the toilet," she repeated in her feeble voice. To no avail, Lilia struggled to get back to her compartment. Once she reached it, she pressed the kind lady's arm.

"Signora, I have to pee badly, but no one will let me into the bathroom!"

The woman sensed Lilia's urgency and accompanied her back down the aisle. "Hey! This young girl needs to use the toilet! Give her some privacy!" she said in a sharp tone.

"Are you blind? Look out there!" one man commented, pointing to the jam-packed aisle. "Where do you want us to go? I'm not losing my place. Tell her to hang out the window like the rest of us." The passengers ignored Lilia and the woman and refused to move.

"I'm sorry, dear. If you can't hold it, you'll have to pee in the hallway between the cars. It's not ideal, but it's dark enough—no one will see you." Like the others, she was tired. The woman returned to her compartment, leaving Lilia to fend for herself.

The motion of the train had Lilia bumping into walls and stumbling over luggage. She held on as best she could so as not to relieve herself inappropriately, which might cause a stir among the other clearly agitated passengers. Her bladder hurt badly, shooting sharp pain into her lower back. The effort of holding it in caused sweat to bead on her lips and her brow to furrow.

Lilia quickly spotted a small clearing behind the last seat, in the far corner at the end of the car. Against all her pride, she crouched low into a nook where she couldn't be seen and emptied her bladder for what seemed an eternity, all the while praying the smell of her urine would not alert those nearby. Lilia wiped herself with the bottom of her dress and returned to her seat. She remained quiet for the duration of the trip. Her eyes stung from tears of humiliation. Her heart was filled with longing—for the now-distant Rome, as well as the ghost of her childhood, which taunted her with the cold realities awaiting in Mussons.

⁂

Upon arriving in Latisana, Lilia caught a glimpse of her father on the platform from her window seat and realized how much she had missed him. She hurried off the train, clutching her suitcase and pushing through the wave of people. Her father's bright smile lit her way like a beacon.

"Papa! Papa!"

Virginio reached out his arms, his bright eyes filled with unmistakable joy at the sight of his little girl, now grown so big. "Liliutti!"

Once in her father's arms, all Lilia's misgivings melted into tears. "I missed you, Papa!"

"We all missed you. Your brothers are excited to see you!"

"And Mama? Is she feeling better? Is she excited to see me, too?"

"Your mother needs rest, but she will be fine. Now, put your suitcase in the wagon and hop on—let's get you home!"

Sitting on the handlebars, Lilia watched a stretch of villages and fields of blossoming wheat and willow trees pass her by. Farmers trailed their cattle, and peasant women worked the rows of cornfields—a day in the life of a villager. To Lilia's eyes, nothing had changed in the year she was away, and yet she felt like a stranger. She was the one who had changed.

As they rode into Mussons and turned onto Via della Chiesa, La Bottega, her school, and Saint Osvaldo Church appeared smaller than she remembered—and the road more narrow, her home less inviting, the street with no color or contrast. It wasn't Rome.

At the sound of the bicycle bell, Giovanni, Riccardo, and Bruno let out a cheer and ran outside to greet their sister. "Lilia! The carnival is coming! The carnival is coming!"

She disregarded the strange greeting and hugged her three brothers. "Oh, look at you! Did you all miss me?"

"We did!"

"I missed you the most!" Bruno held on to Lilia a little longer than the others.

"The carnival, Lilia!"

Confused, she raised her gaze to her father and shrugged her shoulders. "What's this about a carnival? What is a carnival?"

"The boys have been talking about nothing else aside from this carnival for the past few weeks. From what we've heard, the gypsies are traveling village to village. They erect tents with games, live music, magicians, and men eating fire and swallowing swords." Virginio raised his eyebrows and gave Lilia an incredulous look. "I suspect they will arrive in a few weeks."

"Yes, Papa! It's true! And they have flying horses!" Giovanni insisted with an air of authority.

Virginio ruffled his hair and smiled at him. "Flying horses?"

"And swings flying high in the sky!" added Riccardo.

"Well, it will surely be a sight to see! I guess we'll find out soon enough." Virginio winked at his daughter. "Lilia, the carnival is coming—right in time to welcome you back home!" He pulled her into his arms, happy to have her back. "You can tell me all about Rome later. Right now, I'm sure your mother wants to see you."

Before entering the gate, Lilia looked around the village square, remembering how, at one time, she had believed experiencing faraway places like Rome was an impossible dream. Mussons now felt more like a scene from an old movie than a place where she belonged. As she stepped into her old house, it appeared smaller, darker, like it was closing in around her—the walls held sad memories she had hoped to forget. Lilia could almost feel herself shrink in size, back into the girl that once felt unheard and invisible, the girl that spent her days scrubbing floors, cooking, and tending to her brothers.

Lilia poked her head into her mother's room tentatively. "Mama? Are you awake? I'm home! Can I come in?"

"Yes, yes, come in." Maria pulled herself up against her pillow and managed to flash a modest smile. "You look older."

Lilia sat on the bed next to her mother and gave her a gentle kiss on the cheek. "How are you? Papa said you need bed rest."

"What are you wearing? Stand up, turn around, and let me look at you."

Lilia obeyed her mother's request. "Rome was wonderful, Mama, and Signora Zamparelli was good to me." Lilia spun around. "She gave me this beautiful dress and a few others." Lilia wanted so badly to share her experience with her mother, but something stopped her. An old familiar pit formed in her stomach as she noticed her mother's disapproving glance.

"Well, you worked for it. Nothing is free. Take it off. You're home now, and you'll get it dirty doing your chores."

Lilia cleared her throat and forced a tight smile on her lips. "The Signora wanted you to have this." She pulled a beautiful multicolored, floral, silk scarf out of her suitcase.

Maria raised an eyebrow. "When have you ever seen me wear anything with color?" she chided. "Keep it." She closed her eyes and sank back under the covers. "I'm tired now. I'm going to rest. It's good you're home."

This wasn't the homecoming Lilia had hoped to receive from her mother. Once again, she felt insignificant and small. All she could focus on now were Ermides's parting words—God would not forget her. Lilia knew all roads led home; she prayed it wouldn't always be this home.

⋅୭ଢ ୭ஓ⋅

It was a sweltering hot summer afternoon. The air was abuzz with awe, wonderment, and delight as the high-pitched squeals of children were heard throughout the streets and village square of Mussons. Their long-awaited dreams had all at once unveiled before them—the week-long carnival was underway.

Boys and girls of all ages grew increasingly excited at the massive rides as they inched forward in what seemed to be endless queues of people in the piazza and up and down Via della Chiesa. The grounds were full of wonders—from the Ferris wheel to the swing ride and carousel horses, to tents with various games and prizes, such as stuffed animals, toys, and trinkets, to the popcorn trolley and the candy-floss stall, whose awning dangled frilly, pink, polka-dotted fabric. Lilia marveled at how such a large mound of soft, cotton-like, spun sugar could quickly melt on her tongue.

Maria poked her head out the front gate and spied Bruno running wild, weaving circles on the street with a cone piled high with ice cream in one hand and candy floss in the other. She watched the scoops melt and dribble on to her son's hands. "Virginio, I give it two minutes." Sure enough, the scoops wobbled off and on to the ground. A squeal of panic erupted from Bruno's pouting lips, and tears followed.

"And there it goes." Virginio couldn't help but let out an amused chuckle.

Maria hollered out into the street, waving her arms in the air. "Bruno, slow down before you run into someone with your cloud of sticky sugar!" She gave her husband an irritated look before making her way back into the house. "One ride each. No more, so they'd better enjoy it. We didn't work all summer to throw our earnings away on a silly carnival."

"Maria, it happens once a year." Virginio knew better than to challenge his wife, so he turned his attention to the carnival. Like his children, he also enjoyed soaking up the festivities, the streets saturated with whimsical colors from dazzling tents, the crowds of joy-filled faces, and the sound of accordions, fiddles, and flutes dancing through the air. "When's the last time we went dancing? Why don't we go to the square tonight?"

"Dancing? *Me?*" Maria laughed sarcastically. "We didn't even dance at our wedding! It's a waste of time for foolish people. Do I look foolish?"

"No, you look beautiful."

Maria scoffed, turned her back on Virginio, and stormed inside.

Virginio granted Lilia and the boys two rides each. Unable to contain themselves, and with barely a thank-you to their father, the boys barreled off with their coins to the flying horses. From outside the gate of her home, Lilia gazed around in stupefied amazement at how her street had transformed. Her mind wandered as she lost herself in the colorful rows of wooden horses, watching them glide up and down as though they were galloping to the carousel music. *If I were a horse, wild and free, where would I go? Where would life take me?*

"Papa, I would like to go on there!" Lilia pointed to the swings, which she found most intriguing. She watched boys twist the chains and unravel them, spinning the girls in circles high in the sky.

"Keep your skirt down!" Maria yelled out from the kitchen window. Although she didn't speak her disapproving thoughts aloud, they swam through her mind as she went about her chores. *These carnivals are no place for a girl—no place for children. No doubt, all mine will be coming home with a stomach-ache from all the garbage they're eating. Damn gypsies!*

But Lilia was determined not to let her mother's constant stream of negativity tarnish her joy. Not today.

She gave her father a peck on the cheek, ran up the street, and grabbed an empty seat on the swing ride. Lilia patiently waited to be strapped in, ready for one of the boys to jump on to the swing behind her and twist the chains together. Nervousness and excitement bubbled in her stomach like a million butterflies as the engine revved. Lilia's swing rose higher and higher, and the momentum increased. Her screams pierced the air. She lifted her feet as the boy untangled the chains. Lilia's swing spun in circles at such a velocity, she could barely breathe between bursts of laughter. She was breathless with exhilaration. This was a day like no other.

The hours passed like minutes as dusk fell upon the village. Giovanni, Riccardo, and Bruno huddled in the window with full bellies and satisfied grins spread across their faces. They could still hear the four-piece band as it filtered into their bedroom. The chatter of adults drinking wine and partaking in the festivities continued under the moonlight—the night stretching longer than the day.

Once Maria was asleep, Lilia snuck outside, wanting to linger in the merriment a little longer. Lilia's life had reverted to its old routine of endless chores and responsibilities. She knew her mother would not permit her to attend the carnival during the coming week, so she was determined to soak up whatever pleasures she could.

To her surprise, neighborhood boys offered to buy Lilia a few more rounds on the swings, which she gladly accepted. Nearly an hour transpired, and Lilia worried she might be pressing her luck with her mother. As she passed the piazza, people of all ages were dancing on the wooden platform. Lilia stood for a moment behind the railing with longing eyes. She yearned to be in someone's arms, to be twirled and dipped. Lilia followed the swiftly moving dresses as they swooshed in circles. She observed the men's hands on the girls' waists and the way couples glided across the floor, synchronizing their movements and dancing like one body.

I wish I knew how to dance. No one loves a girl who can't dance.

She was instantly transported back to the cinema in Rome when Rhett Butler bid $150 in gold at an auction in exchange for a dance with Scarlett O'Hara.

"Signorina?" an older boy called out to Lilia, but she was too entranced in her fantasy to hear him. The tall, simple farmer tapped her shoulder. Lilia recognized him—he was from Poiana, the neighboring village.

"Will you dance with me? I'll buy you a ticket!"

Surprise overcame Lilia, as it was the first time a boy had ever approached her! Despite her deep desire to be whisked on to the dance floor, she felt awkward and shy.

"Oh, how kind of you, but no thank you. It's late, and I must be getting home."

The boy's face fell with the force of her rejection, but he simply nodded and went on his way.

Lilia quickly ran home, her previous wishes thwarted by her

embarrassment. As Lilia crept down the hallway towards her bedroom, Maria's voice pierced the air.

"You should be ashamed of yourself! A young girl, going to the piazza alone at night. What will people think?"

Lilia's gait quickened. She had learned it was best to ignore her mother if she wanted to diffuse any tension. Tomorrow, all would be forgotten.

⚬⚬⚬

No sooner did the carnival tour end than Maria was back on her feet. Lilia was once again employed as a maid and server, but this time at the bar, catty-corner to her house. Francesca ran La Bottega with her older brother, Ermando. Francesca was in her mid-twenties, nearly ten years older than Lilia. Although the age difference created a cordial distance at first, the two girls quickly became friends.

Francesca lived on the second floor above the bar. She shared the apartment with her brother when he wasn't busy chasing women or was too drunk to find his way home. On occasion, when Francesca felt lonely, she asked Maria to let Lilia sleep over to keep her company. As the families were long-time friends and her daughter was being of service to the bar and making money, Maria approved.

One particular night, Lilia slept over, and was stirred awake at the break of dawn by Francesca, who was unable to sleep.

"Lilia, wake up! Come to the attic with me. I want to show you something!"

Bleary-eyed, Lilia followed Francesca with her lantern down the creaky, narrow hall and up the rickety ladder. Francesca drew the lace curtains aside and pulled back the shutters, letting the early morning light pour across the floor, lighting up every corner of the ample open space. The room was empty and spotless, apart from stacked boxes of supplies and a small table by the window. Several mulberry branches hung from the ceiling.

"Come see what I've been doing. You can help me one day if you like—it would be fun!"

As they neared the table, Lilia peered into a wooden box made up of smaller compartments. Inside each one lay an oval-shaped mound about a half-inch in length.

"What are these? They look like cocoons."

"Yes! They are similar to caterpillar cocoons, but these are from silkworms. I buy the worms and feed them thinly cut strands of mulberry leaves for about a month, until they are old enough to produce silk. They spit the silk threads, which fold into these little mounds. I sell them for a good price, and then they're spun into yarn."

Lilia was impressed by Francesca's months of hard work. "If women knew what went into making their silk! What happens once the cocoons hatch?"

Francesca blurted out in a matter-of-fact way, "The moths mate, reproduce, and die within days."

"Well, that doesn't seem fair, but I guess butterflies don't live long, either."

"It's been a part of their life cycle for millions of years. The females produce a strong-smelling chemical called pheromones, which attract males—they sense the scent with their antennae, which tells them the females are ready to mate. It's funny to watch—the males get so excited. They flutter their wings frantically, which sometimes causes them to fall off!"

"I guess the female lays her eggs and raises them alone? It doesn't seem much different from humans—the woman does *everything*."

Lilia wrinkled her nose in disdain. She had concluded long ago that being born female was the short end of the stick.

"Well, in a way, yes." Francesca giggled at the comparison. "The female lays hundreds of eggs the size of pinheads. Once they hatch, the silkworms feed on the leaves, and the circle of life continues." Francesca paused to gauge Lilia's comprehension.

"Maybe I need pheromones so I can attract a boy!" Lilia excitedly fluttered her arms like a moth as she rolled her eyes, causing Francesca to burst out in laughter.

"In due time, my dear, in due time."

ာလ ၉ာ

July 1950

"Oh, Jesus!" Lilia had been suffering through stomach cramps for days, but nothing compared to the shocking sight before her. She was making the beds when she felt a stream of urine soak her under garments and trickle down her legs. "What is happening?"

Lilia reached inside her panties. They felt warm and wet. When she removed her hand, scarlet blood was dripping between her fingers. Lilia's face turned pale as she stumbled backward, horrified.

I'm fifteen years old and I'm dying!

She quickly washed up in the basin by her bed, mopped the drops on the floor, replaced her undergarments, and placed a rolled-up towel between her legs. Panic-stricken. Lilia waddled down the stairs.

"Mama! Something's wrong!" Lilia threw the kitchen door open to find her mother gathered with a few of her lady friends drinking their morning coffee.

"What happened?" Maria's concern grew as Lilia's face flushed red as a beetroot.

"I'm bleeding, Mama! There's blood everywhere!"

Maria quickly scanned her daughter and saw no signs of a cut or wound. "Bleeding? Where?"

"Down *here*!" Lilia pointed between her legs and uncurled her fingers to reveal the scrunched-up bloody undergarments in her hand.

The women burst into laughter when one of them yelled out, "It's your *menstruation*, dear. You got your menstruation!" The woman shot a baffled look at Maria. "You didn't *tell* her?"

"I got my *what*?" Still holding her cramped belly, Lilia's eyes darted around the room—she was confused and becoming increasingly annoyed at the smug looks on the women's faces, as well as the word she didn't understand.

Maria threw her hand up nonchalantly, delivering a brief explanation through her friends' giggles. "Your menstruation means you'll be bleeding every month like the rest of us. It means you're an adult now, Lilia, and your body is preparing your womb for a baby for when you become pregnant one day." Her face turned serious. "And don't even *think* about getting pregnant before you're married, young lady, do you hear me? That's all we need! Now go wash those soiled undergarments at the pump before anyone sees them."

Lilia stood there soaking in the cruel laughter. She felt shamed and mocked, not solely by her mother, but also by the neighbors. She wanted to burst into tears.

Why didn't Mama tell me? Prepare me? When will this happen again? How will I know? I don't want to bleed every month!

Lilia immediately felt a rush of panic, knowing her privacy was at stake. "Please, Mama, don't tell Papa!" Lilia peeled out into the street to wash and wring out the bloody garments before the stain set in. The chuckling echoed out the window, while Lilia died a slow and agonizing death inside.

Hours later, she passed her father on the stairs. He shot her a wink and a broad smile. "I heard you became a *woman* today!"

Lilia was mortified and nearly froze on the spot. Despite his congratulatory grin, her father's expression seemed to have changed. *I'm no longer his little girl, but a woman now . . . who bleeds!* Lilia wanted the earth to open up and swallow her whole. Sweltering embarrassment and anger burst through her pores as her eyes welled with tears once again.

Her mother's act of betrayal seared her brain. *How could she! What if the whole village knows? I hate my life!*

Lilia ran to the outhouse, the one place where her mournful cries wouldn't be heard.

The following night, after she completed her chores at home, Lilia helped Francesca tidy up the bar. She was collecting the empty glasses, putting clean ashtrays on the tables, washing dishes, and sweeping the floor.

"Francesca . . . something happened yesterday," Lilia hesitated as she spoke and ducked her head in embarrassment, unsure as to how much she wanted to confide in her friend.

"Something not good, I take it?"

It was difficult for Lilia to come to terms with the recent changes in her body, but even saying the word made her feel dirty, "I got my men—I got my—"

"You got your what?"

Lilia stopped sweeping. "I started *bleeding*, all right? I became a *woman*!" Lilia lifted her watery eyes to Francesca, waiting for her to respond or laugh.

Francesca put her wet rag on the bar and removed the broom

from Lilia's hands to hug her. "And here I thought it was *bad* news!" She cupped Lilia's sad face in her hands. "This is a natural part of life—growing up and becoming a woman. It's an important rite of passage, one you should never feel ashamed of but embrace with excitement! You'll have beautiful babies one day, Lilia, and you'll make a most excellent mother!"

"Does this mean I have pheromones now, and I'll attract a man?"

Francesca let out a gentle laugh and placed her arm around Lilia's shoulder.

"Well, in a way, yes! But remember this, my dear. Women are the strongest and bravest creatures of humanity and deserve to be honored and treated with respect. When it comes to men and relationships, men tend to run around, not knowing how to act like gentlemen. They can take a while to grow up and usually don't know a good thing until it smacks them in the face. Whomever your pheromones *do* attract one day, hold out for a good man—you're too precious for anything less."

To Lilia, this was a unique moment and a rite of passage—to have a woman, and one she admired profoundly, share this special message with her, a message of self-respect and self-love, which Lilia knew she would never receive from her mother.

"You know, since Arturo died, I haven't connected like this with anyone . . . until I met you. Even my sisters and I don't *talk*. I'm forever their *little* sister, whereas I feel you as my friend."

Francesca's glowing heart showed on her face, and a hint of sorrow haunted her eyes as she thought of Lilia's beloved brother. "All right, my womanly friend! I'm going to hide out in the backroom for a while, counting the day's earnings. If you could make the beds and sweep upstairs, you'd be a lifesaver!"

Lilia spent the next hour fulfilling Francesca's request. The final sweeping of the landing remained before she could close out her night and go home. While Lilia shuffled her broom, her thoughts turned towards Francesca's words of encouragement. *Women are the strongest and bravest creatures of humanity.* She cherished their friendship; having a sisterly figure in her life gave Lilia a haven where she could be herself.

Lilia glanced at her reflection in a mirror on the wall, smoothing her hands over her dress and keenly observing the newly formed curves on her adolescent body. Perhaps she could embrace her womanhood with pride and not see it as a bane, a source of powerlessness and shame. Lilia no longer felt trapped inside her cocoon. She could almost feel her wings emerge and unfurl.

The sudden sound of footsteps pounded at the bottom of the stairs.

"Francesca? Is that you?" called Lilia. No one replied. The noise stopped, silencing Lilia's breath. "Who's there?" she called again.

The boards creaked, step by step. Ermando appeared out of the shadows, at the top of the landing and hovered. His eyes blinked open and shut in the dim light. He was clearly drunk.

"Ermando, you frightened me! Why didn't you say anything?"

His vacant stare and penetrating eyes sent chills down Lilia's spine. She felt naked and uncomfortable in his presence. Lilia had never liked Ermando, but she had never feared him, either . . . until now. She instinctively gripped the broom, sensing she was no longer safe, as a wicked smile curled on his lips. Ermando lunged forward, yanking the broom out of Lilia's hands, and pushed her to the floor. Her heart accelerated as she lay pinned under his weight. She felt his creeping hands slide past her hips and up her thighs. Incensed and frantic, Lilia kicked furiously.

"What are you doing? Get off me!"

He slammed his hand over her mouth and leaned into her face. Lilia could feel the coarse stubble on his cheek and smell the whiskey and cigarettes on his breath.

"You're going to keep quiet and keep your mouth shut!" His drunken eyes gleamed with vile anticipation.

Lilia tried to scream, but her voice was muffled under his hand. She jammed her nails into his face until he yelped with pain. Ermando wiped the blood off his cheek and raised his hand to strike her.

"You bitch!"

"Stop! Stop!" Lilia covered her head and screamed with her whole body.

"Get off her, you monster! Get your filthy hands off her!" Lilia focused her eyes to see Francesca at the top of the stairs, yelling and hitting her brother repeatedly with the broom handle until she herself weakened, gasping for air. "You drunk bastard! What do you think you're doing? She's just a girl!"

Lilia inched to the corner of the hall and wrapped her trembling arms around her dress, pulling it tight down to her ankles. She watched in horror as Francesca pummeled Ermando with a rage Lilia had never seen before. "You're a forty-five-year-old man, you disgusting, miserable pig!"

Ermando shielded himself, cowering under his sister's wrath until she withdrew to catch her breath. He made a quick break and escaped, stumbling down the stairs, muttering profanities while Francesca shook her broom at him. "You can go to hell for all I care, you piece of shit! Get out of my sight! You're a disgrace to our family!"

She ran over to Lilia, her face twisted with panic. "Lilia, are you hurt? Tell me, did he hurt you?"

Lilia nodded silently. Tears welled in her eyes. "Is it my fault? Did I do something wrong? Is it because of my menstruation?"

A tiny sob rose to Francesca's lips. She embraced Lilia with all her might. "Oh, no, no, it's not your fault. My idiot brother is a monster! Thank God he didn't hurt you!"

"Francesca, please don't tell anyone! I don't want to cause you or your bar embarrassment. I don't want people to know. I don't want them to think I'm a naughty girl or that I'm lying. If I tell my mother, she'll kill him!"

Francesca lovingly stroked Lilia's hair and face. "I promise, Lilia! And I also promise you will never be here alone again! If my brother so much as looks at you, I'll kill him myself!"

In the evening before bed, Lilia soaked her hands in the washbasin, scrubbing Ermando's blood from under her fingernails and softening the slivers in her skin which had formed from clawing the wooden floor when she had been trying to escape. Flashbacks of the scene—his sinister words, his vile breath, and the weight of his body—haunted her.

What if Francesca hadn't heard my screams? What would have happened to me? What if I got pregnant? What would have become of me?

In trying to numb the painful memory, Lilia repeatedly scrubbed her fingers until they were nearly raw.

❧

The summer came and went, and an early fall crept like a wild vine stretching across Mussons. Between chores and working at the bar, Lilia had not spent much time socializing, and Maria continued to deny her daughter the pleasures of life.

One Saturday afternoon, from the kitchen window, Lilia saw Solidea, Mariuccia, and Lidia, approaching the front gate on their bicycles. For a moment, she envied their joyful and carefree lives, but she was still thrilled to see them. Lilia ran outside to greet her friends.

"Lilia!"

"Hi, Solidea!"

"The three of us are going to Morsano to see a movie. We're so excited there's finally a theatre nearby!"

"Please come with us?"

"We miss you!"

"I doubt I can go but let me ask my mother." Despite knowing the answer already, Lilia trailed off to the garden to see Maria. On the way, she passed her father, heading towards the house with a bundle of wood he carried from the barn. Lilia noticed he was suffering from a bout of his asthma. "Papa? You don't sound good."

"It's the ragweed. Every August and September, I go through this." Virginio chuckled, shaking his head. "It makes you wonder why anyone has asthma when there is so much air to breathe!"

"I'll make you some tea later, Papa." Lilia took a deep breath and continued on her way. She still had the teeniest flicker of hope. Perhaps this time, her mother would say yes.

"Good afternoon, young ladies! You look extra lovely today," Virginio's words were muffled as he battled a coughing fit. "What's the occasion?"

"No occasion, Signore Meneguzzi," Mariuccia smiled a dreamy smile. "We're going to Morsano to see *Romeo and Juliet*! They have a theatre there now!"

"Yes! It's playing until tomorrow!" Lidia wiggled with excitement, "We're waiting to see if Lilia can come join us."

"Well, you girls enjoy yourselves. I need to bring this firewood inside, and then I'm afraid I need to lie down. I'm wheezing like an old man!"

Lilia approached the gate wearing a long face. Solidea's shoulders drooped and she sighed, knowing what was coming.

"What did she say?"

"What she *always* says—no!" Lilia kicked the gate, casting her forlorn eyes upon her friends. "I'm sorry. Maybe next time."

"Next time, for sure!" Solidea gave her an optimistic look.

The realization of another joyless and busy summer gone by depressed Lilia as she watched the girls ride away, giggling and chanting verses from Shakespeare—their hands pantomiming in the air. *Wherefore art thou, Romeo? My love is deep—the more I give to thee, the more I have.*

To Lilia, their laughter was a double-edged sword.

Virginio had tucked himself inside the doorway and overheard the conversation. He felt his heart collapse watching his daughter melt into her sadness.

"Liliutti, come here."

Lilia lifted her glum face to her father's.

"Tomorrow, your mother is going to stay overnight with the signora who has breast cancer—she's not doing well. Mama needs to administer her shots, change her dressing, and tend to her bedside. How about we coax Cornelia to watch the boys for a few hours, and you and I will go see the movie? And not a word to your mother," Virginio winked conspiratorially.

"Seriously? You mean it?" Lilia's eyes filled with astonishment at her father's unexpected gesture of kindness.

"I keep hearing about these theaters. And we can't let *Romeo and Juliet* slip by! Depending on when your mother leaves, and by the time we get to Morsano, we might end up being a little late, but—"

"I don't care! Yes! Yes!" Lilia's smile practically lit up the sky. She had not been this happy since her time in Rome.

The following day, Virginio and Lilia patiently waited for Maria's departure and their chance at freedom.

"If you need me, you know where I am. Make sure your brothers stay out of trouble! And Lilia, make sure your father gets his borage tea before he goes to bed. You hear me, Virginio?" Maria hollered across the courtyard. "Drink your tea tonight!"

Virginio nodded with a dutiful wave and smile. He continued tidying up the barn, all the while sneaking a thumb's up to Lilia when Maria's back was turned.

"Yes, Mama." Lilia caught her father's signal from the barn and let a giggle escape.

"What are you laughing at?" Maria sternly asked.

"Nothing, Mama." Lilia stretched her mouth into a serious expression, the corners of her lips fighting a smile. "I hope the signora feels better. It's good you're there to help her. See you tomorrow!"

Once Maria was out of sight, both Lilia and her father leaned far out the gate to confirm the stage was set for their escape.

Virginio and Lilia were giddy with excitement to share this experience as father and daughter. At heart, Virginio was child-like, but this day, he felt like a teenager, sneaking away on a new and forbidden adventure.

"Papa, I know you and Mama might think I'm still too young to fall in love, but I hope a love story like *Romeo and Juliet* finds me, without the tragic ending, of course!"

"For as long as I can remember, you've been dreaming of your knight in shining armor," Virginio smiled and kissed his daughter, "Perhaps today is the beginning of something magical manifesting right around the corner. So, are we ready?"

"Yes!"

"All right, you alert Cornelia, I'll grab the bicycle, and we're off!"

Virginio cheerfully whistled as he guided his bicycle through the shadows down the dirt road leading towards Morsano. He watched Lilia as she rode on the handlebars, eagerness shining in her eyes and the evening sun bestowing its last glow of light upon her dark hair. Virginio felt more contented than he had in weeks. He had been able to grant his daughter a moment she would never forget. He knew Maria would not approve, but what harm was there in seeing his girl happy?

"Liliutti, I'm trying to imagine what seeing a movie will be like, even though you and your sisters tried to explain it to me. I'm excited to share this with you."

Lilia was elated to be able to share this moment with her father, knowing he was about to experience something new. They both deserved this taste of freedom. If only her mother were more like him!

"Papa, I've read *Romeo and Juliet* many times, but to see it in a movie?" Careful not to lose her balance, Lilia stretched her arms out and threw her head back to catch the warm breeze. "It seems she hangs upon the cheek of night, as a rich jewel in an Ethiop's ear . . . Oh, Romeo!" Lilia turned to her father and giggled. "We're going to the movies! If Mama only knew!"

They both let out a victory howl as Virginio pedaled faster, peeling around the bend.

"We're almost there, sweet Juliet!"

Virginio followed his daughter's lead and crept into the dark theatre, careful to not draw attention to their late arrival. Once they were in their seats, Virginio's eyes slowly adjusted to the dark. Amazement seized him as he marveled at the rows of people, couples arm in arm, and the image projected on to the giant white screen—actors who were moving and speaking!

"So, this is the movies. Will you look at that!" Virginio whispered as a raspy wheeze rose from his throat. He bumped Lilia with his shoulder, giving her a giant grin. Despite the crackling sound escaping his lungs, Virginio was right where he wanted to be.

"Isn't this wonderful, Papa?" Lilia's eyes were aglow with delight. Her heart filled with love and gratitude as she squeezed her father's hand. She couldn't wait to share her night at the movies with Solidea and the girls.

Hours later, Virginio and Lilia arrived back to Mussons, writhing with laughter, proud of their well-planned escape from Maria's typical inescapable eagle eye. Nearing their home, Virginio dismounted his bicycle and helped Lilia off the bars.

"This was a special night."

"Oh, Papa, it truly was!"

"If not for my asthma, I would have bought us two more tickets to see the beginning of the movie! I'm sorry we missed it."

Lilia leaned into her father, resting her head on his chest. She looked up at him, admiring the stars. "Papa? Do you believe in fate and destiny? Do all star-crossed lovers eventually meet and fall in love?"

"Yes, and then they die!" Virginio laughed at his jest, thinking back on Romeo and Juliet's tragic fate. "There are many different types of love, Lilia: romantic love, passionate love, marriage, and even forbidden and unrequited love. When you eventually meet your true love, pray for unconditional love—it may be a noble idea, but it's the only kind worth having." Virginio laid his cheek against her hair. "To answer your question, yes, I believe in fate, and although our destiny may not always turn out as we hoped, I feel everything happens for a reason."

"Well, I'm going to meet my Romeo one day, Papa. It won't be star-crossed, forbidden, or unrequited. It will be true love—*forever love!*"

Virginio rang his bicycle bell repeatedly as they entered the gate, his voice bellowing into the air in celebration of Lilia's destiny. "Here's to Lilia's forever love!"

The courtyard radiated with their merriment, which up until this moment had been dead silent.

Giovanni, Riccardo and Bruno leaned out their bedroom window, frantically waving their arms. "Shhhhh! Mama's home!" Giovanni whispered loudly and pointed towards the kitchen, trying to warn Lilia and his father.

Virginio and Lilia automatically went quiet. All the joy, which had been present, dissipated.

"We're doomed," Lilia sighed.

Virginio gave his daughter an apologetic look, knowing they were about to be found out. "I'm so sorry. I had no idea she would be home tonight."

"Papa! Listen to me—don't say a word! The more you ignore her, the sooner she'll stop! Be smart and don't even try to argue with her!"

Virginio took heed of his wise daughter's words as they slunk inside the house. Although they were prepared for the verbal beating, Maria's anger was still overwhelming after such a blissful day.

"Shame on you both!" Maria barked from behind the open crack of the kitchen door. "What kind of father goes out with his daughter and brings her home late at night? Do you think this looks good? What will the neighbors say? You'd better think hard before you try it again, let alone lie to me!"

Virginio kept his promise to ignore Maria and accompanied Lilia to her room at the end of the hall. He sat next to her on the bed. "Of all the times for your mother to come home early!"

"Papa, it's like she knows everything—always!" Lilia could feel her father's regret for being dishonest before seeing it in his eyes, and it broke her heart. "Tell me something, why did you marry Mama when she's so mean?"

"I married her because I love her."

"But is love enough?"

"Lilia, love is a funny thing. You don't always get what you want, and sometimes you don't know what you want. And sometimes, when you think you've got it right, people change—life changes people. Through it all, I always knew I wanted your mother." Virginio paused in reflection. Looking at his daughter, he decided she was mature enough to understand. "Lilia, what you don't know is . . . your mother didn't want me."

"What? What do you mean?" Lilia had always seen her parents as stark contrasts to each other. Her father was gentle and kind, while her mother was hardened and bitter. And yet, throughout the war, throughout those agonizing months her father was away fighting for his life, Lilia witnessed Maria's suffering in silence as she prayed for his return. She could feel her mother's anguished and broken heart, which is why Lilia knew her mother loved her father.

"She was in love with another man before me—madly in love— but as our families grew up together, they expected your mother and I marry. Her parents felt I was better suited for her, a better father and provider. While your mother and I were dating, we had relations and found ourselves with a big surprise—she became pregnant with Arturo, and the rest is history."

"Oh, I see." Lilia was surprised to hear her parents had conceived her brother out of wedlock, especially given that Maria had always been so religious . . . and so chained to public opinion. "Does she know you knew about this other man?"

"No, I don't think so, but it never mattered. I was grateful your mother chose me in the end, maybe not for the reasons I wanted . . . but she chose me. Your mama loves me the best way she knows how—the best way she can. And I have enough love for both of us."

"Maybe this is why Mama doesn't want her daughters to live happily ever after. Mama forbade Dina to be with the man she loved, Ermides had no choice but to give up her true love, and now it's up to me to fight for mine."

Virginio's eyes watered at his daughter's resoluteness.

"Follow your heart, Liliutti. I did, and I never regretted one moment. I pray when it's your time, the good Lord gives you your happily ever after."

17 | SWEET SEVENTEEN

March 1951

১৯৯ It was early spring, and the villagers were preparing for the annual Festa di San Giuseppe—the Feast of Saint Joseph. This street festival was in honor of the Virgin Mary's husband, the earthly father figure of Jesus, and the family's patron saint. On this occasion, villagers also celebrated Father's Day. In years past, such celebrations were dampened by the tragedies of war and the Nazi occupation, making each new one a grander, and more joyous event. A week in advance, the women of Mussons prepared home-baked, braided bread, a symbol of good luck, as well as cakes and pastries like *zeppole*, deep-fried dough balls sprinkled with sugar. In preparation for the ritual of the food table, meatless dishes such as fava beans, a symbol of health, and shrimp, calamari, and sardines were offered in respect for the month of Lent. The villagers' offerings in devotion to their saint provided a bounty for all.

Days before the celebration, Lilia's girlfriends geared up for the event by purchasing new clothes to flaunt their youthful curves and impress the boys while parading the piazza. Sixteen-year-old Lilia lay awake for nights, envisioning herself walking through a ballroom where everyone but her dressed in elaborate gowns and tailored suits, like a scene from the Cinderella story.

"Once again, I'll blend into the crowd in my old, hand-me-down smock, invisible as always. How will I ever meet anyone special if no one notices me?" she pondered aloud.

Sunday morning came all too early. Partly dreading having to attend the celebration without a new outfit, Lilia sprang out of bed, threw open her armoire, and moaned. There hung the few dresses kindly given to her by Signora Zamparelli, but they no longer fitted her developing figure. Lilia heaved a sigh. "I have nothing to wear!" She swayed her curvaceous hips in the inside mirror of the door and admired her growing bustline. Still, the hint of nipples showing through her nightgown made her feel self-conscious and exposed.

Everyone is wearing a bra but me! I'm the only 16-year-old without one—this is so embarrassing!

Lilia quickly threw on an old spaghetti-strap blouse and skirt, marshaled her confidence, and marched to the kitchen. She was determined to do something she had never done before: ask her mother for help, even as she prepared for rejection.

The harsh early morning light cast dark shadows across the room, deepening the lines around Maria's eyes, making her look sullen and tired. Maria was busily rolling long strands of bread dough on the table. She looked older with the fine dusting of flour on her already grayed hair. Braless, her breasts hung low under her usual button-down black dress, gray apron, and black knee-length hose. She was the picture of the consummate housekeeper, wife, and mother of Mussons.

This will be me one day. Lilia closed her eyes momentarily at the thought. *My life—my miserable life.* The reality of being a peasant girl in a poor family made Lilia hesitant to make her request. She stood watching by the door in silence as her mother entwined the strands to make a braided loaf.

Mama never cared about her appearance—why would she care about mine?

"What's wrong with you?" Maria asked, noticing her daughter's tense, fidgeting hands and the way she stood quietly at the door.

"Nothing's wrong."

"What is it?"

Lilia paused and closed her eyes before pouring her heart out in one fell swoop. "Mama, all my friends are wearing a new outfit for the festival tomorrow, and the clothes from Rome don't fit me anymore. Is there any way you and Papa can afford to buy me one dress?" Lilia's eyes rested on her ugly skirt. "All I have is this old elastic-waist skirt, and—"

"And what?" The note in Maria's voice had a hint of a threat, but Lilia didn't care. Not this time.

"Mama, I want a brassiere!" Lilia crossed her arms across her breasts, showing her discomfort. "You can see everything!"

"So, you need to be like everybody else?" Maria raised an eyebrow.

"Well, yes . . . I mean, no . . . I mean, I want to be me, but I want to feel pretty and don't want anyone making fun of me."

Maria huffed in disdain. "I've never worn a brassiere, and no one's ever said anything to me! You don't need one. As for a dress, I wish your father and I could afford one, but we don't have the money. I'm sorry, Lilia. You'll have to make do with what you have. If your friends are your true friends, they won't care what you wear." Maria could feel the sting of her daughter's disappointment but turned her back to focus on her bread-making. "Lilia, run out to the store and get me some milk."

"Yes, Mama."

Resigned to her defeat, Lilia plodded to the dairy. In the glow of the morning sun, as tears rolled down her cheeks, she prayed for resolution.

Will I ever be happy again? Feel free again? I wish I were back in Rome. I don't belong here any more.

With her milk can filled, Lilia stepped out into the street and spotted Padre Munnini walking from his home towards the church. Lilia gasped, and panic bubbled inside her. She backed inside and hid behind the door, out of his sight.

I can't let Padre catch me with bare shoulders! What would he say? What would he do?

Lilia waited for what she thought was ample time for Padre to pass and be far enough away. Confident she was safe, Lilia exited the dairy and turned the corner towards home when she came face to face with the priest; from the look on his face, it was clear he had been waiting for her. Lilia's eyes widened in shock, and her hands trembled, nearly causing her to lose grip on the metal handle as the can of milk rattled side to side.

"Padre!" She tasted a sudden swish of sour saliva in her mouth and a volcanic rush to her head. "Good morning, Padre."

Without hesitation, Padre Munnini slapped Lilia with such a force that she fell backward, the milk threatening to spill over the edge as it sloshed in waves inside the can. Her face immediately turned red, and a nervous buzz in her stomach made her feel nauseous.

"Why are your shoulders not covered?" His eyes twitched from the wrath which consumed him. "Do you have no shame?"

Lilia raised her hand to ease the sharp sting as the burning sensation traveled across her face.

"I—I'm sorry, Padre. I ran out quickly to get milk for my mama."

The priest frowned as he appraised her attire. He was disgusted as he stared in disdain at her spaghetti-strap blouse, which revealed the swell of her firm and braless breasts. Embarrassed by his disapproving stare, Lilia quickly crossed her arms over her chest while still clenching the handle of the milk can with her hand, careful not to spill its contents.

Padre pointed his index finger threateningly at Lilia as he looked sharply into her eyes.

"If your mother can't afford to dress you, tell her I will buy her the fabric! Never let me see you like this again, or you'll be forced to face the congregation at mass and publicly apologize to them for shaming the village with your disrespectful behavior."

For a moment, Lilia fantasized about lashing out in protest and tossing her can of milk in his face, but she pressed her lips tightly together to hold back the tide of rage and humiliation. She stood immobilized until he was halfway to the church. Then she heaved a sigh of relief and quickly peered around to make sure nobody had witnessed her disgrace. Lilia quickly ran back home, slammed the door, and leaned against it, desperate to catch her breath.

"What's wrong?" Maria grabbed the milk can from her daughter's hands and noticed her eyes were large and watery. "What happened to you? Your face is red."

"Padre caught me outside the dairy. He slapped me, Mama! He was angry I didn't have my shoulders covered—and he kept staring at my breasts!" Lilia lost the battle to hold back her angry and frustrated tears, which poured messily down her face and chest.

"He *slapped* you?" A familiar expression of outrage and pride came over Maria's face, causing Lilia to cease her tears. "I'll be back in an hour. Clean up the kitchen."

"Where are you going?" Lilia watched her mother storm out the gate in the direction of the church. "Mama?" But Maria offered no response.

A torrent of angry thoughts assailed Maria as she walked with determined steps to the church. *Miserable man! How dare he touch my daughter! It's enough he controls the village with his preposterous rules and demands. This time, he crossed a line.*

Maria sat waiting impatiently on a bench outside the church, weaving her fingers together restlessly until mass ended. Forty-five minutes passed, and a seed of fire had grown inside Maria's belly.

The doors of the church finally swung open, and Maria stood tall on her feet, her fists firmly on her hips. Parishioners observed Maria's sweaty face and dark mood as they passed. A curious crowd lingered.

"Look out! Maria's angry again!"

"Yes, and she's about to blow her lid. We should get out of her way!"

"No, let's stay and see what happens!"

Maria ignored greetings and waited silently for Padre to exit. Padre emerged with the exodus of church-goers. He wore a sardonic grin, but one look at Maria's flame-roaring eyes wiped it off. However, his wariness quickly gave way to his customary arrogance.

"Maria, should you not have been in mass repenting for your daughter's behavior?" he chided.

"What kind of man, a *priest* no less, slaps a young girl and lays his eyes on her breasts?" Maria screeched her words with all the fiery breath in her lungs.

People stopped to watch and whisper to one another. *Did he slap Lilia? Why would he look at her breasts when he's a priest? I bet she wasn't wearing a brassiere! You know how Maria is about this sort of thing!*

Maria heard the hush of gossip, but all she saw was red. "Don't you ever, *ever* touch my daughter again, or you will have to answer to *me*! I will not cower at your feet, so you'd best think twice next time you touch my child, *any* child! I won't think twice as my hand slaps *your* face . . . *Padre*!" Maria spat out her words, stunning the crowd around her. She quietly turned and left, her hands clenched by her sides, the flames still surging through her veins.

Moments later, Maria arrived home and stalked into the house, slamming the door behind her.

"Mama, what happened?"

"Here." Maria handed Lilia a small bag.

"What is it?"

"Well, open it, and you'll find out." The bag crinkled between Lilia's fingers as she looked inside. Curious and confused by this mysterious offering from her mother, she gently parted the thin rose-colored tissue paper to expose a few yards of delicate white cotton cloth imprinted with a floral pattern of pale pink and purple.

"It's beautiful, Mama, but I don't understand. What is this for?" Lilia's heart raced. Her mother had given her a gift!

"Eduardo at the fabric store told me I could pay him when we have the money. There's enough cloth there to make you two brassieres. And make sure you thank him! He's kindly agreed to do this for you."

A flush of crimson spread over Lilia's face. She glowed with happiness and surprise—she felt like a giddy child.

"Oh my God, Mama!" Lilia could not hold back the urge to throw her arms around her mother. Caught off guard, Maria gave her daughter an awkward pat on the back.

"All right, that's enough now." Maria shrugged out of the embrace. "I have no experience making brassieres, never having worn one myself." She shook her head, still uncomprehending of these expensive feminine contraptions. At the same time, she was assured Padre would now keep his comments to himself, and village gossip would cease. "Go on, take this to Speme. She's waiting for you. I'm sure she will do a fine job."

"Thank you, Mama! Thank you!" No sooner had Lilia expressed her gratitude than she tore off to her cousin's house a few doors up the street. Speme had already spread out the pattern on her sewing table, ready to cut the fabric. Lilia arrived at the door, beaming with excitement.

"Come in, come in. Your mother explained you want this done for the festival tomorrow. We'd best get busy!"

Speme had spent one torturous year imprisoned in Auschwitz and Flossenbürg. She returned home to Mussons at the age of nineteen to live with her mother, Ada, and Ferruccio. Her father, Natale, and fifteen-year-old brother, Gino, had both perished in separate camps. Faint traces of the innocent woman Speme used to be still lingered in the smile that greeted Lilia. Her sullen eyes spoke of a wounded soul still traumatized by the horrors of war yet longing for love and connection. Lilia had never asked her cousin about what transpired in Germany, but it pained her to see Speme so withdrawn from the world. Once playful and joy-filled, Speme had spent the last six years hiding behind her sewing machine, immersed in the safety of her embroidery. She rarely left home, preferring her solitude to Mussons's crowds and occasional festivities. Her voice and presence were buried in the trauma of her past—a past of insurmountable suffering Lilia knew she could never imagine.

"My dear, you're not a girl any more." Speme reached around Lilia with the tape measure, measuring her cousin's bustline. "Your body is shaping into that of a woman."

"I know. All my friends have been wearing brassieres for two years now!"

"Never worry about what other people are doing, Lilia, or feel anxious about whether or not you fit in. You are uniquely beautiful just as you are, but yes . . ." Speme gave Lilia a soft half-smile, "it's time you step fully into this beautiful body and wear a brassiere!"

As Lilia sat watching her cousin cut and sew the fabric, she noticed a momentary lift in the heaviness she saw in Speme's eyes. Lilia smiled as she realized her presence was offering Speme a necessary window of escape into joy, as well as the chance to feel needed.

Lilia observed the intricate yet delicate process of sewing such a small item of clothing. She was impressed with the details so caringly crafted by her cousin. After a few more passes under the needle, Speme cut the last piece of thread with her teeth and turned Lilia to face the mirror.

"Are you ready?"

"I've been ready forever!" Lilia caught a flicker of contentment in Speme's eyes as she fastened the brassiere on to her; this filled Lilia's heart with both sadness for her cousin's difficult life, as well as hope the spark would grow bigger and never die.

"There. How does this look?" Speme asked.

Lilia stood in front of the full-length mirror, admiring her cousin's work. She turned side to side, sizing up her breasts and profile.

"The fabric is so soft, and I love the colors. I feel sophisticated and respectable!"

Speme caught her own drawn, pale reflection in the mirror, which seemed to reveal her bruised and broken spirit. "Look at me. Where did I go? I've become a sad woman," she sighed quietly.

Lilia couldn't help fixating on the tattooed number on her cousin's arm. Speme caught her cousin's gaze in the mirror. "Yes, 60332— the number which erased my identity." Speme's hand instinctively covered the permanent marking on her skin. "They took everything from me, Lilia. My pride, my dignity . . . my soul."

"I always wanted to ask you what happened, but I was afraid to upset you." Lilia rested a comforting hand on her cousin's shoulder.

"Well, you're old enough to understand now, and it's important you never forget our history." Speme leaned back in her sewing chair and rolled down the arm of her sweater to cover the tattoo. "Marcello and his band of partisan brothers tried to kidnap Signore Maestro, who was a known informant to the Germans."

Shocked, Lilia let out a gasp. Flashbacks of her teacher beating and bruising her hands, and then, her saving his life from the Nazi soldiers, invaded her memory. "He was a *spy?*"

Speme let out an incredulous laugh. "There were *many* spies back then, Lilia. When the band didn't succeed in silencing Signore Maestro, he denounced every partisan he knew. When the Nazis came, my family was captured along with nine other villagers. We were taken in part for aiding the American pilot and for supporting the resistance, even though we were not partisans. You already know Ada was spared the same fate as me when the young German soldier pushed her aside for being pregnant. Sometimes I think she suffered more not knowing what happened to the rest of us. They boarded me, my father, and Gino on separate trains. None of us knew where the others were going—it was terrifying. After being on the train for a while, it stopped on a mountain pass, and people yelled, "Run, get off the train. Run!" But I didn't know where we were or where we were going . . . and so I stayed and faced an unimaginable destiny. I was young, and at first, angry and rebellious. The Germans didn't appreciate my attitude and punished me by taking my daily ration of bread away. If not for the other women coming together and sharing their food, I would have starved. Fortunately for me, I was sent to work in a light-bulb factory the Allies later bombed. The Russian front was approaching, and it was then I escaped with my prison mates. We wandered the countryside in Poland aimlessly until the Allies rescued us."

Speme's expression changed rapidly to reveal layers of sadness and other harder-to-read emotions.

Lilia then remembered both Arturo and Speme had been in

Flossenbürg together, without even knowing it. She felt her brother's sudden calming energy wash over her and envisioned his kind face and soulful blue eyes. Despite all Arturo had endured, he would always be an optimistic and positive light in Lilia's life. She could practically hear his encouraging words to Speme as they rolled off her own lips.

Lilia knelt and grabbed her cousin's hands. "Speme, you're still young and destined for good things. You must believe this! You can't lose hope!"

Speme gave a faint smile. "Lilia, I barely recognize myself, even after all these years. My wounds never seem to heal or scar, no matter how hard I try—this is *my* burden to bear. But you're right; we can't give up, and we need to keep striving for what we believe in. I guess I have to trust love and compassion will prevail over hate and cruelty."

Speme's face brightened as she gently hugged Lilia's bare shoulders. "Promise me, Lilia, you will live fully alive and wildly awake, and not turn into a village ghost like me. Don't waste your time trying to impress these farmer boys. There is a better world out there, waiting for you to embrace it. Wait for the one who will take you there. My wounds run deep, but you have a chance. Find your happiness. Fight for it!"

⁘

Monday arrived, and the Feast of Saint Joseph was underway, beginning with a morning service at the church, followed by a procession. Giovanni, Riccardo and Bruno were helping their father in the piazza to set up the food table, which was dressed in a fine, white, linen cloth and decorated with green, white and red flowers in preparation for the day's festivities. Lilia was tidying up the kitchen after a hearty breakfast. She was proud to be wearing a brassiere; no longer would she have to hide her body away in embarrassment or bemoan her braless status. She might not have the new dress she wanted, but she felt pretty, nonetheless.

Maria called out from the landing. "Lilia! Come up and get ready for mass—you can finish what you're doing later."

Lilia hurried up the stairs and paused at her bedroom door in surprise—a new suspender swing skirt was lying on her bed.

"Mama!" Lilia rushed towards the bed to behold the most beautiful outfit she had ever seen. She held the colorful skirt up to her nightgown as her mother entered the room. "Is this for me? But, where did you—*how* did you?"

"While you slept last night, I stayed up making it for you."

A radiant smile exploded on Lilia's face as she twirled in circles, admiring the multicolored stripes in various textures and fabrics, from cotton to polyester and silk. Bliss flowed through her, filling her body with warmth, like the rays of sunshine beaming over this spring day.

"I leafed through all the pieces of fabric your sisters sent me over the years from Rome and Milan. I cut them up and sewed long strips together. You can wear it with your white blouse, and . . ." Maria rolled her eyes for emphasis as a small smile hovered around her mouth, "your new *brassieres*."

"Mama! I love it!"

"Well, get dressed, or we'll be late for mass. All we need is more irritating comments from Padre Munnini, so let's go!" Unable to hold back, Maria's last words trailed smugly behind Lilia as she disappeared down the hall. "I highly doubt *Signora Zamparelli* knows how to sew."

Mussons had come alive with radiant colors. Villagers draped Italian flags and various colored sheets from their windows, and the center square was bordered with endless carnations, azaleas and Easter lilies. After mass and during the procession, girls scattered hundreds of rose petals from their baskets, blanketing the main street in a sea of red, all framed by a perfect azure sky. The food table was laden with elaborately decorated loaves of bread, some in the shape of a crown of thorns, as well as fig cakes, zeppole, pomegranates, apples and seafood, all blessed by the priest, who sprinkled holy water from his golden bowl. The evening was met with singing and dancing around the piazza bonfire, which illuminated the night.

Throughout the day, Lilia paraded through the Feast of Saint Joseph with her friends. She couldn't help but glow as she felt all eyes on her.

"Where did you get this outfit? The red, blue, and turquoise are striking on you!"

"My mother made it for me."

Solidea's gaze dropped over the stunning fabric again. "I've never seen anything like it!"

Lilia blushed, flashing her a proud grin. As the girls fell over themselves admiring Lilia's multicolored skirt, village boys fell over themselves as they admired the beautiful young girl. Was it the brassiere? Or the skirt? Perhaps both, but Lilia couldn't deny she felt more confident and elegant than she ever had, and the boys were taking notice.

⊷ℰℐℴ

The following morning, a soft soprano voice filled the courtyard and wafted through the house.

Al di la; del bene piu prezioso, ci sei tu
Far beyond; the most precious gift, there you are

"Virginio, come quick, look at your daughter." Maria, Virginio, and the boys huddled at the front door in smiles, quiet snickers and muffled laughter. They watched Lilia in her new striped skirt, twirling in circles with a broom, her father's white shirt draped over the bristles, the left cuff gently gripped in her right hand.

Al di la; delle cose piu belle
Far beyond; the most beautiful things
Al di la; delle stelle, ci sei tu
Far beyond; the stars, there you are

Lilia was singing at the top of her lungs to a bright melody only she could hear. She imagined a chorus of birds chiming along with their tiny chirps, and the accompaniment of a delicate breeze dancing through the leaves. The words flooded out of her like no one was watching. The atmosphere of yesterday's festival still lingered in the air with notes of love and romance.

Al di la; del mare piu profondo, ci sei tu
Far beyond; the deepest sea, there you are
Al di la; de I limiti del mondo, ci sei tu
Far beyond; the limits of the world, there you are

Lilia clutched the shirt to her heart, dropped the broom, raised her head high, and belted out the last heartfelt and powerful notes.

Ci sei tu, al di la, ci sei tu per me!
There you are, far beyond, there you are for me!

Laughter erupted inside the house. "Look at your crazy daughter!" Maria shook her head as she held her stomach and chuckled, while Virginio and the boys fell into hysterics.

Hearing them snicker from the window, Lilia was startled out of her fantasy. She felt mortified beyond measure that she'd drawn such an ungracious audience. She wanted to sink into the earth from embarrassment.

"Ci sei tu, al di la, la la la!" Giovanni and Riccardo threw their arms open and busted out the lyrics as Lilia hid behind her closed eyelids, feeling more awkward than a squawking duck. The boys collapsed at Lilia's feet in a fit of uncontrollable giggles.

"Stop it!" Lilia pleaded as she stomped her foot.

"Stop it!" Giovanni retorted, irritating Lilia even more. "Oh! I forgot to tell you, my friend Paolo has a crush on you."

"What?"

"Muah muah muah," Giovanni mocked his sister as he pretended to kiss his fist.

"Stop it! I don't like him!" Irritated, Lilia shooed him away with the broom and stormed inside the house. Maria and Virginio, and Bruno remained silent as they observed the teasing banter.

"Well, you'd better tell him that! He wants to give you a promise ring."

"A promise for what?"

"Who cares!" Riccardo shrugged. "It's a free ring! Take it!"

"I think your voice is pretty," Bruno smiled at his sister, feeling a bit guilty for having laughed along with his brothers.

"Well, thank you, Bruno," Lilia bowed to him in thanks even as she shot a glare of disapproval at the others.

Virginio sensed her craving for approval and love. "Al Di La is an all-time favorite, Liliutti, and you sang it beautifully."

"Hey! Songbird!" Maria attempted to suppress a bubbling giggle. "Before you run and hide upstairs, take the wheelbarrow of dirty clothes to the river and wash them. Round up your friends. I'm sure the seagulls could use a good concert."

An eager light flashed in Lilia's eyes at the chance to escape her family's mockery of her amateur debut. She wheeled the family's dirty clothes and a cauldron of boiling water to the Tagliamento, where she met up with Solidea, Mariuccia, Lidia and other village girls, who were all there to attend to their own laundry. They spoke about boys, laughed at their childish antics, and threw back their heads in song. As they scrubbed their dirty linens in hot water and pounded them on the marble slabs by the river, Solidea noticed Lilia pulling out a white handkerchief.

"Whose *fazzolettino* does that belong to? *Paolo?*" Solidea started a chain reaction of giggles among the girls.

"You, too?" Lilia shot her friends an annoyed look and rolled her eyes, still exasperated about the day's earlier embarrassment. "He's not my boyfriend! I don't want to date a farmer. I'm waiting . . . waiting for my *Romeo.*" Lilia smiled shyly, expecting more ridicule, but Solidea smiled encouragingly at her friend.

"Your stunning new skirt yesterday gathered a few admirers, so I'm sure you won't have any problems finding the man of your dreams." Solidea winked and snatched the hanky out of Lilia's hands. She curtsied, made a gesture with her hand, twirled the piece of cloth in the air, while singing softly.

> *Amor, dammi quel fazzolettino*
> Love, give me that little handkerchief
> *Vado alla fonte e lo voglio lavar*
> I'm going to the fountain and I want to wash it for you

Te lo lavo alla pietra di marmo
I'll wash it on the marble stone
Ogni sbattuta è un sospiro d'amor
Each stroke like a sigh of love
Te lo stendo su un ramo di rose
I'll lay it to dry on a branch of roses
Per ogni spina è un bacino d'amor
For each thorn is a small kiss of love

The riverbed was alive with voices joining in, ringing strong as the girls continued to pound their laundry on the marble slabs.

Te lo stiro col ferro a vapore
I'll iron it for you with a steam iron
Ogni pieghina è un bacino d'amor
Each fold is a small kiss of love
Te lo porto di sabato sera
I'll bring it to you on Saturday night
Di nascosto di mamma e papa
Secretly from my mom and dad

As the girls bent over to rinse the soapy clothes, an occasional breeze sailed in, blowing up their skirts, drawing in the adjacent farm's men, who offered whistles and cheers of appreciation.

"Great legs!"

Lilia flapped her dress down and threw up her hand in disgust, while the other girls hurled stones at the farmers.

"Go find women your own age to whistle at!"

Lilia sang even more loudly, paying little heed to the gawking farmers.

C'è chi dice "L'amor non è bello'
Those that say, "Love is not beautiful'
Certo quello l'amor non sa far
Clearly, they don't know such love

The river water felt warmer on her hands, and a fragrance of make-believe roses tickled her senses. The mere thought of one day finding her true love lifted Lilia's heart.

⋙⋘

Summer 1952

Lilia and her grandfather, Giovanni, were going through his customary Sunday morning ritual. After the war, he'd moved from Romans to Grions, a small farming village east of Mussons, across the Tagliamento. This alpine community bordered Austria and Slovenia. It was nestled among rambling vineyards, wheat, and cornfields. Unable to make her bi-weekly visit, Maria had sent Lilia in her place to take care of her aging father by helping with meals, cleaning his home, doing his laundry, and keeping him company.

Lilia and Giovanni sat side-by-side on old wooden chairs whose legs were planted in the gravel floor of his cement-arched carport. Giovanni wiggled into a comfortable position, leaned back, and took a deep breath, soaking in the brisk air and allowing the sun's rays to warm his face. He savored the first sip of his coffee and grappa.

"Ah, it doesn't get much better than this, does it? You know, Lilia, I never tire of those snow-capped Alps. There's something magical about them, and I can't seem to put it into words."

Lilia looked up from her book.

"When I look at those magnificent mountains which have stood for hundreds of years, I feel like I'm seeing God. I feel closer to heaven." A smile rose on Giovanni's face. "It's been too long since I've seen you this happy, my dear. So, tell me, how was it working in Yesolo?" Lilia had spent the last school year working for a university professor and his wife, who was an elementary school teacher, in Yesolo, a farming community near Venice. They had posted a bulletin at Morsano's city hall, in search of a maid and someone who would mind their three children. Padre Munnini had gotten wind of the notice and offered up Lilia for the position. In his mind, this request to Maria and Virginio was not out of guilt for his abusive treatment towards Lilia, but more to help them keep their daughter appropriately clothed! The placement had been neither significant nor memorable for Lilia, who much preferred the bustling excitement of a big city like Rome. At the same time, it had offered a much-needed escape from the confines of provincial Mussons.

"It was ten months of awkwardness, Nonno! The cleaning and child-minding were fine, but the couple was oddly peculiar. He's a professor at the university in Venice, and she teaches young students at the school on their farm." Lilia turned to her grandfather, giving him a perplexed look. "They slept in separate bedrooms, and never, I mean never, spoke to each other. She would ask me to ask her husband things like where he was going, when he would be home, what he wanted for dinner, did he pay a certain bill. And in turn, the Signore did the same—I became their go-between." Lilia's brow furrowed in confusion. "What kind of a marriage is that?"

"It's a marriage, albeit a strange one. I sense a lot of sadness there. At least all your adventures further solidify what you do and don't want for *your* life. You may not have had the same revelations had you always lived in Mussons."

"I suppose." Lilia's eyes shimmered as a memory sparked within her. "I did have one pleasant experience there. I would sometimes sit on the porch with the Signore at night after his wife and children had gone to bed. We'd sit in rocking chairs, looking up at the vast starlit sky. He would trace the path of stars forming the constellations. He showed me the Big and Little Dipper and taught me where the planets are and how to navigate by the North Star."

"And let me guess," Giovanni let out a soft chuckle, "you saw a shooting star and wished for love to come save you."

"I wished and prayed for many things, Nonno. I wished Arturo and Erminio were still alive. I wished the world not to suffer another war of unspeakable atrocities. I wished all my family's suffering, all my tears, would one day be written and the world would know, and never forget, what war does to people . . . how it can shred souls, like my mama's—a woman now lost to herself." Lilia sighed. "I wished . . . she loved me more. I want more for myself, Nonno. And yes, I wished for love—a great love."

"Ah, a sweet seventeen-year-old girl and her dreams," Giovanni smiled at Lilia with adoration. "Rest assured, the rain eventually leaves the storm, and there awaits a rainbow, ready to take you wherever you want to go."

Giovanni had a habit of raking his fingers through the long hairs in his bushy black brows when he was deep in thought. After minutes of pulling and twisting, he turned to Lilia, a determined twinkle in his eye, "We need to find you a good man."

Lilia merely rolled her eyes as she considered her grandfather. "A good man? Where? Grions?"

Peering over his silver, wire-rimmed glasses, he raised a brow. "My sweet child, the boys are always asking about you here."

Lilia grabbed his large, wrinkled hand and shot him a loving but skeptical smile. "Nonno, those boys are all farmers. I want a man who has traveled far beyond those mountains—a man of the world. I want a gentleman . . . like you! Look at this three-piece suit, bow tie, and your black fedora. You're the epitome of elegance."

"You, my dear, are too kind, and read far too many romance novels! Does this mean you haven't met any boys?"

"Well, there was this one boy last year. His name is Paolo. He gave me a promise ring given to him by his mother. He was sweet but a few years younger than me. Too young! People in Mussons kept telling me to stay away from him, as he wasn't someone I would want to marry. His sister was mentally challenged, and his father had been in a wheelchair for years with some hereditary illness. They worried if I married him one day, our children wouldn't be *right*. Anyway, he came to the house before I left for Yesolo. Mama ignored him, like she does with any boys who come around. He gave me the ring, and I put it in my dresser drawer and never wore it. He kissed me on the cheek before he left—but there were no sparks, Nonno. I felt *nothing*! When I returned to Mussons ten months later, I gave him the ring back. Paolo almost cried. Now, every time I see him, he gives me sad puppy eyes." Lilia shrugged, "He's not *the one*."

"Well, let's hope when you *do* meet your Prince Charming, he doesn't have one of these huge beaks." Giovanni pointed at his commanding Roman nose. "Or walk with a twisted oak cane like this one!" He shook his cane in a gesture of playful self-deprecation, which made both of them laugh.

Lilia's eyes were filled with palpable admiration and love. "It's no wonder everyone in Grions adores you. You're truly one of a kind, Nonno."

"So, tell me, what should this one-of-a-kind, old fart tell all these inquiring young lads?"

"Keep telling them I have a boyfriend." Lilia waved her hand absentmindedly as she turned back to the book she was reading.

Giovanni's expression turned more serious. "All right, but remember one thing—being a farmer is what people *do*, it's not who they *are*. Pray for a good man. This is what I want for you."

Lilia rested her head on Giovanni's shoulder. "Thank you, Nonno. I love you."

"I love you too, my girl." He smiled softly but quickly shook himself out of the moment, which was a little too sentimental for his liking. "All right, enough of this. I don't want to fog up my glasses. Go run your errands, and I'll be here breaking all those lonely hearts when they come asking for you." Lilia kissed his cheek, and he motioned her away.

It was mid-morning, and the bells of Santa Andrea Church were bouncing off the distant hills as they filled the air with their song. Like in Mussons, a row of family-owned shops and narrow, rustic, unpolished homes with arrangements of flowering plants on the windowsills lined the streets leading to the piazza, where Lilia would be buying groceries for her grandfather.

As the church doors swung open, parishioners streamed through, excited to mill about the sidewalk cafe in their Sunday best. Teenage boys revved up their mopeds while onlooking girls huddled in gossip and coy flirtation, and children pushed their way through to the gelato truck in the center of the square. The sweet sounds of summer were buzzing throughout the village.

As Lilia passed by the piazza pub, the hairs on the back of her neck stood at attention. Although she fixed her gaze straight ahead and didn't stop to greet anyone, Lilia could feel all eyes on her. "Hi, beautiful! Where are you from? What's your name?" Hoots and hollers were followed by whistles and clapping as young men gushed over her beauty.

Lilia winced at the attention and quickened her gait. *Why are they staring? Clapping? They think I'm beautiful?* Lilia cast her eyes downward in the hopes no one would approach her, but the comments continued. "Hey! Come talk to us. We don't bite! Come on!"

Oh, please don't look at me! Stop saying these things! Go away! Lilia broke out into a sprint. Squinting through one eye, she turned her head to see if the men had left. Relieved the coast was clear, she plodded ahead towards the general store.

To the villagers, she seemed unfriendly and aloof, but Lilia's shy nature had always been to deflect attention from men. Still, at her core, she yearned for the attention of one man, her one true love—and she knew he was still out there.

One day my knight will appear and steal my heart. He'll kiss me softly like Romeo kissed Juliet.

Lost in dreamy thought, Lilia paused at what she felt was a safe distance from the obnoxious bar. She closed her eyes and tilted her head up, puckering her lips, as if awaiting a much-anticipated kiss. *I feel his breath come towards me. He cups my face with his gentle hands and presses his lips on to mine.*

A soft smile spread across Lilia's face as she rose on her toes. *He whispers my name, "Lilia." His voice echoes like the ocean waves and—*

Lilia's fantasy was abruptly interrupted by a burst of giggles across the street. A cluster of girls were covering their mouths, pointing and laughing. Lilia's cheeks turned scarlet with embarrassment. She quickly hid behind the corner of a building to escape their scrutiny, burying her hands in her face as despair washed over her.

"What is wrong with you—you're not a Capulet!" she hissed aloud. "You're a nobody from Mussons. A maid, and nothing more."

Finally, Lilia arrived at the general store, glad to shake off a moment she hoped to forget. The store was wedged between two other family-owned shops: a small bank and a pharmacy. The sign above the door was weathered, and the letters faded from the sun and peeling paint.

The daily specials were scrawled on cardboard and displayed in the front window, surrounded by barrels of apples and oranges. Lilia stepped inside. The air was perfumed with produce and the aroma of spices. Lilia paused for a moment to survey the scene as people milled about the aisles. She noticed housewives casually browsing and young couples strolling hand-in-hand. Her nose tingled from the perfume of newly cut roses and sweet-smelling strawberries. *I'll cook Nonno a chicken with roasted potatoes and hearty vegetables which will do him some good—and we'll have this luscious fruit for dessert.*

Finally making her way back to her grandfather's house, Lilia was happy to leave behind the bustling piazza and its nosy onlookers. Her arms were filled with bags heavy enough to pull her down. As she strolled along Via Vittorio Emanuele, the street where Giovanni lived, she heard a man's voice call out from above: "Good morning, Signorina."

Startled, Lilia prepared to ward off the attention of yet another intrusive man. But when she looked up, she was surprised to see a handsome man with wavy blonde hair. His smile seemed to radiate from his sparkling blue eyes. She noted he was also dapper, clad in black, pinstriped pants and a crisp, white shirt. He was tying his polished shoes on the windowsill as he smiled at her and nodded hello.

This man oozed such ease and confidence, it forced Lilia to pause for a moment. Her heart raced, and her cheeks flushed. She felt both utterly self-conscious and inexplicably giddy. She tipped her face dreamily up at his until she had to shield her eyes from the bright sun as she shyly smiled back at the man. "Good morning."

A surge of electricity tingled through her body—a feeling she had never experienced. *Who is he? I've never seen him before! He's incredibly handsome! My God, what do I say? What do I do? I must ask Nonno what he knows about this man!*

Fearing she'd stumble over her words, Lilia chose to nod politely and go along on her way even as a pang of regret crept up in her. Although her back was turned, she could still feel the powerful energetic pull of this man. Lilia imagined tulips in a rainbow of colors springing up with each new step she took. She fought off the urge to look back and soak in his beauty once more.

I wish . . . I wish for us to meet again, she thought to herself.

෨ඐ ෨ඐ

As Lilia walked along, the mysterious man gazed at her from his balcony, utterly enchanted. He was none other than Renzo Ganzini, the most sought-after bachelor in Grions. Without having said so much as a word, this young woman had managed to cast her spell upon him, which was no small feat. Lilia's big brown eyes and soulful gaze left him awed, curious, and determined. He simply watched as her cascading waves of chestnut hair bounced down her back, her floral dress hugging her youthful curves. To him, she was a vision of loveliness and femininity.

Twenty-six-year-old Renzo was a sophisticated world traveler who had recently returned from a year in Argentina. He was a highly skilled stonemason, having worked throughout Europe and

South America. The other skill he took pride in was flirting with women and mesmerizing them with his style and wit. But as much as women swooned over him, he had always felt unmoved by their advances. Renzo was clear about what he wanted—a strong yet feminine woman, with grace and style. A woman with a kind heart and a desire to explore the unknown. A dreamer like him. Although friends and relatives often teased him for being too selective, he knew his woman was out there, somewhere, waiting for him.

And at this moment, judging from the palpitation in his heart, a newfound joy rose to light the sky of his being. Without knowing how he knew, he trusted he had found *her*. His queen.

Renzo turned to his brother Enore, who was also gazing out the window.

"Who is that beautiful creature?"

Enore shook his head and laughed. "Forget about it, Renzo. She's Giovanni's granddaughter from the other side of the river. The word around town is, she has a boyfriend. I've seen her here before, and each time she makes my heart flutter, but she's too good for me—untouchable to men like us. You don't stand a chance."

But Renzo knew he wasn't like other men. With a confident twinkle in his eye, he turned to his brother and flashed him a coquett-ish smile. Renzo felt the same surge of determination he applied to everything else in his life. He was certain. "I'm going to marry that girl."

LA FINE • THE END

| FLOSSENBÜRG, GERMANY

April 2018

Arturo Meneguzzi was my uncle, brother to ten siblings, and son to his adoring parents Maria and Virginio. He was a Northern Italian soldier who saved our family's life by giving up his own. His last words to them were, "Mama, if I don't go now, they will kill us all." My family lived a long life, indebted to Arturo, who had sacrificed his own. Surrendering to the Nazis changed his fate, spared my mother's life, and inspired me to tell this incredible story. Arturo died on 6 March 1945, weeks before the camp was liberated. He was twenty-four years old.

In April 2018, I accepted an invitation to the 73rd Anniversary of the Flossenbürg concentration camp liberation in Germany. This camp was the fourth and third largest established by the Nazis. More than 100,000 men and women were imprisoned there and at its sub camps. Flossenbürg was considered one of the most grueling, labor camps by the dreaded Schutzstaffel (SS).

During this weekend-long celebration, 600 people from twenty countries were in attendance. I admit it was trepidation at first. Traveling alone to this remote village in the middle of the Bavarian forest filled me with uncertainty, and I debated canceling my trip. However, never having met my uncle, I was repeatedly captivated by his photo and felt drawn and connected to his soul.

Arturo never had a chance at life. Knowing how much he suffered, and the grief my grandparents and my mother endured, my desire to honor him triumphed over doubt. My wish to pay my respects to his memory, and the countless others whose lives suffered an unimaginable, unjust fate, paved the way to an experience I will never forget.

Initially, I had conjured up all these dark images of the camp and how the energy might make me feel. The Flossenbürg memorial is somber, indeed, but the grounds are beautiful and serene, which I was not expecting. Flowers line the pathways, and the open spaces are park-like. Some might feel this is a way for the German people to mask the horrors that prevailed here, but I think maintaining the site with respect, amid all the darkness, creates a peaceful environment for people to reflect, pray and pay their respects. Year after year, the compassionate facilitators at Flossenbürg strive to keep the memory of what transpired here alive, so this horrific period in history will continue to be taught in schools and shared with the public—never to be forgotten.

On Saturday, 22 April 2018, my tour guide took me through the arched passageway of the administrative building, once the SS headquarters. I looked around the vast open gravel space where thousands of prisoners were alerted by the sound of an alarm and forced to line up year-round, in the early morning and evening, for daily *appell*, roll call.

This daily routine was how the SS manipulated prisoners: by taking away their power, instilling fear, and subjecting them to violence. Even in the dead of winter, thousands of prisoners stood in freezing temperatures and penetrating wind while their numbers were called, and the dead were documented. Here I was, on the same grounds where SS guards held horrific public executions and where prisoners were forced to watch for endless hours until each victim was confirmed dead. SS Major Max Koegel was the head Nazi commander at Flossenbürg and one of the cruelest of Hitler's officers. On any given day, Koegel rode up on his white horse and shot prisoners dead in order to maintain authority and to terrorize the prisoners into obedience. One was lucky to escape his selection.

Surrounding the old headquarters are hilltop homes adjacent to the main camp, homes now inhabited by the locals of Flossenbürg. These homes once housed the camp officials and other higher-ranking SS officers.

After a day of exploiting, humiliating, and dehumanizing prisoners, the SS lived in these heated, well-stocked homes and spent their evenings in the officer's club, outfitted with a casino and an elegant dining hall. In the warmer months, they rode in their stables and played tennis on their courts. Even as the stench of rotting bodies rose around them, they turned a blind eye and lived like kings. As I looked around, it was hard to fathom all that had taken place here, and not that long ago.

Further ahead, I found the kitchen to my left where my uncle had worked while at the camp. To my right was the laundry building, where I visited the original disinfection and shower rooms. If there was a bone-chilling presence felt this weekend, it was here. As prisoners entered the gate, they lined up outside the laundry building where they were forced to undress. Their clothing was stored in labeled garbage bags, never to be returned. Once their heads and bodies were shaved, hundreds of prisoners were directed to the basement to shower. The water was either extremely hot or extremely cold, which served to disorient them even further.

Like my uncle, the prisoners were issued their striped uniforms and rags to wear on their feet—no socks or undergarments. They were confined to quarantine blocks where they waited for a medical check-up to determine their work capacity. Prisoners were distributed throughout the facility based on where they could best serve the SS. My uncle was fortunate to be placed in the kitchen and not the grueling quarry where men survived on a piece of bread, a cup of coffee, and a small bowl of soup—the only nourishment for twelve straight hours of slave labor six days a week. Men died daily in the quarry from the back-breaking work, the severe temperatures, malnutrition, and abuse suffered at the hands of the SS.

On the upper levels of the laundry building, I saw storyboards containing audio and video, artifacts, and a large white book containing the names of all those who had perished. Leafing through the hundreds of pages in the book, I found my uncle's name.

`Arturo Meneguzzi, Prisoner Number: 38887`
`Born 24.11.1920 Died 6.3.1945`

Running my fingers over his name, a deep wave of sadness washed through me, making his tragic demise undeniably real. I could almost hear Arturo whisper into my heart: "Thank you for coming. Thank you for remembering me."

Each day was humbling. Each man, woman, and child's story forced me to reflect on their lives and redefine gratitude for my own. I could feel the needless suffering that took place here. The personal tragedies and photos were gut-wrenching. I was thankful to exit the building, see flowers, trees, green fields and sunshine. Had it been a harsh Bavarian winter, my visit would have impacted me that much more.

During this weekend-long celebration, I learned my uncle's unimaginable fate began in Buchenwald, and the long road ended with his tragic death in Flossenbürg just weeks before the camp's liberation. I also discovered my uncle had spent his last days with someone special, a man he called "friend." His name was Pepick.

Yosef Kapel (Pepick)
Flossenbürg, Germany, 2018

Photo: Arturo Meneguzzi
Udine, Italy, 1941

On one of the evenings, I attended a dinner for survivors, their families, organizers, volunteers, and honored political guests. It was there I met ninety-two-year-old Jewish survivor, Pepick. Speaking with Pepick and his family, I was amazed to discover he remembered my uncle from the photo I carried in my hands—he remembered his name. They had worked together in the camp kitchen.

Pepick shared with me how Arturo stole food to feed the other prisoners and did his best to keep up morale by singing to them in the barracks. Pepick began singing me the song he'd learned from Arturo those many years ago. We quickly drew a crowd that evening, and our miraculous meeting touched hearts—there wasn't a dry eye in sight. In the history of the Flossenbürg memorial celebrations, ours was the first connection of this kind to be made. Pepick and I embraced each other, both grateful for a moment neither of us will ever forget. If this doesn't make you believe in fate, I don't know what will.

Sunday, 22 April 2018, was my final day at Flossenbürg. It consisted of a religious commemoration and the wreath-laying in the Valley of Death. A large crowd had gathered for the event. What shook and struck me most profoundly were the crematorium and the Valley of Death. When the camp was liberated, a mound of ash was collected and interred into what is known as the Pyramid of Ashes; my uncle's ashes lay there.

Closing out the day, over a hundred people joined in a procession in which they carried flowered wreaths down the steep steps of the valley to the Square of Nations, where tombstones memorialize the prisoners who died. From the valley, I could see two of three stone watchtowers still standing; one led towards the ramp to the crematorium. The last barrack closest to the ramp had housed the weakest prisoners. Upon death, their corpses were piled into a wagon and wheeled down to their final destination.

Adjacent to the oven is the marble dissection table, where doctors extracted prisoners' gold teeth. Standing before this table was the eeriest experience of my life. I could feel the omnipresent chill in the air. Horrific visions filled my mind, and at this moment, I was consumed with feelings of hate and confusion. How could this happen?

A few months before the camp's liberation, the number of executions overtook the crematorium's capacity. Under the orders of Nazi officer, Max Koegel, thousands of prisoners' bodies were stacked in piles, drenched with gasoline, and burned—their ashes left to scatter the grounds. The cruelty was palpable. These were people like you and me, who'd been treated like numbers, slaughtered at the hands of monstrous evil. Bowing my head, I sent Arturo our family's love and prayers.

The people at the Flossenbürg memorial were extraordinary. I was overwhelmed by everyone's openness, kindness, desire to give back, and willingness to help. I well up with tears when I think of their generosity towards me and one another. A camp once filled with horror, and despair was blessed with heroes of love and respect, who walked arm in arm.

This experience was a tremendous journey, filled with discovery and immense gratitude, both expected and unexpected. I feel forever changed. I rediscovered the lesson: "Follow the calling of your heart, and it will take you where you need to go."

Over 30,000 prisoners from over thirty countries lost their lives in Flossenbürg. Never forget. Never again.

For more on the Flossenbürg memorial—a place of remembrance, visit lindaganziniauthor.com

| AUTHOR'S MESSAGE

Love. Resilience. Legacy. These are the lessons my mother taught me in her struggles through poverty and the horrors of World War II. This coming-of-age book provides a window into a period of known history but also reveals an eye-opening account into the tragedies of genocide suffered by northern Italy at the hands of war.

I spent many summers growing up with my grandparents in the heart of the sweet hamlet of Mussons. Sitting with them, I listened as they painted for me the hardships my family endured throughout their lives. Even as a child, I could feel the sadness and grief of their past, especially with my grandmother, whose eyes spoke worlds of suffering.

Despite the darkness thrust upon my mother as a child, the ravages of war never dampened her faith—she never gave up believing the depth of her love would heal her family from layers of loss and despair. Stories like this one don't often make it to the big screen, but it's essential to preserve the legacy of the lessons gathered by the people who came before us while keeping in mind the legacy of twentieth-century wars, which still haunt us today.

I believe this book was birthed at the right time, not only for cultural reasons but also in light of our present political climate. On a global scale, people are motivated by fear. We are afraid of our countrymen, fearful of immigration and our neighbors. My mother was a young girl, coming of age during a time when the world feared its future. May her struggles propel readers into making peace with their childhood scars, rediscovering their voices, and living heroically and fearlessly. May my family's story remind people of the real threat of history repeating itself. Through our shared stories, we can author a more peaceful future by taking responsibility for each chapter and creating a world free of hate—a safe world for our children.

My hope is that *Lilia* will be a source of inspiration moving the younger generation to share it with their parents and grandparents. In the process, may it spark meaningful conversation about our many life experiences, and bring people together across generational and other differences to create understanding and empathy.

| ABOUT THE AUTHOR

Linda Ganzini is a natural-born creative. At a young age, she discovered her talent for art and singing. Over the years, she immersed herself in painting, writing lyrics, recording music that garnered international recognition, and would go on to earn awards for her graphic design work.

A native of Canada, who spent her summers in Italy, Linda caught the travel bug and embarked on the adventure of living and working abroad in the U.S., Canada, and Europe.

In addition to her work, traveling, and exploring the great outdoors, one of Linda's deepest passions is bringing her family's story to life, creating a legacy for them, and providing a voice for the voiceless. Her debut book *Lilia* is a homage to her family and their history.

She makes her home on beautiful Okanagan Lake, Canada.

◦◦҇◦ ҈ ◦҇◦◦

If you have enjoyed my mother's story,
stay tuned for the second book in the *Lilia* series.

Do Lilia's dreams rise above her scars?
Against the challenging barriers of change, does she
find the acceptance she longs for and a life of freedom?
Is Renzo the knight on a white stallion,
who transports her into a world of passion,
adventure, and unconditional love?

Sign up for my newsletter at lindaganziniauthor.com
for exclusive content and connect with me on
Instagram @lindaganzini and Facebook @lindaganziniauthor
to follow Lilia's inspiring and triumphant journey.

We would appreciate it if you take a moment and leave
a review for *Lilia* on Amazon and Goodreads.
Your time and kindness mean the world to us both.

Meet you again between the pages of our next book.